Domination and Global Political Justice

AF766743

Domination consists in subjection to the will of others and manifests itself both as a personal relation and a structural phenomenon serving as the context for relations of power. Domination has again become a central political concern through the revival of the republican tradition of political thought (not to be confused with the US political party). However, normative debates about domination have mostly remained limited to the context of domestic politics. Also, the republican debate has not fully taken into account alternative ways of conceptualizing domination. Critical theorists, liberals, feminists, critical race theorists, and postcolonial writers have discussed domination in different ways, focusing on such problems as imperialism, racism, and the subjection of indigenous peoples. This volume extends debates about domination to the global level and considers how other streams in political theory and nearby disciplines enrich, expand upon, and critique the republican tradition's contributions to the debate. This volume brings together, for the first time, mostly original pieces on domination and global political justice by some of this generation's most prominent scholars, including Philip Pettit, James Bohman, Rainer Forst, Amy Allen, John McCormick, Thomas McCarthy, Charles Mills, Duncan Ivison, John Maynor, Terry Macdonald, Stefan Gosepath, and Hauke Brunkhorst.

Barbara Buckinx is Associate Research Scholar in the Woodrow Wilson School of Public and International Affairs at Princeton University, US. Her work has appeared in *Critical Review of International Social and Political Philosophy*, *Ethics and International Affairs*, and *Global Justice: Theory Practice Rhetoric.*

Jonathan Trejo-Mathys is Assistant Professor of Philosophy at Boston College, US. He has published articles and reviews in journals such as *Philosophy and Social Criticism*, *Constellations*, and *Contemporary Pragmatism.*

Timothy Waligore is Assistant Professor of Political Science and Global Professional Studies coordinator at Pace University, US. He has past or forthcoming publications in *Philosophy, Politics & Economics*; *Public Reason: Journal of Moral and Political Philosophy*; and *Analyse & Kritik*.

Routledge Studies in Contemporary Philosophy

For a full list of titles in this series, please visit www.routledge.com

31 **Civility in Politics and Education**
Edited by Deborah S. Mower, Wade L. Robison

32 **Philosophical Inquiry into Pregnancy, Childbirth, and Mothering**
Maternal Subjects
Edited by Sheila Lintott and Maureen Sander-Staudt

33 **Authenticity as an Ethical Ideal**
Somogy Varga

34 **The Philosophy of Curiosity**
Ilhan Inan

35 **Self-Realization and Justice**
A Liberal-Perfectionist Defense of the Right to Freedom from Employment
Julia Maskivker

36 **Narrative Identity, Autonomy, and Mortality**
From Frankfurt and MacIntyre to Kierkegaard
John J. Davenport

37 **Contemporary Feminist Pragmatism**
Edited by Maurice Hamington and Celia Bardwell-Jones

38 **Morality, Self Knowledge, and Human Suffering**
An Essay on The Loss of Confidence in the World
Josep Corbi

39 **Contrastivism in Philosophy**
Edited by Martijn Blaauw

40 **Aesthetics After Metaphysics**
From Mimesis to Metaphor
Miguel de Beistegui

41 **Foundations of Freedom**
Welfare-Based Arguments against Paternalism
Simon R. Clarke

42 **Pittsburgh School of Philosophy**
Sellars, McDowell, Brandom
Chauncey Maher

43 **Reference and Structure in the Philosophy of Language**
A Defense of the Russellian Orthodoxy
Arthur Sullivan

44 **Civic Virtue and the Sovereignty of Evil**
Derek Edyvane

45 **Philosophy of Language and Webs of Information**
Heimir Geirsson

46 **Disagreement and Skepticism**
Edited by Diego E. Machuca

47 **Philosophy in Schools**
An Introduction for Philosophers and Teachers
Edited by Sara Goering, Nicholas J. Shudak, and Thomas E. Wartenberg

48 A Philosophy of Material Culture
Action, Function, and Mind
Beth Preston

49 A Philosophy of the Screenplay
Ted Nannicelli

50 Race, Philosophy, and Film
Edited by Mary K. Bloodsworth-Lugo and Dan Flory

51 Knowledge, Virtue, and Action
Essays on Putting Epistemic Virtues to Work
Edited by Tim Henning and David P. Schweikard

52 The Ontology of Psychology
Questioning Foundations in the Philosophy of Mind
Linda A.W. Brakel

53 Pragmatism, Law, and Language
Edited by Graham Hubbs and Douglas Lind

54 Contemporary Dualism
A Defense
Edited by Andrea Lavazza and Howard M. Robinson

55 Reframing the Intercultural Dialogue on Human Rights
A Philosophical Approach
Jeffrey Flynn

56 How History Matters to Philosophy
Reconsidering Philosophy's Past After Positivism
Robert C. Scharff

57 The Affordable Care Act Decision
Philosophical and Legal Implications
Edited by Fritz Allhoff and Mark Hall

58 Realism, Science, and Pragmatism
Edited by Kenneth R. Westphal

59 Evidentialism and Epistemic Justification
Kevin McCain

60 Democracy in Contemporary Confucian Philosophy
David Elstein

61 Deleuze and Pragmatism
Edited by Sean Bowden, Simone Bignall, and Paul Patton

62 Mind, Language and Subjectivity
Minimal Content and the Theory of Thought
Nicholas Georgalis

63 Believing Against the Evidence
Agency and the Ethics of Belief
Miriam Schleifer McCormick

64 The Essence of the Self
In Defense of the Simple View of Personal Identity
Geoffrey Madell

65 Personal Autonomy and Social Oppression
Philosophical Perspectives
Edited by Marina A.L. Oshana

66 Domination and Global Political Justice
Conceptual, Historical, and Institutional Perspectives
Edited by Barbara Buckinx, Jonathan Trejo-Mathys, and Timothy Waligore

Domination and Global Political Justice

Conceptual, Historical, and Institutional Perspectives

Edited by Barbara Buckinx, Jonathan Trejo-Mathys, and Timothy Waligore

Routledge
Taylor & Francis Group
LONDON AND NEW YORK

First published 2015 by Routledge

2 Park Square, Milton Park, Abingdon, Oxfordshire OX14 4RN
52 Vanderbilt Avenue, New York, NY 10017

Routledge is an imprint of the Taylor & Francis Group, an informa business

First issued in paperback 2018

Copyright © 2015 Taylor & Francis

The right of the editors to be identified as the author of the editorial material, and of the authors for their individual chapters, has been asserted in accordance with sections 77 and 78 of the Copyright, Designs and Patents Act 1988.

All rights reserved. No part of this book may be reprinted or reproduced or utilised in any form or by any electronic, mechanical, or other means, now known or hereafter invented, including photocopying and recording, or in any information storage or retrieval system, without permission in writing from the publishers.

Notice:
Product or corporate names may be trademarks or registered trademarks, and are used only for identification and explanation without intent to infringe.

Library of Congress Cataloging-in-Publication Data
Domination and global political justice : conceptual, historical, and institutional perspectives / edited by Barbara Buckinx, Jonathan Trejo-Mathys, and Timothy Waligore.
pages cm
Includes bibliographical references and index.
1. Hegemony. 2. International relations. 3. World politics—1989– 4. Justice. I. Buckinx, Barbara C. J., 1979–
JZ1312.D66 2015
327.1′14—dc23
2014035613

ISBN: 978-1-138-79696-6 (hbk)
ISBN: 978-0-367-14413-5 (pbk)

Typeset in Sabon
by Apex CoVantage, LLC

To Jonathan Trejo-Mathys, in loving memory

Contents

Acknowledgements

We met in Bad Homburg during 2010–2011 as the first incoming batch of postdoctoral fellows at *Justitia Amplificata*, a research center funded by the German Research Foundation (DFG) and associated with the Goethe University Frankfurt. We owe a great debt of gratitude to *Justitia Amplificata*'s Director, Stefan Gosepath, and Co-Director, Rainer Forst, without whom we would not have been able to organize the conference that lies at the basis of this book. We thank them for their strong intellectual and financial support of our book project, which continued even after we left Germany. We also thank the staff of the Forschungskolleg Humanwissenschaften in Bad Homburg. It was a wonderful year and we look back on it fondly.

Thanks are also due to the invited speakers of the conference, Duncan Ivison, Catherine Lu, John McCormick, Charles Mills, and Sankar Muthu, and to all others who participated and offered useful commentaries and feedback.

Many thanks go to Catherine French and Melissa Fitzpatrick for their invaluable help with copyediting, and to Jake Bleiberg for indexing the book.

Margo Irvin and Nancy Chen at Routledge have been excellent editors and we are very grateful for their guidance.

One piece in this volume is a reprint, and several others reuse and adapt material that was previously published elsewhere. We gratefully acknowledge the permission of publishers to use material from the following sources:

Bohman, James. "Critical Theory, Republicanism, and the Priority of Injustice: Transnational Republicanism as a Nonideal Theory." *Journal of Social Philosophy* 43, no. 2 (2012): 97–112.

Brunkhorst, Hauke. "Düstere Aussichten—Die Zukunft der Demokratie in der Weltgesellschaft: Sieben Thesen." In *Menschenrechte und Volkssouveränität in Europa. Gerichte als Vormund der Demokratie?*, edited by Gret Haller, Klaus Günther, and Ulfrid Neumann, 159–76. Berlin: Campus Verlag, 2011.

Forst, Rainer. "A Kantian Republican Conception of Justice as Non-Domination." In *Republican Democracy*, edited by Andreas Niederberger and Philipp Schink, 154–68. Edinburgh: Edinburgh University Press, 2013.

Forst, Rainer. "Transnational Justice and Democracy: Overcoming Three Dogmas of Political Theory." In *Political Equality in Transnational Democracy*, edited by Eva Erman and Sofia Näsström, 41–59. New York: Palgrave Macmillan, 2013.

McCarthy, Thomas. "Liberal Imperialism and the Dilemma of Development." In *Race, Empire, and the Idea of Human Development*, 166–91. New York: Cambridge University Press, 2009.
McCormick, John P. "Democratic Republics and the Oppressive Appetite of Young Nobles." In *Machiavellian Democracy*, 36–61. New York: Cambridge University Press, 2011).
Pettit, Philip. "A Republican Law of Peoples." *European Journal of Political Theory* 9, no. 1 (2010): 70–94.

We would like to thank the contributors for writing insightful chapters for our volume.

Finally, Barbara would like to thank Egemen, Simonne, Boudewijn, Nilgün, Osman, Aysuda, Till, and Kerem Leif for their love and support.

Jonathan would like to thank the following for their support and inspiration: Maggie, Maya, Micaela, John, Lera, Amy, and Magdalena.

Tim would like to thank the Scholarly Research Fund from the Provost's office at Pace University (Pleasantville), for providing release time from teaching to finish this volume, and is grateful for the love and support of his mother, father, and sisters, Athena and Josie.

As this volume went to press, Jonathan tragically passed away. This volume is dedicated to him.

1 Domination Across Borders

An Introduction

Barbara Buckinx, Jonathan Trejo-Mathys, and Timothy Waligore

The starting point for this volume is that domination consists in subjection to the will of another or others; it manifests itself both as a personal relation and as a structural phenomenon serving as the context for relations of power. A person who is dominated is vulnerable in a profound way: she is constrained in her choices, unable to freely form life plans, and denied equal, autonomous standing with others in a political community or shared social structures. The paradigmatic example of the dominated person is the slave. Even if she does not actually suffer any ill—because the master is benevolent—she is subjected to the master's whim. More recently, scholars have lamented the status of the undocumented immigrant, who is vulnerable to deportation, the struggles of indigenous peoples who are ruled by the settler states that colonized them, and the predicament of the global poor who live (or die) at the discretion of others.

These are not just examples of misery, deprivation, poor health, or relative inequality. These people are subject to the whims of others, even if they are not actually interfered with. They often lack the status, the voice, or the standing to challenge the laws, institutions, and dominating structures to which they are subject. The question of whether or not they receive a fair distribution of goods and resources is primarily a topic for global *distributive* justice. However, the focus of this volume is on domination and global *political* justice. Global political justice examines the creation and reform of institutions and the fairness of background contexts in which decisions are made.[1] As several of our contributors emphasize, the question of distribution is not the only, or even the first, question of justice: justice is focused on the prior question of power, which asks how decisions are made and who has the standing to make them, rather than simply whether these decisions are correct. On this view, injustice is human produced, and refers first, or

[1] See Terry Macdonald and Miriam Ronzoni, "Introduction: The Idea of Global Political Justice," *Critical Review of International Social and Political Philosophy* 15, no. 5 (2012): 521–33, 521.

also, to relations of domination between human beings and not just to distributional inequity.[2]

Of course, distributive justice and domination are often connected in practice. In order for agents to be sufficiently empowered to withstand domination, or to demand to exercise the power that they are formally granted, they may require certain resources, such as health care or shelter. Ensuring that such agents are granted access to those resources might then serve distributive justice as well as help safeguard their freedom. However, while distributive concerns often follow from concerns of domination, the two can pull in different directions. A just global distribution may result through the benevolent intentions of a dominating agent, for instance, just as the slave may receive goods and resources from a benevolent slave master. And, as some of our contributors emphasize, a lack caused by nature might not be a concern of justice at all, or less so than deprivation caused by relations of domination.[3] Domination across borders remains a problem so long as there is global *political* injustice.

This volume addresses domination across borders in its conceptual, historical, and institutional aspects. Such domination can take various forms. The victims may be individuals or collectivities such as peoples or states, and the dominating agents may be other states, global institutions, non-state actors such as global corporations and international non-governmental organizations (NGOs), or structural elements of the global order. Finally, domination across borders may affect different domains of life—economic, social, or cultural—and its scope may be global, international, or transnational.[4]

Global justice can have a few meanings with reference to justice and non-domination across borders. Global justice can be used as a generic term referring to justice at the global level, leaving open what relations of domination should be focused on to formulate the best theory of non-domination across borders. Global justice can also refer to the idea that there are principles or duties of justice with a global scope, or a single global context of justice, at least given today's interdependent world. It can be used to refer to specifically "cosmopolitan" theories of justice, which focus on achieving non-domination for all individuals. In contrast, *international*

---

[2] For this view, see section 1 of Rainer Forst, "Transnational Justice and Non-Domination: A Discourse-Theoretical Approach" (this volume); Forst, "Two Pictures of Justice," in *Justice, Democracy and the Right to Justification: Rainer Forst in Dialogue* (London: Bloomsbury Academic, 2014); Duncan Ivison, "Indigenous Peoples, Injustice, and Global Politics" (this volume). For a criticism of this view, see Stefan Gosepath, "Deprivation and Institutionally Based Duties to Aid" (this volume), 262–71.

[3] Forst, Ivison, and Gosepath explicitly discuss this distinction in this volume.

[4] Cf. Michael Mann, "Has Globalization Ended the Rise and Rise of the Nation-State?" *Review of International Political Economy* 4, no. 3 (1997): 472–96.

justice focuses on non-domination between states (or nations or peoples), without directly focusing on the domination of individuals. *Transnational justice* focuses on multiple forms of domination.[5] Relations of domination include non-state actors. Transnational actors such as multinational corporations are less affected by state boundaries in their operation and membership, and "pass right through" those boundaries. Domination need not result from any single (individual or collective) agent, as victims can suffer from structural forms of oppression across borders, resulting from the possibly unintentional and overlapping effects of a number of different agents.[6]

Domination of course also occurs *within* states. A person may be at the mercy of an unelected government, she may suffer from the effects of corporate malfeasance and be unable to obtain redress, or she may be subject to the influence of unaccountable cultural and religious organizations. Indeed, many of the political movements of the day crystallize around issues of perceived, actual, or potential domination. Popular outrage about an unaccountable police force, a wealthy and rapacious elite ("the 1%") and a lack of control over immigration, healthcare, or climate change policy can be explained as expressions of concern with domination, both within and across borders. However, the purpose of this volume is to extend the focus of these debates about domination to the global level.

In the current world order, with its multitude of disparate supra-state organizations, private organizations, and states, domination across borders is a matter of serious concern. A person may be dominated when her country of citizenship is invaded by another state. She may be dominated by a global corporation that uses the disproportionate resources that it has at its disposal to disobey domestic labor laws. A global institution or non-governmental organization may dominate a community by imposing a culturally inappropriate program of assistance and evading accountability to the recipients. Domination across borders may entail the destitution of individuals through ill-conceived aid programs that favor the interests of global capital over those of the affected populations. It may be located in the structural conditions that increase global economic inequality or accelerate climate change, leading to impoverishment or displacement. More diffuse forms of structural injustice may lead to the global subordination of women.[7] Domination may also involve racial injustice through a structure

---

[5] Rainer Forst, "Towards a Critical Theory of Transnational Justice," *Metaphilosophy* 32, nos. 1/2 (2001): 160–79.

[6] Amy Allen discusses this in "Domination in Global Politics" (this volume). Cf. Iris Marion Young, *Responsibility for Justice* (Oxford: Oxford University Press, 2011); Nancy Fraser, *Scales of Justice: Reimagining Political Space in a Globalizing World* (New York: Columbia University Press, 2009).

[7] Allen, "Domination in Global Politics"; Young, *Responsibility for Justice*; Fraser, *Scales of Justice*.

of global white supremacy, operating not necessarily through a centralized, organized agent, but through transnational relations.[8]

Our contributors write from the perspectives of, and discuss insights from, critical theory, liberalism, republicanism, power theory, feminism, critical race theory, postcolonial thought, global governance, and international law. We take as our point of departure the concept of non-domination as it appears in neo-Roman republicanism and ask how this might be criticized and how different conceptions of domination could be developed and theorized. What is domination and how does it relate to injustice? What can different conceptions of domination and non-domination explain and, conversely, what do they fail to explain?

A subsequent set of questions pertains to the role of history and context in domination and theorizing about domination across borders. To what extent does non-domination correct existing power relations and to what extent does it take them for granted? To what extent should theorizing about justice begin from the history of domination across borders rather than abstract from it?

Finally, there are questions of global institutional design, which ask how global domination can or should be countered. What role, if any, should non-state actors such as non-governmental organizations (NGOs) play? Should our focus be on founding new institutions rather than reforming existing ones? And is an institutional solution even possible, or must we draw on additional, cultural and other, resources?

The chapters in our volume address these three sets of questions—conceptual, historical, and institutional—in three different sections.

1 DOMINATION AND NON-DOMINATION: CONCEPTUAL ISSUES

Since the revival of the republican tradition of thought, which began with J.G.A. Pocock in 1975,[9] domination has once again become a central concern within political theory.[10] The Roman or neo-Roman republican tra-

---

[8] Charles W. Mills, "Race and Global Justice" (this volume), 189.

[9] J.G.A. Pocock, *The Machiavellian Moment: Florentine Political Thought and the Atlantic Republican Tradition* (Princeton: Princeton University Press, 1975).

[10] Richard Bellamy, *Political Constitutionalism: A Republican Defense of the Constitutionality of Democracy* (Cambridge, UK: Cambridge University Press, 2007); Samantha Besson and Jose Luis Martí, eds. *Legal Republicanism* (Oxford: Oxford University Press, 2009); John Braithwaite and Philip Pettit, *Not Just Deserts: A Republican Theory of Criminal Justice* (Oxford: Oxford University Press, 1990); John Braithwaite, Hilary Charlesworth, and Adérito Soares, *Networked Governance of Freedom and Tyranny: Peace in East Timor* (Canberra: ANU Press, 2012); William Brugger, *Republican Theory in Political Thought: Virtuous or Virtual* (New

dition that this volume draws on, and reacts to, is not to be confused with the Republican political party in the United States. Nor is it to be confused with the Greek republican tradition that is inspired by Aristotle and emphasizes the importance of civic virtue and political participation as an essential component of the good life.[11]

In the contemporary literature on neo-Roman republicanism, the work of Philip Pettit has been especially influential. Pettit argues that freedom is best contrasted with domination rather than with interference. A person is free from interference when no obstacles are placed in her way, and no option is forcibly removed from consideration.[12] Freedom from domination

---

York: Macmillan, 1999); Lena Halldenius, *Liberty Revisited* (Lund, Sweden: Bokbox Publications, 2001); Iseult Honohan, *Civic Republicanism* (London: Routledge, 2002); Iseult Honohan and Jeremy Jennings, eds., *Republicanism in Theory and Practice* (London: Routledge, 2006); Cécile Laborde and John Maynor, eds., *Republicanism and Political Theory* (Oxford: Blackwell, 2007); Cécile Laborde, *Critical Republicanism: The Hijab Controversy and Political Philosophy* (Oxford: Oxford University Press, 2008); Frank Lovett, *A General Theory of Domination & Justice* (Oxford: Oxford University Press, 2010); Eric MacGilvray, *The Invention of Market Freedom* (Cambridge, UK: Cambridge University Press, 2011); Jose Luis Martí and Philip Pettit, *A Political Philosophy in Public Life: Civic Republicanism in Zapatero's Spain* (Princeton: Princeton University Press, 2010); John Maynor, *Republicanism in the Modern World* (Cambridge, UK: Polity Press, 2003); Andreas Niederberger and Philipp Schink, eds., *Republican Democracy: Liberty, Law and Politics* (Edinburgh: Edinburgh University Press, 2013); Adrian Oldfield, *Citizenship and Community: Civic Republicanism and the Modern World* (London: Routledge, 1990); Philip Pettit, *Republicanism: A Theory of Freedom and Government* (Oxford: Oxford University Press, 1999), Paperback ed., with postscript [1997]; Pettit, *On the People's Terms: A Republican Theory and Model of Democracy* (Cambridge, UK: Cambridge University Press, 2012); Pettit, *Just Freedom: A Moral Compass for a Complex World* (New York: W.W. Norton, 2014); Henry Richardson, *Democratic Autonomy* (New York: Oxford University Press, 2002); Quentin Skinner, *Liberty Before Liberalism* (Cambridge, UK: Cambridge University Press, 1998); Martin van Gelderen and Quentin Skinner, eds., *Republicanism: A Shared European Heritage*, 2 vols. (Cambridge, UK: Cambridge University Press, 2002); Maurizio Viroli, *For Love of Country: An Essay on Patriotism and Nationalism* (Oxford: Clarendon Press, 1995); Viroli, *Republicanism* (New York: Hill and Wang, 2002); Daniel Weinstock and Christian Nadeau, eds., *Republicanism: History, Theory and Practice* (London: Frank Cass, 2004); Stuart White, *Building a Citizen Society: The Emerging Politics of Republican Democracy*, ed. Daniel Leighton (London: Lawrence and Wishart, 2008). David Miller, who is sympathetic towards republicanism, has published on citizenship and national identity. See, for example, David Miller, *On Nationality* (Oxford: Oxford University Press, 1995).

[11] Cf. Eric Nelson, *The Greek Tradition in Republican Thought* (Cambridge, UK: Cambridge University Press, 2004). In his chapter in this volume, John Maynor writes that this strand is often associated with so-called communitarian authors such as Michael Sandel and Charles Taylor. See Maynor, "Should Republican Liberty As Non-Domination Be Outsourced?" (this volume), 228–30.

[12] Pettit, *Republicanism*, ch. 2.

is both more and less demanding. Not all interference is considered normatively objectionable: in a republic or democracy, laws restrict choice, but those laws are not imposed on the citizenry without their exercising control over that process. Interference thus need not be dominating. However, conversely, there can be domination in the absence of interference. An early definition of this focused on freedom as 'antipower'; that is, the capacity to emancipate from power. Pettit has since moved away from this term, emphasizing instead that the hallmark of a free person is "not being subject to the arbitrary power of another."[13] A person lacks freedom when another agent interferes arbitrarily in her decision-making, or when that agent has the capacity to interfere in this way. Pettit, in the lead chapter of part I of this volume, says that a person is dominated when under the (active, virtual, or reserve) control of another: domination objectionably "puts you under the will of another."[14] It is intentional and occurs between agents, rather than as a structural feature of the political or economic order.

In recent years, Pettit has explicated the conceptual links between freedom as non-domination, on the one hand, and democracy, on the other.[15] For Pettit, non-domination is the primary political ideal; it can subsume other concerns within it, and in the case of conflict, it has primacy over other considerations and values.[16]

Other republicans, such as James Bohman, offer a more explicitly democratic interpretation of freedom as non-domination, defining it as the normative power of a person to "influence the terms of cooperation with others and not be ruled by them."[17] Cécile Laborde also argues in favor of a critical republicanism, and she draws on Karl Marx, Michel Foucault, and others to highlight *structures*, as well as agents, of domination.[18]

Until recently, the scope of neo-Roman republican political thought remained limited to domestic politics. However, as multiple contributors to this volume also emphasize, globalization has problematized the role of states and rendered an exclusive theoretical focus on domestic politics

---

[13] Pettit, "Freedom as Antipower," *Ethics* 106, no. 3 (1996): 576–604, 576. Note that James Bohman and especially Terry Macdonald, in this volume, prefer the term "antipower" to later formulations. See Bohman, "Domination, Global Harms, and the Priority of Injustice: Expanding Transnational Republicanism" (this volume); Macdonald, "Antipower, Agency, and the Republican Case for Global Institutional Pluralism" (this volume).

[14] See Pettit, "The Republican Law of Peoples: A Restatement" (this volume), 44.

[15] Pettit, *On the People's Terms*.

[16] See, for example, Pettit, "The Domination Complaint," in *Nomos XLVI: Political Exclusion and Domination*, eds. Melissa S. Williams and Stephen Macedo (New York: New York University, 2005), 118–63.

[17] James Bohman, *Democracy Across Borders: From Dêmos to Dêmoi* (Cambridge, MA: MIT Press, 2007), 27.

[18] Cécile Laborde, "Republicanism and Global Justice: A Sketch," *European Journal of Political Theory* 9, no. 1 (2010), 48–69.

implausible. Political and economic decision-making frequently escapes state control, and new agents such as international NGOs and transnational institutions assist states with tasks of global governance.[19] In addition, global agents such as multinational corporations threaten to escape state control. This raises doubts about the validity of the idea of the bounded political community, which is presumed in much neo-republican thought. States may no longer be fully effective public agents, and it may instead be necessary to look beyond the state in order to counter domination effectively.

That republicanism did not theorize domination across borders until recently is perhaps not a surprise. International political theory emerged in the late 1970s and early 1980s, when Charles Beitz and Henry Shue each published monographs about political theory beyond borders,[20] and scholars started identifying these and other works as examples of approaches to *global justice*.[21] Early work focused on questions regarding our responsibilities to help the global poor and reduce global inequality, as well as the ways in which we could meet these obligations.[22] Distributive concerns have understandably—given the amount of misery and inequality that exists worldwide—been a focus of much of the literature on global justice.[23]

However, that the republican tradition has an aptitude for international theorizing has been evident since Nicholas Onuf's historical study on the republican provenance of ideas such as sovereignty, international society, and the democratic peace.[24] In the first chapter in part I of this volume, "The

---

[19] Global governance can be defined as "systems of rule . . . in which the pursuit of goals through the exercise of control has transnational repercussions" (J. N. Rosenau, "Governance in the Twenty-First Century," *Global Governance* 1, no. 1 (1995): 13–43, 13). For an example of a critical-theoretical construal of the features of domination displayed by one crucial, global governance institution, the World Trade Organization, see Jonathan Trejo-Mathys, "Toward a Critical Theory of the WTO: Thinking with Rawls Beyond Rawls," *Constellations* 20, no. 3 (2013): 459–82.

[20] Charles Beitz, *Political Theory and International Relations* (Princeton: Princeton University Press, 1979). Henry Shue, *Basic Rights: Subsistence, Affluence, and US Foreign Policy* (Princeton: Princeton University Press, 1980).

[21] A piece by Peter Singer preceded both books. However, Singer's concern was international ethics, not international justice. Peter Singer, "Famine, Affluence, and Morality," *Philosophy and Public Affairs* 1, no. 1 (1972): 229–43.

[22] See Brian Barry, *Theories of Justice* (Berkeley: University of California Press, 1989), esp. ch. 5; Thomas Pogge, *Realizing Rawls* (Ithaca, NY: Cornell University Press, 1989), part 3; Thomas Pogge, *World Poverty and Human Rights* (Malden, MA: Polity, 2002).

[23] For a collection of important pieces on global justice (with a distributive focus), see Thomas Pogge and Darrel Moellendorf, eds. *Global Justice: Seminal Essays* (St. Paul, MN: Paragon House, 2008). We simplify here, leaving out discussions of just war theory, immigration, secession, and other topics.

[24] Nicholas G. Onuf, *The Republican Legacy in International Thought* (Cambridge, UK: Cambridge University Press, 1998).

Republican Law of Peoples: A Restatement," Pettit extends his influential formulation of the republican ideal of freedom as non-domination to the international level.[25]

Like Rawls, whose title he also draws on,[26] Pettit's intervention in global political thought comes after a number of scholars have already articulated global republican approaches based on the values and institutions of his domestic model.[27] Also like Rawls, Pettit is skeptical about the possibility and desirability of a truly globalized version of his domestic theory, which would substitute global for domestic public institutions as the guarantors of individual freedom. Instead, because he expects that states will continue to exist in more or less their current configuration, he proposes to start with "states as they are" and "the international order as it might be."[28]

In Pettit's view, states are organized along two dimensions: their effectiveness and their domestic character. Only effective, popularly controlled states serve the interests of their citizens, and therefore only the domination of these states is a normative concern. As Pettit sees it, a republican international order has no reason to promote the interests of states that are functionally ineffective or unrepresentative, and such states are therefore excluded from the international regime in question. (This regime loosely resembles Rawls's "Society of Peoples," even though Pettit does not use that term.[29]) The initial question is how those well-ordered states or peoples ought to relate to one another and what collective projects they ought to pursue. A subsequent question, which Pettit does not address here, is how these states ought to relate to the individuals who reside in excluded states. Pettit argues that the global order should be arranged so that peoples can organize both internal and external relations according to the ideal of non-domination, thus achieving "a non-dominated status in relation to other states and other international agencies."[30]

---

[25] His chapter, "The Republican Law of Peoples: A Restatement," is a substantial revision of Philip Pettit, "A Republican Law of Peoples," *European Journal of Political Theory* 9, no. 1 (2010): 70–94. He has also addressed non-domination across borders in Pettit, *Just Freedom*, ch. 6: "States and Sovereignty."

[26] John Rawls, *The Law of Peoples* (Cambridge, MA: Harvard University Press, 1999).

[27] See especially Steven Slaughter, "The Neo-Roman Republican Legacy and International Political Theory," ANU Working Paper 2003/5, 2005, https://digitalcollections.anu.edu.au/bitstream/1885/42688/2/03–5.pdf; Slaughter, *Liberty Beyond Neo-Liberalism: A Republican Critique of Liberal Governance in a Globalizing Age* (New York: Palgrave Macmillan, 2005). However, unlike Rawls and his cosmopolitan critics, such as Thomas Pogge and Charles Beitz, Pettit and Slaughter largely agree on what a global extension of the theory should look like.

[28] Pettit, "The Republican Law of Peoples: A Restatement," 37.

[29] Rawls, *Law of Peoples*, 3.

[30] Pettit, "The Republican Law of Peoples: A Restatement," 38.

How can non-domination be achieved in such a regime? Pettit argues that global institutions might be able to promote common global reasons and foster deliberation and reason-giving. However, such institutions may not be sufficiently powerful to successfully counter domination. An alternative, complementary mechanism is the promotion of 'coalitions of the weak,' whereby weaker states present a united front in the face of a dominating power, be that another state or a corporation. As he sees it, the advantage of his proposal is that it recognizes the problem of domination, even where no interference is present, but that "it is not an unrealistic ideal that we have little or no reason to expect states ever to implement."[31]

James Bohman's chapter further advances the line of argument he developed in a series of articles—including, notably, "Republican Cosmopolitanism"—and his book, *Democracy Across Borders: From Dêmos to Dêmoi*.[32] In those writings, Bohman extended the republican conception of non-domination to the global sphere and interpreted non-domination as a *normative* conception, concerned with statuses and standing rather than merely bilateral, arbitrary interference or the capacity for such interference. Here, he argues that republicanism must prioritize injustice rather than justice, and injustice generally rather than only the injustice of domination. This follows Amartya Sen's book *The Idea of Justice*,[33] which Bohman argues is congenial to republicanism, since republicanism focuses on minimizing domination rather than achieving perfect justice. Focusing on Pettit's notion of "antipower," which Pettit set aside in favor of (the capacity for) arbitrary interference, he interprets it as "the power over those who would dominate us, and thus the control over one's life via the content of one's obligations and statuses."[34] Antipower is the joint exercise of Jürgen Habermas's communicative freedom and communicative power, the former of which is "the exercise of a communicative status, the status of being recognized as a member of a public" while the latter is the incorporation of communicative freedom into "institutionalized processes of decision-making."[35] Freedom as non-domination establishes the kind of equality that allows a person to make claims on others.

---

[31] Ibid., 64.

[32] See, for example, James Bohman, "Republican Cosmopolitanism," *The Journal of Political Philosophy*, 12, no. 3 (2004): 336–52; Bohman, "Is Democracy a Means to Global Justice? Human Rights and the Democratic Minimum," *Ethics and International Affairs* 19, no. 1 (2005): 101–16; Bohman, "From Dêmos to Dêmoi: Democracy Across Borders," *Ratio Juris* 18, no. 3 (2005): 293–314; Bohman, *Democracy Across Borders*; Bohman, "Non-Domination and Transnational Democracy," in *Republicanism and Political Theory*, ed. Cécile Laborde and John Maynor (London: Blackwell, 2008), 190–216.

[33] Amartya Sen, *The Idea of Justice* (Cambridge, MA: Belknap Press, 2009).

[34] James Bohman, "Domination, Global Harms, and the Priority of Injustice," 74.

[35] Ibid., 75.

Bohman argues for the inclusion of various forms of domination, such as epistemic domination, which denies a person's standing as a knower. In addition, in order to combat domination, it is not sufficient to allow for tracking of interests or mechanisms of contestation. Instead, Bohman proposes to use the all-subjected and all-affected principles to shed light on the myriad ways in which a person may be dominated. The all-subjected principle suggests a broad scope for domination, since individuals may be subjected to multiple state and non-state actors. Migrants and refugees are certainly subjected to domination by state authorities, since they lack the status of being a citizen. The all-affected principle can capture instances of domination that occur at a distance, and it takes account of degrees of vulnerability, which is often correlated with poverty. Bohman's example here is vulnerability to climate change. This broadening of the scope of non-domination—beyond the nation-state, but also beyond political domination or interest tracking and contestation—ensures that republicanism can reach its potential as "a critical theory for post-national exclusions and hierarchies."[36]

Rainer Forst's previous works and his chapter here touch on a number of themes that are important for this volume's focus on domination and global political justice.[37] For Forst, the first question of justice is the question of power: justice is focused on *who* determines what goods are received by whom, rather than on the outcome of what is received. The paradigmatic victim of injustice is not someone who suffers miserably due simply to nature. We may have reasons of moral solidarity to aid them. It is another matter if a person's deprivation occurs through relations of domination. For Forst, justice and injustice are relational. The demand for justice is a demand to overcome forms of domination. Forst opposes justice to arbitrariness, and thereby defines domination: "Arbitrary rule is the rule of some people over others without legitimate reason—what I call *domination*."[38]

Forst points to two aspects of domination. The first involves "being subjected to a normative order that cannot properly be justified to you."[39] Justification refers not merely to hypothetical justification, but involves participation in actual institutions. Justice refers to the quality of relations

---

[36] Ibid., 85

[37] Forst, "Transnational Justice and Non-Domination"; Forst, *Justification and Critique: Towards a Critical Theory of Politics,* trans. Ciaran Cronin (Cambridge, UK: Polity Press, 2013); Forst, *The Right to Justification: Elements of a Constructivist Theory of Justice*, trans. Jeffrey Flynn (New York: Columbia University Press, 2012); Forst, "Transnational Justice and Democracy: Overcoming Three Dogmas of Political Theory," in *Political Equality in Transnational Democracy*, eds. Eva Erman and Sofia Näsström (New York: Palgrave Macmillan, 2013), 41–59; Forst, "A Kantian Republican Conception of Justice as Nondomination," in *Republican Democracy*, eds. Andreas Niederberger and Philipp Schink (Edinburgh: Edinburgh University Press, 2013), 154–68.

[38] Forst, "Transnational Justice and Non-Domination," 90.

[39] Ibid., 96

between persons who justify claims to each other within a basic institutional structure that binds them. The second aspect of domination involves "being subjected to a normative order where no proper institutions and possibilities of justification are in place to begin with."[40] Forst's view is *relational* but it is not *institutional*. If there is not a basic structure in which the practice of justification occurs, justice demands that it be set up. He does not limit justice to the state, as there are multiple forms of domination transnationally.

Forst critically engages with Pettit's neo-republican view in two ways. First, he offers an alternative Kantian republican view of non-domination, and favors an interpretation of Pettit's view that brings him closer to this Kantian view. Forst says that Pettit has, at least in the past, offered a view that Forst refers to as "negative republicanism," which says that through the rule of law and other republican mechanisms, actors enjoy a realm of freedom of choice that is protected against arbitrary interference. Forst, however, says that one is not truly free if one simply *receives* freedom of choice in this narrow sense. This is not true freedom. In Kant's terms, citizens must also be authors of the laws to which they are subject. Kant says that every human being has a right of freedom: "*Freedom* (independence from being constrained by another's choice), insofar as it can coexist with the freedom of every other in accordance with a universal law, is the only original right belonging to every man by virtue of his humanity."[41] In Forst's terms, this means that every person has a basic right to justification. Each person is an independent justificatory authority. Forst says: "Justice as justification determines which freedoms are justified and what an arbitrary interference is in the first place."[42] Justice is prior to enjoying freedom of choice in the narrow sense.

Second, Forst sees a tension between two types of realism present in Pettit's view of international justice. The first type of realism limits global justice to the politically "realistic" assumption that the state system will survive, and attempts to reform and achieve non-domination between states on

---

[40] Ibid.

[41] Immanuel Kant, *The Metaphysics of Morals*, in *Practical Philosophy*, ed. and trans. Mary J. Gregor (Cambridge, UK: Cambridge University Press, 1996), 353–603, 393, 6: 237. In different ways, other works interpret and/or are inspired by Kant's innate right of freedom (often referring to it as freedom-as-independence). See Anna Stilz, *Liberal Loyalty* (Princeton: Princeton University Press, 1999), esp. 37f; Katrin Flikschuh, *Kant and Modern Political Philosophy* (Cambridge, UK: Cambridge University Press, 2000), esp. 88f; Arthur Ripstein, *Force and Freedom: Kant's Legal and Political Philosophy* (Cambridge, MA: Harvard University Press, 2009). See also the contributions in "Symposium on Ripstein's *Force and Freedom*," *European Journal of Philosophy* 20, no. 3 (2012). For a survey of views on freedom-as-independence and criticism of Kant or some Kantian views, see Christian List and Laura Valentini, "Freedom as Independence: A Critical Survey," Working Paper, 2012/2013, http://personal.lse.ac.uk/list/PDF-files/Freedom-as-Independence.pdf.

[42] Forst, "Transnational Justice and Non-Domination," 97.

that basis. The second type of realism tracks non-domination in all its forms, even if it is not between states, and pays attention to what we realistically know about how domination works in all its forms. Taking into account realism, in the second sense, Forst questions whether we can expect reforms limited by realism, in the first sense, to solve non-domination globally. Pettit's reliance on coalitions of the weak and other reforms may be achievable, but it may not be enough, given what we realistically know about how power works in transnational institutions. Forst suggests that parties could be accorded standing in justificatory processes in a more thoroughgoing reform of transnational institutions.

Amy Allen does not here concede that domination is the only way to think about power; far from it. Indeed, in other work on feminist perspectives on power, Allen has used the term "domination feminist theorists" to include those who speak about illegitimate and unjust "power-over" relations (even if they use terms like "subjection," "patriarchy," "oppression," or "subordination").[43] In contrast, "empowerment feminists" see power primarily as transformative. They define it as an ability or capacity.[44] Theorists who invoke the latter seem to go beyond a conception of domination, even as broadly defined by Allen in one work.[45] Allen herself has argued elsewhere that we need to move beyond a one-sided emphasis on either domination or empowerment.[46]

In the chapter in this volume, however, Allen's project is to critically interrogate Pettit's neo-republican internationalist account of non-domination. Allen accepts, for the purposes of this chapter, the idea of non-domination as the normative goal of a theory of transnational or global justice. Allen follows Bohman in arguing that Pettit's view of domination as arbitrary interference is overly narrow in its focus on dyadic relations; that is, relations between two or more agents. Drawing on the literature of power theory, she suggests that we should distinguish between four dimensions (or faces) of domination: arbitrary interference, institutional agenda-setting, structuring of interests, and constitution of subject-positions. She argues that Pettit's agent-centered account cannot account for all of these dimensions.

Looking at gender relations in particular, she argues that Pettit's account of non-domination as a master/subject relation is inadequate even within states today. Here, she cites Nancy Fraser's concern about the shift to "more impersonal structural mechanisms that are lived through more fluid cultural

---

43 See Amy Allen, "Feminist Perspectives on Power," *The Stanford Encyclopedia of Philosophy*, ed. Edward N. Zalta (Summer 2014 Edition), http://plato.stanford.edu/archives/sum2014/entries/feminist-power.

44 Ibid.

45 Ibid.

46 Allen, "Rethinking Power," *Hypatia* 13, no. 1 (1998): 21–40. See also Allen, *The Power of Feminist Theory: Domination, Resistance, Solidarity* (Boulder, CO: Westview Press, 1999).

forms."[47] She also refers to Iris Marion Young's idea of structural injustice, which can arise from unconscious assumptions of well-intentioned people, cultural stereotypes, market mechanisms, and other processes of ordinary life.[48] Allen argues that the way Pettit apparently focuses on agents and intentions fails to pay attention to how the overlapping effects of (possibly) unintentional actions by agents may lead to structural oppression. Allen then argues that her alternative account better theorizes the global subordination of women and the complex, multiple, and intersecting structures of domination across borders.

2 HISTORY, IMPERIALISM, AND RACE

The second section of our volume turns to historical injustice, empire, and imperialism—all topics that are of significant interest in political theory today.[49] Republicanism has a problematic history with imperialism, often

---

[47] Nancy Fraser, "Beyond the Master/Subject Model: Reflections on Carole Pateman's *Sexual Contract*," *Social Text* 37 (1993): 173–81, 180

[48] Iris Marion Young, *Justice and the Politics of Difference* (Princeton: Princeton University Press, 1990), 41; Young, *Responsibility for Justice*.

[49] Political theory has not always paid attention to empire and imperialism. For a review of the political theory literature, see Jennifer Pitts, "Political Theory of Empire and Imperialism," *Annual Review of Political Science* 13 (2010): 211–35. More recently, see Sankar Muthu, ed., *Empire and Modern Political Thought* (Cambridge, UK: Cambridge University Press, 2012); Jeanne Morefield, *Empires without Imperialism* (Oxford: Oxford University Press, 2014). For various perspectives on colonialism and its legacies, see Jacob T. Levy with Iris Marion Young, eds., *Colonialism and its Legacies* (Lanham, MD: Lexington Books, 2011); see also the references to postcolonial thought in Thomas McCarthy, "Liberal Imperialism and the Dilemma of Development" (this volume). For summaries of various approaches to and writings on historical injustice, see Cécile Fabre, "Reparative Justice," in *Justice in a Changing World* (Cambridge, UK: Polity, 2007); Lukas Meyer, ed., *Justice in Time: Responding to Historical Injustice* (Baden-Baden, DE: Nomos Verlagsgesellshaft, 2004); Jon Miller and Rahul Kumar, eds., *Reparations: Interdisciplinary Inquiries* (Oxford: Oxford University Press, 2007). Among the many writings on transnational historical injustice, see Daniel Butt, *Rectifying International Injustice: Principles of Compensation and Restitution Between Nations* (Oxford: Oxford University Press, 2009). On indigenous peoples, colonialism, and transnational racial injustice, see, for example, Duncan Ivison, *Postcolonial Liberalism* (Cambridge, UK: Cambridge University Press, 2002); Iris Marion Young, *Responsibility for Justice*, esp. ch. 7; Catherine Lu, "Colonialism As Structural Injustice: Historical Responsibility and Contemporary Redress," *Journal of Political Philosophy* 19, no. 3 (September 2011); Rhoda E. Howard-Hassman with Anthony P. Lombardo, *Reparations to Africa* (Pennsylvania: University of Pennsylvania Press, 2008); Timothy Waligore, "Cosmopolitan Right, Indigenous Peoples, the Risks of Cultural Interaction," *Public Reason: Journal of Political and Moral Philosophy* 1, no. 1 (2009): 27–56; Duncan Ivison, Paul Patton, and Will Sanders, eds., *Political Theory and the Rights of Indigenous Peoples* (New York: Cambridge University Press, 2000).

combining a concern with domination at home and enthusiasm for domination abroad. At the same time, republicans have worried that empire abroad will corrupt republican liberty at home. Pettit explicitly brackets the question of historical justice, saying he will "set aside the question of what certain, powerful states may owe to other states as a matter of historical justice."[50] He appears to believe that this is a question that can be answered *after* we have determined which principles ought to govern the international order. A different approach to political theorizing makes the history of domination across borders more central, focusing from the beginning on specific histories of domination, including imperialism, the use of ideas of modernization and development, settler colonialism, and racial injustice.

All four authors in section II situate struggles for non-domination in a specific historical and political context involving imperialism and domination across borders. John McCormick's piece is historical and interpretative, and touches on the relationship between freedom at home and domination across borders. Thomas McCarthy, Charles Mills, and Duncan Ivison engage in contemporary theorizing, arguing that historical injustice cannot be bracketed in theorizing about justice. All four authors explore how the strategic or political endorsement of imperialism or associated ideas and practices can be used in political struggles to advance equality. This might be done by advocating imperialism as a rhetorical strategy to achieve non-domination at home (McCormick, interpreting Machiavelli), using "race" to engage in non-ideal theorizing, where the starting point is a world shaped by global white supremacy (Mills), using "development" as part of a critical theory given the inescapable conditions of global modernity (McCarthy), or viewing justice as dependent on actual historical practices of domination (Ivison).

Ever since the Roman Republic transformed into the Roman Empire, it has been in doubt whether republics can adequately practice and theorize non-domination abroad. The Italian city-states were often oppressors abroad, pursuing the glory of empire, while proclaiming the importance of republican ideals at home. The Italian city-state of Florence fits this example particularly well, and the Florentine Niccolò Machiavelli is usually thought to share this split outlook. In his book, *Machiavellian Democracy*, and his chapter here, John McCormick challenges this interpretation of Machiavelli.[51] McCormick says that Machiavelli was not an unqualified champion of empire, and did not think that glory should come at the expense of liberty when the two collided. Rather, Machiavelli made his argument to a specific audience with a specific purpose in mind. Machiavelli's apparent endorsement of empire was a rhetorical strategy to convince aristocratically biased

---

[50] Pettit, "The Republican Law of Peoples: A Restatement," 41.

[51] John McCormick, *Machiavellian Democracy* (Cambridge, UK: Cambridge University Press, 2001); John McCormick, "The (In)Compatibility of Liberty and Empire in Machiavelli's Political Thought" (this volume).

republicans to accept a form of constitutionalism they might otherwise be hostile towards, one that would have empowered citizens and protected them from domination. He supported measures promoting socioeconomic equality that would have curbed imperial expansion. McCormick tells us that Machiavelli disapproved of how imperial acquisition corrupted republican virtue and prioritized freedom over imperial expansion.

All four authors discuss imperialism with respect to the relationship between concerns of socioeconomic and political equality and concerns of status, race, identity, or glory. In Nancy Fraser's terms, this could be seen roughly as the concerns of "redistribution" and "recognition."[52] McCormick's Machiavelli emphasizes the former, privileging the reduction of inequality over glory when the two clash. McCarthy does not allow recognition to trump concerns of socioeconomic and political equality. He holds that for most, it is intrinsically desirable to have basic protections, to not live in misery, and to have a voice in their own affairs. He allows that modern ideas and institutions may threaten certain aspects of non-modern worldviews, but accepts this tension as inescapable. Charles Mills says that even if a principle of cosmopolitan distributive justice were applied at a global level, this would not adequately address racial injustice, if this were not seen as a payment of a debt. Relations, not merely distributive outcomes, are important. Past wrongs must be recognized as wrongs and treated differently. The correction of racial wrongs generally must involve the (re)affirmation not simply of personhood, but of racial personhood for the living and the dead. Ivison says that justice should not simply be concerned with claims regarding resources, but with what status we have in relation to others. Focusing simply on the "disadvantage" ignores the importance of the humiliation, failed policies, and embedded racism involved in the history of colonialism.

McCormick's Machiavelli is concerned with the effects of imperialism at home; his rhetorical argument for imperialism is aimed at non-domination at home, and does not seem concerned with the fate of those dominated abroad for their own sake. McCarthy, Mills, and Ivison each advocate for a form of universalism or cosmopolitanism that nonetheless demands the political use of concepts, ideas, practices that were created and shaped through the history of domination across borders. However, they see the relationship between history and theorizing about justice in different ways.

McCarthy's chapter begins by examining how ideas of development and progress have been invoked to justify domination across borders, from the settlement of the Americas to contemporary neo-imperialism.[53] While liberalism purports to be universal, classical liberals have both justified European

---

[52] Fraser, *Scales of Justice*.

[53] McCarthy's chapter here is reprint of chapter 6 of his *Race, Empire, and the Idea of Human Development* (Cambridge, UK: Cambridge University Press, 2009).

domination and have been involved in the practice of it. European domination involves a cognitive dissonance for liberals, which is reduced through developmental theories. Certain types of norms and institutions are held to be universal, but European (and later US) domination over "backwards" non-Europeans is said to be necessary for them to progress and develop to the point where these norms are appropriate and these institutions achieved. This embodies the dilemma of development.

McCarthy discusses how this dilemma appears in the thought of Immanuel Kant and John Stuart Mill, and then discusses how this dilemma, and developmental thought more generally, is relevant today. McCarthy does not reject developmental theory, but uses insights from postcolonial critics of development and Jürgen Habermas's discourse theory of democracy to argue for "a critical theory of global development."[54]

McCarthy draws on Dipesh Chakrabarty's thought that European heritage is now a global heritage: certain modes of thought cannot be avoided. However, Europe's ideas of modernity need to be decentered or provincialized, in that they are not adequate for non-Western peoples' political experiences of modernity. European thought is to be renewed and rethought from the margins, and ideas of modernity pluralized, rather than completely rejected.[55] McCarthy thinks that John Stuart Mill's type of developmental thinking is particularly problematic (as is that of Karl Marx); it turns development into a natural science, portraying progress as something for scientific prediction or technocratic manipulation. Developmental theory can be useful when seen as a practical tool in political struggles to further health, well-being, capabilities, and political voice. Still, McCarthy says that the equal standing of all peoples and individuals is made possible through modern concepts and forms like the rule of law and democracy; these may threaten certain aspects of non-modern worldviews, so the dilemma of development cannot be entirely escaped. McCarthy ends by invoking the Kantian hope that some agreement may nonetheless be reached at the global level.

Like McCarthy, Charles Mills argues for the use of concepts formed by domination across borders. Mills asks whether we should use the notion of race, even though it would not exist in ideal theory, and it is useless as a scientific concept. In other words, should we use this sociohistorical product formed through "politics," a construct that arose through domination? Mills says yes. He invokes McCarthy's discussion of the strategy of critical theory: hegemonic ideas are to be examined on the assumption that they have been shaped through domination, and should be reconstructed, or rejected, with reference to an order without such domination.[56] Race and

---

[54] McCarthy, "Liberal Imperialism and the Dilemma of Development," 172.

[55] Dipesh Chakrabarty, *Provincializing Europe: Postcolonial Thought and Historical Difference* (Princeton: Princeton University Press, 2000).

[56] Mills, "Race and Global Justice," citing McCarthy, *Race, Empire, and the Idea of Human Development*, 14n26.

whiteness are invented, but are still real in how they privilege and disadvantage whites and nonwhites. Invoking these concepts need not justify racial hierarchy, but can be anti-racist: it can form part of a critical race theory critiquing "global white supremacy."[57] Mills claims that it is a problem that race is largely absent from contemporary literature on global justice. This silence contrasts with the writings of older authors, such as Marcus Garvey, Martin Delany, David Walker, W.E.B. Du Bois, and Sun Yat-sen, who recognized the subordination of the "wronged races" of the world, and spoke of white domination of the planet as central to global injustice.

One of the reasons for this silence about race, Mills says, is the dominant position liberalism has assumed, and especially the lack of attention in many prominent liberal theories regarding issues of rectification for racial injustice. In a series of works, Mills has criticized how John Rawls, the preeminent liberal political philosopher, uses "ideal theory," invoking a hypothetical social contract among similarly situated individual parties who start from the assumption that society has not experienced a history of injustice.[58] This idealization in ideal theory obscures from the beginning the need for non-ideal theorizing about compensation for past injustice. Mills invokes a "domination contract," a historical contract that establishes relations of subordination based on race and/or sex.[59] Mills further argues that Rawls's theory can be adapted to non-ideal circumstances. He uses the history of racism and/or gender as part of the contract apparatus, focusing on the need for rectifying racial injustice.[60]

In his chapter here, Mills suggests that a racially informed internationalism is compatible with liberal universalism, but attaches a "not yet" view towards a certain type of race-less cosmopolitanism, arguing we need to work through race to get beyond it. Mills discusses the need for compensation and to repair the legacy of colonialism's past, including repair that pays attention to race. Mills is clear that in non-ideal conditions, we should be guided by a "non-ideal (rectificatory) ideal."[61] It may be attractive to invoke an ideal where a racialized world does not exist, but it would be a mistake to think this applicable in a world with a history of (uncorrected)

---

[57] This concept is discussed in Charles W. Mills, *The Racial Contract* (Ithaca, NY: Cornell University Press, 1997), 3ff.

[58] See especially Mills, "Rawls on Race/Race in Rawls," *The Southern Journal of Philosophy* XLVII (2009): 161–84; and his contributions in Pateman and Mills, *Contract & Domination* (Malden, MA: Polity Press, 2007). See also Mills, "Racial Liberalism," *PMLA* 123, no. 5 (2008): 1380–97.

[59] This invokes Carole Pateman. See Pateman, *Sexual Contract* (Stanford: Stanford University Press, 1988). See also Mills, *The Racial Contract*; Pateman and Mills, *Contract & Domination*; Desmond King, Carole Pateman, Charles Mills et al., "Symposium: *Contract and Domination* by Carole Pateman and Charles W. Mills," *Journal of Political Ideologies* 13, no. 3 (2008): 227–62.

[60] In this he differs from Pateman, who rejects social contract theory.

[61] Mills, "Rawls on Race/Race in Rawls," 178–80.

racial injustice.[62] Still, Mills can be read to suggest that we should at least aspire to overcome these non-ideal conditions through rectification, and create conditions where it is once again appropriate to be guided by an ideal suitable to a situation where injustice had not occurred (or an ideal very close to it). Indeed, Mills thinks the ultimate, long-term goal (if only in aspiration) is still, as in Rawls's ideal theory, a world without race.[63] This contrasts with McCarthy's view that we cannot entirely escape the ideas bequeathed to us by a history of domination, nor should we even strive to do so. Even if the history of domination were overcome, would the ideal in such a world resemble an ideal from a theory of global distributive justice (or an ideal from a theory of global non-domination) that was theorized without reference to this history? Do certain ideals become impossible or difficult to realize, such that a different ideal of justice should and must be striven for? If historical injustice can change the meaning, context, and uptake of various ideas, and political theorizing about justice focuses on claims publicly justified to others, then domination across borders could change what justice publicly amounts to.[64]

Ivison tackles the relationship between history and injustice in yet another manner. In his chapter, Ivison uses the example of indigenous peoples to think about the sources of, and remedies for, domination within and across borders, as well as how this can point to a new standard of cosmopolitan justice. Like Mills and others, Ivison rejects starting from an ideal theory that ignores or marginalizes the history of domination. Indeed, the very category of indigenous peoples did not exist before European imperialism and settler colonialism. However, in his chapter, Ivison does not envision an "end" to indigenous peoples. Ivison adopts a practice-dependent approach to justice, which does not assume that there is one eternally true principle of justice.[65] The content and scope of justice depends at least in part on

---

62 Ibid., 180.

63 Mills makes this claim in "Rawls, Ideal Theory, and Racial Justice," forthcoming. Of course, practically speaking, Mills might say it is difficult, if not impossible, to overcome non-ideal conditions.

64 For an argument to this effect with respect to Rawls and the social basis of self-respect, and including a discussion of Mills, see Timothy Waligore, "Rawls, Self-respect, and Assurance: How Past Injustice Changes what Publicly Counts as Justice," forthcoming in *Politics, Philosophy & Economics*.

65 On practice-dependent approaches to justice, see Andrea Sangiovanni, "Global Justice, Reciprocity, and the State," *Philosophy & Public Affairs* 35, no. 1 (2007): 3–39; Sangiovanni, "Justice and the Priority of Politics to Morality," *Journal of Political Philosophy* 16, no. 2 (2008): 137–64; Aaron James, "Constructing Justice for Existing Practice: Rawls and the Status Quo," *Philosophy & Public Affairs* 33, no. 3 (2005): 281–316; Ayelet Banai, Miriam Ronzoni, and Christian Schemmel, "Global and Social Justice: The Possibility of Social Justice Beyond States in a World of Overlapping Practices," in *Social Justice, Global Dynamics: Theoretical and Empirical Perspectives*, eds. Ayelet Banai, Miriam Ronzoni, and Christian Schemmel (London: Routledge, 2011), 46–60.

interpreting the point of shared practices. Only if people stand in particular "practice-mediated relations" to one another do principles of justice hold. Ivison invokes a form of practice dependence that also examines how practices have had historical impact, for good or ill. While this means there may be principles of justice that are not global in scope, there are other practices that point to universal or cosmopolitan principles. Justice would emerge from the interactions between different units, including ones involving domination. Like Forst and others, and against Thomas Nagel, he does not limit justice to the state.[66] Practices of imperialism and domination within and across borders have shaped the international system and marginalized non-state actors.

Ivison draws upon Seyla Benhabib, who has used the situation of legal and illegal immigrants to point towards "another cosmopolitanism."[67] Ivison thinks that the situation of indigenous peoples and their appeals to international law points to a form of "emergent cosmopolitanism." This requires theorizing about the spaces between the local and the global, and cosmopolitan or universal justice emerges in a way not possible through ideal theorizing. He emphasizes how indigenous peoples have pushed for multiple, overlapping forms of citizenship, and for their recognition as "peoples" in international law, helping to re-theorize what it means to be a "people." This includes disconnecting the idea of self-determination from independent statehood.[68] The situation of indigenous peoples has posed challenges to traditional notions of sovereignty and even inspired theories of "self-determination as non-domination" across borders.[69]

Ivison notes, in a Marxian spirit, that our (mis)conceptions of what constitutes domination may leave important harms in place, and even reify them. While invoking Forst, Ivison also challenges him, saying that particular justificatory schemes can themselves be dominating. Injustice, Ivison says, is not only tied in with concerns about the *standing* to make claims, but is also concerned with the *uptake* of claims. A party's claim may be

---

66 Thomas Nagel, "The Problem of Global Justice," *Philosophy & Public Affairs* 33, no. 2 (2005): 113–47.

67 Seyla Benhabib, *The Rights of Others* (Cambridge, UK: Cambridge University Press, 2004); Benhabib, *Another Cosmopolitanism*, ed. Robert Post (Cambridge, UK: Cambridge University, 2006).

68 See, for example, S. James Anaya, *Indigenous Peoples in International Law* (New York: Oxford University Press, 1996); Will Kymlicka, "Theorizing Indigenous Rights," in *Politics in the Vernacular* (Oxford: Oxford University Press, 2001), ch. 6.

69 Iris Marion Young, invoking Pettit, the Iroquois confederacy, and debates over the draft declaration of the rights of indigenous peoples, distinguishes between self-determination as non-interference and self-determination as non-domination. She favors the latter, and argues that it requires federalism, and could be applied at various levels worldwide. See especially Young, *Global Challenges: War, Self-Determination, and Responsibility for Justice* (Cambridge, UK: Polity, 2006).

misunderstood or may not (easily) be comprehensible as a claim of justice, given the dominant political ideas and forms of justification. The invitation to take part in justificatory processes can seem hollow when participants struggle to make their claims *heard*.[70]

Dale Turner has written about how indigenous peoples are constrained to speak the language of liberalism if they want their claims understood by non-Aboriginal judges and politicians.[71] Further, some indigenous writers argue that indigenous peoples should not aim to be included within institutions shaped by historical injustice, and thereby achieve standing to make justificatory claims *within* them, as this may involve buying into certain dominant discourses, and come at a high cost.[72] Indigenous peoples have developed their own conceptions of "self-determination."[73] Taiaiake Alfred and Jeff Corntassel argue that accepting "self-government" within the constitution of the settler state amounts to consenting to transnational historical injustice.[74] Corntassel discusses an "illusion of inclusion" at the international level; whereas once the United Nations excluded

---

[70] Amy Allen has also criticized Forst in a somewhat related, but different, manner. See the contributions, and Forst's response, in Forst, *Justice, Democracy and the Right to Justification: Rainer Forst in Dialogue* (London: Bloomsbury Academic, 2014).

[71] Turner, *This is Not a Peace Pipe: Towards a Critical Indigenous Philosophy* (Toronto: University of Toronto Press, 2006), 58–59. Cf. Turner, "Oral Traditions and the Politics of (Mis)recognition," in *American Indian Thought: Philosophical Essays*, ed. Anne Waters (Malden, MA: Blackwell, 2004).

[72] Taiaiake Alfred, *Peace, Power, Righteousness: An Indigenous Manifesto* (Oxford: Oxford University Press, 1999).

[73] See, for example, Jeff Corntassel, "Toward Sustainable Self-Determination: Rethinking the Contemporary Indigenous-Rights Discourse," *Alternatives* 33 (2008), 105–32; Val Napolean, "Aboriginal Self Determination: Individual Self and Collective Selves," *Atlantis* 29, no. 2 (2005): 1–21; Grace Ouellette, *The Fourth World: An Indigenous Perspective on Feminism and Aboriginal Women's Activism* (Halifax, NS: Fernwood, 2002).

[74] Taiaiake Alfred and Jeff Corntassel, "Being Indigenous: Resurgences against Contemporary Colonialism," *Government and Opposition* 40, no. 4 (2005): 597–615. Further, it has been argued that indigenous ideas are incommensurable with non-indigenous ideas, so it is futile to attempt to have them recognized appropriately in non-indigenous fora. See Mary Ellen Turpel, "Aboriginal Peoples and the Canadian *Charter*: Interpretative Monopolies, Cultural Differences," *Canadian Human Rights Yearbook* 6 (1989–1990): 3–45. In contrast, Angelia Means has argued that indigenous peoples must risk misrecognition in a multicultural democracy, but that their claims may be heard in the form of narrative argumentation; in this way, indigenous ideas could inform and transform what ideas mean for everyone, rather than indigenous peoples being merely passive recipients of how languages of justification are usually used. For example, Aboriginal ideas of land use might alter everyone's conception of property. Angelia Means, "Narrative Argumentation: Arguing with Natives," *Constellations* 9, no. 2 (2002): 221–45. However, even if intercultural dialogue is possible, it might best be achieved through recognition of indigenous

indigenous peoples, it now includes professionalized indigenous delegates more loyal to the United Nations system than responsive to their communities.[75]

All four authors in section II of this volume do not simply engage in abstract theorizing about justice, but pay attention to the importance of political struggles, dialogue, and how political claims will be made and received in a specific context where domination across borders is an issue. McCormick writes about the audience Machiavelli addresses in making strategic political arguments about imperialism. McCarthy believes the political discourses of modernity—brought about through domination—are inescapable, but these norms are required for groups to have equal standing in making claims; however, postcolonial critics point out how marginalized groups have not agreed, and that we cannot assume that agreement will validate western norms and institutions in a wholesale fashion. Mills invokes Fraser's thoughts on contestation about the appropriate way to "frame" justice, as it can no longer be assumed that justice takes place in the nation-state.[76] Mills says that concerns about the legacy of colonialism have been hidden by what Joe Feagin calls a "white racial frame," which has shaped white cognition and theorizing, and ignored the need to repair the past.[77] Ivison discusses the "uptake" of political arguments, whether indigenous peoples can make their claims heard, and how historical practices point to a new standard of universal justice. In each of these ways, the authors in this section theorize political justice within a historical context of domination across borders.

3 GLOBAL GOVERNANCE, INSTITUTIONS, AND NORMATIVE THEORY

In domestic republican theory, non-domination is realized in the context of the state. Recall the definition of freedom as non-domination and its contrast with freedom as non-interference. A person who is subject to another's arbitrary will is un-free, regardless of whether the dominating person—or institution—actually interferes with their choices. Non-arbitrary law, which is formulated by the people in a constitutional

---

sovereignty with indigenous peoples having their own separate jurisdictions. See Michael Rabinder James, "Tribal Sovereignty and the Intercultural Sphere," *Philosophy & Social Criticism* 25, no. 5 (1999): 57–86.

75 Jeff Corntassel, "Towards a New Partnership? Indigenous Political Mobilization and Co-optation During the First UN Indigenous Decade (1995–2004)," *Human Rights Quarterly* 29, no. 1 (February 2007): 137–66, 161.

76 Fraser, *Scales of Justice*, ch. 2.

77 Joe R. Feagin, *The White Racial Frame: Centuries of Racial Framing and Counter-Framing* (New York: Routledge, 2010).

republic, is, by contrast, interfering but non-dominating. Interference is problematic only to the extent that it is arbitrary, because in this case the interfering agent is "not forced to track the interests and ideas of those who suffer the interference."[78]

Individuals are thus only free as citizens of a republic; that is, as members of a representative polity whose institutions force it to track their interests. The protection against domination that state institutions provide is not conceptually distinct from these institutions themselves; republican freedom is constituted by institutions, and, as Lena Halldenius puts it, "institution-dependent."[79]

Given this strong conceptual link between non-domination and state institutions, the question remains whether the conception of non-domination can be adapted to the global context. However, several global republican theorists have attempted to do just that.

Staying close to Pettit's interpretation of republicanism, Steven Slaughter argues that we must counter domination beyond the state in order to safeguard freedom within it.[80] His global civic republican model relies on a transformation of the state, rather than the addition of global institutions. James Bohman moves beyond the institutional model of the state. Like Slaughter, he argues that the current global order, with its delegation of political authority beyond the state, has much potential for domination. He defines domination by reference to the normative power of citizenship rather than the capacity for arbitrary interference or control.[81] Non-domination is achieved in a democratic system, when "individuals are empowered as free and equal citizens to form and change the terms of their common life together."[82] Bohman argues that, transnationally, the best contexts for the realization of non-domination are multiple, overlapping political communities, or *dêmoi*. Fabian Schuppert largely follows Bohman's global democratic account. He argues in support of dispersing power across institutional levels—local, state, regional, and supranational—but also links the achievement of global democracy to the alleviation of distributive injustice.[83]

---

[78] Pettit, *Republicanism*, 272.

[79] Lena Halldenius, "Building Blocks of a Republican Cosmopolitanism: The Modality of Being Free," *European Journal of Political Theory* 9, no. 1 (2010): 12–30, 12–13.

[80] Steven Slaughter, "The Neo-Roman Republican Legacy and International Political Theory"; Slaughter, *Liberty Beyond Neo-Liberalism*.

[81] Bohman, *Democracy Across Borders*.

[82] Ibid., 45.

[83] Fabian Schuppert, *Freedom, Recognition and Non-Domination: A Republican Theory of (Global) Justice* (Dordrecht, NL: Springer, 2014). For another republican approach that is congenial to Bohman's, see Andreas Niederberger, *Demokratie unter Bedingungen der Weltgesellschaft?* (Berlin: De Gruyter, 2009).

Like Bohman, Lawrence Quill adopts a global republican approach that focuses on citizenship and participatory politics.[84] Quill, however, places little faith in global institutional solutions—at least in the present context, as individuals are not yet educated for cosmo-republican citizenship. This form of citizenship, Quill explains, focuses on dissent and resistance.[85] According to Quill, cosmo-republican freedom is exercised by "communities or individuals interested in protest and dissent, exchanging ideas and proposing policy alternatives to those offered by their own territorially based governments."[86]

In international relations, Daniel Deudney has drawn attention to a tradition he calls republican security theory, according to which we can be secure (or free, in neo-republican parlance) only when both anarchy and hierarchy are avoided.[87] José Luis Martí's article, "A Global Republic to Prevent Global Domination," argues in support of a unified, global institutional solution to domination.[88] It stands out as the primary republican contribution to the recently resurgent literature on the world state,[89] which is part of normative scholarship on global governance.

A recent symposium issue, edited by Duncan Bell, brings together some of the most interesting work that is being done in this emerging, global republican approach.[90] Cécile Laborde has forcefully articulated the problem of global domination and its link to distributive injustice, calling on republicans to tackle the global inequalities that make possible "capability-denying relations of domination between the rich and powerful and the poor and the weak."[91]

As discussed above, while many international political theorists are interested primarily in global norms and distributive concerns, including rights

---

84 Lawrence Quill, *Liberty after Liberalism: Civic Republicanism in a Global Age* (London: Palgrave Macmillan, 2005).
85 In the absence of education for world citizenship, Quill says that it will be necessary to rely on an elite of politically active, concerned citizens.
86 Quill, *Liberty after Liberalism*, 3.
87 Daniel H. Deudney, *Bounding Power: Republican Security Theory from the Polis to the Global Village* (Princeton: Princeton University Press, 2007). Anarchy and hierarchy can be understood as domination by private and public actors, respectively.
88 José Luis Martí, "A Global Republic to Prevent Global Domination," *Diacrítica* 24, no. 2 (2010): 31–72.
89 See, for example, Luis Cabrera, *Political Theory of Global Justice: A Cosmopolitan Case for the World State* (New York: Routledge, 2004); Raffaele Marchetti, *Global Democracy: For and Against* (New York: Routledge, 2008).
90 Duncan Bell, ed., "Global Justice and Republicanism (Special Issue)," *European Journal of Political Theory* 10, no. 1 (2010), with contributions by Lena Halldenius, Duncan Ivison, Cécile Laborde, Philip Pettit, and Quentin Skinner. On a similar topic, see also Besson and Martí, *Legal Republicanism*, especially the section on republican international law.
91 Laborde, "Republicanism and Global Justice: A Sketch," 54.

to goods and responsibilities to provide those, others address more explicitly *political* questions of global governance. Global gover*nance* is best contrasted with global govern*ment* and can be defined as "systems of rule . . . in which the pursuit of goals through the exercise of control has transnational repercussions."[92] Instead of focusing on the substantive content of the moral problems that characterize globalization and the current global order, global governance projects instead engage with the political question of the structure and processes by which the various policies that bear on the moral problems associated with globalization gain acceptance.

Normative global governance scholars tend to focus, first, on the normative deficiencies and challenges of the current order and, second, on the agents, institutions, and processes that may constitute or help facilitate reform. The four chapters in section III of this volume also address these two important, related questions.

The first question pertains to the "new circumstances of politics," and asks in which respects the current global order falls short. Jürgen Habermas has described the effect of globalization on the constitutionalization of international law, which limits the power of states.[93] David Held has noted five "disjunctures" between globalization and democracy which demonstrate the way in which globalization has created a new political reality. He names the emergence of international law, the internationalization of political decision-making, the relationship between hegemonic powers and the international security structures, the tension between national identity and the globalization of culture, and, finally, the importance of the global economy.[94] As John Maynor describes in his chapter in this volume, the efficacy of the state has been impacted by economic globalization and the new global order, which consists not just of states but also non-state actors, such as multinational corporations, and supra-state actors, such as global institutions. This has serious consequences for individual freedom, since states have lost some of their capacity to protect residents against domination. Similarly, Hauke Brunkhorst laments the non-democratic character of global governance, arguing in his chapter that globalization has placed societal decision-making processes beyond the control of democratic legislation. Terry Macdonald in her chapter points more generally to the alienation of powerful group agents—such as those that characterize the global order—from the common goals that motivated individuals to bring them into being. As a result, individuals become affected subjects rather than active participants. Against this concern with the political, Stefan Gosepath in his chapter argues that what matters instead is the extent to which the current global

[92] Rosenau, "Governance in the Twenty-First Century," 13.
[93] Jürgen Habermas, "Does the Constitutionalization of International Law Still Have a Chance?" in *The Divided West* (Cambridge, UK: Polity, 2006).
[94] David Held, *Democracy and the Global Order: From the Modern State to Cosmopolitan Governance* (Cambridge, UK: Polity Press, 1995), 99–135.

order fails to alleviate global deprivation; he thinks that a duty to aid is more important than a duty to not dominate.

The second and related question of global governance asks how the world order can or should be reformed in line with the values we care about. Whereas cosmopolitan democrats such as Held prioritize autonomy and self-determination, the primary republican concern is the realization of non-domination beyond the state. In either case, pertinent questions include which agents ought to perform tasks of global governance and how institutions at various levels of decision-making ought to interact with, and defer to, one another. Within this literature, world state theorists, who propose a globally unified political authority, fall on one end of the spectrum, and political theorists who seek to strengthen the role of the state at the expense of other agents fall on the other. In between are global democrats—notably, Held and Daniele Archibugi—and those scholars, such as Habermas, who advocate for regional or global federalism.[95]

Our volume covers a range of approaches to global governance, both with regard to the *process* of reform and the *agents* of global governance. The agents include states, international NGOs, global corporations, and international institutions. With regard to these agents, John Maynor argues that states are currently best placed to protect individuals against global sources of domination, because genuine democracy is only practiced at the state level. Appropriately, republican global institutions may emerge over time, but at present, states should continue to protect individuals from domination. Terry Macdonald and Stefan Gosepath disagree with Maynor's focus on states, albeit for different reasons. As Macdonald sees it, our world order is already a pluralist one, in which public power—a form of group agency that aims to advance common goods—is exercised by a complex set of state, non-governmental, and intergovernmental (supra-state) agents. Accordingly, republicans ought to focus on creating sources of antipower—a form of agency that counters the "choice-constraining effects"[96] of public power through participation—at those same levels: state, non-governmental, and intergovernmental.[97] Stefan Gosepath, for his part, argues that the duty to

---

95 See, for example, David Held, *Democracy and the Global Order*; Held, *Global Covenant: The Social Democratic Alternative to the Washington Consensus* (Cambridge, UK: Polity, 2004); Daniele Archibugi, *The Global Commonwealth of Citizens: Toward Cosmopolitan Democracy* (Princeton: Princeton University Press, 2008); Jürgen Habermas, *The Divided West* (Cambridge, UK: Polity, 2006); Habermas, *The Crisis of the European Union: A Response* (Cambridge, UK: Polity, 2012).

96 Terry Macdonald, "Antipower, Agency, and the Republican Case for Global Institutional Pluralism."

97 Macdonald's conception of public power rejects a functional interpretation of public power. For an alternative view, see Barbara Buckinx, "Global Actors and Public Power," *Critical Review of International Social and Political Philosophy* 15, no. 5 (2012), 535–51.

alleviate (global) poverty leads to a requirement that collective agents be established. States have been shown to be effective collective agents, so, based on past experience, state-like organizations are preferable, though other candidates are emerging. Hauke Brunkhorst expresses deep skepticism about the role of global institutions in global governance. He argues that institutions are part of the problem rather than the solution, and that the democratization of world society will be spearheaded not by formal agents, but by the politics of global protest.

In addition to theorizing about the agents, global governance theorists also focus on the process of reform itself. The prolific, global democratic approach envisions three related transformations in the global order: the promotion of coordinated state action, support for effective international institutions, and the development of "multilateral rules and procedures that lock in all powers, small and major, into a multilateral framework."[98] Habermas, James Bohman, and others—including John Maynor in this volume—look to the European Union as an exemplar of transnational constitutionalism. However, while Maynor admires the European model, he ultimately stays close to the institutional prescriptions of domestic republicanism. He argues that a world state, or more loosely organized supra-state institutions, cannot easily be brought under citizen control, and that it may thus be counterproductive to assign such institutions the task of safeguarding non-domination. Instead, citizens should be empowered to utilize state institutions to resist domination. The application of republican ideals to global institutions may remain an important goal, but the initial and primary focus should be on the continued development of state institutions in accordance with the ideal of non-domination.

In his chapter, Stefan Gosepath is interested in global institutional reform to the extent that it is necessary for the alleviation of severe poverty. Because individuals lack clarity regarding the specific nature of their individual responsibility to reduce global deprivation, a collective agent must be created or reformed to specify the contours of individual duties to aid. Such an agent can be a loose collection of individuals rather than a formal institution. A collective agent exists when it is formed on the basis of a general consensus, there is a joint definition of shared aims and moral norms, action is voluntary, and an internal organizational framework and decision-making procedure is in place. Powerful agents have a greater duty to create and reform global institutions that will solve for global poverty. The duty to form political institutions comes from the individual duty to aid, not from a duty to not dominate, as with republicans in this volume. Gosepath makes eight arguments in opposition to the neo-republican emphasis on non-domination, providing a valuable contrast to the positions of many authors in this volume. For Gosepath, politics is not the

[98] David Held, *Global Covenant*, 102.

first question of justice; deprivation is the first problem, and politics is the answer.

Terry Macdonald, in her chapter, argues that global institutional design should be responsive to the constraints that the prevailing material structures and cultural artifacts pose on the development of public power and antipower. The existence of these material and cultural preconditions explains why democracy—or any other goal of global governance—is only rarely successfully imposed through external efforts to build institutions. Instead, we must identify existing agencies of political power and then attempt to reform them in accordance with democratic norms.

The volume ends with a chapter by Hauke Brunkhorst, who thinks that the greatest source of global domination is legalization and constitutionalization, the same processes that are often offered as solutions to domination. However, the seeds of reform are contained in the same international legal framework that establishes non-democratic transnational rule. The inclusion of human rights and "democratic constitutional rhetoric" in international legal documents provides the basis for global protest movements that may ultimately help transform international law into law that secures space for democratic politics.[99]

Both republicanism and international political theory have undergone a revival in the late 20th and early 21st centuries. Seen as a personal relation or structural phenomenon that involves subjection to (the will of) another or others, domination is a common concern of both literatures. This volume brings them together in an effort to advance scholarship on domination across borders.

While domination is best seen as just one form of injustice, there are systematic and pragmatic reasons to make domination, and the related ideal of non-domination, the primary locus of concern when theorizing justice and injustice across borders. The republican debate has frequently failed to take into account the various, alternative ways of conceptualizing domination as a political problem. The contributions here further suggest that what counts as domination and injustice can often only be contextually understood with reference to the history of domination. Focusing on such problems as imperialism, racism, and the subjection of indigenous peoples suggests that global institutional remedies and norms may need to reflect the global history of domination across borders. Finally, global domination can be tackled only when the contributions of a myriad of global agents—including NGOs, multinational corporations, and global institutions—to both domination and its reduction are acknowledged. Global institutional design itself must also be attentive to the problem of global domination and the role that global institutions have played, and continue to play.

---

[99] Hauke Brunkhorst, "Democracy and World Law: On the Problem of Global Constitutionalism" (this volume).

BIBLIOGRAPHY

Alfred, Taiaiake. *Peace, Power, Righteousness: An Indigenous Manifesto*. Oxford: Oxford University Press, 1999.

Alfred, Taiaiake, and Jeff Corntassel. "Being Indigenous: Resurgences against Contemporary Colonialism." *Government and Opposition* 40, no. 4 (2005): 597–615.

Allen, Amy. "Domination in Global Politics." In *Domination and Global Political Justice: Conceptual, Historical, and Institutional Perspectives*, edited by Barbara Buckinx, Jonathan Trejo-Mathys, and Timothy Waligore. New York: Routledge, 2015.

Allen, Amy. "Feminist Perspectives on Power." *The Stanford Encyclopedia of Philosophy*, edited by Edward N. Zalta (Summer 2014 Edition). http://plato.stanford.edu/archives/sum2014/entries/feminist-power.

Allen, Amy. *The Power of Feminist Theory: Domination, Resistance, Solidarity*. Boulder, CO: Westview Press, 1999.

Allen, Amy. "Rethinking Power." *Hypatia* 13, no. 1 (1998): 21–40.

Anaya, S. James. *Indigenous Peoples in International Law*, 1st ed. New York: Oxford University Press, 1996.

Archibugi, Daniele. *The Global Commonwealth of Citizens: Towards Cosmopolitan Democracy*. Princeton: Princeton University Press, 2008.

Banai, Ayelet, Miriam Ronzoni, and Christian Schemmel. "Global and Social Justice: The Possibility of Social Justice Beyond States in a World of Overlapping Practices." In *Social Justice, Global Dynamics: Theoretical and Empirical Perspectives*, edited by Ayelet Banai, Miriam Ronzoni, and Christian Schemmel, 46–60. London: Routledge, 2011.

Barry, Brian. *Theories of Justice*. Berkeley: University of California Press, 1989.

Beitz, Charles. *Political Theory and International Relations*. Princeton: Princeton University Press, 1979.

Bell, Duncan, ed., "Global Justice and Republicanism (Special Issue)." *European Journal of Political Theory* 10, no. 1 (2010): 9–102.

Bellamy, Richard. *Political Constitutionalism: A Republican Defense of the Constitutionality of Democracy*. Cambridge, UK: Cambridge University Press, 2007.

Benhabib, Seyla. *Another Cosmopolitanism*. Edited by Robert Post. Cambridge, UK: Cambridge University, 2006.

Benhabib, Seyla. *The Rights of Others*. Cambridge, UK: Cambridge University Press, 2004.

Besson, Samantha, and Jose Luis Marti, eds. *Legal Republicanism*. Oxford: Oxford University Press, 2009.

Bohman, James. *Democracy Across Borders: From Dêmos to Dêmoi*. Cambridge, MA: MIT Press, 2007.

Bohman, James. "Domination, Global Harms and the Priority of Injustice: Expanding Transnational Republicanism." In *Domination and Global Political Justice: Conceptual, Historical, and Institutional Perspectives*, edited by Barbara Buckinx, Jonathan Trejo-Mathys, and Timothy Waligore. New York: Routledge, 2015.

Bohman, James. "From Dêmos to Dêmoi: Democracy Across Borders." *Ratio Juris* 18, no. 3 (2005): 293–314.

Bohman, James. "Is Democracy a Means to Global Justice? Human Rights and the Democratic Minimum." *Ethics and International Affairs* 19, no. 1 (2005): 101–16.

Bohman, James. "Non-Domination and Transnational Democracy." In *Republicanism and Political Theory*, edited by Cécile Laborde and John Maynor, 190–216. Oxford: Blackwell, 2008.

Bohman, James. "Republican Cosmopolitanism." *The Journal of Political Philosophy*, 12, no. 3 (2004): 336–52.

Braithwaite, John, Hilary Charlesworth, and Adérito Soares. *Networked Governance of Freedom and Tyranny: Peace in East Timor*. Canberra: ANU Press, 2012.
Braithwaite, John, and Philip Pettit. *Not Just Deserts: A Republican Theory of Criminal Justice*. Oxford: Oxford University Press, 1990.
Brugger, William. *Republican Theory in Political Thought: Virtuous or Virtual?* New York: Macmillan, 1999.
Brunkhorst, Hauke. "Democracy and World Law: On the Problem of Global Constitutionalism." In *Domination and Global Political Justice: Conceptual, Historical, and Institutional Perspectives*, edited by Barbara Buckinx, Jonathan Trejo-Mathys, and Timothy Waligore. New York: Routledge, 2015.
Buckinx, Barbara. "Global Actors and Public Power." *Critical Review of International Social and Political Philosophy* 15, no. 5 (2012): 535–51.
Butt, Daniel. *Rectifying International Injustice: Principles of Compensation and Restitution Between Nations*. Oxford: Oxford University Press, 2009.
Cabrera, Luis. *Political Theory of Global Justice: A Cosmopolitan Case for the World State*. New York: Routledge, 2004.
Chakrabarty, Dipesh. *Provincializing Europe: Postcolonial Thought and Historical Difference*. Princeton: Princeton University Press, 2000.
Corntassel, Jeff. "Towards a New Partnership? Indigenous Political Mobilization and Co-optation During the First UN Indigenous Decade (1995–2004)." *Human Rights Quarterly* 29, no. 1 (February 2007): 137–66.
Corntassel, Jeff. "Toward Sustainable Self-Determination: Rethinking the Contemporary Indigenous-Rights Discourse." *Alternatives* 33 (2008): 105–32.
Deudney, Daniel H. *Bounding Power: Republican Security Theory from the Polis to the Global Village*. Princeton: Princeton University Press, 2007.
Fabre, Cécile. "Reparative Justice." In *Justice in a Changing World*. Cambridge, UK: Polity, 2007.
Feagin, Joe R. *The White Racial Frame: Centuries of Racial Framing and Counter-Framing*. New York: Routledge, 2010.
Flikschuh, Katrin. *Kant and Modern Political Philosophy*. Cambridge, UK: Cambridge University Press, 2000.
Forst, Rainer. *Justice, Democracy and the Right to Justification: Rainer Forst in Dialogue*. London: Bloomsbury Academic, 2014.
Forst, Rainer. *Justification and Critique: Towards a Critical Theory of Politics*. Translated by Ciaran Cronin. Cambridge, UK: Polity, 2013.
Forst, Rainer. "A Kantian Republican Conception of Justice as Nondomination." In *Republican Democracy*, edited by Andreas Niederberger and Philipp Schink, 154–68. Edinburgh: Edinburgh University Press, 2013.
Forst, Rainer. *The Right to Justification: Elements of a Constructivist Theory of Justice*. Translated by Jeffrey Flynn. New York: Columbia University Press, 2012.
Forst, Rainer. "Towards a Critical Theory of Transnational Justice." *Metaphilosophy* 32, nos. 1/2 (2001): 160–79.
Forst, Rainer. "Transnational Justice and Democracy: Overcoming Three Dogmas of Political Theory." In *Political Equality in Transnational Democracy*, edited by Eva Erman and Sofia Näsström, 41–59. New York: Palgrave Macmillan, 2013.
Forst, Rainer. "Transnational Justice and Non-Domination: A Discourse-Theoretical Approach." In *Domination and Global Political Justice: Conceptual, Historical, and Institutional Perspectives*, edited by Barbara Buckinx, Jonathan Trejo-Mathys, and Timothy Waligore. New York: Routledge, 2015.
Forst, Rainer. "Two Pictures of Justice." In *Justice, Democracy and the Right to Justification: Rainer Forst in Dialogue*. London: Bloomsbury Academic, 2014.
Fraser, Nancy. "Beyond the Master/Subject Model: Reflections on Carole Pateman's *Sexual Contract*." *Social Text* 37 (1993): 173–81.

Fraser, Nancy. *Scales of Justice: Reimagining Political Space in a Globalizing World.* New York: Columbia University Press, 2009.

Gosepath, Stefan. "Deprivation and Institutionally Based Duties to Aid." In *Domination and Global Political Justice: Conceptual, Historical, and Institutional Perspectives*, edited by Barbara Buckinx, Jonathan Trejo-Mathys, and Timothy Waligore. New York: Routledge, 2015.

Habermas, Jürgen. *The Crisis of the European Union: A Response.* Translated by Ciaran Cronin. Cambridge, UK: Polity, 2012.

Habermas, Jürgen. *The Divided West.* Cambridge, UK: Polity, 2006.

Habermas, Jürgen. "Does the Constitutionalization of International Law Still Have a Chance?" In *The Divided West*, edited and translated by Ciaran Cronin, 115–93. Cambridge, UK: Polity, 2006.

Halldenius, Lena. "Building Blocks of a Republican Cosmopolitanism: The Modality of Being Free." *European Journal of Political Theory* 9, no. 1 (2010): 12–30.

Halldenius, Lena. *Liberty Revisited.* Lund, SE: Bokbox Publications, 2001.

Held, David. *Democracy and the Global Order: From the Modern State to Cosmopolitan Governance.* Cambridge, UK: Polity Press, 1995.

Held, David. *Global Covenant: The Social Democratic Alternative to the Washington Consensus.* Cambridge, UK: Polity, 2004.

Honohan, Iseult. *Civic Republicanism.* London: Routledge, 2002.

Honohan, Iseult, and Jeremy Jennings, eds. *Republicanism in Theory and Practice.* London: Routledge, 2006.

Howard-Hassman, Rhoda E., with Anthony P. Lombardo. *Reparations to Africa.* Pennsylvania: University of Pennsylvania Press, 2008.

Ivison, Duncan. "Indigenous Peoples, Injustice, and Global Politics." In *Domination and Global Political Justice: Conceptual, Historical, and Institutional Perspectives*, edited by Barbara Buckinx, Jonathan Trejo-Mathys, and Timothy Waligore. New York: Routledge, 2015.

Ivison, Duncan. *Postcolonial Liberalism.* Cambridge, UK: Cambridge University Press, 2002.

Ivison, Duncan, Paul Patton, and Will Sanders, eds. *Political Theory and the Rights of Indigenous Peoples.* New York: Cambridge University Press, 2000.

James, Aaron. "Constructing Justice for Existing Practice: Rawls and the Status Quo." *Philosophy & Public Affairs* 33, no. 3 (2005): 281–316.

James, Michael Rabinder. "Tribal Sovereignty and the Intercultural Sphere." *Philosophy & Social Criticism* 25, no. 5 (1999): 57–86.

Kant, Immanuel. *The Metaphysics of Morals.* In *Practical Philosophy*, edited and translated by Mary J. Gregor. Cambridge, UK: Cambridge University Press, 1996.

King, Desmond, Carole Pateman, Charles Mills et al. "Symposium: *Contract and Domination* by Carole Pateman and Charles W. Mills." *Journal of Political Ideologies* 13, no. 3 (2008): 227–62.

Kymlicka, Will. "Theorizing Indigenous Rights." In *Politics in the Vernacular.* Oxford: Oxford University Press, 2001.

Laborde, Cécile. *Critical Republicanism: The Hijab Controversy and Political Philosophy.* Oxford: Oxford University Press, 2008.

Laborde, Cécile. "Republicanism and Global Justice: A Sketch." *European Journal of Political Theory* 9, no. 1 (2010): 48–69.

Laborde, Cécile, and John Maynor, eds. *Republicanism and Political Theory.* Oxford: Blackwell, 2007.

Levy, Jacob T., with Iris Marion Young, eds. *Colonialism and its Legacies.* Lanham, MD: Lexington Books, 2011.

List, Christian, and Laura Valentini. "Freedom as Independence: A Critical Survey." Working Paper. 2012/2013. London, UK. http://personal.lse.ac.uk/list/PDF-files/Freedom-as-Independence.pdf.

Lovett, Frank. *A General Theory of Justice & Domination*. Oxford: Oxford University Press, 2010.
Lu, Catherine. "Colonialism as Structural Injustice: Historical Responsibility and Contemporary Redress." *Journal of Political Philosophy* 19, no. 3 (September 2011): 261–81.
Macdonald, Terry. "Antipower, Agency, and the Republican Case for Global Institutional Pluralism." In *Domination and Global Political Justice: Conceptual, Historical, and Institutional Perspectives*, edited by Barbara Buckinx, Jonathan Trejo-Mathys, and Timothy Waligore. New York: Routledge, 2015.
Macdonald, Terry, and Miriam Ronzoni. "Introduction: The Idea of Global Political Justice." *Critical Review of International Social and Political Philosophy* 15, no. 5 (2012): 521–33.
MacGilvray, Eric. *The Invention of Market Freedom*. Cambridge, UK: Cambridge University Press, 2011.
Mann, Michael. "Has Globalization Ended the Rise and Rise of the Nation-State?" *Review of International Political Economy* 4, no. 3 (1997): 472–96.
Marchetti, Raffaele. *Global Democracy: For and Against*. New York: Routledge, 2008.
Martí, José Luis. "A Global Republic to Prevent Global Domination." *Diacrítica* 24, no. 2 (2010): 31–72.
Martí, José Luis, and Philip Pettit. *A Political Philosophy in Public Life: Civic Republicanism in Zapatero's Spain*. Princeton: Princeton University Press, 2010.
Maynor, John. *Republicanism in the Modern World*. Cambridge, UK: Polity Press, 2003.
Maynor, John. "Should Republican Liberty As Non-Domination Be Outsourced?" In *Domination and Global Political Justice: Conceptual, Historical, and Institutional Perspectives*, edited by Barbara Buckinx, Jonathan Trejo-Mathys, and Timothy Waligore. New York: Routledge, 2015.
McCarthy, Thomas. "Liberalism and the Dilemma of Development." In *Domination and Global Political Justice: Conceptual, Historical, and Institutional Perspectives*, edited by Barbara Buckinx, Jonathan Trejo-Mathys, and Timothy Waligore. New York: Routledge, 2015.
McCarthy, Thomas. *Race, Empire, and the Idea of Human Development*. Cambridge, UK: Cambridge University Press, 2009.
McCormick, John. "The (In)Compatibility of Liberty and Empire in Machiavelli's Political Thought." In *Domination and Global Political Justice: Conceptual, Historical, and Institutional Perspectives*, edited by Barbara Buckinx, Jonathan Trejo-Mathys, and Timothy Waligore. New York: Routledge, 2015.
McCormick, John. *Machiavellian Democracy*. Cambridge, UK: Cambridge University Press, 2001.
Means, Angelia. "Narrative Argumentation: Arguing with Natives." *Constellations* 9, no. 2 (2002): 221–45.
Meyer, Lukas H., ed. *Justice in Time: Responding to Historical Injustice*. Baden-Baden, DE: Nomos Verlagsgesellshaft, 2004.
Miller, David. *On Nationality*. Oxford: Oxford University Press, 1995.
Miller, Jon, and Rahul Kumar, eds. *Reparations: Interdisciplinary Inquiries*. Oxford: Oxford University Press, 2007.
Mills, Charles W. "Race and Global Justice." In *Domination and Global Political Justice: Conceptual, Historical and Institutional Perspectives*, edited by Barbara Buckinx, Jonathan Trejo-Mathys, and Timothy Waligore. New York: Routledge, 2015.
Mills, Charles W. *The Racial Contract*. Ithaca, NY: Cornell University Press, 1997.
Mills, Charles W. "Racial Liberalism." *PMLA (Publications of the Modern Language Association of America)* 123, no. 5 (2008): 1380–97.

Mills, Charles W. "Rawls, Ideal Theory, and Racial Justice." Forthcoming.
Mills, Charles W. "Rawls on Race/Race in Rawls." *The Southern Journal of Philosophy* XLVII (2009): 161–84.
Morefield, Jeanne. *Empires without Imperialism*. Oxford: Oxford University Press, 2014.
Muthu, Sankar, ed., *Empire and Modern Political Thought*. Cambridge, UK: Cambridge University Press, 2012.
Nagel, Thomas. "The Problem of Global Justice." *Philosophy & Public Affairs* 33, no. 2 (2005): 113–47.
Napolean, Val. "Aboriginal Self Determination: Individual Self and Collective Selves." *Atlantis* 29, no. 2 (2005): 1–21.
Nelson, Eric. *The Greek Tradition in Republican Thought*. Cambridge, UK: Cambridge University Press, 2004.
Niederberger, Andreas. *Demokratie unter Bedingungen der Weltgesellschaft?* Berlin: De Gruyter, 2009.
Niederberger, Andreas, and Philipp Schink, eds. *Republican Democracy: Liberty, Law and Politics*. Edinburgh: Edinburgh University Press, 2013.
Oldfield, Adrian. *Citizenship and Community: Civic Republicanism and the Modern World*. London: Routledge, 1990.
Onuf, Nicholas G. *The Republican Legacy in International Thought*. Cambridge, UK: Cambridge University Press, 1998.
Ouellette, Grace. *The Fourth World: An Indigenous Perspective on Feminism and Aboriginal Women's Activism*. Halifax, NS: Fernwood, 2002.
Pateman, Carole. *Sexual Contract*. Stanford: Stanford University Press, 1988.
Pettit, Philip. "The Domination Complaint." In *Nomos XLVI: Political Exclusion and Domination*, edited by Melissa S. Williams and Stephen Macedo, 118–63. New York: New York University, 2005.
Pettit, Philip. "Freedom as Antipower." *Ethics* 106, no. 3 (1996): 576–604.
Pettit, Philip. *Just Freedom: A Moral Compass for a Complex World*. New York: W. W. Norton, 2014.
Pettit, Philip. *On the People's Terms: A Republican Theory and Model of Democracy*. Cambridge, UK: Cambridge University Press, 2012.
Pettit, Philip. "A Republican Law of Peoples." *European Journal of Political Theory* 9, no. 1 (2010): 70–94.
Pettit, Philip. "The Republican Law of Peoples: A Restatement." In *Domination and Global Political Justice: Conceptual, Historical, and Institutional Perspectives*, edited by Barbara Buckinx, Jonathan Trejo-Mathys, and Timothy Waligore. New York: Routledge, 2015.
Pettit, Philip. *Republicanism: A Theory of Freedom and Government*. Oxford: Oxford University Press, 1997. Paperback ed., with postscript [1999].
Pitts, Jennifer. "Political Theory of Empire and Imperialism." *Annual Review of Political Science* 13 (2010): 211–35.
Pocock, J.G.A. *The Machiavellian Moment: Florentine Political Thought and the Atlantic Republican Tradition*. Princeton: Princeton University Press, 1975.
Pogge, Thomas. *Realizing Rawls*. Ithaca, NY: Cornell University Press, 1989.
Pogge, Thomas. *World Poverty and Human Rights*. Malden, MA: Polity, 2002.
Pogge, Thomas, and Darrel Moellendorf, eds. *Global Justice: Seminal Essays*. St. Paul, MN: Paragon House, 2008.
Quill, Lawrence. *Liberty after Liberalism: Civic Republicanism in a Global Age*. London: Palgrave Macmillan, 2005.
Rawls, John. *The Law of Peoples*. Cambridge, MA: Harvard University Press, 1999.
Richardson, Henry. *Democratic Autonomy*. New York: Oxford University Press, 2002.
Ripstein, Arthur. *Force and Freedom: Kant's Legal and Political Philosophy*. Cambridge, MA: Harvard University Press, 2009.

Rosenau, J. N. "Governance in the Twenty-First Century." *Global Governance* 1, no. 1 (1995): 13–43.
Sangiovanni, Andrea. "Global Justice, Reciprocity, and the State." *Philosophy & Public Affairs* 35, no. 1 (2007): 3–39.
Sangiovanni, Andrea. "Justice and the Priority of Politics to Morality." *Journal of Political Philosophy* 16, no. 2 (2008): 137–64.
Schuppert, Fabian. *Freedom, Recognition and Non-Domination: A Republican Theory of (Global) Justice.* Dordrecht, NL: Springer, 2014.
Sen, Amartya. *The Idea of Justice.* Cambridge, MA: Belknap Press, 2009.
Shue, Henry. *Basic Rights: Subsistence, Affluence, and US Foreign Policy.* Princeton: Princeton University Press, 1980.
Singer, Peter. "Famine, Affluence, and Morality." *Ethics and Public Affairs* 1, no. 1 (1972): 229–43.
Skinner, Quentin. *Liberty Before Liberalism.* Cambridge, UK: Cambridge University Press, 1998.
Slaughter, Steven. *Liberty Beyond Neo-Liberalism: A Republican Critique of Liberal Governance in a Globalizing Age.* New York: Palgrave Macmillan, 2005.
Slaughter, Steven. "The Neo-Roman Republican Legacy and International Political Theory." ANU Working Paper 2003/5. Canberra, AU. https://digitalcollections.anu.edu.au/bitstream/1885/42688/2/03–5.pdf.
Stilz, Anna. *Liberty Loyalty.* Princeton: Princeton University Press, 2011.
"Symposium on Ripstein's *Force and Freedom.*" *European Journal of Philosophy* 20, no. 3 (2012): 447–96.
Trejo-Mathys, Jonathan. "Toward a Critical Theory of the WTO: Thinking with Rawls Beyond Rawls." *Constellations* 20, no. 3 (2013): 459–82.
Turner, Dale. "Oral Traditions and the Politics of (Mis)recognition." In *American Indian Thought: Philosophical Essays*, edited by Anne Waters. Malden, MA: Blackwell, 2004.
Turner, Dale. *This is Not a Peace Pipe: Towards a Critical Indigenous Philosophy.* Toronto: University of Toronto Press, 2006.
Turpel, Mary Ellen. "Aboriginal Peoples and the Canadian *Charter*: Interpretative Monopolies, Cultural Differences." *Canadian Human Rights Yearbook* 6 (1989–1990): 3–45.
Van Gelderen, Martin, and Quentin Skinner, eds. *Republicanism: A Shared European Heritage*, 2 vols. Cambridge, UK: Cambridge University Press, 2002.
Viroli, Maurizio. *For Love of Country: An Essay on Patriotism and Nationalism.* Oxford: Clarendon Press, 1995.
Viroli, Maurizio. *Republicanism.* New York: Hill and Wang, 2002.
Waligore, Timothy. "Cosmopolitan Right, Indigenous Peoples, the Risks of Cultural Interaction." *Public Reason: Journal of Political and Moral Philosophy* 1, no. 1 (2009): 27–56.
Waligore, Timothy. "Rawls, Self-Respect, and Assurance: How Past Injustice Changes what Publicly Counts as Justice." Forthcoming in *Politics, Philosophy & Economics.*
Weinstock, Daniel, and Christian Nadeau, eds. *Republicanism: History, Theory and Practice.* London: Frank Cass, 2004.
White, Stuart. *Building a Citizen Society: The Emerging Politics of Republican Democracy.* Edited by Daniel Leighton. London: Lawrence and Wishart, 2008.
Young, Iris Marion. *Global Challenges: War, Self-Determination, and Responsibility for Justice.* Cambridge, UK: Polity, 2006.
Young, Iris Marion. *Justice and the Politics of Difference.* Princeton: Princeton University Press, 1990.
Young, Iris Marion. *Responsibility for Justice.* Oxford: Oxford University Press, 2011.

Part I

Domination and Non-Domination

Conceptual Issues

2 The Republican Law of Peoples

A Restatement

Philip Pettit

This essay tries to provide a sketch of the international arrangements that we ought to recommend as means for coordinating and organizing the behavior of national states, as they currently exist.[1] Rousseau argued for taking men as they are and looking at the law as it might be.[2] Taking states as they are, in a variation on that principle, I ask about the international order as it might be. There is room for debate, of course, as to whether there ought to be national states of the kind with which we are familiar, or whether such states ought to have their existing territories or powers. But that is not the sort of discussion that I shall be pursuing here. For good or ill, I shall assume that there is unlikely to be a sea change in the configuration of national regimes and ask only about how those regimes ought to be internationally ordered.

I approach the topic from the viewpoint of the long republican tradition, using ideas developed in recent versions of a neo-republican philosophy of politics.[3] The core thesis in that tradition is that freedom is the paramount

---

[1] This is a thoroughly revised version of Philip Pettit, "A Republican Law of Peoples," *European Journal of Political Theory* 9, no. 1 (2010): 70–94. For a further discussion of the issues addressed see Pettit, *Just Freedom: A Moral Compass for a Complex World* (New York: W. W. Norton, 2014), ch. 6.

[2] Jean-Jacques Rousseau, *The Social Contract and Discourses* (London: J. M. Dent & Sons Ltd., 1973).

[3] An up-to-date list of English works in neo-republican thought should include these books: William Brugger, *Republican Theory in Political Thought: Virtuous or Virtual?* (New York: Macmillan, 1999); Iseult Honohan, *Civic Republicanism* (London: Routledge, 2002); Frank Lovett, *A General Theory of Domination & Justice* (Oxford: Oxford University Press, 2010); Jose Luis Martí and Philip Pettit, *A Political Philosophy in Public Life: Civic Republicanism in Zapatero's Spain* (Princeton: Princeton University Press, 2010); John Maynor, *Republicanism in the Modern World* (Cambridge: Polity Press, 2003); Eric MacGilvray, *The Invention of Market Freedom* (Cambridge: Cambridge University Press, 2011); Maurizio Viroli, *Republicanism* (New York: Hill and Wang, 2002); Philip Pettit, *Republicanism: A Theory of Freedom and Government* (Oxford: Oxford University Press, 1997), Paperback ed., with postscript [1999]; Quentin Skinner, *Liberty Before Liberalism* (Cambridge: Cambridge University Press, 1998); Lena Halldenius, *Liberty*

ideal in political life, and that freedom requires, not just the absence of arbitrary interference by others in your affairs, but also the absence of a power of arbitrary interference on their part: the absence of domination. Here I look at the international arrangements that might provide each people with a collective version of individual freedom, giving it a non-dominated status in relation to other states and other international agencies.

The paper is in seven sections. In section 1, I present an assumption about the nature of different states that shapes later discussion. In sections 2 and 3, I look at the nature and disvalue of domination in the interpersonal relations of individuals and the international interactions of peoples. In the following two sections, 4 and 5, I consider the sources of international domination and rehearse the sorts of remedies that might help to alleviate it. And then in section 6, I look at the advantages of highlighting the ideal of non-domination in this context rather than the thinner ideal of non-interference or the richer ideal of cosmopolitan justice.

Revisited (Lund, SE: Bokbox Publications, 2001); Pettit, *Just Freedom: A Moral Compass for a Complex World*; Pettit, *On the People's Terms: A Republican Theory and Model of Democracy* (Cambridge: Cambridge University Press, 2012); Fabian Schuppert, *Freedom, Recognition and Non-Domination: A Republican Theory of (Global) Justice* (Dordrecht, NL: Springer, 2014); these collections of papers: Samantha Besson and Jose Luis Martí, eds. *Legal Republicanism* (Oxford: Oxford University Press, 2009); Iseult Honohan and Jeremy Jennings, eds., *Republicanism in Theory and Practice* (London: Routledge, 2006); Cécile Laborde and John Maynor, eds., *Republicanism and Political Theory* (Oxford: Blackwell, 2008); Andreas Niederberger and Philipp Schink, eds., *Republican Democracy: Liberty, Law and Politics* (Edinburgh: Edinburgh University Press, 2013); Daniel Weinstock and Christian Nadeau, eds., *Republicanism: History, Theory and Practice* (London: Frank Cass, 2004); Martin van Gelderen and Quentin Skinner, eds., *Republicanism: A Shared European Heritage*, 2 vols. (Cambridge: Cambridge University Press, 2002); and a number of studies that deploy the conception of freedom as non-domination, broadly understood: Richard Bellamy, *Political Constitutionalism: A Republican Defense of the Constitutionality of Democracy* (Cambridge: Cambridge University Press, 2007); James Bohman, *Democracy Across Borders: From Dêmos to Dêmoi* (Cambridge, MA: MIT Press, 2007); John Braithwaite and Philip Pettit, *Not Just Deserts: A Republican Theory of Criminal Justice* (Oxford: Oxford University Press, 1990); Henry Richardson, *Democratic Autonomy* (New York: Oxford University Press, 2002); Steven Slaughter, *Liberty Beyond Neo-Liberalism: A Republican Critique of Liberal Government in a Globalising Age* (London: Macmillan Palgrave, 2005); Stuart White, *Building a Citizen Society: The Emerging Politics of Republican Democracy*, ed. Daniel Leighton (London: Lawrence and Wishart, 2008); Cécile Laborde, *Critical Republicanism: The Hijab Controversy and Political Philosophy* (Oxford: Oxford University Press, 2008); John Braithwaite, Hilary Charlesworth, and Adérito Soares, *Networked Governance of Freedom and Tyranny: Peace in East Timor* (Canberra: ANU Press, 2012). For a recent review of work in the tradition see Frank Lovett and Philip Pettit, "Neorepublicanism: A Normative and Institutional Research Program," *Annual Review of Political Science* 12 (2009): 11–29.

1 STATES, REPRESENTATIVE AND UNREPRESENTATIVE

States divide on two dimensions relevant to the issue of how they ought to be organized internationally. One bears on the measure in which they operate effectively, the other on the measure in which they are controlled by their peoples.

The first distinction marks the divide between effective states that have the capacity to provide for basic services to their populations and ineffective states that lack this capacity. Signs that a state is functionally ineffective in this sense will be civil war, unchecked famine, continuing genocide, a class of warlords, and general lawlessness. A state that is functionally ineffective will be unable, intuitively, to claim to speak or act for its people. It will not have the capacities required in a state that can count as "the political organization of the people," in Rawls's phrase,[4] or as I shall say, a state that is representative of its people.

The second distinction divides functionally effective states into those that satisfy a further requirement for being representative of their peoples and those that do not. Even an effective state will be unable to speak or act as a proper representative of its people unless it gives its members institutional resources—in the ideal, rights of election, contestation, accountability, and the like—that enable them to exercise more or less equally shared control, though perhaps only at a general level, over what it says and does in their name. Some effective, popularly controlled states may fail occasionally and contingently to be controlled by their peoples, but they will remain representative insofar as the people at least retain the means of exposing and correcting such failures. Effective states that fall too far short of popular control to be able to claim to speak and act for their peoples will fail more widely and more deeply, denying their members the means required for such interrogation and invigilation.

Applying the distinction between states that are subject to equally shared popular control and those that are not raises particularly tricky issues. Popular control comes in degrees on two distinct fronts: the control may be more or less determinative of government policy, on the one hand, and it may be more or less equally shared among members, on the other. At one extreme, we might regard only fully democratic states—and perhaps only states that approximate a high ideal of democracy[5]—as popularly controlled. At the other extreme, we might hold that any state that respects the internationally recognized human rights of subjects[6]—in particular, their rights of expression and association—is subject to popular control; after all, such a state will

[4] John Rawls, *The Law of Peoples* (Cambridge, MA: Harvard University Press, 1999), 26.
[5] Pettit, *On the People's Terms.*
[6] Charles R. Beitz, *The Idea of Human Rights* (Oxford: Oxford University Press, 2009).

presumably be responsive in some measure to the opinions and criticisms freely expressed among the population. The argument that follows presupposes that we can draw the distinction between popularly controlled and uncontrolled states—and, of course, the distinction between functionally effective and ineffective states—but the argument will go through, no matter where exactly the divide is located. I shall generally assume that it should be located at a point nearer the less demanding extreme, but nothing much hangs on that assumption.

However functional effectiveness and popular control are interpreted, the distinction between representative and non-representative regimes directs us towards real differences between states, and these differences are crucial for the question as to what international arrangements should be put in place. If a state is functionally ineffective or popularly uncontrolled, there is no reason why the international order should seek to promote its interests as a state. Or at least there is no reason for it to do so, assuming that the ultimate goal of that order should be to serve the interests of individual human beings; serving the interests of an ineffective or uncontrolled state may hurt, rather than help, the individuals who live under it. If a state is fully representative of its people, however, then things will be very different. Such a state will look after its own members, on terms that they themselves impose, and it would be objectionably intrusive of other agencies in the international order to assume responsibility for those individuals. The concern in the international order should be to accommodate that state appropriately, this being the way to accommodate the people that it represents.

Assuming that we have identified representative states, the first problem in international normative theory is to identify the basis on which we should assess the different dispensations under which those states might operate and relate to one another. And the second problem is to determine how the international order established among such states can and should deal with the harms and losses suffered by the members of functionally ineffective and popularly uncontrolled regimes.[7]

In this paper I shall look at the first of these issues only. But it is worth noting, for the record, that the ideal of non-domination to be supported in discussing the first issue has important lessons for the second as well.[8] It would argue that representative states, operating through the international

[7] The sequencing of issues into primary and secondary problems is broadly in the spirit of John Rawls's work on the law of peoples, though he tends to make it a matter of stipulation, not something for which argument is needed. See Pettit, "Rawls's Peoples," in *Rawls's Law of Peoples: A Realistic Utopia*, eds. Rex Martin and David Reidy (Oxford: Blackwell, 2006); Rawls, *The Law of Peoples*.

[8] Philip Pettit, "Legitimate International Institutions: A Neorepublican Perspective," in *The Philosophy of International Law*, eds. Samantha Besson and John Tasioulas (Oxford: Oxford University Press, 2010), 139–60; Pettit, "A Republican Law of Peoples"; Pettit, *Just Freedom*.

order, ought to protect the peoples of oppressive states against human rights abuses by their governments; protection might involve diplomatic isolation, an economic embargo, or even military intervention. It would argue that they ought to safeguard the peoples of ineffective states against destitution, insecurity, and the like. And it would require that whatever actions representative states take, they should take them only when the collateral costs do not outweigh the prospective benefits, only on a basis that allows for the development of independent, representative states among the peoples they mean to serve, and only in multilateral exercises that guard against making the people helped dependent on the goodwill of any single donor state.[9]

The discussion that follows, then, is limited in two distinct ways. It operates on the assumption that states will remain in place, more or less as they are, and it looks only at the form that the international order ought to assume in arranging relations between those states that can count as representative of their peoples, being more or less functionally effective and popularly controlled. But the discussion, it should be noticed, is limited in other ways too. I set aside the question of what certain, powerful states may owe to other states as a matter of historical justice. I set aside the question as to how, independently of international arrangements, states ought to treat those who seek asylum or refugee status within their boundaries. And finally I set aside explicit questions about the actions that ought to be taken in various scenarios by non-governmental organizations and other such international bodies.

There are two ideals that often figure in the assessment of international arrangements amongst representative states. At one extreme, there is the very minimal ideal under which representative states—indeed all states—should enjoy non-interference in their internal affairs, where this will require the absence of military intervention and subversive infiltration, but also perhaps the absence of economic pressure, cultural manipulation, and the like. At the other extreme, there is the rather richer ideal under which representative states—and again, perhaps, all states—ought to arrange for the achievement of distributive justice across the peoples of the world, not just in their own countries. On this cosmopolitan picture, justice has the same relevance in the international as in the national scene, although for contingent, institutional reasons it may not make the same demands in the two domains.[10]

I want to argue that a much more attractive ideal is a regime in which representative states are enabled to avoid domination, whether by another

[9] I assume that while there may be abuses of human rights and shortfalls of human welfare in representative states, there will normally be effective legal and political means of contestation and correction available within those countries themselves; thus, in normal circumstances, they will not constitute issues that the international order has to address.

[10] Charles R. Beitz, *Political Theory and International Relations* [1999 ed.] (Princeton: Princeton University Press, 1979); Thomas Pogge, "An Egalitarian Law of Peoples," *Philosophy & Public Affairs* 23, no. 3 (1993): 195–224.

state, or by a non-state body. This is an attractive ideal, as we shall see, because it is required for the protection of the individual members of representative states against domination from outside. The ideal is richer than that of non-interference, yet not so utopian as the cosmopolitan ideal of justice. It supports the Rawlsian proposal that representative states ought to live in mutual respect, but it focuses attention, unlike Rawls himself, on the preconditions that must be fulfilled to make such a regime of respect possible.

Non-domination is equated with freedom within the long republican tradition and so the argument I sketch can be cast as the development of a republican or neo-republican perspective on international normative theory. It takes a rather different line from other republican approaches, however, because it starts from states as they are, and sequences the issues discussed in a broadly Rawlsian way. Other republican approaches tend to look more radically at how individuals can be better served by transformations in the international order.[11] The approach taken here is not necessarily inconsistent with the lines argued in those other treatments; it shares a common insistence on the importance of non-domination and differs mainly in the questions it addresses.[12]

2 THE NATURE OF DOMINATION

The Domination of Individuals

Before looking at domination in an international context it will be useful to provide a more general account of what domination involves. I will deal first with the domination of individuals, looking at what it means for one person to dominate another in a particular choice, and then at what it means for one person to dominate another, period.

I dominate you in a particular choice, say one involving the options, X, Y, and Z, to the extent that I have a power of interfering in that choice. But

[11] Lawrence Quill, *Liberty after Liberalism: Civic Republicanism in a Global Age* (London: Palgrave Macmillan, 2005); Slaughter, *Liberty Beyond Neo-Liberalism*. Bohman, in *Democracy Across Borders*, focuses on the transformation of democracy that can and should be achieved in the international forum and how this can affect national states. I am very sympathetic to his reworking of various democratic concepts but believe that those of us who work in the frame adopted here can also make use of many of those ideas.

[12] For an exploration of the significance of the republican tradition on quite another front see Daniel H. Deudney, *Bounding Power: Republican Security Theory from the Polis to the Global Village* (Princeton: Princeton University Press, 2007). His concern is with ideas about the institutions whereby "republican security" can be ensured: "The tradition of republican security theory begins in classical antiquity, not the modern Enlightenment, and its Enlightenment culminations are in Montesquieu and the American founding, not Kant. Three of the most powerful ideas in contemporary international Liberalism, democratic peace, commercial peace, and international unions, are the legacies of Enlightenment republican security theory" (269).

what is interference? We may take it to involve any one of three sorts of intervention in the choice. First, it may involve removing one or more of the options, via force or agenda-setting or whatever, whether or not the removal is made known to the agent affected. Second, it may involve replacing one or more of those options, say by imposing a penalty on its choice, whether or not this replacement is made known to the agent. And third, it may involve misrepresenting one or more of the options, say by deceiving the agent as to relevant facts about the options or by manipulating the agent's perception of the options by underhand means. Interference in this sense is not an on-off matter of preventing the choice of an option, but rather it comes in degrees; this is because the replacement of an option may involve a lower or a higher penalty, and the misrepresentation of an option may be more or less serious and inescapable.[13]

Understood in this way, interference contrasts with three other forms of intervention. One is the offer in which I reward you for choosing a particular option, say X. This leaves you in a position still to choose between X, Y, and Z; it merely adds a fourth option, which is to choose X and take the reward: in short, to choose X-plus.[14] Another non-interfering intervention is the nudge, as it is now sometimes called, in which I change the structure or architecture of the choice in a way that affects you, without removing or replacing or misrepresenting any option; while leaving you with a choice between healthy and unhealthy food, for example, I may put the healthy food in a more salient position.[15] And a third, non-interfering intervention is the act of persuasion in which I seek to inform you of the respective merits of the options, and to lead you thereby to the choice of a particular alternative; if there is no misrepresentation, then this intervention too leaves you with your original choice.

---

[13] Sometimes interference is equated with prevention only: that is, the removal of an option. See Ian Carter, *A Measure of Freedom* (Oxford: Oxford University Press, 1999); Matthew H. Kramer, *The Quality of Freedom* (Oxford: Oxford University Press, 2003); Hillel Steiner, *An Essay on Rights* (Oxford: Blackwell, 1994); and, for a debate on the issue with republican thinkers, see Laborde and Maynor, *Republicanism and Political Theory*.

[14] What of the exploitative offer: the offer that drives a hard bargain with someone in a weak bargaining position, persuading them to accept an arrangement on the grounds that there is no acceptable alternative and they do not have a voluntary choice in the matter? (See Serena Olsaretti, *Liberty, Desert and the Market* (Cambridge: Cambridge University Press, 2004).) That such an offer is accepted is a sign that the person who is made the offer is already in a vulnerable position where domination is likely to occur. The offer itself will perpetrate a harm if, as is common in such circumstances, it sets up a relationship where further domination is facilitated; if it does not set up such a relationship, then it may better the exploited person's position, though it will hardly reflect well on the character of the exploiter. I am grateful for some discussion of this point with Arudra Burra.

[15] Richard Thaler and Cass Sunstein, *Nudge: Improving Decisions About Health, Wealth and Happiness* (London: Penguin Books, 2008).

What distinguishes interference, on the face of it, from such other interventions and makes it unwelcome? In a phrase: because it puts you under the will of another. Thus I do not interfere with you in the intended, objectionable sense if my action is non-intentional, as when it results from a slip or an oversight.[16] I do not interfere with you in that sense if my action is involuntary, as when my public office requires me to do something that frustrates you and I have no choice in the matter.[17] And I do not interfere with you in that specific sense if my action is non-arbitrary, as it used to be put; if it is conducted on your terms, as when you have instructed me to deny you something—if it is like the imposition of Ulysses's sailors when they keep him bound to the mast.[18] Interference in the sense intended here is either pursued for its own sake, out of sheer malice, or as a means to, or as a foreseen byproduct of, advancing a distinct, discretionary end.

While my interference in your choice involves an intentional, voluntary, and arbitrary action of removing, replacing, or misrepresenting one or more of your options, any domination I enjoy over you in that choice is a result of my having a power of such discretionary interference in the choice. And that power may belong to me, of course, not because of my intentional efforts, but as a byproduct of inherited resources, physical or psychological, legal or cultural. Indeed, having the power of discretionary interference in your choice may not even be something I take pleasure in; I may wish I did not have it.

Anticipating discussion in the next section, why is domination, like interference, likely to be unwelcome? The core reason is that, like interference, it puts you under the will of another. If I have a power of interference in some choice on your part, then whether or not I actually interfere, your capacity to act according to your own wishes will depend on my being and remaining good-willed towards you. Thus, you will depend on the state of my will, and whatever you manage to do, you will do by my implicit or explicit permission. My will, not yours, will be in ultimate charge of how you behave.

The domination I enjoy over you may obtain in one or another degree insofar as the interference I can practice comes in degrees. But it will also obtain in one or another degree to the extent that my power of interfering in your choice comes in degrees. The degree to which I enjoy a power of interference will be determined by how far I can practice interference—whether

---

[16] Isaiah Berlin, *Two Concepts of Liberty* (Oxford: Oxford University Press, 1958), 1.
[17] Serena Olsaretti, *Liberty, Desert and the Market.*
[18] Pettit, *On the People's Terms,* ch. 1. Notice that on the usage adopted here, whether or not an act involves interference in the unwelcome sense is established by a matter of fact: by whether it is pursued without awareness of the effect on the victim, or for reasons that *by accepted criteria* leave the agent no choice, or under terms established by the victim. This observation is particularly important in the case of arbitrariness, since others have offered normative accounts of the idea: see Bohman, *Democracy across Borders*; Richardson, *Democratic Autonomy*. For a distinct, but still non-normative, account of arbitrariness, see Lovett, *A General Theory*.

or not I am aware of this—without difficulty and without cost: how far I can practice it at will and with impunity, as it used to be said. The difficulty or cost that reduces my power of arbitrary interference may be imposed from within my own makeup, as a result of physical or psychological limitations, or as a result of outside factors—say, the hurdles of nature or the hindrance of a system of law that protects you from my intrusion.

These observations mean that you or someone acting in your interest may reduce my domination of you in relation to any choice by putting difficulties or costs in the way of my interfering, or by misleading me into thinking that you have done so; being misled on this matter will constitute a difficulty for me in the exercise of my power. Otherwise put, you can reduce my power of domination by interfering with the interference option that my power gives me: you can remove that option by a sufficiently large difficulty, replace it by a cost that you impose, or misrepresent things so that I do not fully appreciate the possibility of interfering.

The lessons about ways in which you can reduce my domination are matched by parallel lessons about ways in which you cannot hope to do so. Thus you cannot reduce my domination, my power of interfering in your choice, by making me an offer, imposing a nudge that structures the choice so that I am less likely to interfere, or by persuading me that there are good reasons why I should not interfere. All such interventions leave my power of interference in place, even though they may affect the chances of my actually interfering with you. They may make it less probable that I will interfere but they all leave me with access to the option of interfering, should I wish to do so.

I hope that these remarks suffice to show what makes it the case that one person dominates another in a particular choice. But what makes it the case, to go to a stronger possibility, that one person dominates another, period, and not just in this or that choice? The more or less obvious answer is that one person will dominate another as a person to the extent that he dominates that other in choices that have a salient significance in relations between people. But what, then, are the choices that deserve to be given such significance?

My response is: those choices that have traditionally been described, particularly in the republican tradition, as the fundamental or basic personal liberties.[19] These are the liberties associated generally with being able to think as you will, being able to say what you think, being able to associate with anyone who will associate with you, being able to move wherever you wish within the society, being able to take any of a number of available occupations, being able to use your leisure time as you will, and of course being able to exercise the rights of ownership that local, presumptively fair, property conventions give you.

[19] John Lilburne, *The Legal Fundamental Liberties of the People of England, Asserted, Revived, and Vindicated* (London: 1646).

These personal liberties are distinguished by a number of features. First, they are personally important choices: they hold out the prospect, for anyone who can exercise them, of achieving a full and meaningful life. Second, they need to be specified in every society by public law, so that various ambiguities are resolved as a matter of common awareness: for example, the ambiguity in whether hate speech is to count as a basic liberty, or in whether owning land means owning the mining rights in the land. Third, they have to be specified in a way that makes them accessible simultaneously to all; otherwise it would make no sense to look, as the republican tradition looks, for a world in which people equally escape domination. This means that the liberties cannot be competitive choices such that one person's enjoying them reduces the likelihood of others doing so. They should be publicly specified so that, manifestly, people are able to exercise any one of them at the same time that others exercise it and someone's exercise of any one liberty does not take from the satisfaction of others in exercising that or other liberties.[20]

If public law is to specify people's basic liberties, it must equally be expected to protect people—and even perhaps resource them—in the exercise of those liberties; it must be expected in this way to guard them against private domination or *dominium*. And if it is to do this effectively, of course, it had better not dominate the very people for whom it sets up such a protective order, perpetrating public domination or *imperium*. This requires, intuitively, that people can share equally in controlling the very law that serves to identify and guard their liberties. The law had better not be imposed, for example, at the will of a benevolent despot; it ought not to reflect the *arbitrium*, or will, of such an independent agent. It must be imposed, however this is understood, on terms that all are ready to support.[21]

If we restrict the choices in which my domination of you in various choices makes for domination, period, then a number of things follow. First, I will dominate you as a person to the extent to which I dominate you in any of your personal liberties. Second, I will not dominate you as a person if I dominate you in a choice that does not fall under a personal liberty: if, for example, I have a power of interfering with you should you try to harm someone else. And third, I will dominate you to a greater or lesser degree, depending on how many of your basic choices I am able to interfere with. We saw earlier that for two distinct reasons I may dominate you in a choice to one or another degree: first, the interference that I have the power to impose may be more or less intrusive and, second, the power that I have to impose that interference may be subject to greater or lesser cost or difficulty. We see here that when it comes to the issue of whether I dominate you as a person there is also a third respect in which the domination may be a matter of degree.

---

[20] Pettit, *Just Freedom*; Pettit, *On the People's Terms.*
[21] Pettit, *On the People's Terms.*

The Domination of States

A state is an agent insofar as it satisfies the basic template for agency. It endorses certain purposes or goals, forms judgments or representations of the opportunities, means, and merits of advancing those goals, updates such judgments and purposes as new evidence and the like becomes available, and acts in a manner that promotes those purposes according to those judgments. Or at least it is disposed to do this in a more or less reliable, if sometimes stuttering, pattern. And if it fails to live up to the expectations to which we hold agents, it is disposed to acknowledge, or at least try to explain, the failure in response to criticism; it recognizes that if correct, such criticism would be relevant.

The sensitivity to criticism means that the state is an agent more akin to a human being than a mute animal, or indeed a robot. Not only does it conform to our expectations that it should be evidentially reliable in forming and updating its purposes and representations, and executively reliable in acting for those purposes according to those representations, it also has the capacity to recognize the expectations to which we hold it and the ability to take intentional steps to ensure that it lives up to those standards. It is an agent that speaks through its office-holders, and that can use their words to avow attitudes we may expect it to display and to promise actions we may expect it to deliver.

As a corporate agent of this kind, the state belongs with a large set of group agents, including churches and companies, voluntary associations and town councils. These are bodies that recruit a more or less large number of individuals, under a suitable charter or constitution, so that they perform together like a single agent in pursuing a certain agenda.[22] Such corporate agents may dominate individual agents, as our discussion of personal domination should make clear: they may stand over individuals, having a power of interfering more or less at will, and with more or less impunity, in the exercise of their personal liberties. But the more important point to register now is that they themselves may also be dominated.

Any corporate agent, and any state in particular, will face a variety of choices in its day-to-day existence, registering that there are a number of options in each choice and that it can determine whether this or that option is realized. If a corporate body did not face such choices, then it would not count as an agent. And so it should be clear that any such agent, and in particular a state, may be dominated in one or another choice, as certain other agents enjoy a power of interfering with it in making that choice. More or less at will, and with greater or lesser impunity, those other agents or agencies are able to remove or replace an option in the choice, or to mislead the corporate body about the options at its disposal.

[22] Christian List and Philip Pettit, *Group Agency: The Possibility, Design, and Status of Corporate Agents* (Oxford: Oxford University Press, 2011).

But while a corporate agent, like a state, may be dominated in one or another choice, the next question is whether there is any sense in which it may be dominated as a corporation, as a person may be dominated as a person. I argue that there is. In order to operate without problems in the context of other agents—individual and corporate—each corporate agent must have a designated range of choices within which it may choose as of a right: as of a right, established by public convention or law, that is recognized within the community of agents to which it belongs. A community of agents within which such rights were not established and generally recognized would be exposed to potentially disruptive instability and conflict. It would represent a moderate form of Hobbes's state of nature.

Corporate agents might be given rights of choice without those rights being appropriate, of course, just as individuals might be given rights of choice that were not appropriate: say, rights that gave superior liberties to members of a certain class, as the Ancien Régime gave members of the aristocracy and clergy special privileges. That raises the question as to what rights of choice, what designated liberties, ought to be given to corporate agents, in particular to states. The answer to that question will vary with the sorts of corporate agents involved, but we need only concern ourselves with the issue in the case of states.

I suggested earlier that in elaborating on the idea of domination we need to use the law to define a set of personal liberties such that it is just the domination of an individual within that set that amounts to domination of the person. In the same way, I think that we need to define a set of sovereign liberties such that it is just the domination of a state within that set that amounts to its domination as a state. That immediately suggests that we can extend the notion of domination to states only insofar as the international order implicitly or explicitly specifies choices that any state can exercise at the same time as others, and that any state can exercise without jeopardizing the satisfaction that other states can derive from the exercise of such sovereign liberties. The choices to be designated as special, in other words, should be co-exercisable as single liberties and should be co-satisfying as a set.

Defensive or punitive measures aside, these choices obviously ought not to include any choices of a hostile nature, such as those involved in invading a state or holding it to ransom in any way. And equally they ought not to include choices that would destroy the global commons: say, exhaust the fishing resources in international waters, or lead to wholesale pollution of the atmosphere. In order to establish what states may and may not do on such fronts, the international order has to mimic the way that local legal systems identify personal liberties. It has to set up public rules that identify choices that each can exercise without jeopardizing their exercise by others, and without undermining the satisfaction that others derive from such choices. Moreover, it presumably has to protect states against suffering domination from other states or international bodies—or license them to take action in order to ensure this result—without itself imposing a form of public domination on any of those states.

But there is a special constraint that the sovereign liberties of states, as distinct from the personal liberties of individuals, ought to satisfy. This is that no state should be given a sovereign liberty that impacts on the personal liberties that its members must enjoy if they are to escape individual domination. Assuming that it is individual human beings who really matter—more on this shortly—it would be clearly inappropriate for the international order to allow states, as of recognized right, to have liberties inimical to the liberties of their members. Thus to invoke the language of human rights, it would be inappropriate for states to have the right to impose on the human rights of their subjects. Or at least this would be inappropriate with those basic human rights that have a more or less justiciable status in contemporary practice; they are such that any violation serves *pro tanto*— and so, subject to being overridden by associated costs—to justify international action of some kind.[23]

With the idea of sovereign liberties in place, there is no difficulty about introducing the idea of a state being dominated as a state, in parallel to the idea of a person being dominated as a person. To the extent that any agency—say, another state, a multinational corporation, or an international agency—dominates a state in the domain of its sovereign liberties, it will dominate the state as a state.

Must the international order have already specified a set of basic liberties, then, if we are to determine that some external agency dominates a representative state? No, it does not. We can speak of the domination of a state in relation to its sovereign liberties, as they are articulated in actual international practice, or in relation to its sovereign liberties as they would be articulated in the international practice that we favor. This is like the situation on the personal front where we can speak of the domination of an individual with respect to personal liberties, referring either to the liberties that are defined in actual law or to the liberties that would be defined in ideal law.

3 THE DISVALUE OF DOMINATION

The Domination of Individuals

The disvalue of domination in the personal case is registered in the fact that the freedom of a choice, and the freedom of a person have been equated in the long republican tradition with the absence of domination. In the first case, freedom requires the absence of domination in the relevant choice; in the second, it requires the absence of domination in the domain of those

[23] Beitz, *The Idea of Human Rights*.

personal choices identified as the fundamental liberties that ought to be available to the citizen of a republic.

Freedom as non-domination contrasts with two other views of freedom: that is, freedom in relation to agents. On a first conception, you are free in a choice between certain options, X, Y, and Z, insofar as you do not suffer the interference of others in choosing what you actually want or prefer. This conception is defended by Thomas Hobbes, who says that someone is free when he "is not hindered to do what he has a will to"; that is, is not hindered to do what he prefers to do.[24] Hobbes's conception equates freedom with being able to satisfy your actual preference. It might be called the favored-door view of freedom, because if we think of each option in a choice as a door, it requires only that the door you push on be open.

Isaiah Berlin rejects the favored-door view of freedom for a view that requires all the doors in a free choice to be open.[25] He argues that freedom requires, not just that you should be able to get what you want among the options, but that you should be able to get what you want regardless of what it is that you want. He argues that otherwise you could gain freedom in a choice where your preferred option is blocked but an alternative is open just by working on your own preferences and getting yourself to want the alternative; you could gain freedom within prison, even if you wanted to live outside, by focusing on the good things about incarceration and by adapting your preferences to prison life. He rightly holds that this is absurd: "to teach a man that, if he cannot get what he wants, he must learn to want only what he can get may contribute to his happiness or his security; but it will not increase his civil or political freedom."[26]

Where Berlin's view associates freedom with having all the doors in a choice open, not just the door you push on, the republican view imposes a stronger condition still. It certainly requires all doors to be open, since you would be subject to the power of another if the other could deny you access to any of the options on offer in a choice. But it also requires that no one else be in the position of a doorkeeper who is able to close any door in your face, should they happen to be so inclined. You will not be free in a choice, according to this view, if your access to the options—your ability to pass through any of the doors on offer—is dependent on the grace or leave of someone else. To be able to do something, but only *cum permissu*—only with permission—is not to enjoy freedom proper in the choice. If you

---

[24] Thomas Hobbes, *Leviathan: with Selected Variants from the Latin Edition of 1668*, ed. Edwin Curley (Indianapolis: Hackett, 1994), ch. 21.2.

[25] This view is consistent with holding that although you do not have a free choice between three alternatives, X, Y, and Z—Y and Z are closed doors—still if you choose X without knowing that Y and Z are closed, you do so freely and can be held responsible for the choice. See Harry Frankfurt, "Alternate Possibilities and Moral Responsibility," *Journal of Philosophy* 66, no. 23 (1969): 829–39.

[26] Isaiah Berlin, *Four Essays on Liberty* (Oxford: Oxford University Press, 1969), xxxix.

manage to satisfy your own will, that is only because it accords with the will of another that you should be able to satisfy your own will. It is that will that is in ultimate control, then, and not your will.

The first view suggests that it is enough for freedom in a choice if you are able to choose what you actually prefer. The second view argues that you must also be able to choose what you prefer, regardless of what it is that you prefer to choose. The third, republican view argues that you must be able to choose what you prefer, not only regardless of what you prefer to choose, but also regardless of what others prefer that you choose. You will enjoy that sort of freedom just to the extent that there is no one who can get in the way of your realizing your preference in the choice: there is no one in the position of a master, or *dominus*.

The appeal of this conception of freedom should be enough to make clear what the disvalue of domination is. If you are subject to interference with what you actually prefer, you are put under the active control of another. If you are subject to interference with what you might prefer but do not, you are put under the virtual control of another: the other rides herd on your choice, being prepared to let you have your way but only provided your way is their way. And if you are subject to another's capacity to interfere, even when the person does not interfere with any option in a relevant choice, you are under the reserve control of another: the other is in a position of having the say-so on whether or not you can choose as you wish.

These forms of control are all ruled out under the ideal of freedom as non-domination. And with good reason, especially when it comes to domination in the domain of your personal liberties. It is bad by all accounts when another actively restricts your choice, denying you the satisfaction of your preference. It is bad, if not equally bad, when another restricts what you might have preferred in a choice, if not what you actually prefer to do. And it is bad, if again not quite so bad, when another stands over you, ready to restrict your choice in the event of turning hostile. In all these situations, your will is not in charge of what you choose. You are subject to the will of another in the sense of depending for the ability to act as you wish on that will being congenial.

It is bad to be subject to the active, virtual, or reserve control of another, even when you are not aware of such subjection. But this subjection will normally be accompanied by an awareness of the subjection, thus making things even worse. For when you are manifestly subject to the power of another, even a power that is held in reserve, that gives you a reason to be wary of the other and to seek to keep the other sweet. And if it is manifest to each of you that you are aware of your dependence, then that reinforces the effect; it means that you will appear "uppity" if you act as if you were not dependent. Thus, subjection to another is likely to lead you to behave in a slavish way, and to display a range of vices castigated in traditional republican writing. These are the vices of allowing yourself to be intimidated and ingratiating, as you go through the motions of deference and devotion, and seek thereby to humor and placate the other.

These observations should make ready sense of why domination is objectionable. And they give obvious support to the claim that to be dominated in your personal choices—to be dominated as a person—is particularly objectionable. Freedom as a person is cast in the republican tradition as requiring the absence of domination in all basic choices. It is equated institutionally with the freedom you enjoy by virtue of living under a public rule of law—and an associated regime of social norms—that defines personal liberties suitably, offers you protection against private domination in the exercise of those liberties, and does so under such constraints that it does not itself subject you to public domination.

Given your freedom as a person in this sense, it will be manifest to all that you enjoy the required protections and immunities. And so you can walk tall, in the traditional idiom, and deal with others without reason for fear or deference. The law guards you against private domination, or *dominium*, and it is subject to a form of control that you share equally with others so that it does not impose public domination, or *imperium*, either; it is not like the rule of a benevolent despot who might turn against you or others, and on whose goodwill you would therefore depend. It may not redress all the material and other inequalities that arise in any society as a result of natural and social fortune. But it must at least ensure the equality of objective and subjective status that enables each of you in that society to affirm your equal standing with others, recognizing that short of personal timidity, you have every reason to be able to look them in the eye without fear of their interference or deference to their power.

The Domination of States

Let us agree, as I think most of us will, that domination is an evil for individual human beings, restricting the extent to which they can relate to one another as persons who live on equal terms in a relationship of mutual respect. But why should the lesson carry over to the agents that human beings construct when they incorporate? Why should it carry over, in particular, to the states that they create? Why should it be bad that those entities endure domination, and good that they avoid it?

It is natural to think that what happens at the institutional level does not matter unless it makes a difference at the level of individual human beings—or perhaps, though we can put aside this possibility, at the level of other animals. Most people embrace a normative individualism or humanism, as we might describe it. They are committed to the idea that there can be no difference in the value of two institutional arrangements unless there is a difference in the value for individual human beings of those arrangements.[27]

[27] Chandran Kukathas and Philip Pettit, *Rawls: A Theory of Justice and Its Critics* (Cambridge/Stanford: Polity Press/Stanford University Press, 1990); List and Pettit, *Group Agency*.

This normative individualism means that there will be no difference of value between an arrangement under which a corporate agent is dominated and an arrangement under which it is not, unless there is a difference of value in the impact on individual human beings. And so there is a sharp question as to why the domination of corporate entities, particularly states, should matter.

My response to the question is that the domination of corporate agencies will matter insofar as those agencies are organizations whereby individual human beings combine to act together. If the things that the members do as a corporate entity are subject to the dominating control of another agent or agency, then those members are themselves subject to such control. The lesson for representative states is straightforward. Let there be external control of a representative state and there will be external control of the citizens in whose name and interest it acts, since that control will put the operations of the state beyond the effective influence of those individuals. The domination of a representative state is bad or evil as such and it will not generally be justifiable—as it might be in the case, say, of an oppressive state—by any compensating effects on members.

According to standard republican doctrine, individuals are meant to enjoy freedom as non-domination by virtue of being protected against the domination of others by an undominating state. What we now see is that this actually leaves something out. A full statement of the requirements for individual freedom, under a constitutional arrangement, should read: the free individual ought to be protected against the domination of others by a state that is not only internally undominating but also externally undominated. It is the requirement that the state be undominated that explains why the domination of representative states is *pro tanto* bad.

4 SOURCES OF DOMINATION

Let us assume that we have a good idea of the sovereign liberties that ought to or might be given to representative states under an international order in which they figure as equals and, allowing for the relevant differences that variations in territory or population may trigger, can expect to receive evenhanded treatment. These will include some more or less salient liberties, paralleling the personal liberties of individuals, such as the liberty to form one's own views, express such views freely, associate with any other countries, and so on. But equally they will include liberties established under international negotiation or law to exercise restricted, potentially competitive liberties in areas that bear on the global commons and the global good. For example, they will include the liberty of having fishing fleets operate under certain restrictions in international waters or the liberty of releasing harmful gases into the atmosphere up to a certain limit determined by the level of population or the nature of the territory. Assuming that the sovereign liberties are suitably defined, we now ask about how a representative state might suffer domination in the exercise of such liberties.

There are three sorts of bodies that might plausibly exercise dominating control over a representative state: first, and most prominently, other states; second, non-domestic, private bodies that compare in resources to many states, such as corporations, churches, terrorist movements, even powerful individuals; and third, non-domestic, public bodies that are often created by states, such as the United Nations, the World Bank, the International Monetary Fund, the European Union, or the North Atlantic Treaty Organization.

There are many means whereby a stronger state, A, itself representative or non-representative, might dominate a representative state, B, on the basis of active control. Military intervention is one vivid possibility, the infiltration of secret agents another, the bribing or blackmail of officials a third. There is also a possibility of resort to economic pressure, as in threatening to dump goods on the world market in competition with B's products, to sell off holdings in B's currency, thereby depreciating it, or to freeze B's holdings in banks that are under A's control. Relatedly, there is a possibility of A exploiting B by taking advantage of its dependency on A for access to some necessity—say, an important energy source or water supply—in order to ensure that B does not trade with a competitor and/or in order to drive a hard bargain with B (one, intuitively, that denies B what might have been presumed to be a sovereign liberty). And of course there is a possibility of using diplomatic pressure by creating bad publicity for B, triggering problems with its allies and trading partners, and working to deny it influence in world bodies. Depending on the sort of extra strength that A has in relation to B, it may adopt any or all of these measures in an attempt to force B's hand in some way.

But A may also dominate B without resorting to active control, by means of the power that gives it virtual or reserve control over B's exercise of some sovereign liberties. Even if B is not aware that A can interfere in its choices—and in most plausible circumstances, of course, B will be aware of A's power—A can exercise invisible forms of virtual or reserve control over B. A can allow B to follow its head, but keep open the possibility of interfering where that proves necessary to get B to behave congenially. And if B is aware of this possibility, or is misled into positing it, A can rely on B's second-guessing its wishes and adjusting its behavior to A's taste.

A need do nothing to ensure that B complies with its wishes in non-active forms of control; just the fact that those wishes are more or less manifest or apparent will ensure that B falls in line. This invidious form of control requires nothing of A and allows B to pretend to its independence, as it may wish to do for a variety of reasons. A show of independence may have the incidental effect of avoiding domestic contestation or international condemnation, so that the regime of virtual or reserve control will be reinforced in a way in which a regime of active control might not be.

Among the private, international agencies that compare in resources with states, multinational corporations are the outstanding examples, even if they are less colorful than church bodies or terrorist networks. The means whereby they may actively seek to control a representative state are various. Having established itself as a source of employment, a corporation may threaten to move offshore or out of area. This will constitute a serious economic problem for smaller countries and even in larger countries, it may create a problem for a local community and thereby a problem for a government that depends on the electoral support of that community. Again, having established itself as a local corporate citizen, a corporation may exercise alien control over a state by being able to contribute to the campaign financing of politicians, and so holds the capacity to threaten uncollaborative politicians with financing electoral opposition. Or it may exercise powerful influence of a dominating kind by being able to lobby government and politicians from a position of power where it can launch negative publicity campaigns against government or create endless legal hassles for the implementation of government policy.

As with the dominating control that an outside state can practice, this sort of control may be exercised, without resort to active control, in a virtual or reserve fashion. The powerful corporation may never need to make a threat of moving elsewhere or of financing an opposition or of supporting negative publicity in order to control the government of a representative state. It will already enjoy control just insofar as the state is disposed to go along with its wishes, say because of wanting to court the corporation's goodwill. As in the first case, this is the most powerful sort of dominating control. It may enable the corporation to secure a favorable tax rate, easy regulatory conditions, or a lowering of environmental standards, without the corporation being exposed to a danger of whistle-blowing. It will not require even the legally available flexing of corporate muscle, let alone the resort to illegal modes of influence.

Finally, representative states may be subject to the dominating control of public, international bodies, as well as to control by other states or corporations. Although such bodies are set up under a treaty involving a number of states, or established by an existing international organization, there is no guarantee that they will deal with an individual state on a basis that leaves its sovereign liberties intact. Such a body can deny the state a benefit that it makes available to comparable others, thereby changing the previously available option of competing on equal terms. The penalty, to take an example from the world of finance, may be the loss of access to a source of funding, the increase of interest rates on loans, or a decline in its rating as a credit-worthy entity.

This control by international agencies may be enjoyed on the basis of any form of control, active, virtual, or reserve. Non-active control will not require any initiatives on the part of the agency other than that of being there in a stand-by mode, ready to interfere should that prove necessary for furthering its actual or possible preferences. And since non-active control may have an effect as silent as gravity, at least outside the corridors of government power, it can escape the problems of triggering local challenge or international criticism.[28]

5 REMEDIES FOR DOMINATION

What are the safeguards that we might think of seeking against the domination of representative states? I shall consider this question in relation to the domination of states by states, not their domination by other bodies, and at the end of the discussion turn to the question raised by other forms of domination. I will look first at some negative lessons and then at some more positive implications.

Negative Lessons

The first, negative lesson is that it would be foolish to rely on what we might describe as the benevolent despot solution. This would consist, most plausibly, in allowing a single state to assume the role of a world police-officer, trusting it to prevent domination among other states and not to dominate those states itself. This is a non-starter, because a hegemonic state of that kind would be the most unconstrained source of domination, however benevolent its intentions. It would have total control of an alien kind over other states, being able to interfere at any point in order to steer them along congenial paths. It would hardly ever have to resort to such interference, of course, since in the scenario envisaged other states would have every reason to try to keep it sweet, adjusting their plans and initiatives to its taste. Not even needing to interfere in pursuit of its interests, it would attain the most attractive form of power imaginable.

The observation about the benevolent despot solution may seem unnecessary, since it is almost unthinkable that other states would ever willingly grant a single state, or even a set of states, that sort of recognition. But it is worth recalling that liberals from the 17th to the 19th century appear to have been quite complacent about the imperial role that they thought their national states could play.[29] And it is worth remembering that under the

[28] Of course the control exercised by such an agency may well be justified by the effects it promises to have, say in orienting a country towards better economic policies and motivating politicians to resist short-term electoral pressures. And, more important, it may be rendered non-dominating, as argued in the next section, if it is imposed on terms accepted by all parties.

[29] Duncan Bell, "Empire and Imperialism," in *The Cambridge History of Nineteenth Century Political Thought*, eds. Gregory Claeys and Gareth Stedman Jones (Cambridge: Cambridge University Press, 2011); Jennifer Pitts, *A Turn to Empire: The Rise of Imperial Liberalism in Britain and France* (Princeton: Princeton University Press, 2005).

George W. Bush administration, the government of the United States often came close to putting itself forward in such a role. It presented itself as a country of entirely benevolent intentions, interested only in furthering democracy and human rights, and willing to cooperate with allies. But it suggested at the same time that it was committed to maintaining military superiority and invulnerability.[30] That attitude is forthrightly endorsed in a 2000 document from a neoconservative group that was closely associated with the government: "At present the United States faces no global rival. America's grand strategy should aim to preserve and extend this advantageous position as far into the future as possible."[31] This self-conception and self-presentation is entirely hostile to the prospect of reducing domination among representative states.

The most obvious alternative to the benevolent state solution would set up an international regime, on the model of the domestic state, with a constitutional, effective authority over member states. In the domestic context the republican state naturally presents itself as the solution to problems of private domination by some members of the society over others. This state would guard against the problem of *dominium*, or private power, by establishing a non-dominating form of public power, or *imperium*. It would empower the weak and restrain the strong, thereby reducing private domination. But unlike the benevolent despot it would not be itself a source of public domination, being subject to the equally shared control of its people and operating only on terms accepted by all its citizens—all its adult, able-minded, more or less permanent members. The checks envisaged in the tradition involve election to and rotation in office, the separation of powers, the rule of law, exposure to public invigilation, and a raft of other devices. Might an international regime of some kind play an analogous part?

A world state might serve effectively in the role envisaged, at least in principle, but nothing even approaching such a state is feasible in current circumstances and, given the diversity and distrust between cultures, it is doubtful if such a state ever could be successfully established.[32] But what about relying on international, state-supported bodies like the United Nations in order to provide the non-dominating restraints that might block the domination of states by other states? Could the networks of authorities and officials that currently determine so much of what happens in the world

---

[30] Ian Shapiro, *Containment: Rebuilding a Strategy Against Global Terror* (Princeton: Princeton University Press, 2007), ch. 2; US Government, *National Security Strategy of the United States of America*, (Washington, DC: White House, 2002), http://www.whitehouse.gov/nsc/nss.html.

[31] Thomas Donnelly et al., "Rebuilding America's Defenses: Strategy, Forces and Resources for a New Century," http://www.newamericancentury.org/RebuildingAmericasDefenses.pdf.

[32] But see Alexander Wendt, "Why a World State is Inevitable," *European Journal of International Relations* 9, no. 4 (2003): 491–542.

order[33] ever assume the power, deriving from a checked and non-dominating form of control, that would effectively reduce such domination? Could they ever impose a rule of international law and convention—a global, quasi-constitutional arrangement—that would substantially reduce the prospect of domination by states of states?

There are two questions here. One is whether such networked control over states can be non-dominating. And the other is whether such a network could ever exercise the policing power that might restrain state-state domination. I am relatively optimistic on the first question, believing that there are many factors whereby the control exercised by international agencies and their officials can be rendered non-arbitrary, despite the democratic deficits on which critics have seized.[34] States normally appoint to the crucial positions on these bodies; appointments come with specific, restricted briefs; there are usually high bars of accountability to cross; global civic movements—non-governmental organizations—often exercise a significant degree of oversight; and decisions are routinely subject to objection and review by the states affected. The control enjoyed by the relevant authorities and bodies, then, is often more circumscribed than the control enjoyed by domestic, democratic governments; and certainly it is capable of being made so. Were election the only means of keeping tabs on those in power, of course, we would have good reason to worry about these figures. But the states and peoples of the world can control international agencies quite effectively without popular election to the membership of those agencies.

While these bodies might be relatively accountable and non-arbitrary, however, I do not think that in themselves they could have the policing power sufficient to resolve our problem. Even buttressed by a recognized body of public international law,[35] they will not have the resources to provide for the effective regulation of state-state domination. National states come in enormously different sizes, and with greatly different degrees of strength. It would be utopian to expect the more powerful to allow others an equal stake in the control of such bodies and, even if they allowed this, to let such bodies exercise any intrusive degree of jurisdiction over their behavior. A regional body like the European Union may achieve a high degree of discipline in relation to member states—and even here the effect on larger states is limited—but there is no prospect of such heavy-duty discipline being imposed by the United Nations or, in their more insulated domains, by the World Trade Organization, the World Bank, the International Criminal Court, or even the World Health Organization.

---

33 Anne-Marie Slaughter, *A New World Order* (Princeton: Princeton University Press, 2004).

34 Pettit, "Democracy, National and International," *Monist* 89, no. 2 (2006): 301–24; Pettit, "Legitimate International Institutions."

35 D. W. Greig, *International Law,* 2nd ed. (London: Butterworths, 1976).

An example makes the point quite powerfully. In 1986 the International Court of Justice found in favor of Nicaragua, and against the United States, in arguing that customary international law made it an offence for the United States to have supported guerillas against the Nicaraguan government and to have mined Nicaraguan ports. The United States responded by rejecting the idea that the Court had jurisdiction in this case; indeed, it had anticipated that result and temporarily withdrawn from the jurisdiction of the court.[36] The US Ambassador to the United Nations described the court at the time as a "semi-legal, semi-juridical, semi-political body, which nations sometimes accept and sometimes don't."[37]

The contingent difficulty with securing a policing form of regulation by international agencies is compounded by one of a more inescapable character. The forms whereby more powerful states can control less powerful states are so various that no form of central regulation, and certainly not the sort that is associated with currently existing bodies, could effectively prevent state-state domination. It might illegalize and inhibit intervention or infiltration by one state in the affairs of another, but how could it inhibit the sort of control exercised on the basis of greater economic power, wider diplomatic clout, or the enjoyment of some strategic advantage? There are many forms of domination between individuals that the domestic state cannot regulate, deriving from cultural or psychological resources, but these are secondary to the forms of domination it can restrain. In the international sphere, the forms of state-state domination that would escape the policing of any central authority include the most important forms of domination that are possible outside of conditions of war.

Positive Lessons

But while the international bodies do not promise much in the way of central policing and regulation, they are important in another, indirect connection. Such agencies naturally generate discussion in different quarters about how things should be organized globally; their very existence will give extra point to such discussion, whether in international forums, in more informal meetings between governments and civic movements, or in the world media. And even though such discussion will never lead to consensus, it can establish a currency of considerations or standards that all sides recognize as relevant to global organization. Those considerations emerge as the terms in which

---

[36] T. D. Gill, "Litigation Strategy in the Nicaragua Case at the International Court," in *International Law at a Time of Perplexity: Essays in Honour of Shabtai Rosenne*, ed. Yôrām Dinšṭein with the assistance of Mala Tabor (Dordrecht: Kluwer Academic Publishers, 1989), 197–224, 211. See also page 2 of the introduction to that edited volume.

[37] Howard N. Meyer, "When the Pope Rebuked the U.S. at the World Court," *The Baltimore Sun*, March 18, 1997, http://articles.baltimoresun.com/1997–03–18/news/1997077033.

the different sides succeed in arguing—as distinct from coming to blows—even as they weight those terms differently or allow them to lead in different directions as a result of different empirical assumptions. They constitute common reasons such that anyone who learns his or her way around in the circles of debate on international issues will recognize them as the considerations to bring forward in support of any policy position. They will count as relevant in policy debates and they will be recognized as such in common or mutual awareness: each party will acknowledge their pertinence, recognize that everyone acknowledges it, recognize that everyone recognizes that everyone acknowledges it, and so on.[38]

The existence of a currency of common global reasons and the valorization of those reasons as the terms of debate and exchange between countries is of great importance in making it possible for countries to relate to one another in a reasoned manner, seeking a non-dominating influence on one another's positions and holding out the possibility of an unforced, cooperative solution to many problems. The availability of that mode of regulating interstate matters, together with the existence of the forums that international agencies provide, can ensure that there is an onus of justification on states that resort to other dominating modes of influence, particularly when such other initiatives—especially outright wars—prove as costly as they often do. It can make reasoned deliberation on the basis of commonly recognized reasons—and the resolution of differences on the basis of procedures supported by those reasons—into the default option in the mutual accommodation of states.

One ground for thinking that shared global standards can play this role is the disesteem that will attach to any state that spurns those standards in dealing with others.[39] This disesteem may materialize within a state itself, as members find it a matter of shame that the state that acts in its name should not be willing to relate to others in the space of common reasons. Or it may materialize in the international community, as unwilling states and their spokespersons find themselves subject to ignominy and ostracism.

We must grant, of course, that providing for interstate deliberation on the basis of commonly endorsed terms will not ensure in itself against domination. Deliberation in the presence of a manifest asymmetry of power may only cover

[38] John Rawls, in *The Law of Peoples*, may often have common reasons in mind when he speaks of public reasons, and my ideas have clearly been influenced by his discussion. But the language of common reasons, as used here, may be more in the spirit of Habermas than Rawls. See Jürgen Habermas, *A Theory of Communicative Action*, vols. 1 and 2 (Cambridge: Polity Press, 1984, 1989); J. Donald Moon, "Rawls and Habermas on Public Reason: Human Rights and Global Justice," *Annual Review of Political Science* 6 (2003). For an extension of the Rawlsian idea to the international forum, see Joshua Cohen on global reason in Cohen, "Minimalism About Human Rights: The Most We Can Hope For?" *Journal of Political Philosophy* 12, no. 2 (2004): 190–213.

[39] Geoffrey Brennan and Philip Pettit, *The Economy of Esteem: An Essay on Civil and Political Society* (Oxford: Oxford University Press, 2004).

up a deeper game of intimidation by the strong. But the possibility of such deliberation is still significant. It creates a base for determining the sovereign liberties that states should each be able to enjoy, as a matter of international law and understanding, protected against the dominating control of others. And the possibility of deliberation on the basis of commonly acceptable reasons should establish a culture in which international law can strengthen and serve as a discipline for inhibiting potential dominators, and for protecting states from one another. Let states accept a regime of common reasons and they will be able to endorse international law as a set of regulations that can be seen from within as a law that they share in common with others. This can raise international law from a set of convenient standards, binding only when they are convenient, to a system of norms that each state views, and takes others to view, as a base for legitimate expectations. It can give each state what H.L.A. Hart takes to be an essential, internal perspective on that law.[40]

We have been focused on state-state domination and I have been arguing that while no simple solution is on offer, there are grounds for limited enthusiasm about recourse to international agencies. There is ground for enthusiasm insofar as these agencies can promote a currency of common global reasons and foster a reasoned relationship as the default option for states. There is ground only for limited enthusiasm insofar as the agencies may be unable to provide the sort of power needed to protect against domination. More powerful states may have too much influence to be capable of being fully restrained by international bodies. And some forms of domination, associated with economic power and diplomatic clout, may be too elusive to be regulated by such an agency.

Where to turn for extra remedies against the domination of states? The only recourse is a possibility that some see as distinctively republican in its origins.[41] States that are so weak in any dimension that they are subject to the domination of others can unite in common cause in order to give themselves the required muscle to resist the power of the stronger. Consider the military, economic, or diplomatic domain. No matter how great the power of one country, A, in relation to another, B, that power will be reduced or nullified in the event that B manages to secure a credible alliance with enough other countries against A. The point is as old as the adage that there is strength in numbers. And it is borne out in recent international experience, as the forums that allow the weak to band together—and banding together will involve the usual free-rider difficulties—have begun to prove a thorn in the side of more powerful states.[42] Those states have

---

[40] H.L.A. Hart, *The Concept of Law* (Oxford: Oxford Unviersity Press, 1961).
[41] Deudney, *Bounding Power*, 152–54.
[42] There may be more powerful, dominating states within any such league of relatively weaker states, of course. But there may be—though alas there won't necessarily be—a possibility of guarding against this via alliances between the less powerful states in the league.

responded by trying to shift forum when things are not going to their taste, or by trying to opt out of multilateral discussions in favor of bilateral, one-by-one arrangements with the other states.[43] But it is unlikely that such stratagems will prove successful over the long haul, as weaker countries become aware of how they are used.

It is customary to the point of seeming fatuous to emphasize the importance of deliberation, but the perspective provided by the ideal of non-domination does more than that: it also makes clear that in a world of grossly unequal power, deliberation is not going to be enough. It will have to be matched by the groupings that enable the weak to deliberate from a position of strength. States will relate to one another in a truly deliberative mode, eschewing all resort to dominating control, only in the measure that they respect one another. And states will respect one another only in the measure that they command one another's respect; they each have enough power to leave others no choice but to respect them.

This brief overview of possible remedies for state-state domination suggests, then, that the best hope may lie in a dispensation with two aspects. On the one hand, a set of international agencies and forums by means of which states can work out their problems and relations in a space of more or less common reasons and by resort to procedures for resolving intractable difficulties that such reasons support. And on the other, a set of linkages whereby states that are weaker in some dimension and are thereby exposed to domination—including the sort of domination that can hide in a deliberative guise—may band together to reduce the advantages of the strong. Each aspect of the package recommended involves multilateral action: on the one side, the "totilateral" organization of all states behind international agencies and, on the other, the "plurilateral" organization of different subgroups of states into blocs that can effectively compete with their stronger rivals. The scenario sketched does not put an analogue of the domestic state in place in the international order but it does have aspects of a constitutional or quasi-constitutional arrangement for reducing domination.

The two dimensions to the solution proposed are each of vital importance and just to emphasize this importance, I make one further observation. In the world as it is now every state is liable to be indirectly and adversely affected by what in an earlier period would have been innocent initiatives on the part of others. These may involve subsidizing domestic business, creating artificial barriers to imports, fostering the use of scarce fuels, failing to curb carbon emissions, allowing the use of certain herbicides, or not regulating the medical or agricultural use of antibiotics. It is only by means of international debate, grounded in the acceptance of certain common reasons, that

---

[43] John Braithwaite and Peter Drahos, *Global Business Regulation* (Cambridge: Cambridge University Press, 2000).

states can hope to establish where, as in such cases, they may be harming one another and where the limits should naturally be set to the freedom as non-domination they may claim; it is only by such means that states can identify a domain of sovereign liberties that they can each simultaneously enjoy. But international debate will not be able to enforce against stronger states the limits it may in this way identify. And at that point the organization of other states against the relatively strong is bound to be of the utmost importance. That organization is going to be indispensable for giving effect to the lessons forthcoming in debate.

Other Sources of Domination

States may be dominated, not just by other states, but also by non-state bodies. The most obvious candidates are multinational corporations and other private but international bodies. These raise very much the same sorts of problems for individual states that are raised by other, stronger states. The problems may be put in useful perspective by the existence of international agencies and by the culture of common reasons—and ultimately the culture of public international law—that such agencies can nurture. But they will be substantially resoluble, it seems to me, only to the extent that states, in particular weaker states, can join in common cause against corporations and other such bodies. In dealing with states that are isolated from one another, the powerful corporations may be able to dictate lower levels of corporation tax, or lesser environmental restrictions, or indeed a reduced concern for human rights; they may be able to force those states into a race towards lower standards.[44] But they will not be able to do this with states that effectively unite in order to face the threat.

What, finally, of the domination that is possible at the hands of international agencies? I have already addressed this issue in passing. International agencies do not represent a threat on a par with the dangers from other states and from private bodies like corporations, despite the many outcries about the democratic deficit that those agencies display. Their membership is normally subject to the vetting of affected states, their operations are typically exposed to demanding measures of review and accountability, and their decisions are often conditional on the approval of other bodies. Would that domestic states generally performed under comparable restraints. There may well be dangers of domination associated with international agencies, of course, but only a perverted sense of priority would suggest that they are the principal problems in the area.

---

[44] John Ruggie, *Business and Human Rights: Mapping International Standards of Responsibility and Accountability for Corporate Acts* (United Nations Human Rights Council, 2007).

6 THE BENEFITS OF HIGHLIGHTING DOMINATION

Even these quick observations suggest that a republican or neo-republican criterion for assessing international arrangements between representative states is a very attractive one. The non-interference criterion would identify a small cluster of evils that ought to be removed or reduced by an appropriate international order: specifically, the evils associated with active intervention or infiltration by other states and perhaps with economic or diplomatic bullying. The ideal of non-domination would agree that those initiatives represent a failure of international order, at least when they affect the presumptive, sovereign liberties of states. But it would be much more radical in identifying a range of other failures as well. It would indict, not just active intervention in the domain of a state's sovereign liberties, but the sort of non-active control that would make in equal measure for the domination of that state.

The republican ideal would join with the Rawlsian approach in hailing the possibility of representative states relating to one another under a regime of common reasons, treating one another with the respect that is universally recognized as an ideal in the relations between persons.[45] But it would break with that approach in emphasizing that in order for such a dispensation to come into being, in order for a deliberative mode of exchange to be genuinely deliberative and respectful, there are preconditions of equalized power that must first be realized amongst those states. A state that has a power of interference in the affairs of another will enjoy control over that other that no deliberative motions, and no protestations of goodwill, can expel. In order for the ideal of mutual respect to be reliably and credibly honored, so the lesson goes, the representative states that figure in the matrix of international relationships must be powerful enough to command respect from each other: to force one another to display respect.

But if the ideal of non-domination raises the bar that an international order ought to pass, it is not an unrealistic ideal that we have little or no reason to expect states ever to implement. In this respect it scores much better than the ideal often canvassed as a rival to that of non-intervention: the ideal of global distributive justice, understood on cosmopolitan lines.[46] This ideal would argue that states are required to remedy the ills suffered by people in other countries on just the same basis as they are required to remedy ills at home. The ideal is unrealistic in the sense that the governments of representative states can hardly be expected to be able to realize it. The government of such a state might seek to realize the ideal with or without the endorsement by its own citizens, but in either case it is likely to run into difficulties. If it does not seek the endorsement of citizens for

[45] Rawls, *The Law of Peoples*.

[46] Stefan Gosepath, "Deprivation and Institutionally Based Duties to Aid" (this volume), prioritizes distributive justice over non-domination.

pursuing the ideal, then it can expect electoral rejection. And if does seek that endorsement, then it is likely to be limited in the actions it is licensed to take. The citizens of a representative state may well license their government to deal with pressing crises in other countries—say, to relieve the subjects of ineffective or oppressive regimes—but they are unlikely to allow it to use coercively extracted taxes to deal with outsiders and insiders on the same basis.

The ideal of non-domination between representative states contrasts with this unrealistic vision insofar as it is, in economic language, incentive-compatible. Those states that acknowledge it as a normative target at which to aim in their relationships with others can see it as a goal that they and other representative states each have a variety of prudential reasons to pursue. Under the most cynical accounts of motivations in *realpolitik*, states and those who act for states are plausibly ascribed an interest in seeing that other international bodies, states and non-states alike, do not hold sway over them, whether in active recourse to intervention and pressure, or in the silent exploitation of the associated power. That interest ought to provide adequate reason for expecting that if the ideal of non-domination is recognized among representative states, then it ought to assume a motivating role for relevant agents.

This is not to say, of course, that the ideal will be unchallenging and easy to implement. First of all, the ideal will entail costs that states may often be reluctant to bear, as in helping out one of their number against an offender, and in punishing an offender. Second, the stronger states may have an interest, as they surely do, in preventing the weaker from organizing in blocs that would give them suitable standing in international deliberation. And third, the weaker states may face the problem of keeping their members disciplined in face of the free-rider temptation to defect from a bloc stance: say, to win a sweetheart deal from a stronger state by agreeing to laxer terms than were dictated by the bloc, or to attract a multinational corporation to its shores by agreeing to a lower rate of corporation tax than the bloc demanded. Those are real difficulties in the way of achieving a dispensation of international non-domination, but they do not constitute obstacles of the kind that might make the ideal seem utopian.

Incentive compatibility is not the only constraint of feasibility for normative ideals, although it is the only one that is acknowledged in most discussions. Equally important, or important in only a slightly reduced degree, is something that we might describe as discourse compatibility.[47] A proposal or ideal will fail to be discourse compatible to the extent that it is not one that can be supported in a deliberative forum by reasons that are accepted on all sides as relevant to the issue. The most egregious examples would present one side in the deliberations as unequal in some significant

[47] Pettit, *Rules, Reasons, and Norms: Selected Essays* (Oxford: Oxford University Press, 2002), 276.

manner to the other.[48] Consider in this connection the memo by Lawrence Summers, then chief economist to the World Bank, which was leaked in 1991. This made a case for exporting heavy polluting industries to the third world on the ground, roughly, that the anti-pollution preferences of poorer, shorter-lived individuals would not be as strong as those of the richer and longer-lived. The memo caused indignation worldwide, precisely because the proposal was incompatible with the assumptions of equality that underpin deliberation. A Brazilian official wrote in understandable incredulity that the reasoning was "perfectly logical and totally insane."[49]

Is the ideal of non-domination between states likely to be discourse compatible? Might it be internalized in debates between different countries as an ideal that they ought each to embrace and to honor in their dealings with one another?

At this point we return to the republican observation that freedom is well conceptualized as requiring non-domination: the absence of relationships in which the agent is controlled in a dominating way by others. The ideal of non-domination amongst states is nothing more or less, then, than an ideal of freedom. In not dominating their own citizens—in representing popularly checked forms of political control—representative states will pass on one count as free states. But in not being dominated by other states or other international bodies—in being subjected, at most, to the checked control of international agencies—they will pass as free states on a second count too.[50]

As an ideal of freedom, the ideal supported here is bound to be discourse compatible as well as incentive compatible. Freedom is universally accepted as an ideal that any party may claim for itself, and present as a good for every party to the table, in its deliberations with others. Even when a state enters international arrangements that bind it to a certain regulatory order, and that it may find very difficult to leave, freedom as non-domination remains a guiding ideal.[51] The arrangements will not deprive a state of its standing as a free state if they are voluntarily entered and if they give the

---

[48] The importance of discourse compatibility appears in the fact that while parties in a bidding process may come to accept common arrangements that give very different levels of advantage to different sides, those arrangements might prove to be unacceptable in a deliberative process where each is restricted to presenting arguments in the currency of common reasons. We might bargain our way to a seven–three division of 10 units, where the stronger could credibly stick at the offer of three, but it might be very difficult for us to agree that such a division was supported by commonly accepted reasons.

[49] For the content of the memo and criticism of it, including mention of this response, see Jim Vallette, "Larry Summers' War Against the Earth," *CounterPunch* (June 15, 1999), http://www.counterpunch.org/summers.html.

[50] This is congenial with John Maynor's argument in "Should Republican Liberty as Non-Domination Be Outsourced?" (this volume).

[51] And its taking those steps may actually improve the freedom as non-domination of its citizens, as when they are protected against the power of their own state by being able to appeal to an international body against it. See Pettit, *Republicanism*, 153.

state an equal stake and status with other states in determining how the arrangements operate: if, in that sense, the state shares to the highest feasible degree in checking the regulatory powers that the arrangements establish.

This observation enables us to see the ideal we have been discussing as truly a republican ideal. It directs us to a dispensation in which representative regimes come to deserve the old name of "free state," not just because of how they treat their members, but also because of how they treat one another. They will count as republics, whether or not they embrace that title, on two counts: both because their publics are in charge on the domestic front, not some elite or faction, and because their publics are allowed to maintain such control by the relations sustained with similar regimes.[52]

[52] My thanks to Barbara Buckinx for discussion on topics related to an ancestor of this paper, to Duncan Bell, Samantha Besson, John Maynor, and John Tasioulas for comments on that earlier version, and to the very useful discussion at a conference in Cambridge University where it was presented in May 2007. I also benefitted from comments received when it provided the basis for a lecture at the University of Sydney in July 2009.

BIBLIOGRAPHY

Beitz, Charles R. *The Idea of Human Rights*. Oxford: Oxford University Press, 2009.

Beitz, Charles R. *Political Theory and International Relations* [1999 ed.]. Princeton: Princeton University Press, 1979.

Bell, Duncan. "Empire and Imperialism." In *The Cambridge History of Nineteenth Century Political Thought*, edited by Gregory Claeys and Gareth Stedman Jones. Cambridge: Cambridge University Press, 2011.

Bellamy, Richard. *Political Constitutionalism: A Republican Defense of the Constitutionality of Democracy*. Cambridge: Cambridge University Press, 2007.

Berlin, Isaiah. *Four Essays on Liberty*. Oxford: Oxford University Press, 1969.

Berlin, Isaiah. *Two Concepts of Liberty*. Oxford: Oxford University Press, 1958.

Besson, Samantha, and Jose Luis Marti, eds. *Legal Republicanism*. Oxford: Oxford University Press, 2009.

Bohman, James. *Democracy Across Borders: From Dêmos to Dêmoi*. Cambridge, MA: MIT Press, 2007.

Braithwaite, John, Hilary Charlesworth, and Adérito Soares. *Networked Governance of Freedom and Tyranny: Peace in East Timor*. Canberra: ANU Press, 2012.

Braithwaite, John, and Peter Drahos. *Global Business Regulation*. Cambridge: Cambridge University Press, 2000.

Braithwaite, John, and Philip Pettit. *Not Just Deserts: A Republican Theory of Criminal Justice*. Oxford: Oxford University Press, 1990.

Brennan, Geoffrey, and Philip Pettit. *The Economy of Esteem: An Essay on Civil and Political Society*. Oxford: Oxford University Press, 2004.

Brugger, William. *Republican Theory in Political Thought: Virtuous or Virtual?* New York: Macmillan, 1999.

Carter, Ian. *A Measure of Freedom*. Oxford: Oxford University Press, 1999.

Cohen, Joshua. "Minimalism About Human Rights: The Most We Can Hope For?" *Journal of Political Philosophy* 12, no. 2 (2004): 190–213.

Deudney, Daniel H. *Bounding Power: Republican Security Theory from the Polis to the Global Village*. Princeton: Princeton University Press, 2007.

Donnelly, Thomas et al. "Rebuilding America's Defenses: Strategy, Forces and Resources for a New Century." http://www.newamericancentury.org/RebuildingAmericasDefenses.pdf.

Frankfurt, Harry. "Alternate Possibilities and Moral Responsibility." *Journal of Philosophy* 66, no. 23 (1969): 829–39.

Gill, T. D. "Litigation Strategy in the Nicaragua Case at the International Court." In *International Law at a Time of Perplexity: Essays in Honour of Shabtai Rosenne*, edited by Yôrām Dinšţein with the assistance of Mala Tabor, 197–224. Dordrecht: Kluwer Academic Publishers, 1989.

Gosepath, Stefan. "Deprivation and Institutionally Based Duties to Aid." In *Domination and Global Political Justice: Conceptual, Historical, and Institutional Perspectives*, edited by Barbara Buckinx, Jonathan Trejo-Mathys, and Timothy Waligore. New York: Routledge, 2015.

Greig, D. W. *International Law,* 2nd ed. London: Butterworths, 1976.

Habermas, Jürgen. *A Theory of Communicative Action,* vols. 1 and 2. Cambridge: Polity Press, 1984, 1989.

Halldenius, Lena. *Liberty Revisited*. Lund, SE: Bokbox Publications, 2001.

Hart, H.L.A. *The Concept of Law*. Oxford: Oxford Unviersity Press, 1961.

Hobbes, Thomas. *Leviathan, with Selected Variants from the Latin Edition of 1668*. Edited by Edwin Curley. Indianapolis: Hackett, 1994.

Honohan, Iseult. *Civic Republicanism*. London: Routledge, 2002.

Honohan, Iseult, and Jeremy Jennings, eds. *Republicanism in Theory and Practice*. London: Routledge, 2006.

Kramer, Matthew H. *The Quality of Freedom*. Oxford: Oxford University Press, 2003.

Kukathas, Chandran, and Philip Pettit. *Rawls: A Theory of Justice and Its Critics*. Cambridge/Stanford: Polity Press/Stanford University Press, 1990.

Laborde, Cécile. *Critical Republicanism: The Hijab Controversy and Political Philosophy*. Oxford: Oxford University Press, 2008.

Laborde, Cécile, and John Maynor, eds. *Republicanism and Political Theory*. Oxford: Blackwell, 2008.

Lilburne, John. *The Legal Fundamental Liberties of the People of England, Asserted, Revived, and Vindicated*. London: 1646.

List, Christian, and Philip Pettit. *Group Agency: The Possibility, Design and Status of Corporate Agents*. Oxford: Oxford University Press, 2011.

Lovett, Frank. *A General Theory of Justice & Domination*. Oxford: Oxford University Press, 2010.

Lovett, Frank, and Philip Pettit. "Neorepublicanism: A Normative and Institutional Research Program." *Annual Review of Political Science* 12 (2009): 11–29.

MacGilvray, Eric. *The Invention of Market Freedom*. Cambridge: Cambridge University Press, 2011.

Martí, José Luis, and Philip Pettit. *A Political Philosophy in Public Life: Civic Republicanism in Zapatero's Spain*. Princeton: Princeton University Press, 2010.

Maynor, John. *Republicanism in the Modern World*. Cambridge: Polity Press, 2003.

Maynor, John. "Should Republican Liberty As Non-Domination Be Outsourced?" In *Domination and Global Political Justice: Conceptual, Historical, and Institutional Perspectives*, edited by Barbara Buckinx, Jonathan Trejo-Mathys, and Timothy Waligore. New York: Routledge, 2015.

Meyer, Howard N. "When the Pope Rebuked the U.S. at the World Court." *The Baltimore Sun*, March 18, 1997. http://articles.baltimoresun.com/1997-03-18/news/1997077033.

Moon, J. Donald. "Rawls and Habermas on Public Reason: Human Rights and Global Justice." *Annual Review of Political Science* 6 (2003): 257–74.
Niederberger, Andreas, and Philipp Schink, eds. *Republican Democracy: Liberty, Law and Politics*. Edinburgh: Edinburgh University Press, 2013.
Olsaretti, Serena. *Liberty, Desert and the Market*. Cambridge: Cambridge University Press, 2004.
Pettit, Philip. "Democracy, National and International." *Monist* 89, no. 2 (2006): 301–24.
Pettit, Philip. *Just Freedom: A Moral Compass for a Complex World*. New York: W. W. Norton, 2014.
Pettit, Philip. "Legitimate International Institutions: A Neorepublican Perspective." In *The Philosophy of International Law*, edited by Samantha Besson and John Tasioulas, 139–60. Oxford: Oxford University Press, 2010.
Pettit, Philip. *On the People's Terms: A Republican Theory and Model of Democracy*. Cambridge: Cambridge University Press, 2012.
Pettit, Philip. "Rawls's Peoples." In *Rawls's Law of Peoples: A Realistic Utopia*, edited by Rex Martin and David Reidy. Oxford: Blackwell, 2006.
Pettit, Philip. "A Republican Law of Peoples." *European Journal of Political Theory* 9, no. 1 (2010): 70–94.
Pettit, Philip. *Republicanism: A Theory of Freedom and Government*. Oxford: Oxford University Press, 1997. Paperback ed., with postscript [1999].
Pettit, Philip. *Rules, Reasons, and Norms: Selected Essays*. Oxford: Oxford University Press, 2002.
Pitts, Jennifer. *A Turn to Empire: The Rise of Imperial Liberalism in Britain and France*. Princeton: Princeton University Press, 2005.
Pogge, Thomas. "An Egalitarian Law of Peoples." *Philosophy & Public Affairs* 23, no. 3 (1993): 195–224.
Quill, Lawrence. *Liberty after Liberalism: Civic Republicanism in a Global Age*. London: Palgrave Macmillan, 2005.
Rawls, John. *The Law of Peoples*. Cambridge, MA: Harvard University Press, 1999.
Richardson, Henry. *Democratic Autonomy*. New York: Oxford University Press, 2002.
Rousseau, Jean-Jacques. *The Social Contract and Discourses*. London: J. M. Dent & Sons Ltd., 1973.
Ruggie, John. *Business and Human Rights: Mapping International Standards of Responsibility and Accountability for Corporate Acts*. New York: United Nations Human Rights Council, 2007.
Schuppert, Fabian. *Freedom, Recognition and Non-Domination: A Republican Theory of (Global) Justice*. Dordrecht, NL: Springer, 2014.
Shapiro, Ian. *Containment: Rebuilding a Strategy Against Global Terror*. Princeton: Princeton University Press, 2007.
Skinner, Quentin. *Liberty Before Liberalism*. Cambridge: Cambridge University Press, 1998.
Slaughter, Anne-Marie. *A New World Order*. Princeton: Princeton University Press, 2004.
Slaughter, Steven. *Liberty Beyond Neo-Liberalism: A Republican Critique of Liberal Government in a Globalising Age*. London: Macmillan Palgrave, 2005.
Steiner, Hillel. *An Essay on Rights*. Oxford: Blackwell, 1994.
Thaler, Richard, and Cass Sunstein. *Nudge: Improving Decisions About Health, Wealth and Happiness*. London: Penguin Books, 2008.
US Government. *National Security Strategy of the United States of America*. Washington, DC: White House, 2002. http://www.whitehouse.gov/nsc/nss.html.

Vallette, Jim. "Larry Summers' War Against the Earth." *CounterPunch* (June 15, 1999). http://www.counterpunch.org/summers.html.
Van Gelderen, Martin, and Quentin Skinner, eds. *Republicanism: A Shared European Heritage*, 2 vols. Cambridge: Cambridge University Press, 2002.
Viroli, Maurizio. *Republicanism*. New York: Hill and Wang, 2002.
Weinstock, Daniel, and Christian Nadeau, eds. *Republicanism: History, Theory and Practice*. London: Frank Cass, 2004.
Wendt, Alexander. "Why a World State is Inevitable." *European Journal of International Relations* 9, no. 4 (2003): 491–542.
White, Stuart. *Building a Citizen Society: The Emerging Politics of Republican Democracy*. Edited by Daniel Leighton. London: Lawrence and Wishart, 2008.

3 Domination, Global Harms, and the Priority of Injustice

Expanding Transnational Republicanism

James Bohman

Because of the vast inequalities in life prospects for people situated in various locations across the globe, many recent cosmopolitan discussions of social justice have, for good reason, been primarily concerned with the distribution of social goods. The distributive model has shaped discussion of political justice, where distributive justice becomes an indicator of basic concern and respect for all citizens. Given the fact of growing interdependence, it is no longer possible to think of these issues as concerned merely with distant peoples, whose interests, in the final analysis, always seem to be subordinated to those of members of our own political community. Some nationalist republicans have explained the priority given to fellow citizens in terms of a shared national-political identity, or bounded political community that provides the basis for universal values with regard to the common good shared by all fellow citizens.[1] Many cosmopolitan republicans have rejected such a view, however capacious its universalism may seem.[2] While my sympathies lie with the cosmopolitans, my task here is to propose a more radical alternative that asks republicans to shift the terms of the debate and see that the primary virtue of republican theory is not patriotism or some common identity, but rather the priority of overcoming domination and injustice. It can always be asked on any policy that promotes the common good whether or not it increases and decreases domination. But if republicanism requires minimizing domination and injustice, which I believe it does, then it gives priority to injustice more generally and not just to the injustice of domination. Hence, current circumstances of justice demand a broadening of the scope of republicanism, which I take to have already been extended to include the transnational achievement of non-domination.

This shift to the priority of injustice is part of a recent trend in theories of justice. In his book, *The Idea of Justice*, Amartya Sen criticizes the prevalent

---

[1] See Cécile Laborde, "Republicanism and Global Justice," *European Journal of Political Theory* 9, no. 1 (2010): 48–69.

[2] On the limits of nationalist republicanism, see Sophie Guérard de Latour, "Reworking the Neo-Republican Sense of Belonging," *Diacrítica* 24, no. 2 (2010): 91–112.

view that injustices are simply departures from existing forms of justice and from the normative background of the basic structure, against which they can be measured and criticized.[3] Indeed, Sen has long argued against ideal theory, along with Judith Shklar and others, that "the greatest relevance of the idea of justice lies in the identification of patent injustice, on which reasoned agreement is possible, rather than in the derivation of some extant formula for how the world should be precisely run."[4] Indeed, turning our focus on those practices that we deem just may often make us blind to existing forms of injustice, holding the better hostage to the putative best. But once we give priority to injustice instead of justice, it is possible for moral and political reflection to become richer in empirical detail and to begin to address the persistent and sometimes unrecognized normality of injustice. Shklar argues that it is a grave philosophical and moral error to think that injustice is simply the absence of justice, and so that "once we know what is just, it is all that we need to know."[5] We miss precisely the very normality of injustice and the constant adaptation of most of the world's population to the normal, everyday injustices that they suffer under and to which they adapt their preferences.

The criticism that ideal theories can leave out real injustices by focusing on the normative ground of ideal justice is hardly new. This is because republicanism, with its emphasis on non-domination, already takes the practical and methodological priority of injustice to be a fundamental, methodological requirement for improving people's political situations. Unlike Sen's emphasis on non-ideal theory, republicans seek to show the ways in which domination is pervasive in many different social settings and institutions, and as such ought to be minimized. Because of the possibility of undetected domination, injustice has always had analytic primacy over justice in republican political thought. In fact, recent republics take such an account of non-domination as the means to develop a workable conception of freedom, the main task of which is to reduce injustice by minimizing domination within the republic. At the same time, modern republicans have to squarely face the consequences of the emergence of functioning democracies, within which non-domination still refers back to the presence or absence of basic forms of injustice and harms. In this sense, modern republicanism has always been concerned with political inequality rather than political equality, because justice consists in remedying existing injustice rather than establishing justice once and for all.

[3] Amartya Sen, *The Idea of Justice* (Cambridge: Harvard University Press, 2009), 26. Sen rejects "transcendental institutionalism" as inadequate precisely for assessing injustices.
[4] Ibid., 1–2, 12.
[5] Judith N. Shklar, *The Faces of Injustice* (New Haven: Yale University Press, 1990), 19; see also Miranda Fricker, *Epistemic Injustice* (Oxford: Oxford University Press, 2007), 7.

As concretely realized in those institutions able to establish the normative power or standing sufficient for avoiding the ills and harms of domination, non-domination is manifested in the ability of each member of any such institutional scheme to avoid the injustice of being subject to the will of others, while potentially, if not actually, being able to exercise a minimum of control over one's own life. Following, for the moment, Philip Pettit's view of domination as arbitrary interference, we may think of the indefiniteness of authority and social action in modern societies and in transnational settings as allowing new and wider opportunities for others to arbitrarily interfere in our lives, where those who are dominated have no effective legal means of resisting such interference. Pettit includes among potentially arbitrary influences "financial clout, political authority, social connections, communal standing, informational access, ideological positions, cultural legitimation and the like."[6] Even if the exact nature of the sources of dominating power remains a matter of dispute, the core republican idea is that people are dominated to the extent that others are able to deny the standing and statuses that make it possible for them to live without control, threat, or coercion. On this view, it is important, *contra* Pettit, to see that domination is not fully captured by the bilateral case of arbitrary interference. Rather, it is the lack of standing and statuses in some domains (even if they have it in others) that makes people vulnerable to various injustices.

Much has been written about how global interdependence creates new "circumstances of politics." But those circumstances also suggest to republicanism something very different, the new "circumstances of injustice." For this reason, we should first focus on various methodological and explanatory issues related to distinctly transnational forms of the injustice of domination. Second, these circumstances of injustice have to be examined in order to see how they are sustained. My working hypothesis is that there are no persistent injustices without forms of domination. Domination is exercised at the normative level: some persons, such as undocumented workers, are dominated because they lack the most basic communicative statuses, and without such the injustices they suffer lead to persistent and deep forms of injustice. Third, and finally, republicanism must offer its own remedies for domination, specifically the requirements of non-domination as a political ideal, now in transnational settings. According to neo-republicans such as Pettit and Quentin Skinner, the institutions of a republic ought to be designed so as to promote freedom as non-domination, so that these institutions in fact constitute, rather than simply bring about causally, "the very non-domination which citizens enjoy under them."[7] Even if this is correct, the issue remains how a constitutional legal order can be brought about to make it constitutive of robust non-domination. Here the commitment to

---

[6] Philip Pettit, *Republicanism: A Theory of Freedom and Government* (Oxford: Oxford University Press, 1997), 52.
[7] Ibid., 107.

such a constitutive account leaves us in need of a richer understanding of the normative and social basis for non-domination. It also seems to ignore the fact that many constitutional states have, in the past, tolerated (and still do) great inequalities internally and domination externally, even as they purport to establish relations of non-domination within the political community.[8]

TRANSNATIONAL INJUSTICE: NEW FORMS OF DOMINATION

For current purposes, I accept the main thrust of Pettit's argument that non-domination must be understood as a certain form of power. As Pettit puts this more general understanding, non-domination "represents a form of control that a person enjoys in relation to their own destiny," or, more specifically, he explains non-domination as the power of agents to prevent "various ills from happening to them."[9] There are two possibilities for achieving non-domination: either it is in virtue of being a citizen of a free state, or it is that the agent himself possesses such control over his own destiny. Instead of settling this issue, I will return to an older conception that Pettit defended, where non-domination is not power, but "antipower." While this conception no longer figures prominently in Pettit's constitutive view, it has certain advantages over his settled understanding of domination as arbitrary interference.[10] According to Pettit, antipower is "the capacity to command noninterference as a power."[11] Antipower cannot be the simple control of the other, or even the mere capacity to resist the imposition of obligations. Instead, it must be the power over those who would dominate us, and thus the control over one's life via the content of one's obligations and statuses. In other words, as the most basic normative power necessary for non-domination, it is the positive and creative power to interpret, shape, and reformulate the contents of common obligations with others.

In order to make this point, Habermas's distinction between communicative freedom and communicative power is helpful.[12] Democratization has two main dimensions: first, it requires institutions, publics, and associations in which communicative freedom is realized and, second, it requires that this communicative freedom is exercised in institutions that link such

---

[8] James Bohman, "Nondomination and Transnational Democracy," in *Republicanism and Political Theory*, eds. Cécile Laborde and John Maynor (Oxford: Blackwell, 2008), 190–216.
[9] Pettit, *Republicanism*, 67.
[10] Terry Macdonald also prefers the term "antipower." See Macdonald, "Antipower, Agency, and the Republican Case for Global Institutional Pluralism" (this volume).
[11] Pettit, "Freedom as Antipower," *Ethics* 106, no. 3 (1996): 576–604, 589.
[12] On this distinction applied to the global order, see Bohman, "Democratizing the Global Order: From Communicative Freedom to Communicative Power," *Review of International Studies* 36, no. 2 (2010): 431–47.

freedom to the exercise of normatively generated, communicative power. As a preliminary definition, communicative freedom is the exercise of a communicative status, the status of being recognized as a member of a public. Communicative freedom is transformed into communicative power when it is incorporated into institutionalized processes of decision-making. Communicative power is thus a decisional status that is regularized in access to influence in an authoritative institution. Under these conditions, the communicative freedom to initiate deliberation becomes the communicative power to place an item on an institution's agenda. It is the constructive aspect of communicative freedom, the capacity to create and to modify obligations among speakers and hearers, the acceptance of which "creates a new social fact."[13] Thus, when two speakers promise each other that they will meet at a certain place and time tomorrow on the condition that the other will, they have together freely imposed a new obligation that binds themselves and the other. Antipower is thus that form of self-binding and shared obligation that is in our common interests. Communicative freedom requires communicative status; communicative power is based in decisional status. In both aspects of democratization, inequality in antipower could lead to the failure of such obligations or decisions to reflect common concerns and interests.

In democratic communities, non-domination is manifested in the ability of each member of such a scheme to avoid having its terms set by the other members, and thus having potentially, if not actually, a minimum of normative and political control over one's statuses. In order to develop these possibilities further and suggest why something like antipower is the appropriate remedy to domination, it is first necessary to develop the related conception of non-domination. As many critics have noted, Pettit's definition of "arbitrary interference" makes sense only against the normative background of rights, duties, roles, and institutions that actors mutually take for granted in their social action, and which do indeed make agents correspondingly and differentially powerful, with respect to the capacity to dominate others.

If domination and non-domination are instead inherently normative notions, then "the purported exercise of a normative power—the power to modify the rights and duties of others—is essential to the idea of domination."[14] Domination is thus not just the capacity to interfere arbitrarily in another agent's life, but also the capacity to make use of distinctly normative powers that operate against this institutionalized background of legitimate norms. It is the ability to impose obligations and duties arbitrarily. Domination on this view refers to the use of normative powers by the dominator to purport to impose duties and to change the statuses of others. Dominators stand in some *normative relation* to the dominated in the web of authority

---

[13] Jürgen Habermas, *Between Facts and Norms: Contributions to a Discourse Theory of Law and Democracy* (Cambridge: MIT Press, 1996), 147.
[14] Henry Richardson, *Democratic Autonomy: Public Reasoning About the Ends of Policy* (Oxford: Oxford University Press, 2002), 34.

and roles, such as administrator, king, or *pater familias*, all of whom can, in virtue of their authority, exercise the normative power to change the normative statuses of the dominated arbitrarily. Even if the "rational" administrator may seek to impose new duties impartially for the sake of the putative common good, this exercise of normative power can thus be dominating in virtue of the lack of a capacity of those who are subjected to exercise antipower. Such a normative approach more clearly distinguishes between cases of systematic normative domination and the dyadic conception of x arbitrarily interfering with y, and is for that reason better able to analyze the structural and normative features of *institutions* that enable domination.

This conception is insufficient for understanding the costs of domination, particularly given the rather narrow, dyadic account that Henry Richardson develops. First of all, such an account presupposes the central features of citizenship in generating communicative power. In no other role or location than as citizens in democratic institutions do members of modern societies exercise their normative powers of changing shared obligations and statuses under the condition of common liberty. In this case, obligations are not purported to be imposed, but they are the product of the joint exercise of the normative powers and communicative freedom that shape them. Certainly, other forms of authority exist in modern societies than political institutions, and can make it possible for these statuses and obligations to change without popular influence or the discursive control of citizens. Democracy organizes the *joint* exercise of these powers and capacities, so that they are not under the control of any given individual or group of citizens, but are jointly exercised by all. Some of these preconditions are institutional, such as the existence of a free and open public sphere in which all may participate with others in expressing and informing their opinions. But this example also reveals that there are even more fundamental statuses that are necessary in order to exercise citizenship and other statuses. These include mutually granted communicative status, the normative power to address and be addressed by others without loss or dependence. The loss of this power is typical of severe forms of domination, where speakers do not have the standing to speak, much less to make claims concerning the extent of their freedom.

This analysis can be extended to different domains. A republican epistemology, for example, is concerned with the multitude of ways in which domination is expressed by the unjust denial of epistemic status to certain groups. On this view, it is important, *contra* Pettit, to see domination as having many forms beyond arbitrary interference. Rather, the harms to those who are dominated are best understood as the loss of standing and status that makes such injustices possible across many different domains. One such domain is one's standing as a knower, the harm of denying one's epistemic status or capacity to participate as an equal in the social exchange of information. This could significantly broaden Pettit's account. In her analysis of epistemic injustice, Miranda Fricker examines two primary forms of epistemic injustice, testimonial and hermeneutical injustice, in which "someone is wronged in their capacity as a giver of knowledge" in the first case, and in which "someone is wronged in their capacity as a subject of social understanding" in the second case.[15] This approach is significant for broadening republicanism because it exhibits a clear methodological commitment to the priority of injustice that is similar to Sen's capability theory. As she puts it, the way the priority of injustice matters in analyzing epistemic practice is that "there is a lot to be gained philosophically by concentrating on the normality of injustice, and one of the gains might be that we achieve a better grasp of what is required in practice to operate in a way that works against it."[16] Epistemic injustice is in fact then a form of domination, and for this reason we should not expect the individual exercise of epistemic virtues to be sufficient for rectifying its injustice. In epistemic injustice, people are denied not only the status of knowers, but they are also harmed by being excluded from sharing in the generation and exchange of knowledge in the epistemic community.

Even in cases in which there is an extant constitutional order, these protections would be insufficient to achieve non-domination for all who are subject to the exercise of its authoritative institutions. These constitutional arguments neglect the ways in which the lack of resources (rather than the lack of power) is also the basis for domination. Pettit and other republicans have overlooked the strong connection between poverty and domination, which emerges more clearly when we consider not just poverty's effects on the poor, but also the political and structural consequences of pervasive inequalities in transforming communicative freedom into communicative power; that is, how one's status as a member of a public is transformed into access to political influence. Pettit agrees that "ensuring your social freedom will require eliminating those material and related disadvantages that expose you to control by others."[17] Destitution clearly makes us systematically vulnerable to domination and also reduces the worth of liberty. But these disadvantages produce more structural, rather than bilateral, domination as control. According to Andrew Hurrell, inequalities among states give rise to substantial differences in political influence and bargaining power between the rich and the poor and between rich and poor states.[18] This inegalitarian basic structure results in global poverty, its institutions so shaped by inequalities of power and resources as to lack even minimal justice. These conditions of extreme destitution within a putative republic, it should also be noted, are on my view "functionally equivalent to tyranny and the absence of political rights."[19] Moreover, the lack of citizenship common among refugees and migrants exposes them to many forms of domination, since their

---

[15] Fricker, *Epistemic Injustice,* 7.
[16] Ibid.
[17] Pettit, *Republicanism*, 77.
[18] Andrew Hurrell, "Global Inequality and International Institutions," *Metaphilosophy* 32, no. 1/2 (2001): 34–57.
[19] Bohman, "Is Democracy a Means to Global Justice? Human Rights and the Democratic Minimum," *Ethics and International Affairs* 19, no. 1 (2005): 101–16.

status and identity is defined by others without their influence, with little or no recourse.[20] Thus, destitution is certainly one of the great causes of vulnerability to domination and injustice across the whole spectrum of possible forms. Thus, obligations to act so as to overcome such domination resulting in capability failure remain the core of a republican motivation for distributive justice.[21] Regardless of the strength of other causal claims about global inequalities, it is clear that destitution itself makes those who suffer from it vulnerable to many manifest forms of domination and injustice. Eliminating destitution is itself essential to the moral and political goal of minimizing the fundamental injustice of domination, a domination which has for quite a while been a structural feature of modern states.

The upshot of this argument is that there are basic statuses and powers, such as communicative and epistemic statuses, that all persons must possess in order not to be dominated. These statuses are essential to that form of equality that is a necessary condition for non-domination, for the condition in which no person is subjected to another. In some cases, domination is in fact also institutionally mediated, so that all those who lack such statuses and powers are subjected to injustices across a number of domains. If this is true, then non-domination can be understood not just as the absence of interference, but also as a kind of equality, in which claims can be made on me only if I can make claims on others. While such principles are familiar, my aim is to give them a republican interpretation. Pettit takes tracking conditions and contestation to be sufficient for equality (although he would not put it in exactly this way). However, neither tracking nor contestation is sufficient for non-domination. Instead of looking solely at such conditions, broader conditions need to be identified, and here the all-subjected and all-affected principles do just this work (even if they do not state positively the scope of the people, who have the right to exercise communicative power).[22] Under the current circumstances of domination, many different types of actors and institutions can act as dominators, and they in turn may also be dominated, sometimes at a distance.

SUBJECTION, AFFECTEDNESS, AND INJUSTICE: ON THE SCOPE OF DOMINATION

One difficulty with the traditional republican emphasis on citizenship is that its entitlements against the state are no longer broad enough for the sort of security and equality that non-domination demands. Indeed, an increasing

---

[20] Bohman, "Constituting Humanity: Universal Political Rights and the Human Community," *Canadian Journal of Philosophy* (2007), Supplementary Volume 31 on *Global Justice and Global Institutions*, ed. Daniel Weinstock, 227–52.

[21] See also Laborde, "Republicanism and Global Justice."

[22] On these principles and the philosophical problems with both of them, see Sofia Näsström, "The Challenge of the All-Affected Principle," *Political Studies* 59, no. 1 (2011): 116–34.

number of people, such as undocumented and illegal noncitizens, lack communicative and other basic statuses even in democratic societies, with the consequence that they are exposed to domination and injustices meted out by a variety of actors, including citizens, without the protections of non-domination that republics seem to be able to offer. Thus, the condition of illegality renders such persons vulnerable to domination without legal and political recourse. Even when they do attract legal attention, they are in a catch-22, since to expose such domination leads to deportation; thus, domination inevitably exposes them to a variety of further cascading harms and injustices. Without status in such proceedings, they lack the capacity to participate in legal forms and institutional processes that aim at non-domination. Thus, the current bases for non-domination within states are remarkably inegalitarian, making subjection more common now than in the postwar era of states, to the extent that the number of private and institutional dominators has proliferated. The all-subjected and the all-affected principles serve to identify at least two types of domination in the face of greater interdependence and less institutional security.

As it is commonly understood, the all-subjected principle refers to states and other authoritative political units that can demand obligations from its members. Given that members are subjected or bound in this sense, non-domination seems to require that they all have some say concerning the rules, laws, or edicts that bind them. Interpreted in this way, the all-subjected principle would have a broader scope than previously thought, since people can be subjected to a variety of non-state actors (such as private corporations). Under current circumstances of injustice, there is no single form of subjection, and no single actor or institution which has the power of subjection over all others. Rather, powers of subjection are dispersed across various institutions and various units.

However, while subjection to a democratic state neutralizes domination to the extent that people have broad powers and a say over how the state operates these functions, subjection by many other institutional actors now has an even broader scope, especially if it remains unchecked by constitutional and other political means. As Sen argues, subjection can thus only be remedied by norms, powers, and practices with an equally broad scope, and powers and statuses that are sufficient to operate as antipower. Indeed, one of the major purposes of republican political practice is to transform subjection of others into equal standing (among all those who are affected, both citizens or noncitizens, so that the political inclusion of all those subjected is necessary to avoid injustice). Here the capability approach focuses on the freedom of a person to achieve things people have reason to value. As the state loses the sole power of subjection, more locations for practices of non-domination need to be established. The International Criminal Court provides one kind of institution of non-domination in light of the all-subjected principle.

More restricted in scope, the all-affected principle addresses specific forms of domination rather than the full range of statuses and powers suggested by the all-subjected principle. Here the paradigmatic case is action at a distance, such as harmful downstream pollution, in which some set of agents imposes opportunity costs (related to cleanup) and also thereby eliminates options (such as eating fish taken from the river). Similarly, consider the fate of those who live on low-lying islands or river deltas with respect to climate change. While we are all affected by climate change (and all subjected to states which emit harmful greenhouse gases), priority here is given to domination that is both intensive and extensive. Climate change is a great harm, and one with numerous consequences. In such cases, inclusion requires a variable geometry that aligns citizens, noncitizens, and some decision-making authority (extant or not). The republican interpretation of the all-affected principle is still concerned with "all those dominated," and thus, in the case of climate change, with the scope and intensity of domination. Climate change mitigation is just when it minimizes domination. This is an issue of affectedness across a variety of domains. Certainly, poorer regions tend to be more vulnerable than richer ones. Therefore, climate change mitigation must reflect the demands of equality if it is not itself to create a form of domination. Instead, it must give priority to the worst off.

While I cannot here settle the complex issues concerning the all-subjected and all-affected principles, I have offered the minimization of domination as the decisive criterion in these discussions. Since one historically confirmed premise of republicanism is that democracies can be dominators, democratic self-rule is a necessary but not sufficient condition for non-domination. Democracies can be judged by the same criterion of minimizing domination. I have in previous work answered this question in terms of the democratic minimum, the achievement of a normative status sufficient for citizens to exercise their creative powers to reshape democracy according to the demands of justice. The account that I have offered is ultimately deliberative; one that depends on the relationship between deliberation, accountability, and the capacity of citizens to introduce novel demands and claims. However, current extreme inequalities among various politically organized communities make non-domination very difficult to achieve in many parts of the world. These inequalities are not only inequalities in the distribution of political power, but also of primary goods. Given their metric of freedom, neo-republicans have largely been silent on this issue. How might the ideal of minimizing domination apply to inequalities in distributive justice? Gross inequalities in distributive justice surely produce greater political inequalities and insecurity from domination. In general, republicans could understand distributive justice in terms of a threshold based on the capacity of persons to occupy certain moral and political statuses that minimize domination and promote more extensive liberty.

Perhaps the most direct account that would take the minimization of domination as its goal might be a more republican version of Thomas Pogge's institutional argument that attempts to establish that violations of justice are intrinsic to the global basic structure and its way of organizing statuses and membership.[23] For my purposes, the exact causes need not be identified, except to establish that the global basic structure, as it is constituted now, is one in which the minority of the rich dominate the vast global poor (and they can be shown to benefit thereby). But at the very least, Pogge's argument suggests that the political legitimacy of any global basic structure requires that it accept the demand to minimize domination among the poorest of the poor. On republican grounds, the current global basic structure is for this reason illegitimate, since it does not minimize domination accordingly. Given its metric of freedom, the minimum threshold would be one in which all persons in the global basic structure fulfill the necessary conditions for inhabiting statuses of individual and collective control and self-direction, and for achieving the social bases of self-respect.

In this respect, current global economic arrangements promote domination in the form of capability failure; that is, the lack of opportunity to develop basic powers and capabilities necessary for non-domination. Severe poverty is a form of capability failure, including the ability to achieve basic functioning, a diversity of options, and well-being. One such capability is political capability to participate in public life, which is interestingly related to equality. Sen borrows a formulation of the fundamental basis of all democratic life from Adam Smith: the capability to appear in public without shame and thus to participate fully in democratic deliberation. As a matter of domination, the lack of this capability means that some routinely speak on the behalf of others; this is itself a fundamental form of domination, to the extent that it removes the basis for independent participation and recognition in the public sphere. This is in fact a form of domination that can now be present within republican polities, particularly those that move from a bounded and relatively homogenous political community to an open and pluralist polity in which existing relations of non-domination cannot be adequately generalized to extend non-domination to all citizens and residents. This possibility raises a paradoxical question: if the circumstances of politics change sufficiently over time, might it be possible that the existing forms of identification and belonging in bounded political communities themselves contribute to the overall increase of domination? Just as the limits of the conception of domination must be expanded beyond arbitrary power, so too must the conception of non-domination be broadened under the new circumstances of politics. These new circumstances of justice and the emergence of now global harms and other forms of pervasive domination suggest that nationalist forms of republicanism fail to meet the priority of injustice.

---

[23] See, for example, Thomas W. Pogge, *World Poverty and Human Rights* (Malden, MA: Polity, 2002).

TRANSNATIONAL AND NATIONALIST REPUBLICANISM: INEQUALITY AND PARADOXES OF NON-DOMINATION

Taking Pettit as our guide, the standard republican account of non-domination is guided by two premises. First, he argues that, for Hobbesian reasons, more or less equal, "reciprocal power sufficient to check each others' interference" can never achieve a state of non-domination.[24] If non-domination is the supreme political value, the modern state ineluctably requires that freedom is robustly realized in its institutions to the extent that the capacity of others to dominate is currently absent, but it also requires that such dependence is rendered "structurally impossible" in the constitutional state. What is important here is that non-domination thereby becomes a fully common good, so that it would become more or less impossible for any individual to increase his enjoyment of the good without everyone else increasing their enjoyment at the same time. Although this aspect of non-domination has been less prominent, Pettit argues that non-domination demands distinctive forms of "republican" equality and community. "To want republican liberty, you have to want republican equality; to realize republican liberty you have to realize republican community."[25]

The normative interpretation of domination and non-domination that I have developed here helps us extend the conception of domination beyond the bilateral or interpersonal case (modeled on the master dominating the slave) to cases in which collective control is exercised in deliberation. This advance also puts a greater emphasis on legal and civil status, precisely when such statuses are now guarded very closely. Indeed, republican political communities may now become violators of republican equality by drawing membership and limits of the political community too strictly. This is particularly true for republican nationalism, which would ideally combine both the commitment to universal political principles, such as equality, with a strong allegiance to particular political communities. This example reveals a tension in republican thinking on minimizing domination, precisely as the potential for domination—the prevalence of *imperium* and *dominium* in republican nationalism—rises in the face of increasing cultural pluralism within contemporary republics.

How one looks at this new political reality depends on both substantive and methodological issues. But it seems very clear that the issue of the methodological priority of justice or injustice is central to the internal dispute between nationalist and transnationalist republicanism. Nationalist republicans give priority to justice, seeing the nationalist polity as independent of the basic claim to shared belonging and mutual commitments in the republic, with its commitment to the common good. Under the current circumstances of justice, however, these commitments no longer provide a

[24] Pettit, *Republicanism*, 93.
[25] Ibid., 125–26.

basis for minimizing domination. Indeed, accepting the priority of injustice in this case requires expanding the scope of republican theory and its normative commitments. For the point of view of the priority of injustice, the republican-rationalist polity increases rather than decreases overall domination under current circumstances of justice. Other values may be at stake, but they are gained at the cost of increasing domination at home and abroad, especially given the emergence of political inequalities among those who reside in the republic. Republican nationalism is thus caught on the horns of a dilemma: to the extent that it is nationalist, it cannot minimize domination, and to extent that it minimizes domination for *all* those who suffer injustice, it cannot be nationalist. Nationalists may be able to admit that the external circumstances of politics have changed, but they do not acknowledge that this is also true for the circumstances of justice. This is the dilemma of pluralism for some forms of republican justice.

Rawls employs the idea of the circumstances of justice to describe the "normal conditions under which human cooperation is both possible and necessary," so that a society is a cooperative venture for mutual advantage. People share some physical space, in which natural resources "are not so abundant that schemes of cooperation become superfluous, nor are conditions so harsh that fruitful ventures must inevitably break down."[26] Moreover, given certain economic facts about growth, we can assume that future generations will, in general and up to a certain point, live more affluent lives than previous generations. While Rawls does not simply presuppose that the parties have obligations to immediate descendants, and those descendants to theirs, and so on, he does endorse the "motivational assumption" that they will care about some of those in the next immediate generation. As Rawls puts it, justice requires that "for anyone in the next generation, there is someone who cares about him in the previous generation."[27] While intergenerational continuity is not among the circumstances of justice, it is a "motivational assumption" that makes it possible for succeeding generations to inherit our institutions as the result of a "fair accommodation." While Rawls also endorses humanitarian duties to assist people burdened by unfavorable circumstances even outside of the particular political community, there is neither any clear basis for international accommodation, nor any provision for shared resources and global common goods as part of the inheritance across societies. These circumstances of justice make it likely that those who are not already members will lack the statuses of those who are, even when there are some institutional means to ensure certain basic legal protections of such persons (and not citizens).[28]

---

[26] Rawls, *A Theory of Justice* (Cambridge, MA: Harvard University Press, 1971), 126–27.

[27] Ibid., 129.

[28] Philip Pettit's "The Republican Law of Peoples: A Restatement" (this volume) is vulnerable to a similar critique.

Under current circumstances, Rawls's societal and nationalist picture becomes increasingly problematic. While debates about the political consequences of globalization have often focused on the constraints that it imposes on policy options, global interdependence goes beyond these impacts and refers more fundamentally to the unprecedented extent, intensity, and speed of social interactions across borders, encompassing such diverse dimensions as trade, cultural exchange, and the migration of large numbers of legal and illegal persons.[29] While the demise of the nation-state has been greatly exaggerated, the political difficulties posed by globalization for republican nationalist states are more properly normative than functional. In order to maintain control over their boundaries, states have to heighten executive powers, and in this regard they often delegate such authority to international institutions such as the World Trade Organization and the International Monetary Fund (or perhaps some future International Climate Organization). Thus, even if states maintain important regulatory functions and even if membership in a state continues to have significant benefits and protections, they cannot both solve pressing transnational problems and maintain their undivided sovereignty and traditional monopoly powers.[30] The situation so described leads to an increasing potential for domination both within and across societies. Indeed, as Dobson puts it, many of the associated social activities and processes "cross boundaries in one direction only."[31] The migration of peoples across borders is not merely a social fact, but a consequence of the current circumstances of justice, making issues of identity and citizenship fraught with new possibilities for republican democracies to become dominators both at home and abroad. Indeed, these forms of asymmetries of status are in fact already present. The question then becomes whether nationalist republicans can sustain the priority of injustice even as they fail to minimize domination within their borders.

Nationalist republicanism fails to minimize domination in at least two respects. First, it fails on republican terms: it does not minimize, but rather increases, domination inside the political community. It thus increases both the state's *imperium* and private *dominium*, and emphasizes the greater differences in status between citizens and noncitizens, making it more likely for large numbers of people to stand in relations of dependency to others, and

[29] On the various positions and controversies over globalization, see David Held et al., *Global Transformations: Politics, Economics, and Culture* (Cambridge: Polity Press, 1999).

[30] See David Held, *Democracy and the Global Order: From the Modern State to Cosmopolitan Governance* (Stanford: Stanford University Press, 1995), 98–101, for an argument of this sort that emphasizes the scope of interconnections and their consequences for the realization of autonomy as the key problem for democratic governments.

[31] For a republican criticism of Held's account of globalization for failing to begin with such asymmetries rather than with mere scope or intensity, see Andrew Dobson, *Citizenship and the Environment* (Oxford: Oxford University Press, 2003), 12–22.

more difficult for noncitizens to resist the domination of citizens and the *imperium* of the state within its borders. Second, it also increases the *imperium* of the state exercised outside the national community in an effort to control the effects of interdependence (such as migration) at home and inside the national community to achieve security. With changes in the patterns of domination and the failures of states to address issues of membership and status, it is likely that republics will be more rather than less exclusive. Such circumstances are structural, and thus not likely to change in the near future.

If this diagnosis is correct, then republican political theory faces new tasks. Having already transformed itself away from the strong emphasis on communitarian concerns with identity, its tasks under the current circumstances of justice require that it become something more like a critical theory for post-national exclusions and hierarchies. The role given to injustice and domination makes republican political theory a central piece of such a critical theory, especially as it begins from the critique of actual injustice and domination. Republicanism provides the basis for a new transnational egalitarian theory that begins with reformulating the demands of the new circumstances of justice. But more than that, domination is not the only harm that it seeks to minimize; other harms centrally include the basic forms of political injustice that are now becoming prevalent in the world. Most importantly, it has to develop an account of the new forms of injustice and domination that come from social relations across polities. In short, the new circumstances of justice demand that we understand the new ways in which injustice concerns new types of social relations of domination within and across polities.

Shklar is surely prescient when she argues that it is a grave philosophical and moral error to think that injustice is simply the absence of justice, and so that "once we know what is just, it is all that we need to know."[32] Critical republican theory is necessary to illuminate new and increasingly prevalent forms of injustice that challenge both liberal and republican assumptions about political order. As the disagreements among republicans show, it is at present not so terribly clear whether we know what is just, much less whether we see ideal justice as all we need to know under changing circumstances of justice. Nor can a critical theory of the present be satisfied with republican nationalism. As I have argued, under current circumstances, such arrangements cannot avoid the domination of noncitizens, both at home and abroad.

CONCLUSION: EXPANDING REPUBLICAN POLITICAL THEORY

Given the new circumstances of justice and of politics, republicanism ought to be expanded in a variety of ways. Much of my work has sought to expand it spatially to include transnational relations among persons and institutions.

[32] Shklar, *The Faces of Injustice*, 19.

Here it is important to understand non-domination as a shared good: one group or person can have it securely only if all do. This is crucial to understanding significant forms of domination that could not be grasped otherwise. While this is especially important in the globalizing era, it is not sufficient. The concept of domination must be expanded if it is to help us understand a variety of other phenomena, including intergenerational domination, which in the current era takes the form of the domination of present over future generations. More importantly, republican theory can be expanded by seeing domination as one form of manifest injustice. Pettit clearly overreaches when he claims that the emergence of constitutional government brings "an end to domination."[33] This claim not only lacks historical plausibility, it also makes it very difficult to expand republican non-domination to other forms of injustice and other great harms that people suffer in a variety of settings, some of which are just now developing. As a critical theory of the present, republicanism ought to endorse the priority of injustice, in order to expand and enrich its moral and political vocabulary so as to articulate "the wishes and struggles of the age."[34]

The second advantage has to do with the limits of the bilateral conception of domination that guides even forms of republicanism that reject the arbitrary power account. While many forms of injustice are closely related to domination, injustice is the broader category needed for a critical theory of the new circumstances of justice. Recent work on epistemic injustice provides valuable lessons on the need for broadening republicanism to include demands for political equality as well as other forms of injustices, such as the lack of access to influence over many transnational institutions. But some of the more severe and normalized injustices of our historical period include the vast exploitation and domination of migrants and refugees who have little, if any, control over their lives, and no real powers with which to resist domination. The same point could be made about existing democratic institutions failing to provide the proper model for democratization in changing circumstances. A transnational order that could recognize in such injustice dispersed forms of subjection and affectedness could at the same time be transformed by creating conditions of non-domination in the form of transnationally recognized claims to human rights. Given the priority of injustice for broadening republicanism, the transnational polity must also address all those complex forms of social and economic inequalities that heighten rather than minimize domination at various levels of the current global basic structure.

---

[33] Pettit, *Republicanism*, 68. For an account that more reasonably sees "minimizing" rather than eliminating domination as the proper, practical aim of republicanism, see Frank Lovett, *A General Theory of Domination & Justice* (Oxford: Oxford University Press, 2010).

[34] In Karl Marx's phrase, as quoted in James Bohman, "Critical Theory," *The Stanford Encyclopedia of Philosophy* (Spring 2013), ed. Edward N. Zalta, http://plato.stanford.edu/archives/spr2013/entries/critical-theory.

BIBLIOGRAPHY

Bohman, James. "Constituting Humanity: Universal Political Rights and the Human Community." *Canadian Journal of Philosophy* (2007), Supplementary Volume 31 on *Global Justice and Global Institutions*, edited by Daniel Weinstock, 227–52.

Bohman, James. "Critical Theory." *The Stanford Encyclopedia of Philosophy* (Spring 2013), edited by Edward N. Zalta. http://plato.stanford.edu/archives/spr2013/entries/critical-theory.

Bohman, James. "Democratizing the Global Order: From Communicative Freedom to Communicative Power." *Review of International Studies* 36, no. 2 (2010): 431–47.

Bohman, James. "Is Democracy a Means to Global Justice? Human Rights and the Democratic Minimum." *Ethics and International Affairs* 19, no. 1 (2005): 101–16.

Bohman, James. "Nondomination and Transnational Democracy." In *Republicanism and Political Theory*, edited by Cécile Laborde and John Maynor, 190–216. Oxford: Blackwell, 2008.

De Latour, Sophie Guérard. "Reworking the Neo-Republican Sense of Belonging." *Diacritica* 24, no. 2 (2010): 91–112.

Dobson, Andrew. *Citizenship and the Environment*. Oxford: Oxford University Press, 2003.

Fricker, Miranda. *Epistemic Injustice*. Oxford: Oxford University Press, 2007.

Habermas, Jürgen. *Between Facts and Norms: Contributions to a Discourse Theory of Law and Democracy*. Cambridge: MIT Press, 1996.

Held, David. *Democracy and the Global Order: From the Modern State to Cosmopolitan Governance*. Stanford: Stanford University Press, 1995.

Held, David, Anthony McGrew, David Goldblatt, and Jonathan Perraton. *Global Transformations: Politics, Economics, and Culture*. Cambridge: Polity Press, 1999.

Hurrell, Andrew. "Global Inequality and International Institutions." *Metaphilosophy* 32, no. 1/2 (2001): 34–57.

Laborde, Cécile. "Republicanism and Global Justice." *European Journal of Political Theory* 9, no. 1 (2010): 48–69.

Lovett, Frank. *A General Theory of Domination & Justice*. Oxford: Oxford University Press, 2010.

Macdonald, Terry. "Antipower, Agency, and the Republican Case for Global Institutional Pluralism." In *Domination and Global Political Justice: Conceptual, Historical, and Institutional Perspectives*, edited by Barbara Buckinx, Jonathan Trejo-Mathys, and Timothy Waligore. New York: Routledge, 2015.

Näsström, Sofia. "The Challenge of the All-Affected Principle." *Political Studies* 59, no. 1 (2011): 116–34.

Pettit, Philip. "Freedom as Antipower." *Ethics* 106, no. 3 (1996): 576–604.

Pettit, Philip. "The Republican Law of Peoples: A Restatement." In *Domination and Global Political Justice: Conceptual, Historical, and Institutional Perspectives*, edited by Barbara Buckinx, Jonathan Trejo-Mathys, and Timothy Waligore. New York: Routledge, 2015.

Pettit, Philip. *Republicanism: A Theory of Freedom and Government*. Oxford: Oxford University Press, 1997.

Pogge, Thomas W. *World Poverty and Human Rights*. Malden, MA: Polity, 2002.

Rawls, John. *A Theory of Justice*. Cambridge, MA: Harvard University Press, 1971.

Richardson, Henry. *Democratic Autonomy: Public Reasoning About the Ends of Policy*. Oxford: Oxford University Press, 2002.

Sen, Amartya. *The Idea of Justice*. Cambridge: Harvard University Press, 2009.

Shklar, Judith N. *The Faces of Injustice*. New Haven: Yale University Press, 1990.

4 Transnational Justice and Non-Domination

A Discourse-Theoretical Approach

Rainer Forst

The title of my contribution could have also been "transnational injustice and domination," since we cannot make progress with respect to thinking about justice beyond the state unless we develop a realistic and critical view of the many and complex relations of domination within, between, and beyond states that mark our current global predicament. But in order to identify this predicament as one of "injustice," we are in need of a proper conception of justice as non-domination.[1] So let me turn to this first. In a second step, I will explain the difference between my Kantian, discourse-theoretical conception of non-domination and Philip Pettit's neo-republican conception of non-domination. In a third step, I will apply my conception of justice as non-domination to transnational contexts. Finally, I explain the difference between my view and Pettit's notion of international justice.

1 JUSTICE AND NON-DOMINATION

Let me start with a brief reflection on the notion of injustice. In my view, injustice means more than a person lacking certain important or even essential goods for a "decent" life. For if we were to only focus on deficiencies of goods, someone who is deprived of possibilities and resources as a result of a natural catastrophe would seem to be in the same situation as someone who experiences the same kind of deprivation as a result of economic or political exploitation. It is true that assistance is required in both cases. However, as

---

[1] Some sections of this paper are based on my previously published "Transnational Justice and Democracy: Overcoming Three Dogmas of Political Theory," in *Political Equality in Transnational Democracy*, eds. Eva Erman and Sofia Näsström (New York: Palgrave Macmillan, 2013), 41–59, and "A Kantian Republican Conception of Justice as Nondomination," in *Republican Democracy*, eds. Andreas Niederberger and Philipp Schink (Edinburgh: Edinburgh University Press, 2013), 154–68. Permission to reproduce these sections is kindly acknowledged. I am grateful to Barbara Buckinx, Tim Waligore, and Dorothea Gädeke for their critical reading of an earlier version.

I understand the grammar of justice, in the first case, assistance is required as an act of moral solidarity, while in the other, assistance is required as an act of justice conditioned by the nature of one's involvement in relations of exploitation and thus of injustice,[2] and by the specific wrong in question. Thus the grounds of assistance, as well as the content of what is required, differ. Ignoring this difference can lead one to misrepresent what is actually a requirement of justice as an act of generous "assistance" or "aid" to the poor or miserable, thereby possibly committing another wrong, namely, that of veiling the true nature of the injustice present.[3] To do justice to those who suffer from injustice, it is necessary to grasp the relational or structural dimension of justice and to liberate oneself from an understanding that is focused exclusively on quantities of goods. Justice must be directed to *intersubjective relations and social structures*, not to *subjective or supposedly objective states* of the provision of goods. Helping a person overcome misery, irrespective of what it is caused by, is a good thing, generally speaking. Yet overcoming forms of domination that lead to misery is a particular demand of justice.[4] The normative difference here is not one of urgency; rather, it is one of distinguishing various parts of our general normative framework of determining moral obligations.

What is it about the concept of justice that gives it this special place in our moral grammar? In my view, the concept of justice possesses a core meaning of which the essential contrasting concept is *arbitrariness*.[5] Arbitrariness can assume the form of arbitrary rule over others by individuals or

---

[2] Here a range of cases should be distinguished, in particular: directly participating in or contributing to injustice; indirectly participating in injustice by profiting from it but without actively contributing to relations of exploitation; finally, the "natural" duty to put an end to unjust relations, even if one does not profit from them but is in a position to put an end to them. I cannot go into these distinctions further here.

[3] I discuss this as a "dialectics of morality" in Forst, *The Right to Justification: Elements of a Constructivist Theory of Justice*, trans. Jeffrey Flynn (New York: Columbia University Press, 2012), ch. 11. See also the following quote by Immanuel Kant: "Having the resources to practice such beneficence as depends on the goods of fortune is, for the most part, a result of certain human beings being favored through the injustice of the government, which introduces an inequality of wealth that makes others need their beneficence. Under such circumstances, does a rich man's help to the needy, on which he so readily prides himself as something meritorious, really deserve to be called beneficence at all?" from Kant, *Metaphysics of Morals,* in *Practical Philosophy*, ed. and trans. Mary J. Gregor (Cambridge: Cambridge University Press, 1996), 353–603, 573, 6:454. Page numbers referencing the English language editions of Kant will be followed by the Academy edition pagination.

[4] For a contrasting view, see Stefan Gosepath, "Deprivation and Institutionally Based Duties to Aid" (this volume).

[5] John Rawls also argues that the concept of justice is opposed to arbitrariness: "Those who hold different conceptions of justice can, then, still agree that institutions are just when no arbitrary distinctions are made between persons in the assigning of basic rights and duties and when the rules determine a proper balance between competing claims to the advantages of social life" from Rawls, *A Theory of Justice*, revised ed. (Cambridge, MA: Harvard University Press, 1999), 5.

by a part of the community (for example, by a class), or the acceptance of social contingencies that lead to asymmetrical social positions or relations of domination as an unalterable fate, even though they are nothing of the sort. Arbitrary rule is the rule of some people over others without legitimate reason—what I call *domination*—and where struggles are conducted against injustice, they are directed against forms of domination of this kind.[6] The underlying impulse that opposes injustice is not primarily that of wanting something, or more of something, but of no longer wanting to be dominated, harassed, or overruled in one's claim and *basic right to justification*. In contexts of justice, this claim involves the demand that no political or social relations should exist that cannot be adequately justified toward those subjected to them. Herein resides the profoundly *political* essence of justice that a purely goods or recipient-oriented view fails to grasp; for justice concerns *who determines who receives what* and not only or primarily who should receive what. The demand for justice as I conceive it is an emancipatory one. Expressed in reflexive terms, it rests on the claim to be respected as an autonomous subject of justification; that is, to be respected in one's dignity as a being who can provide and demand justifications and who is to have a status as a free and equal normative authority within a normative order of binding rules and institutions.[7] The person who *lacks* certain goods should not be regarded as the primary victim of injustice. Instead, the primary victim is the person who does not "count" in the production and allocation of goods. Justice requires that those who belong to a structured social context should be respected as equals. This means that they should enjoy equal rights to participate in the social and political *order of justification* in which they are involved in determining the conditions under which goods are produced and distributed, and in which they ought to have a standing as justificatory equals.

Justice, then, is the human virtue of opposing relations of arbitrary rule. "Arbitrariness" is the term for "groundless" rule; that is, insufficiently justified rule that assumes the form of domination, presupposing that a just social order is one to which free and equal persons could give their assent—not just counterfactual assent, but assent based on institutionalized justification procedures. So two aspects of a political notion of domination are relevant here: rule of some over others without justifiable reasons, and rule over others in a normative order which lacks sufficient institutional or social preconditions and possibilities of justification in the first place. The latter is the more severe form of domination.

That the basic claim of justice is to have a social and political standing as a free and equal agent of justification is a *recursive* implication of

---

[6] For a historical account of struggles against injustice, see Barrington Moore, *Injustice: The Social Bases of Obedience and Revolt* (London: Macmillan, 1978).

[7] On this notion of dignity, see Forst, *Justification and Critique: Towards a Critical Theory of Politics*, trans. Ciaran Cronin (Cambridge: Polity, 2013), ch. 4.

the fact that political and social justice is a matter of norms of an institutional basic structure that claim to be reciprocally and generally valid. Thus *a supreme principle* holds within such a framework—namely, the *principle of general and reciprocal justification*—which states that every putatively valid claim to goods, rights, or liberties must be justified and justifiable in a reciprocal and general manner, where one side may not make claims that they deny to others and no side may simply project its reasons onto others. Instead all must justify their claims discursively—without excluding involved parties. The criteria of reciprocity (of claims as well as reasons) and generality are reconstructed as criteria of the validity of justice norms, and then interpreted as criteria of justifiable norms of justice and of the procedural quality of justice-generating discourses and discursive structures.

The normative grounding of such a conception of justice as non-domination does not rest on any values or norms other than the principle of justification itself as a principle of practical reason (saying that normative claims always have to be justified according to their immanent validity criteria).[8] Thus, the discourse-theoretical conception of justice is *autonomous* with respect to other values or comprehensive doctrines in Rawls's sense, but it also has a moral force of its own, since it rests on an undeniable claim to be respected as a normative agent or authority when it comes to the norms that claim validity over a person.[9] The principle of justification is thus a principle of practical reason in the Kantian sense, as it does not merely imply what it means to justify as a claim to justice, but also that one has a duty of justice when one is part of a context of justice. Contexts of justice are particular forms of moral contexts. A moral context is one where others are affected by my actions in a relevant way, whereas a context of justice is one where we are participants in an order of rule and/or domination[10]—in other words, one where we are subjected to a social normative order. The grounding of the theory of justice as non-domination is therefore "thin" when compared to other ones which use substantive values of liberty or equality, or well-being or the good, as it only relies on the principle of justification or critique itself. However, it is also "thick," as it interprets this principle to ground a categorical and overriding right and duty of justification between those subjected to a normative order of rule and/or domination. And to add another short parenthetical remark on a complex issue, it is a grounding that is as "immanent" to social practices of justification and critique as it is "transcendental" in reconstructing a principle that inheres in and transcends all particular forms of practices of justification, thus opening up the possibility of testing their justificatory quality in radicalizing the criteria of reciprocity

---

[8] See Forst, *Right to Justification*, chs. 1–2.

[9] I explain the difference with Rawls in ibid., ch. 4.

[10] I will later come back to the question of locating such contexts at the transnational level.

and generality. This transcending force is appealed to by those who say "no" to given orders of justification and demand better ones.

Turning to social and political theory on that basis, we arrive at a central insight for the problem of political and social justice, namely, that *the first question of justice is the question of power*. For justice is not only a matter of which goods, for which reasons, and in what amounts should legitimately be allocated to whom, but specifically *how* these goods come into the world in the first place, *who* decides on their allocation, and *how* this allocation is made. Theories of a predominantly allocative kind are "oblivious to power" insofar as they conceive of justice only from the "recipient side," without raising the political question of how the structures of production and allocation of goods are determined. The claim that the question of power is the first question of justice means that the constitutive places of justice are to be sought where the central justifications for a social basic structure must be provided and the institutional ground rules are laid down that determine social life from the bottom up. Everything depends, if you will, on the *relations of justification* within a society. Power, understood as the effective "justificatory power" of individuals, is the higher-level good of justice; it is the "discursive" power to demand and provide justifications and to repudiate false legitimations—whether as single false legitimations, or as systemic discursive complexes or languages of justification.[11] This amounts to an argument for a "political turn" in the debate concerning justice and for a *critical theory of justice* as a *critique of relations of justification*.

A comprehensive theory of political and social justice can be constructed on this basis, something I can only hint at in the present context.[12] First, we must make a conceptual distinction between *fundamental* (*minimal*) and *full* (*maximal*) justice. Whereas the task of fundamental justice is to construct a *basic structure of justification*, the task of full justice is to construct a *fully justified basic structure*. In order to pursue the latter, the former is necessary; that is, a "putting into effect" of justification through constructive, discursive democratic procedures in which justificatory power is distributed as evenly as possible among the citizens. To put it in (only seemingly) paradoxical terms, this means that fundamental justice is a substantive starting point of procedural justice. Based on a moral right to justification, arguments are presented for a basic structure in which individual members have real opportunities to codetermine the institutions of this structure in a reciprocal and general manner. Fundamental justice guarantees all citizens an effective status as justificatory equals.[13]

---

[11] I develop the notion of power relevant here in my "Noumenal Power," *The Journal of Political Philosophy*, forthcoming.
[12] For a more detailed treatment, see Forst, *Right to Justification*; Forst, *Justification and Critique*.
[13] This concerns a set of rights as well as institutional and social preconditions I cannot elaborate on here. See Forst, *The Right to Justification*, part 2.

2 NON-DOMINATION: NEO-REPUBLICANISM VERSUS KANTIAN REPUBLICANISM

The view I have presented is of a Kantian nature, and it provides the basis for what I call Kantian republicanism—though not "Kant's republicanism," since I elaborate on his views. For Kantian republicanism, a particular notion of autonomy in the moral and political realm is foundational. Its main point is to avoid a one-sided focus on the freedom of persons as "users" or "receivers" of legal freedom, or as protected in their legal status as persons with sufficient freedom of choice. After all, Kant insists on the freedom of persons also as lawgivers, as producers and guarantors of freedom; in short, as politically autonomous citizens. The *dignity* of a free person can never merely be understood as "enjoyment" of freedom or certain liberties—it is also always the freedom of giving laws to oneself, the freedom of normative self-determination. This is a kind of freedom that comes in two modes, one moral and one political, but its modus operandi is, despite the difference between these modes, the same. It is a practice of reciprocal and general justification, or a practice of practical reason, if you like, one moral and one political (but both intertwined). The laws that constitute this and those that are generated in that practice do not just protect freedom—rather, they express it.

I cannot go into the details of the Kantian view I have in mind here.[14] Suffice it to say that I translate the idea of the basic respect for autonomous persons into the language of a moral "right to justification," because, according to a Kantian conception, a person has a categorically undeniable subjective claim to be respected as a normative authority who is free and equal to all others. I call such a non-rejectable claim based on the very principle of justification a moral right, binding every other moral person, thus implying a categorical duty of justification. It is not a right to some good or a right based on some interest. Rather, it is based on the status of the person as a reason-giving and reason-receiving being and authority in the space of reasons. It is therefore the ground of all further claims to moral respect and to the validity of more specific moral norms which need to be justified by reciprocally and generally non-rejectable reasons. I call this form of justification *moral constructivism*. It is a discursive and recursive enterprise: It is discursive since justification needs to be a practice between free and equal persons, even if this is only counterfactually possible in an imagined discourse (to the best of our abilities). It is recursive since no other content or value is given than that of the agents and criteria of construction through justification.[15]

---

[14] But see ibid., chs. 1–2.

[15] See Onora O'Neill, *Constructions of Reason: Explorations of Kant's Practical Philosophy* (Cambridge: Cambridge University Press, 1990), ch. 1.

To apply this to contexts of law and politics, we need to take a closer look at Kant's doctrine of right, which provides the principles that help us understand the justifiable forms of freedom under law as well as the political justification of law that establishes that kind of freedom. Kant contrasts law as regards its content with all ethical doctrines of happiness and as regards its form with moral imperatives, because positive law refers only to external actions and not to inner motivation. The essential difference between legality and morality resides less in the content of the respective laws than in the "incentives": positive law is external coercive law and constrains freedom of choice, whereas moral laws determine the moral will.[16] Thus, the supreme principle of law specifies that restrictions on freedom are in need of universal justification: "Right is therefore the sum of the conditions under which the choice of one can be united with the choice of another in accordance with a universal law of freedom."[17] The foundation of this definition of law, according to which all forms of legal coercion are in need of reciprocal and general justification among free and equal persons, is a basic moral human right to *lawful* freedom prior to any positive law: "*Freedom* (independence from being constrained by another's choice), insofar as it can coexist with the freedom of every other in accordance with a universal law, is the only original right belonging to every man by virtue of his humanity."[18] Kant's 'innate right' is the implication the (to use my terminology) moral basic right to justification has with respect to law, as it is the universal right for human beings to be respected as "ends in themselves."

According to the principle of right, only 'general laws' can be laws of freedom, and they can be general only if they are in accordance with the "united will of the people."[19] The citizen can be politically autonomous—and here Kant takes up Rousseau's notion of autonomy—if he obeys only laws that he has given himself. He obeys no law other "than that to which he has given his consent"[20]—"for it is only to oneself that one can never do wrong."[21] As an active member of the polity, as a voting citizen, the person is a *citoyen*, not just a *bourgeois*: She[22] or he is simultaneously author and addressee of the law. Hence, generally and reciprocally binding law can be legitimate only if it can stand the test of being agreed upon in procedures of general and reciprocal justification. The mere "idea of reason, which,

---

16 Kant, *Metaphysics of Morals*, 383–84, 6:220.
17 Ibid., 387, 6:230.
18 Ibid., 393, 6:237.
19 Ibid., 457, 6:313.
20 Ibid., 457, 6:314.
21 Kant, "On the Common Saying: That May Be Correct in Theory, but It is of No Use in Practice," in *Practical Philosophy,* ed. and trans. Mary J. Gregor (Cambridge: Cambridge University Press, 1996), 279–309, 295, 8:294f.
22 As I am phrasing it as a general point, I include both gender terms—which Kant did not.

however, has its undoubted practical reality," states that "the touchstone of any public law's conformity with right" is its ability to command general agreement.[23] In short, just as the moral principle which makes it a duty to justify morally relevant actions and norms in a particular way becomes the foundation of the original right to freedom, in the same way it here becomes the foundation of the requirement to justify coercive laws in the medium of "public reason." Where there is no adequate possibility to generate such discursively justified norms in democratic practice, the first duty of justice is to establish such institutions.

In Kantian republicanism, freedom in the state can only be fully realized if it is the freedom "of obeying no other law than that to which [the citizen] has given his consent."[24] This is the real meaning of legal independence or political-legal non-domination: you are only independent, or non-dominated, if you are at the same time subject *and* author of the law. Otherwise your right to freedom—or your right to justification—is only half realized. You might *receive* freedom or some justification. But if you cannot be the *author* of the laws of freedom, you are not offered real freedom. The laws securing freedom must be reciprocally and generally justifiable, but no one has the authority to fabricate these justifications for you, as you are an autonomous agent of justification.[25]

This I take to be the essence of Kantian republicanism, which stresses independence as a basic moral principle of right for rational, end-setting beings who inhabit a social space together.[26] It implies the right to have all other rights (and duties) justified strictly reciprocally and generally, and thus the right to justification of independent agents grounds all other rights. It does this in a discursive, reflexive way, not by way of a deduction. In the mode of moral constructivism, this leads to a conception of moral rights. In the mode of political constructivism, this leads to a conception of human rights, as well as to a conception of democratic political and social justice. Human rights are all the rights that persons who respect each other as free and equal cannot deny each other within a normative order of legal, political, and social life. The main point is again a reflexive one: no one must be subjected to a normative order that cannot be adequately justified to him or her. This is the basic human right and the basic claim of justice.[27]

---

[23] Kant, "On the Common Saying," 296–97, 8:297 (emphasis omitted).

[24] Kant, *Metaphysics of Morals*, 457, 6:314.

[25] This is why I do not think that Kantian republicanism, especially in its discourse-theoretical version, is subject to the critique that it relies on a purely counterfactual notion of justifiability; for this critique, see Philip Pettit, *On the People's Terms: A Republican Theory and Model of Democracy* (Cambridge: Cambridge University Press, 2012), 147f.

[26] In line with Arthur Ripstein, *Force and Freedom: Kant's Legal and Political Philosophy* (Cambridge, MA: Harvard University Press, 2009), 16f, 371.

[27] See Forst, *Justification and Critique*, ch. 2.

The Kantian republican conception I have sketched uses a discourse-theoretical notion of non-domination. Domination, to repeat, has two aspects; namely, being subjected to a normative order that cannot properly be justified to you, and being subjected to a normative order where no proper institutions and possibilities of justification are in place to begin with. The second is the more severe form of domination, as it structurally takes away the possibility of codetermining the normative order.

How does this relate to Philip Pettit's version of republicanism?[28] For Pettit, republicanism is essentially a theory of legitimate government grounded in a particular idea of freedom as "non-domination," understood as "the social status of being relatively proof against arbitrary interference by others, and of being able to enjoy a sense of security and standing among them."[29] In contrast to freedom as mere "non-interference," non-domination is bound up with being and seeing oneself as someone who is not at the mercy of others' arbitrary will, even if these others were to mostly leave you alone. The republican notion of self-respect and freedom is directed against the *potential* of arbitrary interference.[30] The rule of law is thus important, as is a social status protecting persons "robustly" against social and political vulnerability to the possibility of arbitrary interference. Slavery is the counterpart of the notion of freedom used here, with the slave as the extreme version of a dominated person. Even though Pettit correctly emphasizes that freedom as non-interference is distinct from freedom as non-domination, a negative conception of liberty lies at the center of his view: the argument for non-domination ultimately serves to secure the realm of freedom of choice of persons against arbitrary interference.[31] This is why I refer to this view as *negative republicanism*: the republican infrastructure is primarily a sheltering mechanism for individual liberty understood in this way. In his republican theory, citizens are "law-checkers" interested in their secure freedom of choice, not "law-makers" as in a Rousseauian or Kantian scheme.[32]

So how distinct is my Kantian conception of republican justice as non-domination from Pettit's conception of republican freedom as non-domination? In answering this question, I would like to offer a (somewhat revisionary) reading of Pettit that brings him closer to the Kantian family. My reason for doing so is that, as I see it, the real force of freedom as

[28] I will be brief here. For a more extensive discussion, see my "A Kantian Republican Conception of Justice as Nondomination."

[29] Philip Pettit, *Republicanism: A Theory of Freedom and Government* (Oxford: Oxford University Press, 1997), viii.

[30] Ibid., 5, 22f. In his recent work, Pettit prefers the term "uncontrolled" rather than "arbitrary" interference, yet with the aim of preserving the core meaning. See Pettit, *On the People's Terms*, 58. Cf. Pettit, "The Republican Law of Peoples: A Restatement" (this volume).

[31] See esp. Pettit, "Keeping Republican Freedom Simple: On a Difference with Quentin Skinner," *Political Theory* 30, no. 3 (2002): 339–56, 340.

[32] Pettit, *On the People's Terms*, 15.

non-domination derives from a notion of justice as justification that both grounds and defines it.[33] It grounds it because the basic claim of republican citizens is not one of freedom generally, but one of freedom from *arbitrary*—i.e., *unjust* and *unjustifiable*— interference or rule (that is, domination). The claim is based on one's standing as a free and equal agent of justification. It is a claim to a kind of liberty (and liberties) defined by what oneself and others can justifiably and justly ask from one another in a basic social structure. As Pettit explains in the course of discussing Quentin Skinner's view championing non-interference, justifiable rule is *not* seen as domination.[34] Only *arbitrary* rule is seen as domination, and that means *unjustifiable* rule over others, denying their standing as free and equal agents as normative authorities. Being denied such standing leads to the "grievance . . . of having to live at the mercy of another," which Pettit isolates as the main social and political evil.[35] If interference or rule by others is justifiable between equals, it is not seen as an infringement of freedom. The notion of *justice* referring to the quality of the relations between free and equal participants in a basic structure of justification is thus central and *normatively prior* to that of freedom of choice. Justice as justification determines which freedoms are justified and what an arbitrary interference is in the first place.

This might seem to read into Pettit's approach a Kantian notion of freedom, but this is only a concern if one overlooks the implications of how Pettit distinguishes between the non-arbitrary or "controlled" rule of law, which does not compromise freedom, and domination, which does compromise freedom. The rule of law is seen as "conditioning" freedom, and this is close to Kant's view.[36] Republican freedom is about the "full standing of a person among persons,"[37] and, explicitly referencing Kant, Pettit goes on to explain: "The terrible evil brought about by domination, over and beyond the evil of restricting choice, and inducing a distinctive uncertainty is that it deprives a person of the ability to command attention and respect and so of his or her standing among persons."[38] Thus the main evil is that of not being regarded as "a voice worth hearing and an ear worth addressing"[39]—that is, in my words, as a person with a right to justification. As Pettit formulates it: "To be a person is to be a voice that cannot properly be ignored, a voice which speaks to issues raised in common with others and which speaks with

---

[33] I thus take issue with the way Pettit distinguishes between justice and legitimacy in ibid., chs. 2–3. For my own view, see Forst, "Legitimität, Demokratie und Gerechtigkeit: Zur Reflexivität normativer Ordnungen," in *Deliberative Kritik—Kritik der Deliberation. Festschrift für Rainer Schmalz-Bruns*, ed. Daniel Gaus et al. (Baden-Baden, DE: Nomos, 2014).

[34] Pettit, "Keeping Republican Freedom Simple."

[35] Ibid., 4f.

[36] Ibid., 342.

[37] Ibid., 350.

[38] Ibid., 351.

[39] Ibid., 350.

a certain authority: enough authority, certainly, for discord with that voice to give others reason to pause and think."[40] Every person is to be respected as a justificatory authority in this way, and this is the essential meaning of freedom as autonomy: to have a *categorical* right not to be subjected to norms that cannot reciprocally be justified.[41]

In my view and in my preferred Kantian reading of Pettit, we have gone quite a bit beyond a negative conception of freedom without also adopting a controversial positive conception of freedom. Thus, what matters in a republican account of non-domination is freedom as autonomy; that is, freedom *from* unjustifiable subjection or coercion and freedom *as* a self-determining agent of (moral, as well as political) justification. Only where practices of justification exist that prevent some from dominating others is freedom as non-domination guaranteed. Rather than focusing on the "robust" legal state of enjoying freedom of choice, we should focus on the relational freedom of being a codetermining agent of justification within the normative order that binds us.

3 TRANSNATIONAL CONTEXTS OF JUSTICE

If we want to locate the Kantian, discourse-theoretical view of justice as non-domination in contexts beyond the state, we must use a broader definition of a context of justice than Kant's, which focuses on subjection to legal coercion within a state. What we have to hold onto, however, is the insight that justice, whether "political" or "social," presupposes in the first instance specific practices of justification—that is, a basic structure of justification—and this political praxis of reciprocal and general justification is essentially what we mean by 'democracy'; those who are subjected to general and binding norms should also be the authority who justifies these very norms—as active subjects of justification and not just *in mente* or in proxy or expert discourses. The goddess *Justitia* does not come into the world to dispense gifts; her task is instead to banish arbitrary rule, i.e., domination. Democracy is the form of political order capable of accomplishing this in the right way. The task of democracy is to secure the political autonomy of those who are supposed to be both subjected to and authors of binding norms.

How can this be extended to transnational contexts? Until now, I have stressed that the aim of justice is to create justified social relations and political structures, and to this effect it first calls, reflexively speaking, for the creation of a basic structure of justification. It follows that justice has its proper place wherever a threat of arbitrary rule exists, where a social context is degenerating, or where it could degenerate into a context of

[40] Pettit, *Republicanism*, 91.

[41] I will not go into a discussion of whether that kind of basic moral-political status can be grounded in a consequentialist theory, which I doubt.

domination. One might conclude from this that the existence of a specific social *context of cooperation* is a necessary presupposition of a context of justice.

A number of theories have drawn this conclusion. In the first place, we must mention that of John Rawls. Rawls locates social justice in the national sphere and views the international domain as one in which merely a minimal list of human rights is valid and otherwise only duties of assistance exist.[42] This is not so much a state-centered as a specifically cooperation-centered view. Interpreters often mistakenly underestimate how much weight Rawls attaches to the "most fundamental" idea of a "society as a fair system of social cooperation over time from one generation to the next," which he consistently situates at the center of his theory.[43] According to Rawls, only such a society provides the resources—in the twofold sense of material and normative resources—that a "well-ordered society" presupposes. Here alone are to be found the reciprocity conditions and the economic, political, and moral cohesion that a just society requires.

Some theorists develop this idea in a communitarian direction so that "common sentiments"[44] or "shared understandings"[45] within a nation, understood as a political and cultural *community*, become a necessary presupposition for a complete context of justice. Others, by contrast, adopt an institutionalist perspective that emphasizes the *state* as the central context of justice. Thomas Nagel expresses that justice "is something we owe through our shared institutions only to those with whom we stand in a strong political relation. It is, in the standard terminology, an associative obligation."[46] The essential aspects of such a "strong political relation" are the existence of a collectively authorized source of law and the fact that the relation is not voluntary—that is, that the relation expresses the will of those involved as citizens and that this must also be so if they are not to be subjected to illegitimate coercion.[47] Positive normative authority and factual coercion must coexist in order to form a context of justice—as a context of law.

Rawls and Nagel's arguments carry considerable weight because a social context of justice is in fact a demanding one and presupposes certain relations among those involved. Nevertheless, these arguments are problematic because they employ a *conclusion* as a *premise* when they argue that a

---

[42] Cf. John Rawls, *The Law of Peoples* (Cambridge, MA: Harvard University Press, 1999).

[43] Rawls, *Justice as Fairness: A Restatement* (Cambridge, MA: Harvard University Press, 2001), 5.

[44] David Miller, *National Responsibility and Global Justice* (Oxford: Oxford University Press, 2007).

[45] Michael Walzer, *Spheres of Justice* (New York: Basic Books, 1983).

[46] Thomas Nagel, "The Problem of Global Justice," *Philosophy & Public Affairs* 33, no. 2 (2005): 113–47, 121.

[47] Michael Blake emphasizes the aspect of coercion. See "Distributive Justice, State Coercion, and Autonomy," *Philosophy & Public Affairs* 30, no. 3 (2001): 257–96.

particular social or legal institutional context of cooperation or legal force is a necessary precondition of justice. For, as explained above, Justitia is a man-made deity who comes into the world to banish social arbitrariness, and this means that she has her (combative) place wherever arbitrariness prevails (or poses a threat) among human beings. In such cases, she calls for specific institutions—for example, for the rule of law where a "state of nature" of arbitrariness existed—but then she cannot presuppose that these institutions are already in place. She presupposes that persons have the status of beings who have a right to justification and she calls for the creation of a basic structure of justification wherever arbitrary rule prevails; but her calling for this cannot be contingent on a basic structure already existing. Thus, the objection to Rawls, as certain globalist cosmopolitans assume, need not claim that a "global basic structure" already in fact exists,[48] because the comparison between national contexts and a global basic structure is untenable when it comes to the "thickness" of the relevant social relations. And although one can point out, *contra* Nagel, that certain global institutions also exercise state-like legal coercion and claim authority for this,[49] there remains a striking difference from national law here as well. It is instead important to move beyond thinking in terms of the dichotomy between "state" and "world" and to assume a plurality of contexts of (in)justice that differ with regard to their relational quality, so that justice can be correctly located or "grounded" specifically, in a way informed by an appropriate social-scientific analysis of actually existing social relations.[50]

Viewed from a critical perspective, to assume that a context of justice exists only where norms of law and justice are already institutionalized in positive law, or only where positive, mutually beneficial forms and institutions of cooperation already exist,[51] would amount to a twofold "practice positivism." These two forms of positivism can be called "positive institutionalism" and "positive cooperationalism." Against this, it must be objected that a context of justice exists wherever relations of political *rule* and social *cooperation* exist *and* wherever forms of *domination* exist, whether or not they are legally institutionalized. The latter include various relations of *negative* cooperation; i.e., forms of (legal, political, economic, or cultural) coercion and/or exploitation. This provides the entry point for a critical and "realist" theory of justice, and such a theory presupposes an

---

[48] Compare the original (and later differentiated) views of Charles Beitz, *Political Theory and International Relations* (Princeton: Princeton University Press, 1979), part 3, and Thomas Pogge, *Realizing Rawls* (Ithaca: Cornell University Press, 1989), ch. 6.

[49] Joshua Cohen and Charles Sabel, "Extra Rempublicam Nulla Justitia?" *Philosophy & Public Affairs* 34, no. 2 (2006): 147–75.

[50] See my original argument for a critical theory of transnational justice, now in Forst, *The Right to Justification*, ch. 12.

[51] Such a cooperation conception can be found in Andrea Sangiovanni, "Global Justice, Reciprocity, and the State," *Philosophy & Public Affairs* 35, no. 1 (2007): 3–39.

informed social-scientific analysis.[52] It recognizes a complex system of rule and of forms of domination at the national, international, and transnational levels. As a result, it sees the primary task of justice as the creation of corresponding transnational and supranational structures of justification. Such structures must be capable of converting complex relations of domination into relations of reciprocal justification not marked by grave power asymmetries, and they must open up space for discourses, and above all for critique, where the nature of existing conditions and appropriate responses are matters of dispute.[53] Justice tracks, as it were, arbitrariness in forms of domination and coercion wherever they occur. The assumption that this would first require an already existing, positive social or legal context of cooperation fails to appreciate the correct order of things: first and foremost, there is concrete injustice in the world, and justice calls for structures of justification and banishes human arbitrariness. Justice is a relational, as well as an institutional, virtue; it does not refer to all asymmetrical relations between human beings without discrimination, but it does refer to those exhibiting forms of domination and social arbitrariness—whether in contexts involving only sparse legal regulation or in thicker institutional contexts, within and beyond the state.

The question of the extent to which a relational, discursive conception of justice can be described as "practice-dependent" must therefore be answered in a differentiated manner. "Practice-dependence" is the term used by Andrea Sangiovanni to describe approaches that, in contrast to "practice-independent" definitions of justice (such as those of luck egalitarianism or the universal provision of goods),[54] assume that the "content, scope and justification" of norms of justice depend on the concrete practices these norms are supposed to regulate. These practices thus enjoy normative priority and provide the context of interpretation for what justice requires.[55] Yet which practices these are and how they should be interpreted, it must be pointed out by way of criticism, is not revealed by these practices themselves, but is a prior requirement in need

---

[52] See, for instance, Andrew Hurrell, *On Global Order: Power, Values and the Constitution of International Society* (Oxford: Oxford University Press, 2007); Deborah D. Avant, Martha Finnemore, and Susan K. Sell, eds., *Who Governs the Globe?* (Cambridge: Cambridge University Press, 2010).

[53] I agree with Nancy Fraser that the latter condition is important; see Fraser, *Scales of Justice: Reimagining Political Space in a Globalizing World* (New York: Columbia University Press, 2009), esp. chs. 2 and 4. Nevertheless I believe that a critical social-scientific analysis is capable of adequately describing existing relations and structures and their need for justification in order to mark the entry point for discursive justification.

[54] Examples are Simon Caney, *Justice Beyond Borders: A Global Political Theory* (Oxford: Oxford University Press, 2005), and Stefan Gosepath, "The Global Scope of Justice," in *Global Justice*, ed. Thomas Pogge (Oxford: Blackwell, 2001), 145–68.

[55] Thus also Aaron James, "Constructing Justice for Existing Practice: Rawls and the Status Quo," *Philosophy & Public Affairs* 33, no. 3 (2005): 281–316.

of justification—they could be legally regulated, democratic, or cooperative practices, for instance, but they could also be practices of domination or negative cooperation. Hence the identification and interpretation of the practices to be regulated in accordance with justice must occur in light of principles of justice themselves, where these principles cannot follow from specific social practices alone but must be related to these practices in the right way. Otherwise there would be a threat of regress that could be broken off only in an arbitrary way through an abstract definition of which actual concrete practices are practices of justice.

Hence, a non-positivist approach that avoids a status quo bias which threatens to insulate existing contexts from external demands of justice (and often idealizes them into contexts of cooperation or self-determination)[56] must distinguish between different notions of "practice." The higher-order principle of justification, which gives rise to the principle of reciprocal and general justification in contexts of social rule and domination, is itself a principle of practical reason which states that intersubjective validity claims must be justified in an appropriate way. This principle is thus practical in nature (because *immanent* to the practice of justification), yet it also *transcends* concrete practices. Only in this way can the necessary proximity and distance to existing practices be generated by referring to the fundamental practice of justification.

Besides the basic notion of the practice of justification, various other notions of "practice" must be distinguished: practices of legal regulation, of political codification, and of economic and general social cooperation. Each of these can assume a *positive* or a *negative* form. Here it is a mistake to opt for a positive or a negative version of "practice-dependence," for both positive and negative practices give rise to duties of justification and justice. Contexts and practices of justice exist wherever there are—more or less institutionalized—forms of collective rule *or* domination that are

---

[56] See on this also the critique of "justice positivism" in Darrel Moellendorf, *Global Inequality Matters* (New York: Palgrave Macmillan, 2009), 36. Miriam Ronzoni tries to avoid a national status quo bias by criticizing international asymmetrical relations that arose in the context of positively established practices of economic exchange and of international commerce and no longer fulfill the internal purpose of these practices, as long as new global regulatory structures have not been erected; Ronzoni, "The Global Order: A Case of Background Injustice? A Practice-Dependent Account," *Philosophy & Public Affairs* 37, no. 3 (2009): 229–56. It should be noted, however, that without a higher-order principle of discursive justice it would remain open how to resolve disputes over the meaning of certain exchange practices, for example, and whether justice is done to this meaning and how one should respond to it—if one thinks, for example, of conflicting libertarian and egalitarian interpretations of current practices. Also, the question of whether individual practices of this kind are even worth preserving would lack any basis. However, Ronzoni rejects a higher-order principle (244), so that the view remains fixated on positive practices, and thus the analysis of injustice remains confined to a conventional analysis and interpretation of these principles.

in need of justification in accordance with the principle of reciprocal and general justification. This conception can be called a *discursive and critical practice approach* that does not refer exclusively to already existing positive contexts of justification. It incorporates positive practices and their content just as it designates negative practices—and to both it applies the principle of justification, which states that nobody may be subjected to norms or institutions that cannot be appropriately justified to him or her. Hence, the content and scope of norms of justice are defined in this way; namely, always with reference to relational social contexts, but not in a one-sided or selective manner.

A theory of transnational justice along these lines does not paint an idealized picture of perfect global distribution as an "end state," nor does it start from a Rawlsian "original position" that includes all human beings. Instead, it pursues the existing forms of subjugation and exploitation, of structural asymmetries and arbitrary rule, in order to demand relations of justice, and hence of justifiability, wherever such forms are to be found. This opens up a panorama of relations, structures, actors, and necessary institutions that appears to be highly confusing.

The appropriate response to this problem is a theory of *fundamental transnational justice*.[57] The basic structure of justification to which this theory refers aims to create structures of participation and legitimation that can assume and perform the tasks of opening and critique, culminating in the justification and adoption of binding transnational and international norms. The guiding principle is that of political autonomy and equality, though consistency also requires that this principle should hold within states, which often deny their citizens this autonomy, and as a principle that seeks to counterbalance the asymmetries between stronger and weaker states. The essential players in this process are in the first instance states, but reflexive forms of participation must be found that prevent these actors from continuing to dominate parts of their own population, other states, or parts of other states. Therefore, where existing supranational, international, and transnational organizations reproduce specific asymmetrical relations of rule, they can only provide the starting point for more participatory and reflexive political forms. The principle of fundamental transnational justice gives every political community the right to participate in cross-border, normative discourses on an equal footing, and affected parties below the state level simultaneously have the right to demand participation in such discourses if the latter would otherwise ignore or perpetuate specific relations of domination. This means that corresponding fora must be opened up to opposition parties from states,[58] though also to civil society actors as organized in the

[57] On this, see Forst, *The Right to Justification*, chs. 10–12.

[58] On this, see the corresponding proposal of Michael Zürn in the context of international institutions; Zürn, *Regieren Jenseits des Nationalstaats* (Frankfurt am Main: Suhrkamp, 1998), 352.

World Social Forum, for example.[59] In this way, transnational mechanisms of domination can also be uncovered and denounced through transnational critical alliances that constitute a politically relevant *demos* in virtue of being subjugated under specific structures of domination.[60] The political communities with corresponding means at their disposal have a duty to establish such a basic structure of justification. However, this does not give them the right to determine what forms this structure takes. Rather, it is a fundamental demand of justice and of human rights[61] that relations of justification should be established in which the opportunities to generate and exercise justificatory power are fairly distributed.[62]

As a result, the first task of justice is to create structures of justification in which arbitrary rule is banished—structures in which those who are subjected to rule or domination, whether of an economic, political, or legal kind, can bring the "force toward the better argument" to bear against those who exercise such rule or domination. Democracy as a practice of justice acquires special importance in this context. In the first place, it must be liberated from the narrow choice between a "world state or world of states." It is best understood as a normative order in which those who are subject to rule or norms should also be the normative authority, and this in an active sense within a practice of justification. Thus the question of the relevant *dêmoi* is answered in terms of the existing structures of rule, and the answer to the question of codetermination and the requisite institutional form depends on the degree of subjection. Democratic rule is a discursively justified form of rule, which means a form in which structures of justification exist that are adequate to the scope of the rule exercised. This already extends the question of democratic rule conceptually beyond national borders according to the relations of rule in which a state is embedded—whether as ruler or ruled (or, in complex systems, both simultaneously to different extents). Here a principle of political proportionality holds, according to which a structure of justification must be sufficiently open to participation and sufficiently effective to react to a given situation of subjection. However, this principle does not decide which model of order—ranging from a multilevel system to global federalism—follows. That must be decided with a view to the situation that is supposed to be

[59] Corresponding modes of participation based on relevant involvement or subjugation must be sought in this context, though I cannot discuss this further in the present context.

[60] On this, see the analysis of transnational politicization in Zürn, "Vier Modelle einer Globalen Ordnung in Kosmopolitischer Absicht," *Politische Vierteljahresschrift* 52, no. 1 (2011): 78–118, 100–104.

[61] For a detailed account, see Forst, "The Justification of Human Rights and the Basic Right to Justification: A Reflexive Approach," *Ethics* 120, no. 4 (2010): 711–40.

[62] On this, see James Bohman, *Democracy Across Borders: From Dêmos to Dêmoi* (Cambridge, MA: MIT Press, 2007). However, Bohman does not define his concept of the demos in the sense I propose.

transformed from an unregulated form of domination into a regulated form of justification or rule.[63]

Understanding democracy in processual terms, it expresses the collective aspiration to subsume the exercise of rule under relations of effective justification and authorization of norms by those who are subjected to them. To assume that this requires a *demos* defined in terms of the state (or nation) would be to reify democracy. After all, the *dêmoi* that are constituted as states are already integrated into such diverse networks of international and transnational arbitrary rule (including non-state actors) that the "congruence condition"[64] of the authorization and exercise of rule is no longer satisfied. In a world scarred by colonialism and grave social asymmetries, there are *dêmoi* that, to simplify, are subjected to external power in different ways, nationally and transnationally, as well as internationally and supranationally, and there are *dêmoi* that profit from such subjugation—and there are hybrid forms of the two.[65] Justice and democracy are primarily recuperative and processual in nature and are not justified *ex nihilo*. *Dêmoi* generally take shape through prior social relations that stand in need of justification. Jürgen Habermas once coined the image of "besiegement" for the exercise of communicative power: public discourses generate justifying reasons that the political system cannot ignore.[66] The concept of "justificatory power" that takes up these reflections, by contrast, is agnostic when it comes to the question of whether the mode of producing and exercising communicative power is an institutionalized one or not. What is essential, however, is that the force *toward* the better argument that challenges privileges and domination can in this way be exerted.

---

[63] Jürgen Habermas proposes a division of labor between a supranational world organization that would be authorized to deal with questions of international security and human rights within the framework of a global constitution, and a transnational "global domestic policy" that would presuppose negotiation systems in which questions of the global economy and the environment would feature centrally. See Jürgen Habermas, "Does the Constitutionalization of International Law Still Have a Chance?" in *The Divided West*, ed. and trans. Ciaran Cronin (Cambridge: Polity, 2006), 115–93, 136–37, and *The Crisis of the European Union: A Response*, trans. Ciaran Cronin (Cambridge: Polity, 2012), 56ff. In the more recent version, Habermas emphasizes that institutions are needed to prevent such negotiation systems from reproducing existing asymmetries of power, and he proposes oversight by a "world parliament" (67ff). That is one possible way to bring about more symmetrical relations of justification, but other possibilities for representing those affected or subjected are also conceivable.

[64] Zürn, *Regieren Jenseits des Nationalstaats*, 17.

[65] See Pogge, *Politics as Usual* (Cambridge: Polity, 2010); Iris Marion Young, *Responsibility for Justice* (Oxford: Oxford University Press, 2011).

[66] Jürgen Habermas, "Popular Sovereignty as Procedure," in *Between Facts and Norms*, trans. William Rehg (Cambridge, MA: MIT Press, 1996), 463–90, 486–87; Habermas subsequently revised this conception in favor of a more institutionally mediated one. However, it is especially applicable at the transnational level.

The recuperation of relations of rule and domination and their transformation into relations of justification is rightly called "democratization" when it succeeds in generating structures that put a brake on arbitrary rule, for instance through effective "contestation."[67] This is so even if there is still a long way to go to their complete recuperation and containment. Whenever privileged actors are forced to surrender their prerogatives because these lose their legitimation—after exposure within a system of justification and the formation of counter-power—this represents an increase in democracy. Democracy progresses—often only in modest steps—where non-legitimized rule, be it political, legal, or economic, is subjected to the justificatory authority of those affected. Democracy as practice is always a matter of *democratization*, of expanding and equalizing justificatory power.

4 TWO KINDS OF REALISM

In a number of recent texts, Philip Pettit has developed a republican conception of international justice.[68] At its core we find an ideal of "globalized sovereignty" that is animated by the idea of non-domination among states and that shares major assumptions with Rawls's account of a law of peoples. In the first place, it is based on a respect for peoples as separate and autonomous political units (ideally forming representative states, the first part of the construction of international justice, as in Rawls) and it thus entails a rejection of political cosmopolitanism and far-reaching arguments for global distributive justice. Pettit's approach takes the different forms of domination that exist or are possible at the international level into account, but believes that the dominating effects of a highly integrated, global political and legal structure would be higher than the dominating effects of an international system that leaves states and their different powers mostly intact, though bound by an entrenched, internationally-recognized set of rights and obligations of states and human beings. Above all, Pettit is a political realist who does not believe that it is possible, given the fact of global cultural plurality, to move further beyond distinct political communities. Furthermore, he makes the normative argument that citizens of a state have obligations toward one another that they do not have towards outsiders.[69]

---

[67] Pettit, "Democracy, Electoral and Contestatory," in *Designing Democratic Institutions*, ed. Ian Shapiro and Stephen Macedo (New York: New York University Press, 2000), 105–44.

[68] I refer to the most recent version of the conception to be found in Pettit, *Just Freedom: A Moral Compass for a Complex World* (New York: W.W. Norton & Company, 2014), ch. 6. Cf. Pettit, "The Republican Law of Peoples: A Restatement" (this volume).

[69] Pettit, *Just Freedom,* 158f.

I suggest that we call this form of realism *Realism 1*. It places certain constraints on the normative horizon of thinking about global justice, restricting it to international justice as a law of sovereign peoples. I believe, however, that some of the conclusions that follow from these constraints are in tension with another kind of realism that is also implicit in Pettit's republicanism. This form, *Realism 2*, is the source of much of the strengths of Pettit's view, as far as I see it. Realism 2 details the actual and possible forces of social and political domination and tracks domination wherever it occurs or can realistically occur; i.e., in asymmetries of power that lead to unjustifiable interferences with the liberty of subjects, persons, or states. As one can see, these two realisms might pull in different directions. While Realist 1 constructs a limited form of international republican justice as globalized sovereignty, Realist 2 identifies domination in its many international, transnational, or supranational forms—just as he or she would within a state—and demands "robust" structures of the rule of law, democratic legitimacy, or distributive justice to overcome and safeguard against political or social domination in contexts beyond the state. Obviously, a lot depends on an evaluation of the existence or threats of domination at these levels beyond the state, and empirical considerations play a major role. Still, this assessment is guided by normative evaluations. For a non-domination republican, there are difficult questions here: is the proposed realistic (in the sense of realism 1) account of international justice sufficient to secure non-domination given what we realistically (in the sense of realism 2) know about domination beyond the state?

As Pettit's work shows, he is in many ways a Realist 2. He spells out the many dangers and forms of domination of states by other states, in many dimensions of power—economic, political, military, as well as by international agencies and multinational corporations that "beggar the economy" of weaker states.[70] As a result, a system of entrenched protections is required, "entrenched in quite a deep manner," as Pettit adds.[71] Realist 2 thus argues that there must be mutually justifiable "suitable rules" for the exploration of resources, for trade as well as climate policy, and for limiting the power of multinational corporations and banks.[72] Yet Realist 1 then seems to counter that such rules and "universal standards" must be "negotiated in international forums."[73] However, here, Realist 2, who knows about the reproduction of power asymmetries in such contexts, asks about the justificatory standing of weaker states (as well as oppositional groups of states) in these negotiations—and I am not sure whether the notion of justice in negotiations of Realist 1 is sufficient to answer that.

When it comes to the question of implementation, Pettit argues that the recognition of the proposed general liberties by some states will motivate

70 Ibid., 162.
71 Ibid.
72 Ibid., 164.
73 Ibid., 164f.

others to follow suit, aspiring to be well recognized and in good standing internationally—or trying to avoid pressure and criticism. Apart from such esteem-based motivations, pure self-interest will also help, as states would have reason to want to be treated according to such norms. There will not be, as exists in a state, a robust system of sanctioning institutions—rather, a system of institutions through cooperation will emerge. But here Realist 2 wonders whether Realist 1 would truly want to describe international institutions like the World Trade Organization or the International Monetary Fund as such cooperative schemes, and to what extent they reproduce structural asymmetries and forms of international domination. And if they do, would we not argue for a thorough reform that transformed them into institutions of justice?

In the section where Pettit discusses the relevance of interstate inequality, he stresses what he calls the "norm of norms," i.e., that of discursive equality and justificatory generality and reciprocity (as I would phrase it). However, he does not conceive of a stronger form of democratic order that could impose such reciprocity (as Realist 2 would prefer). Instead, he argues that it is a "lesson of history" that stronger states will only use "soft power" of persuasion and no other means to influence such rule-making and implementation. Again, Realist 2 wonders whether that is realistic.

When it comes to dealing with impoverished states, Pettit argues for a policy of solidarity and help according to the principle "pouvoir oblige," though states are not allowed to force their citizens into "involuntary beneficence"[74] or "one-sided philanthropy." At this point Realist 2 objects, as he sees a global system of economic interdependence with a significant amount of power asymmetries, forced cooperation, and exploitation which create duties of justice on the side of the powerful and dominating agents instead of duties of beneficence. A lot depends, of course, on how we describe global economic relations, but Realist 2 here is of the opinion that Realist 1 is unrealistic and that he gets the demands of justice wrong.

In sum, critical Realist 2 does not argue against Pettit (or Nagel) that dominant states, multinational corporations, or international organizations have "the same" power over other states or peoples,[75] such that there already exists a basic structure of domination that must be turned into the basic structure of non-domination of a world state. But Realist 2 is convinced that there is *sufficient* domination inter- and transnationally that must be tracked, and that it must be overcome by establishing appropriately *robust* structures of justification that can curb such power asymmetries and realize basic forms of justice. This kind of realism strikes me as being more in tune with the basic republican idea of non-domination, but the theory of transnational justice that would result is different than the ideal of globalized sovereignty.

---

[74] Ibid., 175.
[75] Ibid., 184.

BIBLIOGRAPHY

Avant, Deborah D., Martha Finnemore, and Susan K. Sell, eds. *Who Governs the Globe?* Cambridge: Cambridge University Press, 2010.

Beitz, Charles. *Political Theory and International Relations*. Princeton: Princeton University Press, 1979.

Blake, Michael. "Distributive Justice, State Coercion, and Autonomy." *Philosophy & Public Affairs* 30, no. 3 (2001): 257–96.

Bohman, James. *Democracy Across Borders: From Dêmos to Dêmoi*. Cambridge, MA: MIT Press, 2007.

Caney, Simon. *Justice Beyond Borders: A Global Political Theory*. Oxford: Oxford University Press, 2005.

Cohen, Joshua, and Charles Sabel. "Extra Rempublicam Nulla Justitia?" *Philosophy & Public Affairs* 34, no. 2 (2006): 147–75.

Forst, Rainer. *Justification and Critique: Towards a Critical Theory of Politics*. Translated by Ciaran Cronin. Cambridge: Polity, 2013.

Forst, Rainer. "The Justification of Human Rights and the Basic Right to Justification: A Reflexive Approach." *Ethics* 120, no. 4 (2010): 711–40.

Forst, Rainer. "A Kantian Republican Conception of Justice as Nondomination." In *Republican Democracy*, edited by Andreas Niederberger and Philipp Schink, 154–68. Edinburgh: Edinburgh University Press, 2013.

Forst, Rainer. "Legitimität, Demokratie und Gerechtigkeit: Zur Reflexivität normativer Ordnungen." In *Deliberative Kritik—Kritik der Deliberation. Festschrift für Rainer Schmalz-Bruns*, edited by Daniel Gaus, Oliver Flügel-Martinsen, Tanja Hitzel-Cassagnes, and Franziska Martinsen. Baden-Baden, DE: Nomos, 2014.

Forst, Rainer. "Noumenal Power." *The Journal of Political Philosophy*, forthcoming.

Forst, Rainer. *The Right to Justification: Elements of a Constructivist Theory of Justice*. Translated by Jeffrey Flynn. New York: Columbia University Press, 2012.

Forst, Rainer. "Transnational Justice and Democracy: Overcoming Three Dogmas of Political Theory." In *Political Equality in Transnational Democracy*, edited by Eva Erman and Sofia Näsström, 41–59. New York: Palgrave Macmillan, 2013.

Fraser, Nancy. *Scales of Justice: Reimagining Political Space in a Globalizing World*. New York: Columbia University Press, 2009.

Gosepath, Stefan. "Deprivation and Institutionally Based Duties to Aid." In *Domination and Global Political Justice: Conceptual, Historical, and Institutional Perspectives*, edited by Barbara Buckinx, Jonathan Trejo-Mathys, and Timothy Waligore. New York: Routledge, 2015.

Gosepath, Stefan. "The Global Scope of Justice." In *Global Justice*, edited by Thomas Pogge, 145–68. Oxford: Blackwell, 2001.

Habermas, Jürgen. *The Crisis of the European Union: A Response*. Translated by Ciaran Cronin. Cambridge: Polity, 2012.

Habermas, Jürgen. "Does the Constitutionalization of International Law Still Have a Chance?" In *The Divided West*, edited and translated by Ciaran Cronin, 115–93. Cambridge: Polity, 2006.

Habermas, Jürgen. "Popular Sovereignty as Procedure." In *Between Facts and Norms*, translated by William Rehg, 463–90. Cambridge, MA: MIT Press, 1996.

Hurrell, Andrew. *On Global Order: Power, Values and the Constitution of International Society*. Oxford: Oxford University Press, 2007.

James, Aaron. "Constructing Justice for Existing Practice: Rawls and the Status Quo." *Philosophy & Public Affairs* 33, no. 3 (2005): 281–316.

Kant, Immanuel. "The Metaphysics of Morals." In *Practical Philosophy*, edited and translated by Mary J. Gregor, 353–603. Cambridge: Cambridge University Press, 1996.

Kant, Immanuel. "On the Common Saying: That May Be Correct in Theory, but It is of No Use in Practice." In *Practical Philosophy*, edited and translated by Mary J. Gregor, 279–309. Cambridge: Cambridge University Press, 1996.
Miller, David. *National Responsibility and Global Justice*. Oxford: Oxford University Press, 2007.
Moellendorf, Darrel. *Global Inequality Matters*. New York: Palgrave Macmillan, 2009.
Moore, Barrington. *Injustice: The Social Bases of Obedience and Revolt*. London: Macmillan, 1978.
Nagel, Thomas. "The Problem of Global Justice." *Philosophy & Public Affairs* 33, no. 2 (2005): 113–47.
O'Neill, Onora. *Constructions of Reason: Explorations of Kant's Practical Philosophy*. Cambridge: Cambridge University Press, 1990.
Pettit, Philip. "Democracy, Electoral and Contestatory." In *Designing Democratic Institutions*, edited by Ian Shapiro and Stephen Macedo, 105–44. New York: New York University Press, 2000.
Pettit, Philip. *Just Freedom: A Moral Compass for a Complex World*. New York: W.W. Norton & Company, 2014.
Pettit, Philip. "Keeping Republican Freedom Simple: On a Difference with Quentin Skinner." *Political Theory* 30, no. 3 (2002): 339–56.
Pettit, Philip. *On the People's Terms: A Republican Theory and Model of Democracy*. Cambridge: Cambridge University Press, 2012.
Pettit, Philip. "The Republican Law of Peoples: A Restatement." In *Domination and Global Political Justice: Conceptual, Historical, and Institutional Perspectives*, edited by Barbara Buckinx, Jonathan Trejo-Mathys, and Timothy Waligore. New York: Routledge, 2015.
Pettit, Philip. *Republicanism: A Theory of Freedom and Government*. Oxford: Oxford University Press, 1997.
Pogge, Thomas. *Politics as Usual*. Cambridge: Polity, 2010.
Pogge, Thomas. *Realizing Rawls*. Ithaca: Cornell University Press, 1989.
Rawls, John. *Justice as Fairness: A Restatement*. Cambridge, MA: Harvard University Press, 2001.
Rawls, John. *The Law of Peoples*. Cambridge, MA: Harvard University Press, 1999.
Rawls, John. *A Theory of Justice*, revised ed. Cambridge, MA: Harvard University Press, 1999.
Ripstein, Arthur. *Force and Freedom: Kant's Legal and Political Philosophy*. Cambridge, MA: Harvard University Press, 2009.
Ronzoni, Miriam. "The Global Order: A Case of Background Injustice? A Practice-Dependent Account." *Philosophy & Public Affairs* 37, no. 3 (2009): 229–56.
Sangiovanni, Andrea. "Global Justice, Reciprocity, and the State." *Philosophy & Public Affairs* 35, no. 1 (2007): 3–39.
Walzer, Michael. *Spheres of Justice*. New York: Basic Books, 1983.
Young, Iris Marion. *Responsibility for Justice*. Oxford: Oxford University Press, 2011.
Zürn, Michael. *Regieren Jenseits des Nationalstaats*. Frankfurt am Main: Suhrkamp, 1998.
Zürn, Michael. "Vier Modelle einer Globalen Ordnung in Kosmopolitischer Absicht." *Politische Vierteljahresschrift* 52, no. 1 (2011): 78–118.

5 Domination in Global Politics

A Critique of Pettit's Neo-Republican Model

Amy Allen

In his recent work, Philip Pettit has argued for an extension of his republican conception of justice as non-domination to the global level. This extension not only fills in a gap that was left in his earlier, state-centric account of freedom as non-domination, but is also offered as an attractive alternative to thin notions of liberal non-interference, on the one hand, and thicker cosmopolitan demands for global distributive justice on the other hand. Extended to the international level, Pettit's republican ideal of non-domination yields a conception of global justice that aims to achieve two goals: first, an international order in which non-dominating, representative states relate to one another and to other multinational and international agencies in non-dominating ways and, second, the inclusion of individuals into non-dominating, representative states and into a non-dominating, international order.

For the purposes of this chapter, I will assume, with Pettit, that a theory of global justice would do well to take non-domination as its normative goal. I realize that the ideal of non-domination may be criticized for being insufficient in other ways,[1] but I would like to set these criticisms aside for now in order to concentrate on Pettit's conception of domination. For if we are to take non-domination to be an attractive normative orientation for political theorizing, then it matters a great deal how we understand the concept of domination. To be sure, this is not limited to the context of global politics—and I will have some things to say in what follows about the limitations of Pettit's account of domination more generally—but it is crucially important for thinking about this context, hence for theorizing domination across and beyond the boundaries of nation-states.

In this chapter, I critically analyze the usefulness of Pettit's neo-republican account of domination for theorizing domination in the context of global politics. After reviewing Pettit's conception of domination in the first section, I assess his account by comparing it to the four-dimensional conception of domination offered by power theorists such as Peter Digeser and Mark

---

[1] See, for example, Patchen Markell, "The Insufficiency of Non-Domination," *Political Theory* 36, no. 9 (2008): 9–36.

Haugaard, where the four dimensions (or faces) are: arbitrary interference, institutional agenda-setting, the structuring of interests, and the constitution of subject-positions. I argue that, as a result of its agent-centered or action-theoretic focus, Pettit's conception cannot encompass either the third or fourth dimensions of domination. In the third section, I examine the issue of structural relations of domination in global contexts in more detail, and argue that Pettit's inability to adequately theorize the third dimension of power leads him to offer a dyadic, internationalist conception of global domination relations that leaves equally important structural, transnational relations of domination untheorized. In other words, section two aims to show that Pettit's account is limited to the first two dimensions of domination, while section three attempts to show why this constitutes a problem for an account of domination in global politics.

1 PETTIT'S CONCEPTION OF DOMINATION

Let me begin by reviewing Pettit's account of domination. For the republican tradition that Pettit's work aims to recover, the opposite of freedom is slavery; hence, domination or non-freedom is exemplified by the relationship between master and slave. As Pettit understands that relationship, it means "that the dominating party can interfere on an arbitrary basis with the choices of the dominated: can interfere, in particular, on the basis of an interest or an opinion that need not be shared by the person affected. The dominating party can practise interference, then, at will and with impunity: they do not have to seek anyone's leave and they do not have to incur any scrutiny or penalty."[2] Accordingly, Pettit defines domination as "a relationship in which one party enjoys a degree of alien control over another," where "alien control" is further defined as "a power of arbitrary interference" in the choices of that other.[3] On this definition, A has control over B just in case: 1) A has desires regarding how B chooses; 2) A's desires move him or her to further desire a certain pattern or outcome in B's choices; and 3) A makes the desired difference with respect to B's choices. Such control of

---

[2] Philip Pettit, *Republicanism: A Theory of Freedom and Government* (Oxford: Oxford University Press, 1997), 22.

[3] Philip Pettit, "A Republican Law of Peoples," *European Journal of Political Theory* 9, no. 1 (2010): 70–94. In the revised and expanded version of this piece, included in this volume, Pettit mostly drops the language of "alien control" and makes a few other terminological shifts. See Pettit, "The Republican Law of Peoples: A Restatement" (this volume). As far as I can tell, these changes do not alter the substance of his view, at least not in any way that bears on the argument made here. Hence, I will continue to refer to the earlier version, though I will also provide references to the new version where the two versions are the same. For further discussion of the definition of domination, see also Pettit, *Republicanism*, 52–66; and Pettit, "Three Axioms, Four Theorems," in *Republicanism and Political Theory*, eds. Cécile Laborde and John Maynor (Oxford: Blackwell, 2008).

B's choice is *alien* control just in case "it involves making the assumptions presupposed by the choice untrue or leading B to think they are untrue."[4] In other words, "A will exercise alien control over B's choice insofar as A undermines the truth and/or the endorsability"[5] of one of B's assumptions about what he or she is capable of doing. A may exert alien control over B through these ways: through interference (that is, through intentional obstruction, coercion, deception, and manipulation), through what Pettit calls invigilation (that is, standing by, ready to interfere in the event that B chooses contrary to A's desires), or through intimidation (that is, by leading B to believe that A has invigilatory control over him or her).[6]

Domination understood as a relationship of alien control is contrasted with relations of non-alien control, in which "A can raise the probability that B will choose in a desired pattern, but without undermining the truth or endorsability of any can-do assumption" on B's part.[7] On the one hand, non-alien control can take the form of reasoned or deliberative control, in which A offers B reasons for choosing as A desires, but those reasons do not undermine the truth or endorsability of any of B's can-do assumptions. On the other hand, non-alien control can take the form of checked or non-arbitrary control, in which A's interference with B is carried out with B's permission, and B is able to bring an end to the interference if he or she wishes and is aware of being so able.

Why is domination, so defined, a bad thing? In the case of individuals, the answer is rather obvious: a relationship of domination fails to treat those who are dominated as creatures who are capable of making choices and forming beliefs in a reason-sensitive way; hence, it fails to treat them with respect for their rational nature. As he puts it in the piece included in this volume, domination is an evil for individuals inasmuch as it restricts "the extent to which they can relate to one another as persons who live on equal terms with one another in a relationship of mutual respect."[8] If the evil of domination is understood in this way, then how can this be extended to account for the domination of supraindividual entities, such as states? Insofar as states are organizations in which individuals combine to act together, it follows that the members of states are subject to alien control

---

[4] Pettit, "A Republican Law of Peoples," 74.

[5] Ibid.

[6] In the revised version of his "Republican Law of Peoples" included in this volume, Pettit makes a slightly different tripartite distinction between active, virtual, and reserve control. See Pettit, "Restatement," 51ff. Virtual and reserve control seem to be variations of what Pettit earlier called invigilatory control, since they both involve A standing by, ready to intervene should B's choice not be to A's liking. Hence, not much of a consequence for my argument hangs on the subtle differences between these two sets of distinctions, so I will not discuss them further here.

[7] Pettit, "A Republican Law of Peoples," 75.

[8] Pettit, "Restatement," 52. Note that this is somewhat different than the more instrumental account of the value of non-domination for individuals that Pettit offers in his earlier work. See Pettit, *Republicanism*, 82–89.

if "the things that the members do as a corporate entity are subject to the dominating control of another agent or agency."[9] It further follows that "the domination of a representative state is bad or evil as such and it will not generally be justifiable—as it might be in the case, say, of an oppressive state—by any compensating effects on members."[10]

Hence, whereas Pettit had previously emphasized that, in the standard account of republicanism, "individuals are meant to enjoy freedom as non-domination in virtue of being protected against the domination of others by an undominating state,"[11] he now sees that this account is incomplete because individuals cannot be fully free if the state of which they are members is dominated by another state (or other entity). In other words, Pettit's earlier conception of freedom tacitly presupposed the nation-state as the ultimate frame of reference for assessments of freedom or domination, and thus failed to acknowledge the ways in which individuals might suffer domination indirectly as a result of being a member of a state that is dominated by another state (or other entity). The full conception of freedom as non-domination is now stated thus: freedom as non-domination requires that individuals be "protected against the domination of others by a state that is not only internally undominating but also externally undominated."[12] The most obvious source of the domination of a representative state is another state, but private entities such as corporations and churches, and public entities such as international institutions can also exercise such alien control. As with individuals, State A can dominate State B through interference, invigilation, or intimidation. State A can interfere, for example, through military action, the operation of intelligence agencies, or economic sanctions or other forms of pressure. State A can dominate through invigilation by standing by, ready to interfere in such ways should B fail to comply with A's wishes. State A can dominate through intimidation by leading B to believe that A does have invigilatory control. Multinational corporations can exercise alien control over states through economic pressure (for example, by moving their operations elsewhere or by lobbying governments or representatives within a government) and also through the mere ability or threat to do so. International institutions such as the United Nations, the International Monetary Fund (IMF), and the World Bank can exercise alien control over states through military interference (in the case of the United Nations), or through economic interference such as sanctions or conditions on aid or loans, or through the ability or threat of such interference.

---

[9] Pettit, "A Republican Law of Peoples," 76; cf. Pettit, "Restatement," 53.
[10] Pettit, "A Republican Law of Peoples," 77; cf. Pettit, "Restatement," 53.
[11] Pettit, "A Republican Law of Peoples," 77; Pettit, "Restatement," 53; cf. Pettit, *Republicanism*, especially ch. 3.
[12] Pettit, "Restatement," 53.

If we remain within the restricted framework of the relationship between the individual and the nation-state, the most effective remedy for domination, in Pettit's view, is a constitutional state that deprives dominating parties of their power of arbitrary interference while refraining from dominating anyone in doing so. The plausibility of this way of remedying domination turns on the distinction between mere interference, which Pettit's republicanism finds unproblematic, and arbitrary interference, which it finds objectionable. The constitutional state may interfere with dominating parties by preventing them from dominating others (without, of course, dominating those parties), so long as that state is responsive to the common good in doing so.[13] In this way, "in the domestic context the republican state naturally presents itself as the solution to problems of private domination of some members of the society over others."[14] On this model, the remedy for the subordination of women in the United States, for example, would consist in the United States government depriving men of their power of arbitrary interference over women, but without dominating anyone in so doing. This could be done through a variety of legal and administrative means, such as strengthening and enhancing the enforcement of existing laws against sexual assault and domestic violence, funding support services for rape and domestic abuse survivors, enforcing existing laws against sexual harassment, gender discrimination, and wage disparities in the workplace, and so on. These remedies would not themselves be instances of domination, so long as the state, in devising and implementing such remedies, is responsive to the common good and remains open to contestation about what constitutes the common good. This is so, even though these remedies would control the choices of some individuals, by prohibiting them from sexually harassing women, paying women less money for the same work, and committing acts of violence against women, and even by using some of their tax revenue to pay for domestic violence shelters or other social services designed to improve the lives of women. Such measures interfere with the choices of some individuals, but they do not do so arbitrarily.

What about the international context? How is the domination of some states by other states (or by multinational corporations or international institutions) to be remedied, in Pettit's view? Pettit considers the possibility of a world state, modeled on his conception of the republican state, which would fulfill the same role of preventing domination in a non-dominating way in the international context, but rejects this idea on the grounds that it is completely infeasible.[15] He also considers the possibility that existing international institutions such as the United Nations, together with public international law, could fulfill the same function as the domestic

[13] Pettit, *Republicanism*, 67–68, 92–95.

[14] Pettit, "A Republican Law of Peoples," 80; Pettit, "Restatement," 57.

[15] Pettit, "A Republican Law of Peoples," 81; Pettit, "Restatement," 57–58.

state at the international level but without actually necessitating a world state. He worries, however, that such institutions, even when backed with "a recognized body of public international law," "will not have the resources to provide for the effective" regulation of "state-state domination,"[16] both because they will be incapable of constraining the actions of the most powerful states and because some forms of state-state domination, especially those associated with economic power or diplomatic clout, will elude the control of such institutions. However, such international institutions are important in an indirect way, inasmuch as they promote the "currency of common global reasons" and help to make "reasoned deliberation on the basis of commonly recognized reasons—and the resolution of differences on the basis of procedures supported by those reasons—into the default option in the mutual accommodation of states."[17] To be sure, interstate deliberation by itself will not eliminate domination—in fact, "deliberation in the presence of a manifest asymmetry of power may only cover up a deeper game of intimidation by the strong"[18]—but it can create a basis for determining basic sovereign liberties; that is, the common liberties that all states should be able to enjoy. In addition, it can generate an internal, participant perspective on international law. These considerations give us grounds, in Pettit's view, for "limited enthusiasm"[19] for international institutions as mechanisms for remedying state-state domination. But the republican perspective on non-domination also helps us to see why deliberation by itself is not going to be enough in the international context to remedy domination; hence, "it will have to be matched by the groupings that enable the weak to deliberate from a position of strength," for example, military or economic alliances.[20]

2 DOMINATION IN FOUR DIMENSIONS

Drawing on earlier work by Peter Digeser, Mark Haugaard has recently outlined what he calls a four-dimensional conception of power.[21] Haugaard's focus is much broader than my own in this chapter, as he aims to offer an account of normatively harmful and beneficial forms of power-over and power-with across all four of the dimensions. Since my aim in this chapter is the rather limited one of assessing Pettit's conception of domination in a global context, I will limit my focus in what follows to

[16] Pettit, "A Republican Law of Peoples," 81; Pettit, "Restatement," 58.
[17] Pettit, "A Republican Law of Peoples," 82–83; Pettit, "Restatement," 60.
[18] Pettit, "A Republican Law of Peoples," 83; Pettit, "Restatement," 60–61.
[19] Pettit, "A Republican Law of Peoples," 83; Pettit, "Restatement," 61.
[20] Pettit, "A Republican Law of Peoples," 84; Pettit, "Restatement," 62.
[21] Mark Haugaard, "The Three- and Four-Dimensional Power Debates Reconsidered: Power Over as Concerted Power," forthcoming in *Constellations*. See Peter Digeser, "The Fourth Face of Power," *Journal of Politics* 54, no. 4 (1992): 977–1007.

using Haugaard's four-dimensional account to assess Pettit's conception of domination. This should not, however, be taken to imply that I equate power, or even power-over, with domination. On my view, not all instances of exercising power over others count as domination—it is at least possible to exercise power over others in non-dominating ways—and not all instances of exercising power count as exercising power over others. A complete conception of power should encompass individual and collective empowerment, what I call power-to and power-with, as well as power-over.[22] The fact that I am not talking about these other aspects of power relations here should not be taken to mean that I do not think they are important.

Before I return to Pettit, let me briefly review the four dimensions of power, which have emerged out of the power debates that began in the mid-20th century with the influential work of Robert Dahl. The first dimension of power is the one initially theorized by Dahl, characterized by what Pettit calls arbitrary interference. This notion is captured in Dahl's famous definition of power: "A has power over B to the extent that he can get B to do something that B would not otherwise do."[23] The second dimension is that of institutional agenda-setting, as brought out in Bachrach and Baratz's famous critical response to Dahl's original proposal. On this view, A has power over B not only by getting B to do what he would otherwise not do, but also to the extent that A can organize some issues into politics and organize others out, in a way that is beneficial to himself.[24] The third dimension is the structuring of interests, as theorized in Steven Lukes's classic analysis of power. On this view, A has power over B not only by getting B to do what he would not otherwise do, and not only by controlling what gets on the political agenda in the first place, but also by, as Lukes puts it, "shaping and determining his very wants."[25] The fourth dimension is the constitution of subject-positions, as theorized in Michel Foucault's account of subjection. Here we leave behind the language of A and B, since subjection is, for Foucault, not only something that subjects do to one another but also "a form of power which makes individuals subjects."[26] On this view, power does not merely shape the choices, deliberations, desires, and interests of individual subjects, it *constitutes* them as subjects in the dual sense of that term, as both subject to power and subjects who are capable of exercising power. As Digeser puts it, the four

22 As I argue in more detail in Amy Allen, *The Power of Feminist Theory: Domination, Resistance, Solidarity* (Boulder, CO: Westview Press, 1999).

23 Robert Dahl, "The Concept of Power," *Behavioral Science* 2, no. 3 (1957): 201–15, 203–4.

24 Peter Bachrach and Morton Baratz, "The Two Faces of Power," *American Political Science Review* 56, no. 4 (1962): 947–52.

25 Steven Lukes, *Power: A Radical View* (London: Macmillan, 1974), 23.

26 Michel Foucault, "The Subject and Power," in *Power*, vol. 3 of *Essential Works of Michel Foucault*, ed. James Faubion (New York: The New Press, 2000), 331.

dimensions—or faces, in his terminology—can be understood as answering four different questions:

> Under the first face of power the central question is, 'Who, if anyone, is exercising power?' Under the second face, 'What issues have been mobilized off the agenda and by whom?' Under the [third face], 'Whose objective interests are being harmed?' Under the fourth face of power the critical issue is 'What kind of subject is being produced?'[27]

Haugaard further argues that a four-dimensional analysis of power "constitutes an exceptionally useful set of conceptual tools for the analysis of power," particularly in the context of international relations.[28]

How does Pettit's conception of domination stack up against this four-dimensional view? Pettit's account of domination as alien control can best be understood as a version of the basic Weberian understanding of power as the probability that one actor will be able to carry out his own will vis-à-vis another, against resistance.[29] Pettit invokes Max Weber when he introduces his conception of domination,[30] and he also explicitly links his understanding of domination to Dahl's influential Weberian conception.[31] His account of domination is agent-centered—or, we might say, action-theoretic—and it requires some agents, be they individual or corporate agents, intentionally influencing the choices of other agents. As he emphasizes in his piece in this volume, in order to count as an instance of domination, interference in someone's choice must be an "intentional, voluntary, and arbitrary" action.[32] Thus, Pettit seems to flatly rule out the possibility that individuals could be dominated by a structure or a mode of subject-constitution.

Inasmuch as Pettit explicitly models his account of domination on Dahl's Weberian view, it seems fairly straightforward to say that his account of domination as arbitrary interference—whether overt or implied—covers the first dimension of domination pretty easily.[33] However, Pettit also claims that his account of domination includes manipulation, which may "take the form of agenda-fixing, the deceptive or non-rational shaping of people's beliefs or desires, or the rigging of the consequences of people's actions."[34]

---

27 Digeser, "The Fourth Face of Power," 980.
28 See also Michael Barnett and Raymond Duvall, "Power in International Politics," *International Organization* 59, no. 1 (2005): 39–75.
29 Max Weber, *Economy and Society: An Outline of Interpretive Sociology*, vol. 1, eds. Guenther Roth and Claus Wittich (Berkeley: University of California Press, 1978), 53.
30 Pettit, *Republicanism*, 52.
31 Pettit, "Dahl's Power and Republican Freedom," *Journal of Power* 1, no. 1 (April 2008): 67–74.
32 Pettit, "Restatement," 44.
33 Pettit, "Dahl's Power and Republican Freedom."
34 Pettit, *Republicanism*, 53.

Hence, he suggests that his account of domination also covers the second (agenda-setting) and the third (structuring of interests) dimensions as well. Indeed, in his paper, "Dahl's Power and Republican Freedom," Pettit claims that Dahl's original analysis can be regimented and extended in such a way that "enables the account to escape a number of influential critiques," including those of Bachrach and Baratz, and Lukes.[35]

Pettit's extension of Dahl, however, primarily concerns what he calls the "punctual" character of the action that is presupposed by Dahl's original definition, not the agent-centered or action-theoretic nature of the account. The distinction between punctual and extended instances of domination seems to track the distinction in his piece in this volume between domination in this or that choice and domination, period. Domination in this or that choice is a punctual instance of imposing one's will on another, while domination, period is a temporally extended state of affairs in which one individual imposes his or her will on another across a range of significant choices.[36] Once we extend Dahl's account beyond the punctual, Pettit argues,

> there is no reason why A's power should not affect what B does at a given time, or over time, in virtue of initiatives taken earlier or over time; no reason why it should not be exercised over someone in virtue of general initiatives that are not directed at that individual in particular; no reason why the initiatives should not go behind the back of the individual and rig his or her motives or mind-set; and so on.[37]

Also, once we extend it in this way, we can see that "power may be exercised even in cases where there is no active interference,"[38] even where A does not interfere in a positive way in B's choices, and even where B does nothing. These are cases of what Pettit calls invigilation. As explained above, in instances of invigilation, A stands by and does nothing so long as B acts in accordance with his wishes; he interferes only when B does something that does not please him. "A's invigilation may not be a conscious or intentional action that would provide a referent for 'w' in the original schema; it may consist merely in being there, ready to interfere—and interfere intentionally—should B not behave to A's taste."[39] Even when A does not interfere, A's willingness to interfere should B choose against A's taste increases the probability that B will act as A wishes, and thus A exercises power over B even without actively interfering.

How convincing is Pettit's claim that his extended version of Dahl's account responds to the critiques offered by Bachrach and Baratz, and

---

35 Pettit, "Dahl's Power and Republican Freedom," 69.
36 See Pettit, "Restatement," 42–46.
37 Pettit, "Dahl's Power and Republican Freedom," 69.
38 Ibid., 70.
39 Ibid.

Lukes, and thus encompasses the second and third faces of domination? With regard to agenda-setting, one might say that since, even on this view, A is still doing something—namely, including or excluding something on the agenda for political discussion, debate, and action—that has the effect of making it more or less likely that B will do something, Pettit's account seems like it can cover this kind of situation as well. When we get to the third dimension, however, Pettit's claim starts to wear thin. For even though Lukes framed his definition of power in the language of A having power over B, his aim was rather different than either Dahl's or Bachrach and Baratz's. Both of those earlier analyses of power sought to illuminate the give and take of relations of power within a specific political context, namely, representative democracies, whereas Lukes's aim had more to do with making sense of structures of social subordination. As a result, the A/B talk does not fit his analysis of power all that comfortably, since although social subordination can entail the kind of A/B relations of power understood as imposing one's will on another, it also entails something like a more Gramscian notion of hegemony or a Bourdieuian notion of habitus,[40] both of which are structural conceptions of power. As Bourdieu understands it, the habitus constrains both the dominator and the dominated and forms part of the tacit background knowledge by means of which both A and B make sense of their situation; as a result, it is not clear that the simple language of A dominating B—even when A does so without actively interfering with B—suffices any longer. The habitus, for example, is what allows existing relations of domination to be perceived by both dominator and dominated as natural and acceptable and that habitus is ongoingly reproduced through the actions of both but without either necessarily intending for this to be the case. As Bourdieu puts it with respect to the example of masculine domination: "The structure of masculine domination is the ultimate principle of these countless singular relationships of domination/submissions, which, while they differ in their form according to the position in space of the agents concerned . . . separate and unite men and women in each of the social universes."[41] But this way of thinking about domination is not obviously compatible with Pettit's agent-centered view according to which instances of domination must be intentional, voluntary, and arbitrary.

Moreover, in light of the agent-centeredness of Pettit's definition of domination and his rejection of a structural analysis of domination, it seems abundantly clear that his account does not encompass the fourth dimension of domination. For although Foucault's analysis of power does have some

---

[40] On this point, see Haugaard, "The Three- and Four-Dimensional Power," 22; cf. Lukes, *Power: A Radical View*, 2nd ed. (New York: Palgrave Macmillan, 2005), 139–43.

[41] Pierre Bourdieu, *Masculine Domination* (Stanford: Stanford University Press, 2001), 108.

agent-centered or action-theoretic elements, his account of subjection is best understood as a constitutive rather than an agent-centered conception of power, one in which power "is no longer merely the name given to the conditions for the prevention of individual freedom but also to the conditions of possibility for individuality."[42] Domination in this sense is not just a matter of A imposing his or her will on B by interfering with B's choices or standing ready to do so should the need arise, it is also a matter of how A and B are constituted as choosing subjects in the first place. The thought here is that perhaps the most effective form of domination is one that takes hold at the level of subject constitution, shaping and structuring the space of reasons within which subjects choose and the critical capacities that they bring to bear on those choices. As Barnett and Duvall have argued, such a conception of power helps us to understand "how diffuse and contingent social processes produce particular kinds of subjects, fix meanings and categories, and create what is taken for granted and the ordinary of world politics."[43] For example, an analysis focusing on the fourth dimension of power could help to illuminate the discursive and productive relations of power by means of which subjects are constituted as either "civilians" or "combatants" in the context of international humanitarian law.[44]

Thus, whereas Pettit's account may accommodate the first two dimensions of domination reasonably well, it really cannot accommodate the third and fourth dimensions at all, since both of these require something beyond an agent-centered or action-theoretic understanding of domination. If theorists such as Haugaard and Barnett and Duvall are correct that a complete account of power in international relations needs to encompass all four dimensions, then this is a drawback of Pettit's conception. Furthermore, with respect to the third dimension specifically, it shows that Pettit's account fails to accomplish one of the ends that it sets for itself, namely, showing how a modified Dahlian conception of power can be extended in ways that allow it to respond to Lukes's criticisms. In the next section, I discuss the third dimension of domination in the context of global politics in greater detail, and argue that a satisfactory account of domination in the context of global politics must at a minimum include the sort of structural elements picked out by the third dimension of domination.[45] Moreover, and relatedly, such an account needs to go beyond a narrow focus on *inter*national relations to also encompass *trans*national relations of power.

---

[42] Martin Saar, "Power and Critique," *Journal of Power* 3, no. 1 (April 2010): 7–20, 16.
[43] Barnett and Duvall, "Power in International Politics," 57.
[44] Ibid.
[45] On this point, see also Barnett and Duvall: "Analysis of power in international relations . . . must include a consideration of how social structures and processes differentiate differential social capacities for actors to define and pursue their interests and ideals" (42).

3 STRUCTURAL DOMINATION IN TRANSNATIONAL CONTEXTS: CRITIQUE OF PETTIT

Pettit's account offers an attractive starting point for thinking about global justice inasmuch as it starts with an attempt to analyze actually existing injustice and domination. Pettit's approach starts by "taking states as they are"[46] and assumes "that states come in very different demographic and territorial profiles, and have very different powers" all "in keeping with the actual state of world affairs."[47] In so doing, Pettit refreshingly avoids the tendencies toward ideal theory that come to the fore in many accounts of global justice, and thus it also avoids the associated tendency to treat political theory as a branch of applied moral philosophy.[48] However, I do want to question whether Pettit's conception of domination, as presented, is adequate for theorizing domination in a global context. I focus here on two criticisms of Pettit's conception of domination. The first concerns his basic conception of domination, which is modeled on a dyadic, master-subject relationship. This model, I argue, is not even adequate for theorizing all forms of domination within existing nation-states, as the example of the subordination of women shows, and is especially problematic as a way of thinking about domination in a global context. Moreover, I think it can be shown to be problematic by Pettit's own lights, or on the basis of assumptions that he shares. The second has to do with Pettit's restricted focus on states as the subjects of domination at the global level. This restricted focus leaves Pettit unable to render the complexity of global relations of domination, which often take transnational rather than, or in addition to, international forms.

My first criticism of Pettit is that the dyadic, agent-centered, intentional conception of domination sketched out in the previous two sections is insufficient for making sense of the current relations of global domination and injustice that his republican account aims to illuminate.[49] We need a richer and more complex account of domination to serve as the basis for our ideal of non-domination. The limitations of Pettit's dyadic, master-subject conception of domination are evident even if we restrict our focus to the context of an individual nation-state. To see why, consider the applicability of Pettit's

---

46 Pettit, "A Republican Law of Peoples," 70; cf. Pettit, "Restatement," 37.

47 Pettit, "A Republican Law of Peoples," 71.

48 See Raymond Geuss, *Philosophy and Real Politics* (Princeton: Princeton University Press, 2008).

49 For a related critique of Pettit, focusing on modern forms of domination more generally, though not specifically examining the context of global justice, see Michael Thompson, "A Functionalist Theory of Social Domination," *Journal of Political Power* 6, no. 2 (2013): 179–99. Although I agree with much of Thompson's critique of Pettit, I find his own conception of domination overly broad, since it seems to collapse the distinction between legitimate and dominating forms of power-over. For my account of this distinction, see Allen, *The Power of Feminist Theory*, ch. 5.

conception of domination to the subordination of women. Pettit frequently uses the example of women's subordination to illustrate his conception of domination; not only that, he also explicitly argues that his republican conception of non-domination can serve as an ideal for feminists, and he finds important precursors of his own republicanism in the work of early feminists such as Mary Astell, Mary Wollstonecraft, and John Stuart Mill.[50] As Pettit puts it, "if the main problem for women is that cultural, legal, and institutional pressures combine to put them in a position akin to that of slavery—combine to place them under the thumb of men—then the ideal for women is precisely that of being secured against arbitrary interference"; that is, the ideal is freedom as non-domination.[51] Indeed, in large part because of their historical association, Pettit thinks that republicanism and feminism are especially suited to one another, such that republicanism can "offer a persuasive articulation of the central feminist claims" and an articulation that "has had a continuous history within the ranks of feminists themselves."[52]

However, although Pettit is no doubt right that the overarching goal of feminism is to end the subordination of women by men,[53] it is far from clear that his dyadic, master-slave conception of domination is actually suitable for understanding contemporary forms of gender subordination. While this dyadic model may have made more sense in the 18th and 19th centuries, when the republican feminist accounts that Pettit cites were written, and although vestiges of those dyadic master-subject relations no doubt continue to exist, the master-subject model offers an inaccurate picture of gender subordination in contemporary, Western, late-capitalist societies. As Nancy Fraser puts this point, "gender inequality is today being transformed by a shift from dyadic relations of mastery and subjection to more impersonal structural mechanisms that are lived through more fluid cultural forms."[54] Those structural mechanisms of oppression and subordination have been ably theorized by Iris Marion Young, who defines structural injustice as "the vast and deep injustices some groups suffer as a consequence of often unconscious assumptions and reactions of well-meaning people in ordinary interactions, media and cultural stereotypes, and structural features of bureaucratic hierarchies and market mechanisms—in short, the normal processes of everyday life."[55] Inasmuch as Pettit's account requires that a

---

50 See Pettit, *Republicanism*, 138–40.
51 Pettit, *Republicanism*, 139.
52 Ibid., 140.
53 Ibid., 139, quoting Jane Mansbridge and Susan Moller Okin, "Feminism," in *A Companion to Contemporary Political Philosophy*, eds. Robert Goodin and Philip Pettit (Oxford: Blackwell, 1993), 269.
54 Nancy Fraser, "Beyond the Master/Subject Model: Reflections on Carole Pateman's *Sexual Contract*," *Social Text* 37 (1993): 173–81, 180. I discuss Fraser's critique of Pateman in more detail in Allen, *The Power of Feminist Theory*, 11–18.
55 Iris Marion Young, *Justice and the Politics of Difference* (Princeton: Princeton University Press, 1990), 41.

relation of domination be both agent-centered and intentional, it clearly leaves out this kind of conception of structural oppression, which is caused not by a single or a collective agent but rather by the overlapping, unintentional actions of a multitude of different agents.

To be fair to Pettit, I think that his notion of invigilatory control is introduced in an effort to explicate what other theorists call structural mechanisms of domination but without having to invoke shadowy notions such as social structure. If A can dominate B without interfering in any way in B's action, but simply by standing ready to interfere should B choose contrary to A's wishes, and if A and B both know this and further know that A's interference would be effective, then the effect of such invigilatory control can look quite like what Fraser and Young would describe as impersonal, structural mechanisms of oppression. Patterns of domination and subordination can be perpetuated in this way without anyone taking any overt action: a woman might choose to defer to her husband's wishes knowing that she could be beaten with impunity if she does not, and this would be an instance of domination even though the husband takes no overt action to secure his wife's compliance. This account of domination is much more sophisticated than, for example, Catharine MacKinnon's once-prominent view, according to which gender domination is construed as men having their feet on women's necks.[56] But considering a slightly different example shows us the limitations of Pettit's agent-centered and intentional conception of domination. Suppose that a woman chooses to enter a relatively low-pay, low-status occupation because she knows that such work will be more easily combined with child-rearing duties and responsibilities. Such choices are arguably largely responsible for the remaining gender wage-gap, and as such are a crucial element of women's ongoing subordination, related to their lack of representation in high-status professions (law, academia, business, politics) despite their earning college degrees at higher rates than men. But when a woman makes such a choice, who is exercising invigilatory control over her? Who is standing by, waiting in the wings, ready to interfere should she decide to pursue a career in corporate law or a run for the Senate? The answer is: not necessarily anyone. Gender subordination in cases such as this one is the result of the concatenation of a variety of unintentional actions, unconscious beliefs, unstated assumptions, and impersonal market mechanisms that shape the interests and even the critical capacities of those in positions of dominance and those who are subordinated. In order to illuminate such instances of subordination we need an account of domination that goes beyond the intentional acts of individual or collective agents—even

[56] "Take your foot off our necks, then we will hear in what tongue women speak," (Catharine MacKinnon, "Difference and Dominance: On Sex Discrimination," in *Feminism Unmodified: Discourses on Life and Law* (Cambridge: Harvard University Press, 1987), 45). I discuss MacKinnon's conception of domination in Allen, *The Power of Feminist Theory*, 11–18.

if those include acts of refraining from acting—to encompass structural relations of domination along the lines of the third dimension of domination discussed above.

So, the structural nature of domination is important for theorizing domination within nation-states—even the non-dominating, representative states that Pettit assumes for the purposes of his early republicanism—as the example of the subordination of women shows. However, the limitations of Pettit's dyadic, master-subject conception of domination become even more evident when we think about domination in global terms. In order to see this, we first need to consider the second criticism of Pettit's account of domination in global politics that I mentioned above, his focus on state-state relations, and specifically on states as the subjects of domination. Although Pettit acknowledges that non-state actors—whether private, such as multinational corporations, or public, such as international institutions—can be in positions of dominance in global affairs, his account of global domination is modeled on state-state relations and hence doesn't illuminate the role of non-state actors in global politics particularly well.[57] Perhaps this accounts for his rather implausible claim that although it is possible for international institutions such as the United Nations, the World Bank, and the IMF to dominate states, these international agencies "do not represent a threat on a par with the dangers from other states and from private bodies like corporations."[58] Moreover, he consistently speaks of states as the relevant subjects of domination in the global sphere, thus

[57] For a related critique, see Cécile Laborde, "Republicanism and Global Justice: A Sketch," *European Journal of Political Theory* 9, no. 1 (2010): 48–69, 57.

[58] Pettit, "A Republican Law of Peoples," 85; cf. Pettit, "Restatement," 57. With respect to such international institutions, Pettit observes that "their membership is normally subject to the vetting of affected states, their operations are typically exposed to demanding measures of review and accountability, and their decisions are often conditional on the approval of other bodies" (Pettit, "A Republican Law of Peoples," 85–86; Pettit, "Restatement," 63). Hence, Pettit concludes, "only a perverted sense of priority would suggest that they [the international agencies] are the principal problems in the area" (Pettit, "A Republican Law of Peoples," 86; cf. Pettit, "Restatement," 63). The point about accountability may have some truth with respect to the United Nations—though the composition of the permanent members of the Security Council and the role of the veto in its operations renders this claim highly suspect—but it is definitely not true for the extremely powerful international financial institutions such as the IMF and the World Bank, which are largely run and staffed by wealthy, industrialized countries and which are accountable largely to interests in those countries rather than to the interests of the countries that they give or loan money to. This explains how the disastrous structural adjustment policies and loan conditionalities of the last 30 years were possible. Arguably these are the principal mechanisms of domination across borders today; one might even claim, as James Tully has done, that existing international institutions serve to uphold informal imperialism; Tully, "On Law, Democracy and Imperialism," in *Imperialism and Civic Freedom*, vol. 2 of *Public Philosophy in a New Key* (Cambridge: Cambridge University Press, 2008).

leaving relations of domination between non-state actors (for example, between two multinational corporations, between multinational corporations and international financial institutions, between international financial institutions and NGOs, and so forth) out of his conception of global domination. As such, Pettit's conception of global domination is best understood as an *inter*nationalist account.

However, such an internationalist conception of global domination is insufficient for making sense of the current shape of transnational globalization, in which public and private non-state actors dominate not only other state actors but also other non-state actors.[59] In global and transnational contexts, individuals do not only suffer domination indirectly, by being members of states that are dominated by other states, or by multinational corporations or international institutions. They also suffer domination directly by non-state actors—as, for example, when multinational corporations exploit workers in sweatshops in Bangladesh. Hence, a fully satisfactory conception of domination in global politics, if it is to do justice to what Pettit calls "normative individualism" by taking account of the impact of different institutional arrangements on individual human beings,[60] should encompass not only *intra*national (within a nation-state) and *inter*national (between states), but also *trans*national (as Julian Culp explains, "between agents from different states, where at least one of them is a non-state agent")[61] relations of domination.[62] Such an account of domination needs to start from what Rainer Forst has called the "fact of multiple domination": the recognition that the global context is "one of a complex system of power and domination with a variety of powerful actors, from international institutions to transnational corporations, local elites, and so forth."[63] In light of the fact of multiple domination, even Pettit's limited enthusiasm for the role that international institutions can

---

[59] For a helpful and illuminating discussion of the contrast between internationalist and transnationalist conceptions of justice, see Julian Culp, *Global Justice and Development* (Basingstoke: Palgrave Macmillan, 2014).

[60] See Pettit, "A Republican Law of Peoples," 76; Pettit, "Restatement," 52.

[61] Culp, ch. 4.

[62] Pettit might argue that his full account of a non-dominating state can protect against the negative impact of corporations and other entities on individual citizens, since part of the role of the non-dominating state is to protect individual members from domination by other members. But as Pettit himself acknowledges, this account of the non-dominating state presumes the individual nation-state as its context; hence, it is not well suited to making sense of transnational relations of domination exercised by multinational corporations who are not solely members of one state. To tackle this problem, one needs a broader conception of domination at a global level, and Pettit's *inter*national conception, with its narrow focus on relations between and among states, is not equipped to deal with this issue.

[63] Rainer Forst, *The Right to Justification: Elements of a Constructivist Theory of Justice*, trans. Jeffrey Flynn (New York: Columbia University Press, 2012), 256. Cf. Forst, "Transnational Justice and Non-Domination: A Discourse-Theoretical Approach" (this volume).

play in checking global relations of domination seems misguided, since it is unclear how the domination of states (or individuals within states) by such international institutions themselves (such as the IMF) could possibly be ameliorated in this manner.

Related to this is Pettit's relative lack of attention to the role of poverty in producing and reproducing structural domination.[64] Global poverty is the result of multiple, systemic, interrelated relations of domination that are not well illuminated by a simple master-subject model, even if we assume that the masters and the subjects can be collective agents. As Cécile Laborde explains, Pettit's agent-relative model of domination "overlooks the fact that the global system is . . . a (structurally unfair) systemic order which authorizes and aggravates the pre-institutional subservience and dependency of weak states. . . . This structural asymmetry cannot be accounted for in purely agent-relative terms."[65] What Forst calls the multiple domination model highlights the fact that "in a complex network of powers, several agencies influence the actions of others so that a number of them profit, whereas others—collectives or persons—profit very little or not at all."[66]

To speak of a network of powers is, for Forst, to think of multiple domination as a stable and regular system that is not intentionally planned and that does not have a fixed or stable center, but that is "intentionally upheld by various actors for the benefits they receive from it."[67] However, I would follow Young rather than Forst here in holding that such a system need not even be *intentionally* upheld in order to count as a structural form of domination; global economic inequalities can result from the overlapping, unintended consequences of the actions of a multitude of different actors. As Young's extended discussion of sweatshops and the anti-sweatshop movement shows, when I buy a piece of clothing at, say, the Gap, I reinforce and uphold a structure of oppression that is composed of complex legal, economic, and political relations between multinational corporations, international trade organizations, state actors, and garment factory owners in Bangladesh, and the 13-year-old girls who work in those factories in unsafe conditions for below-subsistence-level wages.[68] I need not attempt to intentionally and voluntarily control the choices of that 13-year-old girl, as Pettit's model seems to require, nor need

---

[64] James Bohman, "Domination, Global Harms, and the Priority of Injustice: Expanding Transnational Republicanism" (this volume). For a compelling account of the role of social, economic, and political structures in the genesis of poverty, see Iris Marion Young, *Responsibility for Justice* (Oxford: Oxford University Press, 2011). For an interesting attempt to develop a critical republican account of global distributive justice that draws on, but also modifies, Pettit's conception of domination (precisely by adding a structural dimension to the account), see Laborde, "Republicanism and Global Justice."

[65] Laborde, "Republicanism and Global Justice," 57.

[66] Forst, *The Right to Justification*, 257.

[67] Ibid., 256.

[68] See Young, *Responsibility for Justice*, 123ff.

I intentionally uphold the unjust global trade regimes that oppress her, as Forst's model seems to require. I may not even be aware of the effect of my purchasing decisions on her, and yet my actions, together with the actions of millions of other American consumers, reinforce and maintain a structure of domination from which we systematically benefit—above all by our access to cheap clothing and household goods—and she is oppressed and exploited.[69] It seems to me that although the dyadic, master-subject model of domination may be adequate for illuminating some relations of power in some contexts, including international relations between states, it is inadequate for making sense of relations of structural oppression such as the sweatshop case. In other words, a richer account of domination, one that starts from the fact of multiple domination and illuminates structural features of domination, is needed to make sense of genuinely transnational relations of domination. Only such an account will enable us to take into account all of the relevant relations of domination that have harmful impacts on individuals that our system of international arrangements should attempt to address.

While Pettit's dyadic, master-subject understanding of domination may be helpful for illuminating certain aspects of international power relations, insofar as states can stand in for either master or subject in his dyadic account, it is insufficient for illuminating more complex, multiple, and intersecting structures of domination at the global level, particularly the economic structures that serve to entrench global poverty. These structures are also closely related to the global subordination of women, since women make up a disproportionate share of the world's poor. Such structures and the transnational relations of domination that they enable are crucial for understanding what Barnett and Duvall call "the enduring structures and processes of global life that enable and constrain the ability of actors to shape their fates and their futures."[70]

CONCLUSION

Pettit maintains, plausibly enough, that what we ultimately care about when we criticize relations of domination is the evil done to individuals as a result of such domination. This is the assumption of normative individualism. But if we assume this, then we cannot restrict our account of domination to the

[69] My response to those who would argue that such girls are better off working in sweatshops in the cities of Bangladesh than they would be if they had stayed in their home villages is that even if this were true, it would not follow from this premise that working in such sweatshops is *not* a form of oppression. To see why, consider a simple analogy: if I take a child who is starving in off of the street, feed, clothe, and attend to all of his bodily needs but also make him my personal slave, does the fact that he is in some material sense better off than he was before mean that he is not now oppressed?

[70] Barnett and Duvall, "Power in International Politics," 41.

kind of dyadic, internationalist conception offered by Pettit. To make sense of the myriad ways in which individuals suffer domination in the context of transnational relations of power, we need a structural conception of power that illuminates the role of the overlapping, unintentional actions of a multitude of different agents in creating, maintaining, and reproducing relations of domination.

BIBLIOGRAPHY

Allen, Amy. *The Power of Feminist Theory: Domination, Resistance, Solidarity*. Boulder, CO: Westview Press, 1999.

Bachrach, Peter, and Morton Baratz. "The Two Faces of Power." *American Political Science Review* 56, no. 4 (1962): 947–52.

Barnett, Michael, and Raymond Duvall. "Power in International Politics." *International Organization* 59, no. 1 (2005): 39–75.

Bohman, James. "Domination, Global Harms, and the Priority of Injustice: Expanding Transnational Republicanism." In *Domination and Global Political Justice: Conceptual, Historical, and Institutional Perspectives*, edited by Barbara Buckinx, Jonathan Trejo-Mathys, and Timothy Waligore. New York: Routledge, 2015.

Bourdieu, Pierre. *Masculine Domination*. Stanford: Stanford University Press, 2001.

Culp, Julian. *Global Justice and Development*. Basingstoke: Palgrave Macmillan, 2014.

Dahl, Robert. "The Concept of Power." *Behavioral Science* 2, no. 3 (1957): 201–15.

Digeser, Peter. "The Fourth Face of Power." *Journal of Politics* 54, no. 4 (1992): 977–1007.

Forst, Rainer. *The Right to Justification: Elements of a Constructivist Theory of Justice*. Translated by Jeffrey Flynn. New York: Columbia University Press, 2012.

Forst, Rainer. "Transnational Justice and Non-Domination: A Discourse-Theoretical Approach." In *Domination and Global Political Justice: Conceptual, Historical, and Institutional Perspectives*, edited by Barbara Buckinx, Jonathan Trejo-Mathys, and Timothy Waligore. New York: Routledge, 2015.

Foucault, Michel. "The Subject and Power." In *Power*, vol. 3 of *Essential Works of Michel Foucault*, edited by James Faubion. New York: The New Press, 2000.

Fraser, Nancy. "Beyond the Master/Subject Model: Reflections on Carole Pateman's *Sexual Contract*." *Social Text* 37 (1993): 173–81.

Geuss, Raymond. *Philosophy and Real Politics*. Princeton: Princeton University Press, 2008.

Haugaard, Mark. "The Three- and Four-Dimensional Power Debates Reconsidered: Power Over as Concerted Power." *Constellations* (forthcoming).

Laborde, Cécile. "Republicanism and Global Justice: A Sketch." *European Journal of Political Theory* 9, no. 1 (2010): 48–69.

Lukes, Steven. *Power: A Radical View*. London: Macmillan, 1974.

Lukes, Steven. *Power: A Radical View*. 2nd ed. New York: Palgrave Macmillan, 2005.

MacKinnon, Catharine. "Difference and Dominance: On Sex Discrimination." In *Feminism Unmodified: Discourses on Life and Law*. Cambridge: Harvard University Press, 1987.

Markell, Patchen. "The Insufficiency of Non-Domination." *Political Theory* 36, no. 9 (2008): 9–36.

Pettit, Philip. "Dahl's Power and Republican Freedom." *Journal of Power* 1, no. 1 (April 2008): 67–74.

Pettit, Philip. "A Republican Law of Peoples." *European Journal of Political Theory* 9, no. 1 (2010): 70–94.

Pettit, Philip. "The Republican Law of Peoples: A Restatement." In *Domination and Global Political Justice: Conceptual, Historical, and Institutional Perspectives*, edited by Barbara Buckinx, Jonathan Trejo-Mathys, and Timothy Waligore. New York: Routledge, 2015.

Pettit, Philip. *Republicanism: A Theory of Freedom and Government*. Oxford: Oxford University Press, 1997.

Pettit, Philip. "Three Axioms, Four Theorems." In *Republicanism and Political Theory*, edited by Cécile Laborde and John Maynor. Oxford: Blackwell, 2008.

Saar, Martin. "Power and Critique." *Journal of Power* 3, no. 1 (April 2010): 7–20.

Thompson, Michael. "A Functionalist Theory of Social Domination." *Journal of Political Power* 6, no. 2 (2013): 179–99.

Tully, James. "On Law, Democracy and Imperialism." In *Imperialism and Civic Freedom*, vol. 2 of *Public Philosophy in a New Key*. Cambridge: Cambridge University Press, 2008.

Young, Iris Marion. *Justice and the Politics of Difference*. Princeton: Princeton University Press, 1990.

Young, Iris Marion. *Responsibility for Justice*. Oxford: Oxford University Press, 2011.

Weber, Max. *Economy and Society: An Outline of Interpretive Sociology*, vol. 1. Edited by Guenther Roth and Claus Wittich. Berkeley: University of California Press, 1978.

Part II

History, Imperialism, and Race

6 The (In)Compatibility of Liberty and Empire in Machiavelli's Political Thought

John P. McCormick

Machiavelli appears to be the most unabashed champion of imperialism—literally, of domination across borders—in the history of Western political thought. He seems to measure political success by the extent of a polity's territorial expanse rather than its quality of civic life or even temporal continuity; i.e., he seems to care only how much *imperium* a regime possesses rather than how it is wielded, or even for how long.

Moreover, Machiavelli was fixated on, and exceedingly annoyed by, the following historical contrast: while the ancient Italians militarily conquered and compelled to obedience foreign peoples like the French, the Germans, and the Spanish, contemporary Italians are consistently invaded and molested by these very same, former subject peoples. One could interpret a certain strand of Machiavelli's work as a provocation for overturning this situation and for restoring Italy's heretofore supreme geopolitical status.

At the more subtle level of principle, Machiavelli's greatest work, the *Discourses*,[1] champions both liberty and glory as the ultimate ends of republican politics. When these ends seem to collide, even the most sensitive commentators conclude that the Florentine chooses glory, best achieved through the acquisition of empire, as the goal that republics should pursue

---

[1] See Niccolò Machiavelli, *Discorsi Sopra la Prima Deca di Tito Livio* [circa 1513–1519], in *Opere I: I Primi Scritti Politici*, ed. Corrado Vivanti (Torino: Einaudi-Gallimard, 1997), 193–525; hereafter cited as "D" in the main text with book and chapter numbers in parentheses. In English, see Machiavelli, *Discourses on Livy*, eds. and trans. Harvey C. Mansfield, Jr. and Nathan Tarcov (Chicago: The University of Chicago Press, 1997) and Machiavelli, *Discourses on the First Decade of Livy*, in *The Sweetness of Power: Machiavelli's* Discourses *and Guicciardini's* Considerations, eds. and trans. James. B. Atkinson and David Sices (DeKalb, IL: Northern Illinois Press, 2002). See also Machiavelli, "Il Principe (De Principatipus)" [composed circa 1513 and published in 1532], in *Opere I: I Primi Scritti Politici*, ed. Corrado Vivanti (Torino: Einaudi-Gallimard, 1997), 114–92; this is abbreviated as "P," cited with chapter numbers within the text. I rely on the following translations, emended where noted: Harvey C. Mansfield, Jr., ed. and trans., *Machiavelli's The Prince*, 2nd ed. (Chicago: The University of Chicago Press, 1998), and William J. Connell, ed. and trans., *Machiavelli's The Prince* (Boston: Bedford/St. Martin's, 2005).

above all others. In other words, when push comes to shove, empire trumps liberty for Machiavelli.

I want to call into question the interpretation of Machiavelli as an unqualified champion of empire on two grounds: (1) I show that Machiavelli's ostensible endorsement of empire actually plays an important part in a rhetorical strategy whereby the Florentine persuades aristocratically biased republicans, like those to whom he dedicates the book, to accept a constitutional model more inclusive and empowering of common citizens than they would have otherwise accepted; and (2) I demonstrate that Machiavelli strongly disapproves of the manner in which the Roman Republic, his paragon of republican virtue, was corrupted and brought down precisely by its acquisition of empire, and that Machiavelli endorses measures that would have inhibited Roman imperial acquisition by preserving socioeconomic equality at home.

Thus, when one conceives of liberty in terms of extensive popular participation and equitable socioeconomic conditions, Machiavelli prioritizes freedom over imperial expansion. I demonstrate that Machiavelli uses his reconstructed Roman republic to moderate the oppressive behavior of nobles, aristocrats, and the grandi toward the common people. Machiavelli attempts to convince his declared audience of young grandi to forsake their attachment to the aristocratic republican model exemplified by Sparta and Venice and instead opt for the Roman, popularly inclusive republican model—as Machiavelli reconstructs it, a much more democratic republican model.

In the early chapters of the *Discourses*, Machiavelli attempts to convince the grandi that the best republic is one in which they maximize the material and immaterial benefits they gain from *diminished* political preeminence in such regimes *and* institutional arrangements that protect young patricians from the deleterious results of their own appetite for domination. Machiavelli advises the grandi, against their inclinations, natural and cultivated, to render themselves more accountable to a militarily and civically empowered common citizenry.

Machiavelli sets the parameters of a political bargain, the terms of which he hopes to maneuver his dedicatees into accepting: the grandi constrain their appetite for complete domination of the people at home, granting the latter their own magistracies—the tribunes—with lawmaking authority in popular assemblies and direct judgment over political crimes, so that the people may serve as the regime's "guard of liberty." In return, the young grandi gain the opportunity for increased riches and eternal fame by pursuing empire, that is, by commanding citizen-soldiers in the domination of countless others abroad.

With exemplary models of Roman captains *cum* conquerors, Machiavelli diverts the grandi from short-term domination over their own people to long-term domination over mortality. Whether Machiavelli actually anticipates or even hopes that the nobles make good on this opportunity remains an open question on this reading. Roman-style imperialism may be only one of several military options for Machiavelli—in fact, given the decisive role that imperial expansion plays in Machiavelli's account of liberty's demise and the republic's collapse, it is quite likely not the most preferable.

1 YOUNG ARISTOCRATS AND THE APPETITE TO OPPRESS

In his magnum opus, the *Discourses*, Niccolò Machiavelli famously praises the Roman Republic for attaining incomparable greatness (*grandezza*) and for enjoying unprecedented liberty (*libertà*). The former, he indicates, resulted from the republic's unparalleled acquisition of empire; the latter corresponds with the role played by Rome's common people, the plebeians, rather than its nobility, as the "guardian of liberty" in domestic politics. When interpreters detect, quite rightly, the fact that these principles fundamentally collide in Machiavelli's analysis, most interpreters conclude that greatness, and hence empire, ultimately take precedence over freedom and popular government in the Florentine's preferences. This essay illustrates in further depth the conflict between empire and liberty in Machiavelli's *Discourses* and accentuates the reasons why many readers conclude, with some cause, that Machiavelli favors the former over the latter. But ultimately it demonstrates that Machiavelli, in fact, favors just the opposite; he criticizes imperial conquest, and offers means by which republics might evade the corruption of liberty that inevitably results from the pursuit of empire.

The puzzle of empire and liberty, I suggest, can be solved when one reads the *Discourses* from the perspective of young aristocrats like those to whom Machiavelli dedicates the work: Cosimo Rucellai and Zanobi Buondelmonti. Cosimo and Zanobi were young nobles—*ottimati* in the parlance of the day, *grandi* in Machiavelli's general usage (P 9; D I.4). Both young men belonged to families with long traditions of influence and command in Florence and, more pertinently, families with well-known biases against any republic that was not a *governo stretto*; that is, a polity within which only the very few, wealthiest citizens rule. And yet the interpretive literature generally ignores the class background and social perspective of the young Rucellai and Buondelmonti, tending instead to present Machiavelli's dedicatees simply as "humanists and literati," "republican sympathizers," patriots, and, overwhelmingly, just "friends" of Machiavelli.[2] I demonstrate that Machiavelli uses his reconstructed, *imperial* Roman Republic to moderate the behavior of such young grandi vis-à-vis the people.

[2] See Quentin Skinner, *Past Masters: Machiavelli* (New York: Hill and Wang, 1981), 49–50; Maurizio Viroli, *Founders: Machiavelli* (Oxford: Oxford University Press, 1998), 14, 159; and, e.g., Harvey C. Mansfield, *Machiavelli's New Modes and Orders: A Study of the Discourses on Livy* (Ithaca: Cornell University Press, 1979), 21.

2 AN INCONCLUSIVE DEBATE OVER THE POPOLO VERSUS THE GRANDI

As stated above, the problem of empire and liberty in Machiavelli's analysis arises out of a controversy over which kind of polity is best, an aristocratic or democratic republic, and hence which part of a republic should hold ultimate authority, the nobles or the people. In the early chapters of the *Discourses*, Machiavelli initially attempts to adjudicate this issue with reference to liberty exclusively, and not by invoking empire when he stages a rhetorical debate between aristocratic and popular spokesmen. Machiavelli's immediate audience of young grandi, like most aristocrats before them, will be alarmed by the prospect of the common people's inclusion in government, because such inclusion, they surmise, entails greater prospect of public disturbances on the part of the people. Exemplary for such an audience is the purportedly unruly behavior of the people in democratic Athens and, earlier in Florence's history, during the Ciompi Revolt (1378). Historically, the Athenian *demos* famously ostracized or executed prominent citizens, and, within recent memory, Florence's lower guildsmen and unenfranchised woolworkers violently seized the city for several months.[3]

Consult Felix Gilbert's research on the pro-oligarchic/anti-populist preconceptions of the Florentine ottimati in this era, including members of the Rucellai and Buondelmonti families: Gilbert, "Florentine Political Assumptions in the Period of Savonarola and Soderini," *Journal of the Warburg and Courtauld Institute* 20, no. 3/4 (1957), 187–214; Gilbert, "The Venetian Constitution in Florentine Political Thought," in *Florentine Studies: Politics and Society in Renaissance Florence*, ed. Nicolai Rubinstein (Evanston, IL: Northwestern University Press, 1968), 442–62; and Gilbert, "Bernardo Rucellai and the Orti Oricellari: A Study on the Origin of Modern Political Thought," in *History: Choice and Commitment*, ed. Felix Gilbert (Cambridge, MA: Harvard University Press, 1977), 215–46. On the Florentine ottimati's general contempt for Machiavelli, see Robert Black "Machiavelli, Servant of the Florentine Republic," in *Machiavelli and Republicanism*, eds. Gisela Bock, Quentin Skinner, and Maurizio Viroli (Cambridge: Cambridge University Press, 1990), 71–99, 97; John M. Najemy, "The Controversy Surrounding Machiavelli's Service to the Republic," in *Machiavelli and Republicanism*, eds. Gisela Bock, Quentin Skinner, and Maurizio Viroli (Cambridge: Cambridge University Press, 1990), 102–17, 117; Felix Gilbert, *Machiavelli and Guicciardini: Politics and History in Sixteenth-Century Florence* (Princeton, NJ: Princeton University Press, 1965), 172–74; and Roberto Ridolfi, *The Life of Niccolò Machiavelli*, trans. C. Grayson (Chicago: The University of Chicago Press, 1963), 130–32.

[3] See Gene Brucker, "The Revolt of the Ciompi," in *Florentine Studies: Politics and Society in Renaissance Florence*, ed. Nicolai Rubinstein (Evanston, IL: Northwestern University Press, 1968), 314–56; and John M. Najemy, *Corporatism and Consensus in Florentine Electoral Politics, 1280–1400* (Chapel Hill, NC: University of North Carolina Press, 1982). The purported excesses of the Ciompians' behavior and demands would play an important role in Florentine humanism's efforts to legitimate both the Albizzi oligarchy and the Medici principality that subsequently ruled the city. See James Hankins, ed., *Renaissance Civic Humanism: Reappraisals and Reflections* (Cambridge: Cambridge University Press, 2000), 75–178.

Machiavelli claims that the tumults that often characterize such republics do not result simply from inappropriately extensive popular participation; there are actually *two* causes of such discord, two seemingly irreconcilable appetites: "[i]n every republic are two diverse humors, that of the people and that of the great, and all the laws that are made in favor of freedom arise from their disunion" (D I.4; cf., P 9). And even when the conflict between the popolo and the grandi generate such tumults, Machiavelli insists, the consequences are not necessarily dire. He suggests that exiles, fines, and capital executions were kept to an absolute minimum in the quite tumultuous Roman Republic and, moreover, were spread out over 300 years (D I.4). The grandi, Machiavelli intimates, need not fear unreasonably the humor of the people, that is, their desire *not* to be oppressed. The people act rambunctiously, he suggests, only when they've actually been oppressed or when they have sufficient reason to be suspicious of being oppressed. Thus, Machiavelli declares, "the desires of free peoples are rarely pernicious to freedom" (D I.4).

Machiavelli cajoles his aristocratic dedicatees further by insisting that the plebs respond only reactively or passively in most cases of oppression anyway. In accord with their nature, Machiavelli insists that the people generally *refrain* from doing something instead of *actively* doing something: in response to actual oppression, for instance, the Roman plebs exit the city or fail to enroll for military service—they do not engage in direct violent action against the grandi. Moreover, he insists that the harshness with which the Athenian *demos* treated their prominent citizens was perhaps a justifiable response to the experience of tyranny (D I.28); and in the *Florentine Histories*, while Machiavelli criticizes the Ciompians for acting in an excessively violent fashion, he nevertheless carefully catalogues their legitimate grievances against the republic's economic and political elites.[4]

Because they desire only *not* to be oppressed, and since they generally act on that desire reactively rather than preemptively, Machiavelli suggests that the people ought to be entrusted with the "guard of freedom" within republics. This is a difficult case to make to an aristocratic audience. Buondelmonti and Rucellai undoubtedly think of republics as regimes within which members of the "best families" circulate political offices among themselves. They act freely vis-à-vis the people in such a regime by exercising command over the latter through these offices, and by refusing to share such offices. The general citizenry might select who specifically among the nobility holds office at any particular time—election being, after all, an aristocratic appointment device—but the people will not exert any further control over them than that.[5]

---

[4] See Niccolò Machiavelli, *Florentine Histories* [1525], trans. Laura F. Banfield and Harvey C. Mansfield (Princeton, NJ: Princeton University Press, 1988), III.12–22.
[5] Bernard Manin, *The Principles of Representative Government* (Cambridge: Cambridge University Press, 1997), 42–93, 132–60.

Machiavelli points out that Sparta and Venice were republics that placed the guard of liberty with the nobles (D I.5); in other words, they reserved all magistracies for the grandi and entirely excluded the people from political participation. Conventional wisdom among the ottimati in Florence insisted that Sparta and, most especially, Venice were the best republics due to their tranquility and longevity.[6] Certainly, Sparta and Venice satisfy the young grandi's definition of liberty: they facilitate the young grandi's exercise of offices over the people on their own terms rather than on terms set by a foreign or domestic prince or, even, on the people's terms.

Machiavelli concedes the longevity of Sparta and Venice's "freedom" (D I.5). But, while emphasizing his own voice ("I say"), Machiavelli argues, on normative and descriptive grounds, for granting the guard of liberty to the people, as he claims the Romans did. The people desire not to be dominated and so, "having a greater will to live free," they have less appetite to usurp or seize liberty. The people can prevent the grandi from seizing liberty through an ensemble of pleb-enabling and noble-constraining institutions; i.e., through practices and behaviors that constitute the political concessions that Machiavelli extracts from the grandi over the course of Book I of the *Discourses*. These include examples of collective plebeian action that stops short of looting and murder, such as those mentioned above: the institution of the plebeian tribunes, practices such as public accusations and popularly judged political trials, assemblies where the people deliberate over and enact laws, eligibility to stand for and actually hold noble-dominated magistracies, and—most painfully for the grandi, as it turns out (D I.37)—claims for equitable distribution of property.

After making his personal case for Rome as the republic to be emulated, and for the people as worthy guards of liberty—a speech in which Machiavelli assumes the role of a plebeian magistrate, a tribune perhaps[7]—Machiavelli relinquishes the floor to an unnamed party, first singular, then possibly plural ("he . . . says," "they give as examples"). This spokesman or these spokesmen make the case against Machiavelli's Rome and in favor of an aristocratic guardianship of liberty. Although taken by some commentators to be Machiavelli's true opinion, the views expressed by the spokesman/spokesmen for the grandi amount to little more than the typical "aggrandizing plebs'" interpretation of Roman history that was

[6] For representative views of Venice in the Florentine political imagination, see Gilbert, "The Venetian Constitution in Florentine Political Thought"; and Francesco Guicciardini, *Dialogue on the Government of Florence* [1524], trans. Alison Brown (Cambridge: Cambridge University Press, 1994). On views of Venice more widely, see William J. Bouwsma, *Venice and the Defense of Republican Liberty: Renaissance Values in the Age of the Counter Reformation* (Berkeley: University of California Press, 1968); and Eco O.G. Haitsma Mulier, *The Myth of Venice and Dutch Republican Thought in the Seventeenth Century*, trans. Gerard T. Moran (Assen, NL: Van Gorcum, 1980).

[7] Mansfield, *Machiavelli's New Modes and Orders,* 46.

found in, for instance, Livy before and Montesquieu after Machiavelli,[8] an interpretation that was prevalent among ottimati like Guicciardini and the elder Rucellai in his own day.

The noble spokesmen, who for all intents and purposes could be the two dedicatees with whom Machiavelli converses here, make no pretense of justifying a monopoly of power in the patrician hands on the grounds that they are "the best" or that they "deserve" it. Through this admission by the noble spokesman or spokesmen, Machiavelli may signal that his dedicatees have been instructed successfully in this indisputable fact of their nature: they are driven by an appetite to dominate, period. The spokesmen for the grandi admit in an unqualified fashion the fact that the nobles seek to hold the guard of liberty—that is, exclusive or predominant political power—as a "stick in their hand." In other words, they aspire to attain offices and honors to command and oppress others—literally and figuratively, to beat them. If the speech contains anything more than a self-serving justification for noble guardianship, it is the following claim that amounts to a barely veiled threat: when the grandi hold the guardianship, republics "better satisfy [the grandi's] ambitions, and having a greater part of the republic, by holding this stick in their hand, they are inclined to more contentment" (D I.5).

In other words, if given "this stick," the grandi will have their ambitions satisfied "more," but not completely; and thus they will be given cause to be "more" contented, but not necessarily fully content. With this threat, the nobles offer to disrupt a free way of life *less often* if they are given a weapon by which they can deprive other citizens of liberty. But, in their own words, there is no guarantee at all that possession of this weapon will prove sufficient to satisfy their oppressive appetite. Conversely, in Machiavelli's description of a republic where the people guard liberty, it seems as if there exists a greater possibility that liberty can be shared and that each class's definition of liberty can be partially satisfied. But there is no such possibility for anyone but the grandi to be "free" when *they* act as the guardians of liberty.

In any case, in spite of the partisanship implied by the perspective of the plebeian magistrate that Machiavelli adopts at the start of this dispute—or perhaps because of it—Machiavelli does not decide for one side or the other, for Roman popular guardianship or Spartan/Venetian oligarchic guardianship, at the debate's conclusion. While the grandi may reveal that they want to dominate, and while they might confess to harboring an oppressive humor, they will *never* admit that the people are less inclined toward oppression than they are—an admission that would logically necessitate

[8] For instance Titus Livy, *History of Rome (Ab Urbe Condita), Books 1–10*, vols. 1–4, trans. B. O. Foster (Cambridge, MA: Harvard University Press [Loeb], 1919–1926), IV.8–9; and, in general, Charles Louis de Secondat, Baron de Montesquieu, *Considerations on the Causes of the Greatness of the Romans and their Decline* [1734], trans. David Lowenthal (Indianapolis: Hackett, 1999).

that the nobles relinquish to the people the guardianship of liberty. Rather than make such a concession of their own free will, they dissemble, deflect, and feign vulnerability ("we're both the same; they're worse; ok, we want a stick to beat others; no, they want the stick; it is they who threaten *us* with sticks!"). Clearly, the grandi will not cede any power to the people either out of the goodness of their hearts or on the basis of sound reasoning. And while Machiavelli seems willing to leave the dispute a draw, he suddenly resorts to an almost unannounced criterion to break the stalemate: the prospect of empire.

Machiavelli mentioned earlier that republics like Rome that endure tumults and permit extensive popular participation may "avail themselves of the people in important things" (D I.4), but he doesn't specify exactly what that means. Rome, of course, is most famous for the territorial expanse of its empire, and the people's involvement in military affairs mentioned in this section makes this expansive empire possible. Indeed, in I.5, Machiavelli states rather matter-of-factly that Rome is the model of an imperial republic, while Venice and Sparta are the models for self-contained republics. Therefore, the decision in favor of one or the other type of republic depends, *not* on one's view of the respective natures of the people or the great, but ultimately on whether or not empire is a desired goal.

After tossing this tiny explosive into the laps of those whom he's just maneuvered into confessing their appetite to oppress, Machiavelli promises them that he will elaborate further on this tantalizing prospect for expansive oppression in the next chapter.

To summarize what has just transpired: the people's spokesman could not settle the verbal dispute with the aristocratic spokesmen in I.5; he cannot force a conclusion on the grandi who are stronger and better resourced than he is. A seemingly external standard, empire, must be invoked to settle the quarrel.[9] This dialogue displays Machiavelli's impotence in the art of verbally persuading his young patrician interlocutors. To encourage Cosimo and Zanobi in the direction of a more democratic republic, Machiavelli of necessity resorts to the bait of greater advantage based on what the grandi admit that they want most: greater prospects and avenues for oppression. In the next chapter, I.6, empire may motivate young grandi in ways that rational arguments by a plebeian spokesman or magistrate cannot. Before moving on in this vein, it must be noted that, having whet the appetite of his audience with the prospect of imperial rule, Machiavelli happens to mention, almost as an aside, the fact that the grandi cannot "manage" (*maneggiare*) a people enlisted in warfare in just any "mode" the former may please (D I.6).

---

[9] For extensive discussions on the place of empire in Machiavelli's political thought, see David Armitage, *The Ideological Origins of the British Empire* (Cambridge: Cambridge University Press, 2000), 125–45; and Mikael Hörnqvist, *Machiavelli and Empire* (Cambridge: Cambridge University Press, 2004).

3 EMPIRE'S ALLURE AND THE DISCREDITING OF ARISTOCRATIC REPUBLICS

Of the entire *Discourses*, I.6 is one of the most closely studied chapters.[10] Many commentators, on the basis of solid evidence and serious hermeneutic efforts, conclude the following: in light of the many shortcomings and inconsistencies of Machiavelli's analysis of Sparta and Venice, his unjustifiable preference for Rome must be motivated primarily by his desire to unleash human appetite in an unprecedented fashion, and/or by his endorsement of the human pursuit of greatness in history. On this view, Machiavelli subordinates liberty to the necessity of acquisition and/or to a normative preference for greatness.[11]

Does this admittedly puzzling chapter, I.6, look any different when read from the perspective of the book's young patrician dedicatees? At first blush, the chapter disappoints those who turn to it for an immediate discussion of republican imperialism: empire is mentioned in neither the chapter heading nor in the first two, rather long paragraphs. Machiavelli obliquely refers to it in his observation that the Venetian grandi, or "gentlemen," did not put the populace "to work in things in which they could seize authority" (D I.6). This refers back to the opposite kind of republic, Rome, which, as mentioned in I.5, makes use of the people "in important things." In addition, empire, or lack thereof, is pertinent to Machiavelli's discussion in these passages of Sparta's resistance to growth. Rather than empire, the chapter actually continues to investigate the issue of democratic versus oligarchic republics—Rome versus Venice/Sparta—but this time from a different angle; namely, whether the "great effects" (*effetti grandi*) produced in Rome could be achieved without the controversies, tumults, and enmities between the people and the Senate that occurred there.

Yet exactly what are the great effects presented to the grandi at this point? The laws that foster "liberty" that Machiavelli mentions? Or the empire that he invokes at the cessation of the debate between the aristocratic and popular spokesmen? To the frustration of the imperially curious, Machiavelli

---

[10] Leo Strauss, *Thoughts on Machiavelli* (Glencoe: The Free Press, 1958), 110–14; Mansfield, *Machiavelli's New Modes and Orders*, pp. 45–53; Mansfield, *Machiavelli's Virtue* (Chicago: The University of Chicago Press, 1996), 85–92; Victoria Kahn, *Machiavellian Rhetoric: From the Counter-Reformation to Milton* (Princeton, NJ: Princeton University Press, 1994), 50–51, 261 n. 13; Patrick J. Coby, *Machiavelli's Romans: Liberty and Greatness in the Discourses on Livy* (Lanham: Lexington Books, 1999), 39–41; and Armitage, *The Ideological Origins of the British Empire*, 128–32.

[11] Among Strauss-influenced investigations: Markus Fischer, *Well-Ordered License: On the Unity of Machiavelli's Thought* (Lanham, MD: Lexington Books, 2000); Coby, *Machiavelli's Romans*, 261–68, accentuates greatness; the contributors to Paul A. Rahe, ed., *Machiavelli's Liberal Republican Legacy* (Cambridge: Cambridge University Press, 2005) prioritize the appetite for acquisition.

seems to be treating liberty as the great effect, mentioning both Rome's "free way of life" and Sparta/Venice, who were "free for a long while without enmities and tumults" (D I.6). But it seems strange to associate tumults with freedom by pointing out, as Machiavelli does here, that tumults caused the *ruin* of Rome's free way of life after the time of the brothers Gracchus. *This* is their great effect? The republic's decline and fall?

Machiavelli invokes the "time of" the Gracchi, rather than the brothers themselves, and their land reforms aimed at ameliorating economic inequality between the Roman nobility and the plebeians. He later shows, in the midst of an apparent indictment of the Gracchi, that it was the ambition of the grandi and the avarice of the Senate that made the brothers' popular appeal possible, indeed necessary, and set in motion the republic's decline (D I.37). He may reproach their method there, but he does not besmirch the Gracchan cause.[12] Yet this issue of oppression by the grandi and responses to it by the people in Rome relates directly to the issue of "great effects" without tumult in the other type of republic. How did the Venetian and Spartan grandi exclude the people politically so as to avoid tumults, yet restrain themselves from such thorough oppression that the people neither revolted, nor resorted to a Caesar in response?

Machiavelli argues that Venice and Sparta were successful, noble-dominated, and domestically tranquil *governi stretti* because of their small size (D I.6). Small republics may sustain themselves without extensive inclusion of the people; the proportion of nobles to commoners in such regimes remains so large as to keep the latter pacified. One might venture to say that the domestic politics of Sparta and Venice appear to be fantasies from a Machiavellian standpoint: in both cities there are nobles who do not oppress the people, either of their own volition (Venice) or as the result of a separation of the nobles from the plebs imposed by monarchical authority (Sparta). Thus, the grandi are free to govern but not to oppress the plebs in these polities. But given their fundamentally oppressive nature, as Machiavelli defines it, can the grandi really be "free" when they observe a distinction between governing and oppressing?

The people, for their part, seem to exist in what is their natural state in both cities: absent oppression by the nobles they neither agitate against them, nor, for that matter, seek any role in governing whatsoever. Machiavelli notes that Venice formed its aristocracy before a populace, in any real sense of the term, had developed there. Thus, the people never played a role

---

[12] Prejudice against the Gracchi among Florentine patricians is perhaps best typified by Leonardo Bruni, *The Humanism of Leonardo Bruni: Selected Texts*, eds. and trans. Gordon Griffiths, James Hankins, and David Thompson (Binghamton, NY: Medieval & Renaissance Texts & Studies, 1987), 186; and Francesco Guicciardini, "Considerations of the *Discourses* of Niccolò Machiavelli" [1530], in *The Sweetness of Power: Machiavelli's* Discourses *and Guicciardini's* Considerations, eds. and trans. James B. Atkinson and David Sices (DeKalb, IL: Northern Illinois University Press, 2002), 381–438, 395.

in the formation of the regime, as they had in Rome, and consequently never leveraged a significant institutional role for themselves. On closer inspection, however, Machiavelli seems to identify a way of governing the people that actually qualifies as oppression; oppression that merely goes uncontested. The Venetian people apparently never experienced liberty, and hence it is not that they live free from oppression, but rather that they don't know how to contest oligarchic governance *cum* oppression "because nothing had been taken away from them" (D I.6). But people who have experienced a modicum of liberty under a prince-Senate competition, as in early Rome, or under a *governo largo*, as in Florence, will not refrain from challenging grandi domination once they've lost such liberty or experience its diminution (cf. P 5). Moreover, emphasizing the connection between popular liberty and a martial citizenry, Machiavelli notes that Venice undermined social dynamism by prohibiting the people's participation in military affairs (D I.6).

Machiavelli mentions numerous factors that prevented tumults from ensuing in Sparta—insulation from foreigners, a small population, relative equality of conditions, and restrictions on growth. Unlike the Roman Republic, which was a citizen-making machine, elevating allies and former enemies to partial and even full citizenship (cf. D II.30), Sparta actively inhibited the development of a large and diverse populace by excluding foreigners, even as visitors. Two other factors that forestalled civil discord in Sparta are the role of monarchy and the status of rank. With respect to the latter, Machiavelli observes that the ranks of the city (*gradi della città*) were spread among few citizens and kept at a distance from the plebs. But what kind of rank, which entails both distinction and command, can be kept so far away from subordinates as to go unnoticed? What kind of grades, gradations, distinctions actually matter without palpable comparison and contrast? Subordinates must observe rank—they must see it so that they can acknowledge its bearers as superior if the appetite for prestige in its holders is to be at all satisfied. Subordinates must experience rank—they must feel it, if its holder's appetite to order others about can begin to be realized. Could the unrecognized ranks that Machiavelli locates in Sparta really satisfy the grandi?

The answer may be moot in the Spartan context where one or both kings, who were interposed "in the midst of the nobility," defended the plebs from noble-generated injuries (D I.6). Thus, the Spartan people had no cause to defend themselves actively against the nobles because the kings took responsibility to protect them. I would suggest that a regime with such a watered-down exercise of rank, and with a nobility that is effectively constrained by a monarchical actor, is not a republic at all, but rather a principality. The upshot of all of this is, first, that Venice is an unrealizable republican model for grandi who wish to dominate a regime. In such circumstances they must either establish a regime which does not yet contain a people, or find a city in which the people have never enjoyed even a modicum of liberty. Second, Sparta is an undesirable republican model because it is a trifle too reminiscent of precisely the Medici principality to which the young patrician dedicatees already submit. Machiavelli has thoroughly discredited the Florentine ottimati's two paragons of republicanism on the basis of criteria derived precisely from their own preferences.

But Machiavelli already may have diverted the attention of his audience of young grandi away from Spartan and Venetian liberty—that is, mere oppression of the people within their own republic—or at least he may have problematized it, by the introduction of empire. Having described the (unattainable and unsatisfying) liberty of the grandi in Venice and Sparta, Machiavelli suggests that Rome could have avoided tumult only if it had imitated the other two by, respectively, not arming the people and not admitting foreigners (D I.6). But in doing both, Rome strengthened the plebs by, literally, putting sticks in their hands and swelling their numbers. Had it not done so, Machiavelli avers, on the one hand, it would not have come to greatness, and, on the other, it would have been weak. These two very different claims may appeal, respectively, to two different kinds of grandi: chance-taking versus risk-averse nobles. Indeed, this passage establishes the strategy that Machiavelli pursues in the rest of the chapter: grandi who are willing to forsake some domination of their own citizens for greater oppression of others abroad (and the greater wealth and fame that accompanies such exploits) will cede some domestic, political role to the people. Grandi who still cling to a definition of liberty whereby they wholly exclude the people from politics and exercise domination over them will be made to fear that such a republic is inherently weak, and hence made to live in constant danger of being annexed by another regime—an eventuality which would certainly curtail the grandi's domestic "liberty."

The latter term does not appear in the balance of the chapter, but its realization may yet be Machiavelli's main objective. He entices the grandi to compromise their notion of liberty (the monopoly on "a political way of life" at home) through appeals to the greatness or necessity of expansion and, in so doing, bargains for the people an unnamed and undefined new kind of liberty: the people assume a larger role in politics than they had been granted previously in republics. As a result the people will be empowered to protect themselves from oppression by the grandi and protect the whole regime from the collapse that domination by the grandi portends. On reflection, then, the comparison of the liberty practiced and guarded in Sparta and Venice, on the one hand, and in Rome, on the other, may have been inappropriate from the start, since they are qualitatively different in important respects. When liberty is conceived as independence from other regimes, the two models are the same; when it is conceived as the play of domestic forces, they are different in kind. Yet Machiavelli often casts the comparison as if "liberty" in both cases were equivalent, adding the element of empire to induce the grandi to tolerate a transition from the one kind of liberty to the other.

Interpreters often assume that the desire for domination that Machiavelli attributes to the grandi in these early chapters of the *Discourses* necessarily entails a desire for eternal fame.[13] But this is not an assumption that Machiavelli makes about either grandi in general or his noble dedicatees a priori. If it were, then the strenuous effort to elevate the Roman over the Spartan and Venetian republics would have been unnecessary. The grandi's appetite to oppress the people of their own polity is *not* in and of itself the same as the desire for worldly glory through imperial conquest. Machiavelli certainly labors to move them from the one to the other, the former to the latter, and in this chapter I have shown that much of the argument and action of the early discourses strategically serves that attempted manipulation. As the history of ancient and early-modern city-states generally shows, most grandi prefer a predominance of men of virtue (that is, wealth and prominence) in magistracies, defensive security over empire, and domestic stability over class conflict.[14] In other words, the grandi within most oligarchies were content with dominating their own regimes and acquiring modest renown within them. The assumption that Machiavelli is encouraging his elite to follow their most basic nature, understood as a desire for glory, is then one step removed from what is actually their more fundamental inclination. They have a humor to dominate, according to Machiavelli, *not* a humor to be famous.

The desire to oppress or command has no inherent link with the desire for glory; it pertains to the pure pleasure of making others do something in accord with one's own will that they would not have done otherwise, or of lording over others a privilege or status that they themselves do not possess. It does not mean, first and foremost, striving to have one's name revered eternally. Bullies do not ordinarily think about eternity (e.g., D III.1). Machiavelli's gambit is to pique such bullies' interest in domination over *mortality and time*, and offer it to them in exchange for some relinquishing of their domination over their own poorer citizens. The first six chapters of the *Discourses* induce the young grandi to include common citizens in politics so that they may be conscripted into the army, which the grandi can use to expand their regime and possibly achieve eternal fame for themselves. While ordinary nobles might require enticements to pursue eternal glory, it is Machiavelli's "founders" or would-be founders who could be said to be driven naturally by a desire for eternal glory—for them, the appetite for oppression and for glory are entwined. But it is doubtful that history demonstrates this or that Machiavelli assumed that this also applies to the

[13] Strauss asserts that Machiavelli's nobles are consumed by "the insatiable desire of each for eternal glory in this world." Leo Strauss, *Thoughts on Machiavelli*, 134; cf., 250.

[14] Daniel Philip Waley, *The Italian City-Republics* (London: Longman Press, 1969), 88–157; Raphael Sealey, *A History of the Greek City-States, 700–338 B.C.* (Berkeley: University of California Press, 1976), 66–133, 238–68; and Anthony Molho, Kurt Raaflaub, and Julia Emlen, eds., *City-States in Classical Antiquity and Medieval Italy* (Ann Arbor: University of Michigan Press, 1991), 33–52, 93–169, 289–354, 565–640.

grandi as a class.[15] In this case, Machiavelli's inspiring examples of illustrious Roman magistrates and commanders in the *Discourses* are prescriptive, not descriptive.

4 DEMOCRATIC REPUBLICS: IMPERIAL OR MERELY MARTIAL?

Machiavelli's choice for Rome, his "belief," as he professes repeatedly at the climax of I.6, in the imperial republican model rules out the possibility of a militarily strong but non-expansive republic. Why might we have cause to doubt his profession of faith in this respect? After all, he uses as the examples of "weak" republics those with a "weak foundation," Sparta and Venice, which are republics with the greatest longevity ever recorded. Perhaps the quality of their internal liberty pales in comparison with Rome's, but their stability, longevity, and, in the Spartan case, martial virtue is incompatible with any conventional understanding of weakness. Perhaps their exploits did not rise to the level of Roman *grandezza*, but they did not lack for renown.

Machiavelli makes a rather unreserved claim about the human condition when he states that the rise and fall of worldly events necessarily requires regimes to expand or fail. This would seem to compel a republic to acquire empire by necessity. Yet Machiavelli's claim is not, in fact, as unequivocal as it first seems. At the conclusion of a highly rhetorical consideration of self-containment versus expansion, and after insisting that necessity *will* inevitably compel a republic to expand, Machiavelli concludes with the less definitive phrase: "*if indeed* necessity brings [a republic] to expand" (D I.6, emphasis added). This is a curiously hesitant way for Machiavelli to discuss a topic like necessity—a topic that he treats so emphatically elsewhere (e.g., I.1).

In total, Machiavelli's endorsement of Rome over Sparta or Venice does not completely disparage the accomplishments of aristocratic republics. He acknowledges that the latter type of republic may enjoy even greater longevity than did Rome (D I.2). Sparta lasted 800 years as a republic; Rome lasted only 300. (Indeed, Machiavelli could not have known that Venice's republic would ultimately last *twice* as long as Rome's.) But when viewed as potential vehicles by which young grandi might satisfy their appetite to oppress, Machiavelli has thoroughly discredited the Spartan and Venetian republican models. Moreover, for Machiavelli himself, I would argue, whatever might be the benefits of aristocratic and socially harmonious republics in terms of longevity, those republics are deficient with respect to the substance of

---

[15] Therefore, like Strauss, Mansfield and Tarcov may too easily collapse the grandi appetite to dominate with the appetite for glory: without qualification they equate "those whose natures insist on [ruling]" with "those who want glory." See Harvey C. Mansfield and Nathan Tarcov, *Machiavelli's Discourses on Livy*, xxviii; cf., Mansfield, *Machiavelli's Virtue*, 238.

political culture, the quality of public policy, and efficacy in military affairs. These can only be achieved through the antagonistic relationship between the grandi and the people that occurs in a *governo largo*, where the people are armed. Sparta, no matter how successful, was not as great as Rome because it did not enjoy as rich a civic life, nor did it acquire as much empire (D I.6). Thus, the active civic life enjoyed by Machiavelli's popularly based Rome is not a peaceful, bucolic, or tranquil arrangement of social interaction. Though he never distinguishes the two conceptually, discord seems to be good both in itself—as a preferred way of conducting public life—and as a means to better policy and military success.

But given the history of republics, most of which look more like Sparta or Venice than Rome, and based on the political prejudices of the Florentine ottimati discussed above, it is safe to assume that many grandi will *not* be seduced by the promise of imperial glory into tolerating popular inclusion and public tumults "as necessary inconveniences for the greatness achieved by Rome" (D I.6). Therefore, besides the carrot (glory or greatness) and the stick (the necessity of expansion), an added element—the fear that weakness will lead to regime collapse—is required to encourage most grandi to accept such inconveniences. At the end of the chapter Machiavelli reminds his audience of one of those inconveniences—a plebeian tribunate that enables the people to guard liberty—and he introduces public accusation by which common citizens, but especially the tribunes, could bring other citizens to account. So besides being opposed by the plebs and their tribunes, the grandi are now encouraged to allow themselves to be indicted by and tried before the people for suspicion of usurping liberty.

In light of these institutional prescriptions, while appetite and greatness play no small role in the *Discourses*, I would suggest that greatness and appetite are inducements that Machiavelli uses to motivate a grandi audience to pursue empire, not for its own sake, but as a mechanism that encourages greater popular participation in politics. The Roman model promises more liberty for citizens at home, but diminution of it for the citizens of other republics abroad. The Spartan/Venetian model promises virtually no liberty for most citizens at home, but it does not, for the most part, threaten republics abroad. Machiavelli is quite possibly ambivalent about both maximum longevity without popular liberty, on the one hand, and, on the other, maximum expansion that destroys liberty elsewhere and corrupts it at home. But he explicitly endorses the Roman model that portends the latter, because it, and *not* the former model—presumably preferred by his dedicatees before reading the *Discourses*—encourages popular inclusion and empowerment.[16]

[16] The aristocratic liberals of the 19th century reversed this logic, endorsing empire, in part, as a way of protecting themselves from the plebeians: e.g., Mill and Tocqueville endorsed imperial projects as a way of channeling outward the domestic threats posed by mass democratization. See Jennifer Pitts, *A Turn to Empire: The Rise of Imperial Liberalism in Britain and France* (Princeton, NJ: Princeton University Press, 2005).

In this respect, the exclusion of the Swiss and the Athenians from the context of the debate over liberty, power, and greatness in I.6 is quite curious. Machiavelli's neglect of Athens cannot be attributed simply to the fact that, as he states in I.2, it is a "simple" popular regime or democracy as opposed to a properly "mixed" republic (i.e., that the Athenians did not institute a proper senate): after all, Machiavelli subsequently refers to Athens as a republic (e.g., I.28). The Athenian republic is an example of a regime that entrusted the people with the guard of liberty and that achieved greatness and fame commensurate with Rome's, and yet whose expansionary policies led to the enslavement of much of Hellas and a devastating collapse of the regime domestically. Athens is a democratic republic that rivals Rome in greatness but that, even more dramatically than Rome, highlights the drawbacks of expansion.

The Swiss are an even more interesting case because Machiavelli sometimes intimates that he admires them as much as he does the Romans and, given their historical and geographic proximity, fears them more.[17] The Swiss are as powerful militarily as were the Romans, but they do not expand, or at least do not expand imperially: when not needed for domestic defence, they lease their troops to other regimes, such as France, which does not arm its people. Additionally, the Swiss augment themselves through enlargements of their confederation—i.e., in a way that preserves or enhances the liberty of new territories, rather than extinguishing it. The Swiss, who constitute a confederation of democratic republics, rival the Romans in power, but they illustrate the fact that imperial expansion is *not* necessary, even as they amplify Machiavelli's preference for military prowess derived from citizen-soldiers.

In light of these considerations, many commentators may accept too readily Machiavelli's association of the Swiss republican confederation with the ancient Etruscan ("Tuscan") one that Rome defeated (D II.4).[18] Machiavelli's examples of how the ancient French seized Lombardy from the Tuscans and how the Romans overwhelmed the latter (D II.4) may be, respectively, an ironic commentary on contemporary French-Swiss relations and an angry underscoring of the present plight of the militarily weak republics of north-central Italy. Machiavelli often remarks that the French monarchy is now the virtual puppet of the Swiss republics (e.g., D II.30), and Tuscan republicanism (under a league or a hegemonic city) is constantly undermined by the Catholic Church's alternating collusions with France, Spain, and the German Emperor to maintain and/or expand the Papal States (see, e.g., P 7, 12, 24). (One must also consider the ramifications for

---

[17] Read I.12, II.4, II.12, II.16 in light of Machiavelli's exchange with Vettori in John M. Najemy, *Between Friends: Discourses of Power and Desire in the Machiavelli-Vettori Letters of 1513–1515* (Princeton, NJ: Princeton University Press, 1993), 156–75.

[18] See, e.g., Strauss, *Thoughts on Machiavelli*, 182.

Machiavelli's endorsement of empire, his less than favorable emphasis on Rome's elimination of liberty in virtuous cities in Tuscany and throughout the ancient Mediterranean (D II.2–3)).

So why does Machiavelli fail to praise or endorse the Swiss republican-military model more openly in the *Discourses*? Quite simply, I suggest, because there is no inducement for his young patrician addressees to adopt it in practice: it promises advantages for the people and none for them. The Swiss model provides the popolo with liberty and equality without in any way compensating the grandi in return. Machiavelli must, on the contrary, entice them with a republican model that entails empire so as to encourage them to accept more egalitarian and participatory politics at home.[19] With the carrot of glory and the stick of necessity, Machiavelli compels his dedicatees to pursue empire, and in the process leverages more populist domestic politics, a Machiavellian democracy,[20] out of them. This is not to say that the grandi will cease their attempts to oppress their own citizens, both at home and on the field of battle, once they enlist the plebeians in the project of empire-building. Machiavelli makes plain the fact that the Roman nobility will continue to try to oppress the plebs directly while they are fighting wars away from the domestic jurisdiction of the tribunes (D I.39), and indirectly through exacerbating socioeconomic inequality in the republic by monopolizing the fruits of empire (D I.37).

Conversely, however, to what extent will the people abide by patrician direction of imperial expansion in the long run, once they've been politically empowered domestically? The grandi might be heartened by the elite manipulation of the plebeians as citizens and troops that Machiavelli describes throughout the *Discourses*, but peoples might learn how to resist it precisely on the basis of Machiavelli's descriptions. Ultimately, whatever the idiosyncratic advantages or inherent deficiencies of the Swiss confederate-republican model invoked by Machiavelli, they are no more peculiar or deleterious than those that he ascribes to the Roman imperial-republican model. Therefore, I suggest that the common assumption that empire trumps liberty in the *Discourses* remains deeply problematic. Indeed, when extolling the virtues of the Roman people in a later chapter, Machiavelli praises them as lovers of *both* "the glory and the common good" of their city (D I.58). If it remains possible to separate liberty or the common good from imperial acquisition, then the model of a popularly and militarily empowered but non-imperial republic would seem to remain a viable option as well.

In sum, expanded popular participation not only improves the lot of common citizens by enabling them to contest and contain the grandi's

[19] For a fine-grained examination of Machiavelli's estimation of the pros and cons of Swiss military policy, see Coby, *Machiavelli's Romans*, 119–20, 138–39.

[20] See John P. McCormick, "Machiavellian Democracy: Controlling Elites with Ferocious Populism," *American Political Science Review* 95, no. 2 (2011): 297–314.

ambition—this is liberty in practice, or what Machiavelli calls a "free way of life"—but also helps both grandi and popolo by better ensuring the longevity of regimes, longevity endangered by the grandi's desire to oppress. Republics must not permit the grandi to oppress the people so thoroughly that they jeopardize the very regime structure that makes some satisfaction of their oppressive appetite possible. After all, in the *Discourses*, Machiavelli insists that the grandi's oppressive appetite is the most serious threat to a republic, just as he declares it to be the primary threat to a principality in *The Prince*.

Republics are usually ruined because the grandi empower a prince to help them dominate the people when laws and institutions are no longer at least partially sufficient to this end (D I.16). Or, they are ruined because the people enlist a prince to protect them from the grandi when laws and institutions no longer do so (D I.7). Either way, the fault lies with the oppressive nature of the grandi. In case they miss it, to emphasize his point to Cosimo and Zanobi about their appetite to dominate the people, Machiavelli frequently insists that *young* nobles, the "sons of Brutus" (e.g., D I.16, D I.46, D III.3), incessantly venture to satisfy their oppressive desires on more vulnerable citizens. One of Machiavelli's principle intentions as far as the dedicatees are concerned is to make them ponder whether there is more to be gained in the long term as Brutuses rather than as his ill-fated and rightfully ill-regarded sons.

5 EMPIRE, SENATORIAL GREED, AND THE CORRUPTION OF LIBERTY

Machiavelli's seemingly straightforward endorsement of imperialism early in the *Discourses* is undermined by his subsequent treatment of the topic throughout the rest of the book. Indeed, in Machiavelli's account, the decline of the Roman Republic can be attributed directly to aspects of its imperial expansion: in particular, the impoverishment of her citizen-soldiers and the prolongation of her officers' military commands.

As mentioned above, Machiavelli famously defies consensus among commentators on the Roman Republic by attributing the flourishing of Rome's freedom and greatness to the tumults resulting from the conflict between the grandi and the popolo. But he also concedes that tumults ultimately contributed to the ruin of Rome's free way of life after "the time" of the Gracchi and the latter's revival of the Agrarian Laws (I.4). The Agrarian Laws, sponsored by Tiberius and Gaius Gracchus, limited the amount of public lands citizens could hold, and redistributed to the plebs public lands already held in custody by wealthy Romans. Senators and their clients murdered Tiberius in the Roman Forum after he successfully resisted their efforts to block passage of the laws. A decade later, they desecrated the body of his brother, Gaius, who had committed suicide after failing to prevent a conservative rollback of his brother's and his own agrarian and judicial reforms. Apparently taking these lessons to heart, all future "reformers" would enter the Forum accompanied by armed legions.

It is worth noting that Machiavelli's description of Rome's descent into corruption after these events invokes the "time of" the Gracchi, or the "scandals" and "contentions" that arose in response to their policies (I.37, III.24). Machiavelli attributes that corruption and decline to neither the brothers themselves, nor to the content of their land reform proposals. Indeed, he concludes his description by criticizing the brothers' prudence rather than their intentions, and by validating the necessity of such laws (I.37).

According to Machiavelli, the nobility, "the greater part" of which was, in fact, constituted by the wealthiest Romans, apparently refused to recognize that the public good necessitates a minimizing of economic inequality within the republic (I.37). Rather, the nobility associate the common good with their own economic privilege: as Machiavelli observes, "it appeared to them that they were defending the public in opposing" agrarian legislation. Moreover, Machiavelli declares that the nobles were angered at the prospect of losing new revenue sources since the agrarian reforms mandated that subsequently conquered lands would be distributed among the plebs, rather than be entrusted to the custodial care of senators and their clients.

Thus, according to Machiavelli, the prospect of agrarian legislation led the Senate to send Roman armies "to the farthest parts of Italy or outside of Italy" so that they might acquire lands that poor plebeians could not feasibly make profitable even under ownership. This senatorial strategy, as described by Machiavelli, worked in the following way: "the fields possessed by the enemies of Rome, being distant from the eyes of the plebs and in places where it was not easy for them to cultivate, came to be less desired by them" (I.37). Distant lands would become an unlimited source of revenue for the few wealthiest Romans who could afford to maintain them—a source of revenue that would inevitably exacerbate the inequality that already existed at home between the nobles and the plebeians.

In fact, as Livy reports in greater detail, while plebeian soldiers were in the field, senators and their clients foreclosed on their lands at home; the soldiers simply could no longer pay their debts, lacking yields from the lands they had left uncultivated while marching off to war. The Senatorial class then worked these lands with the cheap labor of slaves such that increasingly impoverished and unemployed citizen-soldiers stopped having children who could repopulate the army.[21] This was the socioeconomic *cum* military crisis that the Gracchi tried to address.

Through such self-enriching policies, the nobles aggravated the republic's sociopolitical problems, not only by perpetuating conditions of economic

---

[21] See Livy, *History of Rome*, e.g., IV.49, 51, VI.5, 35; cf. also, Plutarch, *Lives* (London: Macmillan Press, 1921), X.145–241.

inequality, but also by making military commanders inordinately powerful (III.24). According to Machiavelli, senatorially driven acquisition of territory farther and farther afield from Rome and Italy necessitated the prolongation of military commands. This in turn laid the groundwork for Caesarism: fewer and fewer captains received military experience, hence necessitating reliance on a smaller and smaller cadre of commanders. Furthermore, the increasingly proletarianized citizen-soldiers became economically dependent on the generals with whom they lived for years at a time away from the city.

Machiavelli concedes that the plebeians initiated the practice of prolonging commands: they reelected tribunes who most effectively defended them against the oppressive behavior of the nobility and who most deftly resisted the obstructionist efforts of the latter against pro-plebeian reforms. But he argues that the Senate converted repeated reappointment into the practice that eventually undermined the republic's "free way of life:" the Senate encouraged the creation of proconsuls who required more than the usual annual term of office to conquer and maintain the distant lands that were the source of the nobility's steady streams of revenue. In the end, Machiavelli suggests, the controversies surrounding Agrarian legislation "altogether ruined Roman freedom" because the nobles' wealth and power had increased to the point where they could only be overcome with force (I.37). As a result, both the Senate and the plebs began supporting armed champions, who now possessed unprecedented military authority, like Sulla and Pompey, on the one hand, and Marius and Caesar, on the other; that is, oligarchically or popularly inclined warlords who commanded armies more loyal to their commanders than to the republic.

As mentioned above, interpreters building on the work of Leo Strauss[22] often suggest that Machiavelli understood the Roman nobility to be driven by a desire for glory or honor rather than by the base appetite for acquiring and preserving wealth. Yet Machiavelli declares quite explicitly in the chapter on the Agrarian Laws that, in the Roman context, the grandi, after protracted delays, "always yielded honors to the plebs without extraordinary scandals," but that they defended "property" with the utmost "obstinance" (I.37). This is a clear but understated reference to the butchery committed by the senators against the Gracchi and their supporters. Machiavelli suggests that this fact demonstrates "how much more men esteem property than honors," and, as he often uses the term, 'men' here refers euphemistically to members of the nobility (see, e.g., D I.3). Clearly, Machiavelli understands the nobles to value material goods much more highly than they do their reputation and prestige, their honor and their dignity. The senatorial greed that manifested itself in extensive imperial acquisition more than any other factor is the cause of the decline and fall of the Roman republic.

---

[22] Strauss, *Thoughts on Machiavelli*, 134, 169, 250.

CONCLUSION

After establishing Rome as the republican model most conducive to the oppressive appetite, now directed toward imperial conquest, of his young patrician audience, Machiavelli elaborates on the following themes throughout the balance of the *Discourses*: the restoration and preservation of liberty entailed by the grandi's elimination of monarchical rule; the rewards of riches and fame that result from the grandi's command of an armed populace in the pursuit of empire; and the prospect that the grandi will continue to hold the chief magistracies, even if they share such positions with members of the common people. Through these and other political concessions mentioned above (such as the plebeian tribunate, public accusations, direct popular judgment over political trials and lawmaking) the plebeians expand and enhance their role as the republic's "guardian of liberty." These developments and institutions allow the people to win many domestic skirmishes with the grandi in defending and broadening their "free way of life."

The war that the Roman people never win, however, is the contest over economic inequality: they lose many minor battles as the Senate consistently fabricates military conflicts that postpone consideration of Agrarian legislation until some later date (D I.13, I.37, I.39). By the time the Gracchi actually enact such legislation, the nobility had amassed from the fruits of empire such economic power, and the citizen-soldiery had been reduced to such egregious poverty and abject servility, that no successful recourse short of a wholesale refounding of the republic is available to potential reformers. The Senate may win two notable battles in causing the death of each Gracchus brother (and many of their supporters), but the Roman Republic as a whole is destined to lose this war: the Senate loses its authority and the people their liberty. While the Senate's economic and political choices spelled doom for that particular republic, Machiavelli's reflections on Rome raise the possibility that future citizenries might learn from this example and better constrain the senatorial orders of their own republics with respect to imperial expansion and socioeconomic inequality.

I hope that my remarks here at the very least seriously problematize the depiction of Machiavelli as an unqualified advocate of empire who favors republican glory over civic liberty. Machiavelli initially uses the prospect of empire to induce aristocratically biased republicans to grant common citizens institutions by which they effectively govern themselves and curtail the oppressive behavior of the grandi in domestic politics. Subsequently, Machiavelli intimates that the best way to preserve the potency of popular liberty and the vitality of the democratic institutions that secure it is the following: the early and consistent pursuit of policies that "keep the public rich but the citizens poor" (D I.37), and that curtails as much as possible a republic's pursuit of empire.

BIBLIOGRAPHY

Armitage, David. *The Ideological Origins of the British Empire*. Cambridge: Cambridge University Press, 2000.

Black, Robert. "Machiavelli, Servant of the Florentine Republic." In *Machiavelli and Republicanism*, edited by Gisela Bock, Quentin Skinner, and Maurizio Viroli, 71–99. Cambridge: Cambridge University Press, 1990.

Bouwsma, William J. *Venice and the Defense of Republican Liberty: Renaissance Values in the Age of the Counter Reformation*. Berkeley: University of California Press, 1968.

Brucker, Gene. "The Revolt of the Ciompi." In *Florentine Studies: Politics and Society in Renaissance Florence*, edited by Nicolai Rubinstein, 314–56. Evanston, IL: Northwestern University Press, 1968.

Bruni, Leonardo. *The Humanism of Leonardo Bruni: Selected Texts*. Edited and translated by Gordon Griffiths, James Hankins, and David Thompson. Binghamton, NY: Medieval & Renaissance Texts & Studies, 1987.

Coby, Patrick J. *Machiavelli's Romans: Liberty and Greatness in the Discourses on Livy*. Lanham: Lexington Books, 1999.

Connell, William J., ed. and trans. *Machiavelli's The Prince*. Boston: Bedford/St. Martin's, 2005.

De Secondat, Charles Louis, Baron de Montesquieu. *Considerations on the Causes of the Greatness of the Romans and their Decline* [1734]. Translated by David Lowenthal. Indianapolis: Hackett, 1999.

Fischer, Markus. *Well-Ordered License: On the Unity of Machiavelli's Thought*. Lanham, MD: Lexington Books, 2000.

Gilbert, Felix. "Bernardo Rucellai and the Orti Oricellari: A Study on the Origin of Modern Political Thought." In *History: Choice and Commitment*, edited by Felix Gilbert, 215–46. Cambridge, MA: Harvard University Press, 1977.

Gilbert, Felix. "Florentine Political Assumptions in the Period of Savonarola and Soderini." *Journal of the Warburg and Courtauld Institute* 20, no. 3/4 (1957): 187–214.

Gilbert, Felix. *Machiavelli and Guicciardini: Politics and History in Sixteenth-Century Florence*. Princeton, NJ: Princeton University Press, 1965.

Gilbert, Felix. "The Venetian Constitution in Florentine Political Thought." In *Florentine Studies: Politics and Society in Renaissance Florence*, edited by Nicolai Rubinstein, 442–62. Evanston, IL: Northwestern University Press, 1968.

Guicciardini, Francesco. "Considerations of the *Discourses* of Niccolò Machiavelli" [1530]. In *The Sweetness of Power: Machiavelli's* Discourses *and Guicciardini's* Considerations, edited and translated by James B. Atkinson and David Sices, 381–438. DeKalb, IL: Northern Illinois University Press, 2002.

Guicciardini, Francesco. *Dialogue on the Government of Florence* [1524]. Translated by Alison Brown. Cambridge: Cambridge University Press, 1994.

Guicciardini, Francesco. *Maxims and Reflections* [1530]. Translated by M. Domandi. Philadelphia: University of Pennsylvania Press, 1965.

Haitsma Mulier, Eco O. G. *The Myth of Venice and Dutch Republican Thought in the Seventeenth Century*. Translated by Gerard T. Moran. Assen, NL: Van Gorcum, 1980.

Hankins, James, ed. *Renaissance Civic Humanism: Reappraisals and Reflections*. Cambridge: Cambridge University Press, 2000.

Hörnqvist, Mikael. *Machiavelli and Empire*. Cambridge: Cambridge University Press, 2004.

Kahn, Victoria. *Machiavellian Rhetoric: From the Counter-Reformation to Milton*. Princeton, NJ: Princeton University Press, 1994.

Livy, Titus. *History of Rome (Ab Urbe Condita), Books 1–10*, vols. 1–4. Translated by B. O. Foster. Cambridge, MA: Harvard University Press (Loeb), 1919–1926.
Machiavelli, Niccolò. "Discorsi Sopra la Prima Deca di Tito Livio" [circa 1513–1519]. In *Opere I: I Primi Scritti Politici*, edited by Corrado Vivanti, 193–525. Torino: Einaudi-Gallimard, 1997.
Machiavelli, Niccolò. "Discourses on the First Decade of Livy." In *The Sweetness of Power: Machiavelli's* Discourses *and Guicciardini's* Considerations, edited and translated by James B. Atkinson and David Sices. DeKalb, IL: Northern Illinois University Press, 2002.
Machiavelli, Niccolò. *Discourses on Livy*. Edited and translated by Harvey C. Mansfield, Jr. and Nathan Tarcov. Chicago: The University of Chicago Press, 1997.
Machiavelli, Niccolò. *Florentine Histories* [1525]. Translated by Laura F. Banfield and Harvey C. Mansfield. Princeton, NJ: Princeton University Press, 1988.
Machiavelli, Niccolò. "Il Principe (De Principatipus)" [composed circa 1513 and published in 1532]. In *Opere I: I Primi Scritti Politici*, edited by Corrado Vivanti, 114–92. Torino: Einaudi-Gallimard, 1997.
Machiavelli, Niccolò. *The Prince*. Translated, edited, and with an introduction by William Connelly. Boston: Bedford/St. Martin's, 2005.
Machiavelli, Niccolò. *The Prince*, 2nd ed. Translated by Harvey C. Mansfield, Jr. Chicago: The University of Chicago Press, 1998.
Machiavelli, Niccolò, and Francesco Guicciardini. *The Sweetness of Power: Machiavelli's* Discourses *and Guicciardini's* Considerations. Edited and translated by James B. Atkinson and David Sices. Dekalb, IL: Northern Illinois University Press, 2002.
Manin, Bernard. *The Principles of Representative Government*. Cambridge: Cambridge University Press, 1997.
Mansfield, Harvey C. *Machiavelli's New Modes and Orders: A Study of the Discourses on Livy*. Ithaca: Cornell University Press, 1979.
Mansfield, Harvey C., ed. and trans. *Machiavelli's The Prince*. Chicago: The University of Chicago Press, 1998.
Mansfield, Harvey C. *Machiavelli's Virtue*. Chicago: The University of Chicago Press, 1996.
Mansfield, Harvey C., and Nathan Tarcov, eds. and trans. *Machiavelli's Discourses on Livy*. Chicago: The University of Chicago Press, 1997.
McCormick, John P. "Machiavellian Democracy: Controlling Elites with Ferocious Populism." *American Political Science Review* 95, no. 2 (2011): 297–314.
Molho, Anthony, Kurt Raaflaub, and Julia Emlen, eds. *City-States in Classical Antiquity and Medieval Italy*. Ann Arbor: University of Michigan Press, 1991.
Najemy, John M. *Between Friends: Discourses of Power and Desire in the Machiavelli-Vettori Letters of 1513–1515*. Princeton, NJ: Princeton University Press, 1993.
Najemy, John M. "The Controversy Surrounding Machiavelli's Service to the Republic." In *Machiavelli and Republicanism*, edited by Gisela Bock, Quentin Skinner, and Maurizio Viroli, 102–17. Cambridge: Cambridge University Press, 1990.
Najemy, John M. *Corporatism and Consensus in Florentine Electoral Politics, 1280–1400*. Chapel Hill, NC: University of North Carolina Press, 1982.
Pitts, Jennifer. *A Turn to Empire: The Rise of Imperial Liberalism in Britain and France*. Princeton, NJ: Princeton University Press, 2005.
Plutarch. *Lives*, vol. 10. New York: Macmillan, 1921.
Rahe, Paul A., ed. *Machiavelli's Liberal Republican Legacy*. Cambridge: Cambridge University Press, 2005.

Ridolfi, Roberto. *The Life of Niccolò Machiavelli*. Translated by C. Grayson. Chicago: The University of Chicago Press, 1963.
Sealey, Raphael. *A History of the Greek City-States, 700–338 B.C.* Berkeley: University of California Press, 1976.
Skinner, Quentin, *Past Masters: Machiavelli*. New York: Hill and Wang, 1981.
Strauss, Leo. *Thoughts on Machiavelli*. Glencoe: The Free Press, 1958.
Strauss, Leo, and Joseph Cropsey. "Niccolò Machiavelli, 1469–1527." In *History of Political Thought*, edited by Leo Strauss and Joseph Cropsey, 271–92. Chicago: Rand McNally, 1972.
Viroli, Maurizio. *Founders: Machiavelli*. Oxford: Oxford University Press, 1998.
Waley, Daniel Philip. *The Italian City-Republics*. London: Longman Press, 1969.

7 Liberal Imperialism and the Dilemma of Development

Thomas McCarthy

Interrogating the tension in liberal thought between norms of equal respect and theories of sociocultural development is critical to understanding the relations of modern Europe to the rest of the world.[1] From the settlement of the Americas and the formation of the East India and Royal African companies in the 17th century to present-day neo-imperialism, European (and later, American) dominion over non-Europeans has repeatedly been justified with conceptions of development, enlightenment, civilization, and progress, which were deployed to reduce the cognitive dissonance between liberal universalism and liberal imperialism. At the same time, as we have been made increasingly aware by postcolonial scholarship, many of the classical liberal theorists were deeply involved with colonial affairs and constructed their political philosophies with a view to them.

In what follows, after (1) assembling a few scattered reminders of this involvement and briefly recalling the systematic formulation of the dilemma of development by Immanuel Kant, I shall (2) examine the form that dilemma assumed in the detranscendentalized atmosphere of John Stuart Mill's utilitarianism and basically retained thereafter. Two contrasting ways of dissolving the dilemma will be reviewed and rejected in sections 3 and 4, leading to the conclusion, in section 5, that it cannot be theoretically eliminated but may, perhaps, be politically displaced to a predicament with which we have to come to terms. Section 5 will consider some conditions for doing so.

1

John Locke, who was an original shareholder in the Royal African Company when it was chartered in 1672, had earlier (1669) coauthored the Fundamental Constitutions of Carolina, which legally recognized negro

[1] This chapter is reprinted from Thomas McCarthy, "Liberal Imperialism and the Dilemma of Development," in *Race, Empire, and the Idea of Human Development* (Cambridge: Cambridge University Press, 2009), chapter 6. Permission to reprint this piece is gratefully acknowledged.

slavery, and later (1682) participated in their revision, which retained the slavery article unaltered.[2] In addition to serving as Secretary to the Lords Proprietors of the Carolina Colony (1669–1675), he also served as Secretary and Treasurer to the English Council for Trade and Foreign Plantations (1673–1674) and as Secretary to the English Board of Trade (1696–1700). His rationalizations of the enslavement of Africans and the expropriation of Native American lands drew upon a narrative of development from the state of nature to political society. In the state of nature, such as obtained in Africa and North America, each is guarantor of his own life, liberty, and possessions; and when attacked, threatened, or resisted in the pursuit of his interests, each may resort to force, which might then legitimately result in conquest, enslavement, or expropriation. Most famously, Locke declared America to be a "vacant land" occupied only by nomadic savages, who had failed to heed God's command to cultivate the earth and Nature's law that conferred ownership upon those who did so—and hence a land morally and legally open to appropriation. "God gave the world to men in common; but . . . He gave it to the use of the industrious and rational (and labor was to be his title to it)."[3] This contrast between the idle, irrational, "wild Indian" wandering the "uncultivated waste" of America and the industrious, rational, civilized planter harvesting its bounty dominates Locke's repeated references to America and its indigenous peoples in the *Second Treatise*, and gives figurative expression to his view of the general development of human forms of life from nomadic hunting and gathering to settled agriculture, for "in the beginning all the world was America."[4]

Locke's involvement with, detailed knowledge of, and liberal apologetics for England's Atlantic empire was later equaled, if not surpassed, by the Mills in their connection with East Indian affairs.[5] James Mill was engaged by the East India Company in 1819, became its Chief Examiner in 1830, and remained with it for the rest of his life. Indebted both to Bentham's utilitarianism and Scottish Enlightenment conceptions of development, he retained only superficial traces of their respective criticisms of colonialism.

---

[2] There is a large literature on the relationship of Locke's liberalism to English colonialism. See, for instance, the discussions of this in James Tully, *An Approach to Political Philosophy: Locke in Contexts* (Cambridge: Cambridge University Press, 1993); Barbara Arneil, *John Locke and America: The Defense of English Colonialism* (Oxford: Oxford University Press, 1996); and David Armitage, *The Ideological Origins of the British Empire* (Cambridge: Cambridge University Press, 2000).

[3] John Locke, *Two Treatises on Government,* ed. Peter Laslett (Cambridge: Cambridge University Press, 1993); *Second Treatise,* 291.

[4] Locke, *Second Treatise,* 301.

[5] From the extensive literature on this connection, see, for instance, the discussions in Eric Stokes, *The English Utitlitarians and India* (Oxford: Oxford University Press, 1959); Lynn Zastoupil, *John Stuart Mill and India* (Stanford, CA: Stanford University Press, 1994); Uday Singh Mehta, *Liberalism and Empire* (Chicago: University of Chicago Press, 1999); and Jennifer Pitts, *A Turn to Empire: The Rise of Imperial Liberalism in Britain and France* (Princeton: Princeton University Press, 2005).

England's dominion in India was, he granted, generally against its own best interests. But it did serve the best interests of the indigenous population: "If we wish for the prolongation of an English government in India ... it is for the sake of the natives, not of England ... Even the utmost abuse of European power is better, we are persuaded, than the most temperate exercise of Oriental despotism."[6] This was in keeping with James Mill's characterization of Indian society as barbaric and of Indians as incapable of self-government—a characterization informed by a scheme of development that flattened Scottish Enlightenment stadial theories onto the plane of utility and reduced the number of importantly different developmental stages to a binary opposition: barbarism versus civilization. The imposition of British rule on backward India was then justified in terms of a tutelary duty to assist it, through colonial administration, in passing from its social childhood to social maturity.

James's son, John Stuart, who was also employed by the East India Company for most of his adult life and rose to Chief Examiner in his last year there, subsequently imported this idea of progressive colonial dominion into the core of his classical formulation of liberal values—hence the sudden admonition in the introductory chapter of *On Liberty* that its principles are "meant to apply only to human beings in the maturity of their faculties," and not to "those backward states of society in which the race itself may be considered as in its nonage."[7] As to the latter, "despotism is a legitimate mode of government in dealing with barbarians, provided the end be their improvement and the means justified by actually effecting that end."[8]

I shall have more to say of John Stuart Mill's views on these matters in section 2. Here it is important to note that, though the use of developmental schemes to justify illiberal and dominating practices toward non-Western societies has been characteristic of the mainstream of classical liberal theory, it is not present in all streams of liberal thought; there are others characterized rather by a deep ambivalence toward, or even an outright rejection of, colonialism.[9] Nor, as we shall see in sections 3 and 4, does the tension between universalism and developmentalism trouble only liberal thought. Given this diversity of views, it seems to me an oversimplification to argue, as many recently have, that imperialism is constitutive for liberalism *as such*, especially since the critiques advanced by anticolonial liberals have typically appealed to liberal values. However, it is undeniable that the mainstream of liberal thought, running from Locke through Mill to contemporary

---

6 Cited from Mill's review of *Voyages aux Indes Orientales* in Pitts, *A Turn to Empire,* 125.

7 John Stuart Mill, *On Liberty,* ed. Elizabeth Rapaport (Indianapolis: Hackett Publishing, 1978), 10–11.

8 Ibid., 10.

9 See, for instance, Sankar Muthu, *Enlightenment and Empire* (Princeton: Princeton University Press, 2003); and Jennifer Pitts's discussions of the Scottish Enlightenment and Jeremy Bentham in *A Turn to Empire.*

neoliberalism, has continually flowed into and out of European-American imperialism, and that ideas of sociocultural development have been integral to that connection. Developmental thinking has proved to be rather adaptable and thus quite serviceable in rationalizing the various truncations of universal rights and obligations that colonial domination and exploitation required. Moreover, the putatively scientific status of theories of development lent a naturalistic aura to socially constructed hierarchies, thus deflecting moral assessment and political critique. In this and other ways, the refraction of liberal ideals in the medium of developmental theory made it rhetorically possible to combine universalism in principle with Eurocentric domination in practice.

The inherent tensions between moral universalism and developmental hierarchy were already recognized and given sharp systematic expression by Kant. From the *moral-legal standpoint* of practical reason, he repeatedly denounced contemporary forms of European imperialism and their purported justifications. At the same time, from the *anthropological-historical standpoint* of reflective judgment, he argued that the only way to make sense of human history was in terms of the gradual diffusion of an asymmetrical progress centered in Europe. The tensions that arose from his uncompromising adherence to both standpoints are a defining characteristic of the Kantian world picture. He lived with the tensions because he believed he could not do otherwise: morally speaking, the fundamental principles of equal dignity, respect, and consideration dictated that we pursue a global kingdom of ends, in which everyone recognized everyone else as an end in him or herself; but anthropologically speaking, the development of our rational nature resulted from the play of our unsocial sociability, with vastly inequitable outcomes. What I am calling the dilemma of development is evident in this construction: the path Kant projects toward the "moral destiny" of humankind is marked, even prepared, by mutual conflict and uneven development, which, from the start of the modern period, has meant European dominance and non-European assimilation. As a result, historical events and tendencies that are unacceptable from a moral-legal perspective often prove to be functional from a developmental perspective, as a means to the perfection of our rational nature. Thus war, conquest, oppression, inequality, exploitation, and the other great evils of the human condition, which are morally despicable, have served as valuable spurs to the development and spread of culture and civilization. In the larger scheme of things, "this splendid misery is bound up with the development of the natural predispositions in the human race, and the end of nature itself, even if it is not our end, is hereby attained."[10]

As we shall see, this dilemma of development can be variously transformed, but cannot easily be eliminated from the liberal world picture. It

---

10 Immanuel Kant, *Critique of the Power of Judgment,* ed. Paul Guyer, trans. Paul Guyer and Eric Matthews (Cambridge: Cambridge University Press, 2000), 299.

haunts liberalism even when ethics are naturalized and well-being is reinstated as its final end, when the teleology of nature and theodicy of history are no longer theoretical concerns, and when history and anthropology are viewed simply as forms of empirical inquiry—as a closer look at the thought of John Stuart Mill will make clear.[11]

2

Kant dealt with the tension between the universality of law and morality, on the one hand, and the unevenness of sociocultural development, on the other, by appealing to "rational" faith and hope in the workings of Divine Providence.[12] He could avoid a moral-political choice between the imperial rule of what he saw as less developed by more developed societies and the self-rule of underdeveloped societies condemned to lasting inequality and subordination, because he could believe and hope that the hidden hand of God/nature-in-history would guide human affairs toward the "ultimate end" of history and the "moral destiny" of humankind. As this sort of progressive eschatology of history lost its credibility, Kant's specific way of defusing the dilemma between liberal universalism and liberal imperialism ceased to be an option. Thus, the more naturalistic resolution to the dilemma offered by John Stuart Mill in the context of 19th-century British imperialism became more typical of the justifications of colonialism within progressive liberal thought until the advent of the postcolonial condition following World War II.[13]

Mill did not appeal to divine providence or to a teleology of nature and history; and he placed general well-being at the center of moral and political theory. At the same time, he transfigured the baser motives for imperial conquest and exploitation into the higher motives of a civilizing mission and a benign paternalism, which was for the good of those subject to it, whether or not they realized it. The *superior force* of European societies, which made

---

[11] I shall be referring primarily to Mill's writings from the years just after the Great Uprising against the British in India (1857), the end of the East India Company, and the institution of direct imperial rule by the British government: *On Liberty* [1859]; "A Few Words on Non-Intervention" [1859], in *Essays on Politics and Culture,* ed. Gertrude Himmelfarb (Garden City, NY: Doubleday, 1962), 396–413; "Civilization" [1836; revised ed. 1859], in *Essays on Politics and Culture,* 51–84; and *Considerations on Representative Government* [1861] (South Bend, IN: Gateway, 1962). References will be given in parentheses in the text by abbreviated titles and page numbers.

[12] See Thomas McCarthy, *Race, Empire, and the Idea of Human Development* (Cambridge: Cambridge University Press, 2009), ch. 2.

[13] See Karuna Mantena, *Alibis of Empire* (Princeton: Princeton University Press, 2010), for qualifications of this generalization having to do with the shift from ethical to sociological conceptions of imperial legitimacy in the closing decades of the 19th century.

empire a real possibility, was thereby combined with their putatively *superior character* to make the case for imperial dominion. Such power-backed paternalism, while admittedly despotic, was at the same time progressive and thus was superior to the indigenous forms of self-rule found in less developed societies, which, while no less despotic, were surely less progressive. As Mill plainly put it, there are conditions of society in which "there being no spring of spontaneous improvement in the people themselves, their almost only hope of making any steps in advance depends upon the chances of a good despot. Under a native despotism, a good despot is a rare and transitory accident; but when the dominion they are under is that of a more civilized people, that people ought to be able to supply it constantly" (*CRG*, 346).

How does he arrive at this view, theoretically speaking? There are several paths, but the main one is marked by his understanding of the basic normative standard of utility: "I forego any advantage which could be derived to my argument from the idea of abstract right as a thing independent of utility. I regard utility as the ultimate appeal in all ethical questions; but it must be utility in the largest sense, grounded on the permanent interests of man as a progressive being" (*OL*, 10). The internal connection between utility and progress is spelled out in the same essay through contrasting liberty with custom. Mill traces a series of links connecting liberty with autonomy, individuality, reason, progress, and the like, on the one side, and on the opposite side, connecting custom with un-freedom, stagnation, and the like. In consequence, the full development of the capacities of the individual and of the species requires individual freedom, while the great enemy of development is conformity to custom, which does not educate any of the distinctive endowments of human beings. In civilized societies, where liberty is given greater scope, each individual becomes "an independent center of improvement," whereas in uncivilized—savage or barbaric—societies, where custom rules, human life becomes stagnant or retrogresses:

> The despotism of custom is everywhere the standing hindrance to human advancement, being in unceasing antagonism to that disposition to aim at something better than customary, which is called, according to circumstances, the spirit of liberty or that of progress or improvement . . . [T]he contest between the two constitutes the chief interest of the history of mankind. The greater part of the world has, properly speaking, no history, because the despotism of custom is complete. This is the case over the whole East (*OL*, 67).

With this characterization of non-European modes of life as just so many forms of the despotism of custom, which blocks the development of human capacities and frustrates the permanent interests of man as a progressive being, we are close to a justification of colonial intervention and superintendence.

There is, however, a palpable tension in this with other elements of Mill's argument in *On Liberty.* For if self-development and self-improvement are ethically enjoined by his brand of perfectionism, the latter simultaneously proscribes interfering with the liberty of others for their own good: "the only freedom which deserves the name is that of pursuing our own good in our own way"; "mankind are the greater gainers by suffering each other to live as seems good to themselves than by compelling each to live as seems good to the rest" (*OL*, 12). But, Mill hastens to explain, this applies only to "human beings in the maturity of their faculties" (*OL*, 9). It does not apply to children or to backward societies, "in which the race itself may be considered in its nonage" (*OL*, 10). For the latter, spontaneous progress is so fraught with difficulties that "a ruler full of the spirit of improvement is warranted in the use of any expedients that will attain an end perhaps otherwise unattainable. Despotism is a legitimate mode of government in dealing with barbarians, provided the end be their improvement and the means justified by actually effecting that end" (*OL,* 10). And as Mill makes clear in other writings from the same period, this civilizing despotism can better be afforded by an already civilized nation with non-self-interested foreign policy aims—such as England—than by indigenous rulers.

Furthermore, Mill tells us, the principle of non-intervention in the internal affairs of other sovereign nations, which stands at the center of modern international law, governs only relations among civilized nations, not relations between them and uncivilized or barbarous peoples:

> The sacred duties which civilized nations owe to the independence and nationality of each other are not binding towards those to whom nationality and independence are either a certain evil or at best a questionable good . . . To characterize any conduct whatever towards a barbarous people as a violation of the law of nations only shows that he who speaks has never considered the subject . . . [B]arbarians have no rights as a *nation* except a right to such treatments as may, at the earliest possible period, fit them for becoming one (*NI*, 406).

If this "right" were applied to British rule in India, Mill is confident that there would be no violation. It was at bottom a non-self-interested, civilizing tutelage aimed at reforming economic, political, and educational institutions, so that India—which must once have been capable of self-development before stagnation set in—might some day again take responsibility for its own improvement.

In general, the proper normative standard for evaluating government is the best possible institutions in the existing state of a society, where "best" is to be understood as "most conducive to progress" (*CRG*, 27). Hence the appropriate institutions will differ according to a society's "stage of advancement." More specifically, the form of government must be such that "its operation is favorable, or not unfavorable, to the next step, which it is necessary for them to take, in order to raise themselves to the next level" (*CRG*, 39). Representative government—"the ideal type of the most perfect society"—is suitable only to societies at advanced stages of improvement (*CRG*, 75). As societies range lower in development, other forms of government are preferable, "when the people, in order to advance in civilization have some lesson to learn, some habit not yet acquired, to the acquisition of which representative government is likely to be an impediment" (*CRG*, 79). In some such situations, what is called for is "the government of dependencies by a free state," under the condition, of course, that the rule be in the best interests of the ruled: "this mode of government is as legitimate as any other, if it is the one which, in the existing state of civilization of the subject people, most facilitates their transition to a higher stage of improvement" (*CRG*, 346). Rule by a "good despot" is "the ideal rule of a free people over a barbarous or semi-barbarous one" (*CRG*, 346). And as colonization was at that time rapidly becoming "the universal condition of the more backward populations" (*CRG*, 347), it was this ideal of good colonial despotism that should govern the relations of the most advanced European nations with the rest of the world, for whom it was typically the best attainable form of government—that is, the most favorable to future development.

Mill's own account of such development is notably thin by comparison to those that came before and after. It is, to begin with, one-dimensional: there is a single axis of development, along which every society can be ranked as more or less advanced. Moreover, the rankings pertain to societies as wholes; all aspects of a society—its art and religion as well as its economics and politics—are held to reflect its general level of development. And these holistic, one-dimensional rankings are further simplified by grouping all differentiations into one overriding, binary opposition: civilized versus barbarian (or savage, rude, uncivilized, etc.). Though Mill does sometimes remark on the differences between nomadic and settled societies, between hunting and gathering bands and the great ancient civilizations, between the indigenous cultures of North America and those of China and India, all such differentiations get reduced to that single dichotomy when he is concerned with colonial relations. Thus, in an essay on "Civilization" written in 1836 and republished with minor revisions in 1859, after enumerating a variety of respects in which societies can be compared, Mill assures his readers that

> though these ingredients of civilizations are various . . . they begin together, always coexist, and accompany each other in their growth. Wherever there has introduced itself sufficient knowledge of the arts of life, and sufficient security of property and person, to render the progressive increase of wealth and population possible, the community becomes and continues progressive in all its elements which we have just enumerated (*C*, 53).

And it is just this characteristic of being "progressive in all its elements" that structures the dichotomy between civilized and uncivilized societies. In this he followed in the footsteps of his father, as he did in his low estimation of the degree of civilization in India.[14] Though clearly different from what he called "savage tribes," India was also a stagnant society that was incapable of progressive self-rule and could thus be improved only with outside guidance. And of course, in terms of Britain's relations to its colonies, that is the attribution that counted. One might conjecture that the practical-political perspective of who colonized whom rendered finer theoretical distinctions insignificant; it was the perspective of colonial rule that framed the description and evaluation from the start.

Mill was not entirely clear in identifying the chief motor of progress. At times he accentuated "material" developments—in property relations, in trade and manufacture, in the division and combination of labor, and the like—and at other times "cultural" developments—in the "powers and acquirements of mind," in the diffusion of intelligence, in opinions, habits, and social practices, and the like—and quite often, both. But he was clear that race was not the decisive factor; and this distinguished him from many other late 19th and early 20th-century developmentalists.[15] He did not, it seems, reject out of hand the existence of "natural" differences among the "various races of men"; rather, he judged the empirical evidence that they were decisive to developmental differences to be weak in the extreme—especially when compared to the evidence for the developmental significance of the sorts of material and cultural factors mentioned above.[16] The factor he most often singled out for attention, "national character," he clearly understood in cultural rather than racial terms. In this respect, he anticipated a line of argument favored by many 20th-century theorists. Indeed, with his "postmetaphysical" rejection of any theodicy or teleology of history, his replacement of laws of nature and commands of reason with utilitarian considerations of well-being and progress, and his reliance—however defective—on empirical history and the human sciences to make his case, Mill could be said to have anticipated in many respects the approaches to development and modernization that came to dominate after World War II.[17]

As noted, even in the desublimated atmosphere of Mill's postmetaphysical liberalism, the dilemma of development does not disappear without a trace. It surfaces repeatedly in the tension between his basic liberal value of autonomy—"If a person possesses any tolerable amount of common sense and experience, his own mode of laying out his existence is the best, not

---

[14] John Stuart Mill proofread the many volumes of his father's *History of British India* (1817)—when he was 11 years old!

[15] See McCarthy, *Race, Empire, and the Idea of Human Development*, ch. 3.

[16] See John Stuart Mill, "The Negro Question," published anonymously in *Fraser's Magazine for Town and Country* in 1850, in response to an earlier article by Thomas Carlyle (reprinted in *Little's Living Age*, vol. XXIV, 465–69); and the discussion of Mill's views on "race" by John Robson, "Civilization and Culture as Moral Concepts," in *The Cambridge Companion to Mill*, ed. John Skorupski (Cambridge: Cambridge University Press, 1998), 338–71.

[17] I discuss some of these approaches in McCarthy, *Race, Empire, and the Idea of Human Development*, ch. 7.

because it is the best in itself, but because it is his own mode" (*OL*, 64)—and the paternalism underwritten by his developmental reading of Europe's relations with non-European peoples, for whom government by a more civilized people is "as legitimate [a mode of government] as any other" and is in fact "their almost only hope in making any steps in advance" (*CRG*, 346). The tension is further heightened when Mill asserts that the comparative evaluation of different modes of life cannot properly be made from a God's-eye view but only "practically, when anyone thinks fit to try them" (*OL*, 54).[18] Or when he castigates the persecutors of Mormons by declaring: "I am not aware that any community has a right to force another to be civilized . . . Let them send missionaries, if they please" (*OL*, 90). Or when he goes so far as to state that "on every principle of morality and justice," Great Britain ought to consent to her colonies separating "should the time come when, after full trial of the best form of union, they deliberately desire to be dissevered" (*CRG*, 342). But such reservations are regularly outweighed by the worry that non-European societies are ruled by "the despotism of custom," which is irremediably opposed to the "free development of individuality," which is in turn not only "one of the leading essentials of well-being" but also "a necessary part and condition" of civilization, education (i.e., *Bildung*), and culture (*OL*, 54). Here one must choose, for "the contest between the two is the chief interest of the history of mankind" (*OL*, 67). And though the tension between them cannot be made simply to disappear, it can, Mill thinks, be reduced considerably by the requirement, in regard to the government of dependencies by free states, that a "government of leading strings" is admissible only if it actually "train[s] the people to walk alone" (*CRG*, 42).[19] That is to say, it belongs to the normative ideal of such government—to which Mill supposed Britain's rule of its colonies approximated—that the dominant people seek to advance the development of the subject people, so that the arrangement is temporary: once the immature people is capable of self-rule and self-improvement, it can be treated as an equal member of the community of civilized nations—but not just yet.

3

Whatever the tensions internal to this ideal, it so evidently diverged from the realities of colonial rule that critics had an easy time debunking it. In this Marx was at the forefront. In two articles on British rule in India written for the *New York Daily Tribune* in 1853 (that is, at about the time Mill was

---

[18] Nevertheless, though he was himself engaged with the governance of India throughout most of his adult life, Mill never deemed it necessary to visit that part of the world.

[19] This remark is made specifically with reference to a type of uncivilized, slave-based society, but it applies to the governance of other types as well.

publishing the views considered above) Marx took it as evident that the East India Company was "actuated solely by the spirit of gain"[20] (June 25, 654). The advancements it fostered in the conditions of life in India were largely the consequences of a basically exploitative relationship. So while they were, as he too believed, necessary to the full development of Indian capacities, they were anything but benign. England had destroyed the entire framework of Indian society for its own purposes and thereby wreaked havoc on traditional institutions, organizations, and communities, and great suffering upon their members. Nevertheless, it remained that England's pursuit of its own self-interest had led to fundamental transformations of Indian life that were a prerequisite to further progress—"the laying of the material foundations of Western society in Asia" (August 8, 659). England, he assures us,

> in causing a social revolution in Hindostan, was actuated only be the vilest interests, and was stupid in her manner of enforcing them. But that is not the question. The question is, can mankind fulfill its destiny without a fundamental revolution in the social state of Asia? If not, whatever may have been the crimes of England, she was the unconscious tool of history in bringing about that revolution (June 25, 658).

In this the British were no different from other capitalist regimes around the globe: "Has the bourgeoisie ever done more? Has it ever effected a progress without dragging individuals and peoples through blood and dirt, through misery and degradation" (August 8, 662)? Covering over naked self-interest with the mantel of a civilizing mission was just one more instance of the "profound hypocrisy" of capitalism (August 8, 663). So, what Mill regarded as a reconciliation of liberal values with colonial practices, Marx called hypocrisy—and in this he was in agreement with most critics of colonialism to the present. What separates him from many of them, however, and particularly from many postcolonial theorists, is the horn of the universalism/developmentalism dilemma he holds on to. Moral judgments are beside the point. The transformation of the world by capitalism is a necessary stage on the way to the full flowering of human capacities in socialism: "When a great social revolution shall have mastered the results of the bourgeois epoch, the market of the world and the modern powers of production . . . then only will human progress cease to resemble that hideous pagan idol, who would not drink the nectar but from the skulls of the slain" (August 8, 664).

Today Marx's historical confidence in that "great social revolution," like Kant's rational faith in God or nature's plan of history, has largely lost

[20] I shall be citing articles from June 25 and August 8, 1853, both of which are reprinted in *The Marx-Engels Reader,* ed. Robert C. Tucker (New York: W.W. Norton, 1978), 653–58 and 659–64, respectively. References to them are given in parentheses in the text by date and page number.

whatever powers of reconciliation it might once have possessed. Thus, as I shall elaborate in section 3, many postcolonial critics have grabbed on to the other horn of the dilemma: morally condemning neo-imperial relations while dismissing developmental theory as an ideology of empire. Theorists who still hold on to both horns and try to close the gap between them stand accused by both sides of "profound hypocrisy." And it is by no means easy to avoid that charge without surrendering either universal norms or developmental schemes, the ideological combination of which to justify empire was coeval with liberalism.

As we have seen, the problem arises when universal moral principles—such as those Kant derives from pure practical reason or those Mill derives from considerations of utility—are "applied" to a social reality described anthropologically-historically as developing in essential respects. For this purpose, in Kant's formulation, "pure moral principles" have to be "schematized" to take account of relevant differences, if they are to be applied properly, that is, differently in different contexts. As examples of such schematized moral principles, he mentions rules that apply to the treatment of people "in accordance with their differences in rank, age, sex, health, property, or poverty, and so forth," or according to whether they belong to "the cultivated or the crude."[21] Similarly, Mill advises us that, though the "comprehensive science or art of government" yields general principles, the latter have to be applied differently according to "the stage of advancement already reached," for "the one indispensable merit of a government" is that it promotes the development of the people governed (*CRG*, 37–39).

But it is not only such "contexts of application" that connected liberal theory to European imperialism; that connection was already forged in its "contexts of origin."[22] The combination of developmentalism with universalism was deployed by progressive liberalism as a justification for empire from the beginning, and not by chance; for the general accounts of history and society that served this purpose were always interpretations from a practically engaged point of view. They reflected the nature of Europeans' contacts with non-European societies from the voyages of "discovery" onwards. And given a hermeneutic standpoint shaped by their growing superiority of force and by their growing confidence in the superiority of their culture and institutions, that is not surprising. The imbalances of power of various sorts formed a context in which the autonomy and equal respect required in theory could not be effectively demanded in practice. As colonial powers usually could not be forced to negotiate

[21] Immanuel Kant, "The Metaphysics of Morals," in *Practical Philosophy*, ed. and trans. Mary J. Gregor (Cambridge: Cambridge University Press, 1996), 584.

[22] The classic formulations of liberalism postdate the completion of the conquest of Ireland, the founding of the East India Company, and the granting of a charter to Virginia, among other things.

differences on equal terms, they were disposed to interpret them in hierarchical and temporal terms. Other societies and cultures became earlier "stages" of development, salient differences became marks of backwardness, and backwardness meant that a society or culture's time had passed. Correspondingly, the application of liberal ideals could take the form of a temporalizing or, better, temporizing universalism. This produced the familiar "not yet" effect—as in "not yet ready for self-rule," the deferral of equal respect and autonomy until such time as the subjects' needs for education and improvement had been met.[23] From this perspective, when dealing with backward peoples, as with children, it makes no sense to seek the consent of the governed; the most that can be expected is good colonial government—or as Mill bluntly put it, good despotism—that will one day make such consent appropriate. Thus colonial policy, in dealing with institutions and practices that belong essentially to the past, legitimates itself as future-oriented reform. It compensates denial of freedom and equality in the present by issuing a "promissory note" for future freedom and equality—conditional, of course, on the requisite developments actually taking place. The shape of that future is already known: it is, by and large, the present shape of the most advanced societies. What are required now are the use of power for improvement by the colonizers and the acceptance of the (temporary) deferral of self-rule by the colonized. Historically, however, it was all too evident that "good despotism" was always already an ideological cover for domination and exploitation and that "the natives' patience" had always already run out. Against this background, it is not surprising that many postcolonial thinkers today dismiss or deconstruct the very idea of development.

4

Until relatively recently, and with some important exceptions (e.g., Gandhi), critics of liberal developmentalism have, like Marx, tended to remain within the ambit of developmental thinking, broadly conceived. In the 1980s and 1990s, however, outright rejections of developmentalism became widespread. Various forms of postcolonial thought, often appropriating post-Nietzschean and post-Heideggerian critiques of Western humanism, challenged its fundamental assumptions. From these more radical perspectives, even the received forms of Marxist critique appeared to be modernist tropes oriented to the ultimate convergence of all societies and cultures. What were needed, however, were not new forms of critical modernism but "postmodernism," not better forms of development

---

[23] Uday Singh Mehta elaborates upon this temporizing effect in *Liberalism and Empire*, 106–11.

but "postdevelopment." There has since been a continual proliferation of postmodern and postdevelopment critiques, of which I shall briefly note only two broad streams, which in practice often flow together and join other streams.[24]

One, which often uses Foucault's genealogical critique as a point of reference, sees post-World War II development theory and practice as a neocolonial regime of power/knowledge meant to succeed the colonial regime and thus as a central strategy of modern power rather than a path to emancipation from it.[25] It links "universal reason" internally to relations of power: what is rational is right for everyone, what everyone should do, what everyone may be sanctionably expected, even forced, to do. Through multiple, often tacit chains of reasoning of this sort, Western humanist ideals get linked to disciplinary strategies that are embedded in power relations and aimed at subjugating, normalizing, and dominating non-Western peoples. As the practical knowledge of local traditions gets disqualified in the development paradigm, there is a need for outside assistance from already developed societies and the international agencies that implement their policies. Vast armies of officials, planners, and experts are thereby vested with power/knowledge. And given the resultant gradient between expert and local knowledge, development is inherently structured as a top-down field of action. It is the expert who determines what improvements are needed, what will be most beneficial to the "target populations," in short, what is to be thought and what is to be done. The hegemony of "reason" is thus secured by forces beyond the force of the better argument. The task of critical analysis in this genealogical mode is to subvert the constitutive Eurocentrism of discourse formations like "development" and "modernization" by revealing their complicity with technologies of neo-imperial power.

A second broad stream of postdevelopment critique (in practice, often flowing together with others) is deconstructive in tenor and often in conversation with the work of Jacques Derrida. A guiding thought here is that Eurocentrism has so deeply penetrated not only historical and social-scientific modes of inquiry, but also political and popular modes of representation that colonial discourse has been able to outlive the death

---

[24] For a sampling of diverse lines of critique, see these collections: Wolfgang Sachs, ed., *The Development Dictionary* (London: Zed Books, 1992); Majid Rahnema and Victoria Bawtree, eds., *The Post-Development Reader* (London: Zed Books, 1997); and Ronaldo Munck and Denis O'Hearn, eds., *Critical Development Theory* (London: Zed Books, 1999).

[25] See, for example, Arturo Escobar, *Encountering Development: The Making and the Unmaking of the Third World* (Princeton: Princeton University Press, 1995). Earlier on, Edward Said's very influential work, *Orientalism* (New York: Vintage Books, 1979), drew upon Foucault in analyzing colonial discourse as the intrication of particular forms of knowledge with particular relations of power.

of colonialism itself. Development theory, in particular, is a very deep-seated mind-set, and there is no antidote for it but a patient and persistent "decolonization of the mind."[26] Decolonizing the historical and social imaginaries of ex-colonizers and ex-colonized alike requires something different from what even the most humanitarian versions of developmentalism are able to provide; for they attempt only to improve development, to reconstruct development with justice, dignity, democracy—that is, "with a human face." But the development paradigm is *inherently* tied to the project of Western domination and so cannot be remedied by reconstruction. It has, rather, to be ongoingly deconstructed until we have unlearned to think of history in totalizing terms, as a unitary process with a uniform future. The proper tools for this can be found in a form of cultural critique that operates both inside and outside the ambit of Eurocentrism.[27] There is no possibility of thinking outside "the West" altogether; rather, critics can use the alterity and ambivalence that ineluctably inhabits Western thinking about the Other to effect its own deconstruction. For the repeated attempts of colonial and neocolonial discourse to constitute a totality through exclusion or homogenization of the Other inevitably fail; inassimilable elements ineluctably pervade such discourse, ambivalence is intrinsic to it, and deconstructionist critique can exploit that ambivalence to subvert its authority.[28]

Genealogical and deconstructive modes of discourse analysis, as well as other forms of postmodern and postdevelopment critique, pursue a type of cultural politics aimed at resisting the dominance of Eurocentrism and loosening its hold on the imaginaries of postcolonizers and postcolonized alike. But the question is repeatedly raised: in the name of what are these modes of resistance, transgression, and subversion exercised? If postmodern critique is not to end merely in parasitic forms of discursive dissolution and identification through opposition, it should provide some idea of possible alternatives to liberal and Marxist conceptions of development. And then the grip of modern cultural and institutional forms becomes harder to shake; it proves difficult, if not impossible, to think consistently about social and political reconstruction without drawing upon those forms. And if that is so, we have no alternative but to revisit and rethink our dilemma.

[26] As Ashis Nandy, who is, however, no deconstructionist, has famously put it. See his "Colonization of the Mind," in *The Post-Development Reader*, eds. Majid Rahnema and Victoria Bawtree (London: Zed Books, 1997), 168–78.
[27] Robert Young, *White Mythologies: Writing History and the West* (London: Routledge, 1990).
[28] See, for instance, Gayatri Chakravorty Spivak, *In Other Worlds: Essays in Cultural Politics* (New York: Methuen, 1987); and Homi K. Bhabha, *The Location of Culture* (London: Routledge, 1994).

Dipesh Chakrabarty puts the matter this way:

> The phenomenon of 'political modernity'—namely the rule by modern institutions of the state, bureaucracy, and capitalist enterprise—is impossible to *think* of anywhere in the world without invoking certain categories and concepts, the genealogies of which . . . all bear the burden of European thought and history. One simply can't think of political modernity without these and other related concepts . . . This heritage is now global.[29]

That is to say, in consequence of European global hegemony in the modern period, certain forms and matters of thought have become "unavoidable—and in a sense indispensable" (*PE*, 4). They shape scholarship, now also global, in history and the human studies, including the analysis and critique of Western imperialism itself. But though European thought "is now everybody's heritage," it is also "inadequate in helping us think through the experiences of political modernity in non-Western nations" (*PE*, 16). "Provincializing" or decentering Europe thus calls not for rejecting the European thought "to which one owes one's intellectual existence," but for rethinking and renewing it "from and for the margins," which are plural and diverse (*PE*, 16). In particular, the historicist ideology according to which non-Western modernities will merely replicate the Western model, albeit at more or less retarded rates of development, and which still informs development theory and practice in most national and international settings, has to be displaced by more pluralistic modes of thinking about past histories and present possibilities.[30]

This suggests that the "inside/outside" predicament utilized by postmodernist thinkers for deconstructive purposes can also serve as the starting point for a reconstructive undertaking: an attempt to elaborate a critical theory of global development, in which the unreasonable, unjust, and undesirable elements of actually existing development—those which owe their establishment and persistence primarily to force and violence, structural and symbolic, as well as intentional—are corrected or eliminated, while those which are reasonable, just, and desirable—which evince good reasons, basic fairness, and desirable consequences when examined "from and for the margins"—are retained and revised. In short, we need not choose between the ravages of neoliberal and neoconservative globalization, on the one side, and wholesale rejections of modernization, on the other. Beyond this either/or lies the possibility of critically reconstructing developmental theory and practice in the interest of collectively organized action toward

[29] Dipesh Chakrabarty, *Provincializing Europe: Postcolonial Thought and Historical Difference* (Princeton: Princeton University Press, 2000), 4. Cited in the text as *PE*.
[30] For another version of this line of thought, see Partha Chatterjee, *The Nation and Its Fragments* (Princeton, NJ: Princeton University Press, 1993).

democratically defined aims of improving the life conditions of the wretched of the earth. For most of human history, most people, everywhere, have lived their lives under conditions of dire poverty, chronic malnutrition, and narrowly constricted possibilities. Science and technology, modern economies and administrations, individual liberties and democratic self-rule have alleviated these conditions of human suffering in some parts of the world.[31] The vast multitudes now living lives of deprivation and oppression do not need to have every form of development forced upon them; they have not chosen their destitution, powerlessness, suffering, and humiliation. For most, material sufficiency, basic protections, some chance of improving their situations, some voice in the decisions that affect their lives, and the like are intrinsically desirable.

Amartya Sen has captured this thought in his conception of "human development" as the development of people's "capabilities"; that is, as a process of expanding their "substantive freedoms" to lead the kinds of lives they value.[32] To this end, having basic rights and some say in important decisions affecting oneself and one's community are essential, for they condition the exercise of all other capabilities. It is this last thought that Jürgen Habermas has sought to elaborate in his discourse theory of democracy, according to which regimes, laws, programs, and policies can be legitimated in the end only through the reasoned agreement of those affected in open public discussion.[33] And postcolonial critics of classical development theory have made it abundantly clear that such agreement is not to be expected so long as the equation of human progress with Western modernity serves the wholesale validation of its cultural and social forms. Once that is no longer granted, the value of Western values is no longer "given" but has to be ongoingly interrogated and negotiated in culturally hybrid discourses leading typically to hybrid outcomes.

Notwithstanding their considerable differences in history and culture, as well as in colonial and postcolonial experience, the formerly colonized regions of the world now share the problem of having to "provincialize" or decenter Europe, "the original home of the modern" (*PE*, 42). Moreover, they have to do so under conditions of a global capitalism that engulfs them all. In this situation, it seems, voices "from and for the margins" will be effectively heard only to the extent that the dynamics of capital accumulation are again brought under legal-political regulation and management, this

---

[31] Robert William Fogel, *The Escape from Hunger and Premature Death, 1700–2100: Europe, America, and the Third World* (Cambridge: Cambridge University Press, 2004).

[32] Amartya Sen, *Development as Freedom* (New York: Alfred A. Knopf, 1999). Note that this formulation encompasses the basic values of personal autonomy and political self-determination, but is freed from the asymmetrical restrictions liberalism historically placed on their application.

[33] Jürgen Habermas, *Between Facts and Norms: Contributions to a Discourse Theory of Law and Democracy*, trans. William Rehg (Cambridge, MA: MIT Press, 1996).

time at a global and not merely national level. Failing that, the poorest and weakest societies will continue to be dominated and exploited, or at best patronized, by the richest and strongest. The now dominant, neoliberal form of globalization undercuts social goals of every kind: it reduces nature, society, and culture to so many "standing reserves" at the disposal of the most powerful economic interests. And postmodern pessimism saps the hope that this situation can be changed for the better through politically organized, collective action, which is the "good intention" behind at least some forms of developmental theory and practice.

5

Where does this leave us with respect to the dilemma of development that Kant identified and analyzed? Our discussion of Mill has made manifest that it did not dissolve along with natural teleology and historical theodicy. Even the naturalization of ethics did not attenuate it, so long as one or another form of species perfectionism supplied the standard for judging "improvement." But another departure from the Kantian paradigm has substantially altered the way we (should) think about the dilemma: the detranscendentalization of our idea of reason and the general recognition of its constitutive embeddedness in language games and forms of life. Human reason is always already "impure," and the universal can only ever be actual as "concrete." In the absence of a Hegelian Absolute, this leaves us, as Gadamer and others have convincingly elaborated, with a multiplicity of forms of embodied reason, the distances between which can only be bridged by hermeneutic modes of communication. For present purposes, this means that we must rethink the dilemma of development from the perspective of the historical and cultural polyphony of communicative rationality. Whatever "unity of reason" there may be in the "diversity of its voices" is not simply given but also has to be achieved.[34] Thus the idea of cultural convergence that underwrote Kant's cosmopolitan hopes will, if those hopes are to survive, have to be complicated by the idea of negotiating cultural differences in the "struggle over the universal." Neither the arrogance of Enlightenment universalism nor the diffidence of cultural relativism is up to the global challenges that confront us.[35] Once again, we have to think in terms of the unavoidable dialectic of

[34] Jürgen Habermas, "The Unity of Reason in the Diversity of Its Voices," in *Postmetaphysical Thinking,* trans. William Hohengarten (Cambridge, MA: MIT Press, 1992), 115–48. I discuss the implications of reason's constitutive embeddedness for Habermas's own thought in *Ideals and Illusions: On Reconstruction and Deconstruction in Contemporary Critical Theory* (Cambridge, MA: MIT Press, 1993), and in *Critical Theory* (Oxford: Basil Blackwell, 1994), coauthored with David Hoy.
[35] Anthony Appiah, *Cosmopolitanism: Ethics in a World of Strangers* (New York: W. W. Norton, 2006); Seyla Benhabib, *Another Cosmopolitanism* (Oxford: Oxford University Press, 2006).

the universal and the particular: if norms of global justice are to be accepted as legitimate on all sides, they will have to accommodate global-cultural diversity, and that requires leaving institutional space for the reasonable divergences in interpretation and application that are to be expected.[36] For as is evident in the ongoing debates about human rights, agreement on the general validity of norms not only does not preclude, but in fact enables, debate about their meaning both in general and in particular.

The impurity of reason and the space for reasonable pluralism it opens up also mean that any idea of universal history is essentially contestable. Kant was already aware that general historical schemes constructed through "reflective judgments," however informed they might be by the "determinative judgments" of relevant empirical inquiries, neither attained nor could aspire to the status of rigorous science. Nevertheless, owing to the univocal character of practical reason as he understood it, he could propose a single, overarching metanarrative of the realization of reason in history. From our present perspective, it is clear that the irreducible diversity of hermeneutic standpoints and practical orientations informing interpretive endeavors, however well informed, will typically issue in a "conflict of interpretations," and thus call for dialogue across differences. The historically dominant standpoint of European hegemony and orientation to its civilizing mission may no longer be adopted as a matter of course. Among other things, successful struggles for national liberation following World War II and formal recognition of national equality through the United Nations have meant that cultural differences must increasingly be discussed and negotiated rather than assumed a priori to be marks of superiority or inferiority. And this too has rendered developmental schemes essentially contestable—which is not to say arbitrary but, rather, inherently open to reasonable disagreement.[37] This methodological lesson is all the more important for the mainstream of development theory, which followed Mill and Marx rather than Kant in taking itself to be a more or less rigorous empirical science, rather than a practically oriented and empirically informed mode of interpretation. In this regard, the varieties of development theory inflicted upon third world countries after World War II were typically as smug in their assumptions of Western superiority as the classical theories of progress were during the age of empire.[38]

Methodology is supported here by considerations of morality, law, and politics. One characteristic feature of the tension inhabiting Kant's

[36] On the functioning of different types of norms in transnational contexts, see Antje Weiner, ed., "Contested Meanings of Norms—The Challenge of Democratic Governance Beyond the State" (Special Issue), *Comparative European Politics* 5, no. 1 (2007).

[37] See the concluding section of chapter 5 of McCarthy, *Race, Empire, and the Idea of Human Development*.

[38] Colin Leys, *The Rise and Fall of Development Theory* (Bloomington: Indiana University Press, 1996). I discuss this in *Race, Empire, and the Idea of Human Development*, ch. 7.

simultaneous embrace of the functional perspective of anthropological-historical thinking and the normative perspective of moral-legal reasoning is his repeated insistence on the priority of the latter. Thus, the well-known passage in "Perpetual Peace" in which he avers, "nature guarantee[s] that what man *ought* to do by the laws of his freedom (but does not do) will be done by nature's compulsion," so that "the problem of setting up a state can be solved even by a race of devils (so long as they possess understanding)"[39] is closely followed by an appendix in which he proclaims: "A true system of politics cannot therefore take a single step without first paying tribute to morality . . . The rights of man must be held sacred, however great a sacrifice the ruling power may have to make."[40] That is to say, political actors should do what is right and leave the rest to God/Providence/nature. As confidence in providential history waned, however, the split between "right and utility," as Kant termed it, yawned ever larger in international affairs. Pursuing utility in the short run for the sake of right in the long run was the route generally favored by development theory and practice after Mill. But as Chakrabarty reminds us, during the period of decolonization and nation-building following the Second World War, this hoary structure of deferral became increasingly unstable.[41] The tension between the "not yet" of colonial paternalism and the "now" of anticolonial nationalism was superseded, so to speak, not in development theory, where the tension persisted, but in political practice. The need for mass movements to politicize the peasantry and for mass democracies to grant them full citizenship status engendered the political modernity of subaltern classes and the political displacement of development theories concerning them. A related point could be made concerning the changes in international law since the founding of the United Nations. The formal recognition of new nations in every corner of the world and the globalization of human rights regimes have transformed the structure of deferral into what is called in German the *Gleichzeitigkeit des Ungleichzeitigen*, the contemporaneousness of the non-contemporaneous. Struggles for global justice today must proceed on the formal presupposition of the equal standing of all individuals and peoples. Putting that presupposition into legal and political practice is critical to ensuring an effective voice for those who are supposed to be the beneficiaries of development policies and thus for diminishing the ever-present tendencies toward paternalism, benevolent despotism, and worse. More specifically, until the formal recognition of equal standing gets translated into democratic practices—of transparency, accountability, representation,

[39] Immanuel Kant, "Perpetual Peace: A Philosophical Sketch," in *Kant: Political Writings*, trans. H. B. Nisbet (Cambridge: Cambridge University Press, 1991), 93–130, 112.
[40] Ibid., 125. This appears in the section "On the Disagreement Between Morals and Politics in Relation to Perpetual Peace," 116–25.
[41] Chakrabarty, *Provincializing Europe.*

participation, and the like—with a more equitable balance of power, the temptation for liberal progressivism to metamorphose into liberal neo-imperialism will likely remain irresistibly great.

The structure of deferral is not the only aspect of the dilemma of development that, while not dissolvable in theory, is at least displaceable in practice. Kant held that the functional perspective of historical development was subordinate to the normative perspective of moral duty. Not only was his account of human advancement already constructed with a practical interest in the achievement of our moral destiny, it was meant to be "applied," not as a predictive tool or a technical recipe, but as a guideline for moral and political practice. In this respect, I think, Kant was closer to the mark than mainstream development theory has since been. The repeated attempts to construct scientific theories of sociocultural development—whether neo-Marxian theories of historical materialism, neo-Darwinian theories of social evolution, structural-functional theories of modernization, or neoliberal theories of globalization—have not only failed badly as theories but have also been harmful in practice. They have tended to inspire top-down, bureaucratic rule by scientifically trained "development experts," which disqualified local knowledge and treated "target populations" as the objects rather than the subjects of life-transforming decisions.

An alternative approach would be to regard the empirical-theoretical analyses provided by developmental studies as tributary to the practical-political deliberation of collective agents seeking to act on such knowledge, including especially those whose condition is supposed to be improved by it. While acknowledging the interpretive and practical dimensions of development theory undercuts its claim to be part of "a natural science of society," it is compatible with understanding it as an empirically informed and practically oriented analytical framework. One could, I think, only accept the former self-description so long as the main participants in the discourse of global modernity generally shared the same hermeneutic standpoint and the same practical orientation, namely the ones dictated by the realities and interests of European imperialism. But what appeared to be advancement from that perspective, usually looked like conquest, settlement, enslavement, colonization, imperialism, neo-imperialism, or the like from others.

To be sure, the political displacement of the dilemma of development would not eliminate all tensions from it, in particular those arising from the strongly modernist assumptions of democracy, human rights, and the rule of law themselves. These are not cognitively and evaluatively neutral. And they clash with many aspects of non-modern worldviews and forms of life—with viewing social relations in terms of a hierarchical complementarity between genders, castes, classes, or the like; with understanding social status in terms of a scale of intrinsic dignity and value; with regarding the established order as "the" cosmologically or religiously anchored, normal, and proper order of things; with taking the established structure of social functions to be ontologically rooted rather than contingent and alterable; with judging the diversity of worldviews and forms of life in terms not of reasonable pluralism but of truth and error, good, and evil; with rejecting the legitimacy of social arrangements that place limitations on the imperative role of religion in shaping public life; or the like.[42] So the predicament we are left with is marked, at the very least, by a tension between, on the one hand, the preconditions of the modern legal and political forms that underwrite the equal standing and equal voice needed to break the old connection between liberal progressivism and liberal imperialism and, on the other hand, some aspects of the forms of life and social orders most in need of such guarantees. There is no easy exit from this predicament.[43] Kant placed his hope in a gradual "move towards greater agreement on principles . . . [that] will lead to mutual understanding and peace" under conditions of global modernity.[44] In a less providential and less monocultural vein, we may hope at least for a multiplicity of "creative adaptations" to these conditions, as Charles Taylor has put it, drawing on the cultural resources of different traditions and resulting in a degree of overlapping consensus and functional equivalence sufficient to enable global peace and promote global justice.[45]

---

[42] Charles Taylor, *Modern Social Imaginaries* (Durham, NC: Duke University Press, 2004).

[43] For attempts to address aspects of the predicament from the standpoint of a concern to promote non-domination, see the other contributions in this volume. Most germane and complementary to the concerns of this particular chapter are those of Charles Mills and Duncan Ivison.

[44] Kant, "Perpetual Peace," 114.

[45] See Taylor, "Two Theories of Modernity," in *Alternative Modernities*, ed. Dilip Gaonkar (Durham, NC: Duke University Press, 2001), 172–96.

BIBLIOGRAPHY

Appiah, Anthony. *Cosmopolitanism: Ethics in a World of Strangers*. New York: W. W. Norton, 2006.

Armitage, David. *The Ideological Origins of the British Empire*. Cambridge: Cambridge University Press, 2000.

Arneil, Barbara. *John Locke and America: The Defense of English Colonialism*. Oxford: Oxford University Press, 1996.

Benhabib, Seyla. *Another Cosmopolitanism*. Oxford: Oxford University Press, 2006.

Bhabha, Homi K. *The Location of Culture*. London: Routledge, 1994.

Chakrabarty, Dipesh. *Provincializing Europe: Postcolonial Thought and Historical Difference*. Princeton: Princeton University Press, 2000. [Cited in the text as *PE*]

Chatterjee, Partha. *The Nation and Its Fragments*. Princeton, NJ: Princeton University Press, 1993.

Escobar, Arturo. *Encountering Development: The Making and the Unmaking of the Third World*. Princeton: Princeton University Press, 1995.

Fogel, Robert William. *The Escape from Hunger and Premature Death, 1700–2100: Europe, America, and the Third World*. Cambridge: Cambridge University Press, 2004.

Habermas, Jürgen. *Between Facts and Norms: Contributions to a Discourse Theory of Law and Democracy*. Translated by William Rehg. Cambridge, MA: MIT Press, 1996.

Habermas, Jürgen. "The Unity of Reason in the Diversity of Its Voices." In *Postmetaphysical Thinking*, translated by William Hohengarten, 115–48. Cambridge, MA: MIT Press, 1992.

Hoy, David, and Thomas McCarthy. *Critical Theory*. Oxford: Basil Blackwell, 1994.

Ivison, Duncan. "Indigenous Peoples, Injustice, and Global Politics." In *Domination and Global Political Justice: Conceptual, Historical, and Institutional Perspectives*, edited by Barbara Buckinx, Jonathan Trejo-Mathys, and Timothy Waligore. New York: Routledge, 2015.

Kant, Immanuel. *Critique of the Power of Judgment*. Edited by Paul Guyer. Translated by Paul Guyer and Eric Matthews. Cambridge: Cambridge University Press, 2000.

Kant, Immanuel. "The Metaphysics of Morals." In *Practical Philosophy*, edited and translated by Mary J. Gregor. Cambridge: Cambridge University Press, 1996.

Kant, Immanuel. "Perpetual Peace: A Philosophical Sketch." In *Kant: Political Writings*, translated by H. B. Nisbet, 93–130. Cambridge: Cambridge University Press, 1991.

Leys, Colin. *The Rise and Fall of Development Theory*. Bloomington: Indiana University Press, 1996.

Locke, John. *Two Treatises on Government*. Edited by Peter Laslett. Cambridge: Cambridge University Press, 1993.

Mantena, Karuna. *Alibis of Empire*. Princeton: Princeton University Press, 2010.

Marx, Karl. "The British Rule in India." *The New York Daily Tribune*, June 25, 1853. Reprinted in *The Marx-Engels Reader*, 2nd ed., edited by Robert C. Tucker, 653–58. New York: W. W. Norton, 1978.

Marx, Karl. "The Future Results of British Rule in India." *The New York Daily Tribune*, August 8, 1853. Reprinted in *The Marx-Engels Reader*, 2nd ed., edited by Robert C. Tucker, 659–64. New York: W. W. Norton, 1978.

McCarthy, Thomas. *Ideals and Illusions: On Reconstruction and Deconstruction in Contemporary Critical Theory*. Cambridge, MA: MIT Press, 1993.

McCarthy, Thomas. *Race, Empire, and the Idea of Human Development*. Cambridge: Cambridge University Press, 2009.

Mehta, Uday Singh. *Liberalism and Empire*. Chicago: University of Chicago Press, 1999.

Mill, James. *The History of British India*, 6 vols., 3rd ed. London: Baldwin, Cradock, and Joy, 1826.

Mill, John Stuart. "Civilization" [1836; revised ed. 1859]. In *Essays on Politics and Culture*, edited by Gertrude Himmelfarb, 51–84. Garden City, NY: Doubleday, 1962.

Mill, John Stuart. *Considerations on Representative Government* [1861]. South Bend, IN: Gateway, 1962.

Mill, John Stuart. "A Few Words on Non-Intervention" [1859]. In *Essays on Politics and Culture,* edited by Gertrude Himmelfarb, 396–413. Garden City, NY: Doubleday, 1962.

Mill, John Stuart. "The Negro Question." *Fraser's Magazine for Town and Country* XLI, January 1850, 25–31. Reprinted in *The Collected Works of John Stuart Mill*, vol. 21: *Essays on Equality, Law, and Education*, edited by John M. Robson. Toronto: University of Toronto Press, 1984.

Mill, John Stuart. *On Liberty* [1859]. Edited by Elizabeth Rapaport. Indianapolis: Hackett Publishing, 1978.

Mills, Charles W. "Race and Global Justice." In *Domination and Global Political Justice: Conceptual, Historical and Institutional Perspectives*, edited by Barbara

Buckinx, Jonathan Trejo-Mathys, and Timothy Waligore. New York: Routledge, 2015.
Munck, Ronaldo, and Denis O'Hearn, eds. *Critical Development Theory*. London: Zed Books, 1999.
Muthu, Sankar. *Enlightenment and Empire*. Princeton: Princeton University Press, 2003.
Nandy, Ashis. "Colonization of the Mind." In *The Post-Development Reader*, edited by Majid Rahnema and Victoria Bawtree, 168–78. London: Zed Books, 1997.
Pitts, Jennifer. *A Turn to Empire: The Rise of Imperial Liberalism in Britain and France*. Princeton: Princeton University Press, 2005.
Rahnema, Majid, and Victoria Bawtree, eds. *The Post-Development Reader*. London: Zed Books, 1997.
Robson, John. "Civilization and Culture as Moral Concepts." In *The Cambridge Companion to Mill*, edited by John Skorupski, 338–71. Cambridge: Cambridge University Press, 1998.
Sachs, Wolfgang, ed. *The Development Dictionary*. London: Zed Books, 1992.
Said, Edward. *Orientalism*. New York: Vintage Books, 1979.
Sen, Amartya. *Development as Freedom*. New York: Alfred A. Knopf, 1999.
Spivak, Gayatri Chakravorty. *In Other Worlds: Essays in Cultural Politics*. New York: Methuen, 1987.
Stokes, Eric. *The English Utitlitarians and India*. Oxford: Oxford University Press, 1959.
Taylor, Charles. *Modern Social Imaginaries*. Durham, NC: Duke University Press, 2004.
Taylor, Charles. "Two Theories of Modernity." In *Alternative Modernities*, edited by Dilip Gaonkar, 172–96. Durham, NC: Duke University Press, 2001.
Tully, James. *An Approach to Political Philosophy: Locke in Contexts*. Cambridge: Cambridge University Press, 1993.
Young, Robert. *White Mythologies: Writing History and the West*. London: Routledge, 1990.
Weiner, Antje, ed. "Contested Meanings of Norms—The Challenge of Democratic Governance Beyond the State" (Special Issue). *Comparative European Politics* 5, no. 1 (2007).
Zastoupil, Lynn. *John Stuart Mill and India*. Stanford, CA: Stanford University Press, 1994.

8 Race and Global Justice

Charles W. Mills

The theme of this volume is "domination and global political justice" in its multiple possible dimensions. So I want to begin with a striking global analysis from less than a century ago, from the 1920s. I will conceal for the moment the author's identity, except to say that he is a well-known historical figure. See if you can guess who it is before you turn the page:

> Of the billion and a half people in the world, the most powerful are the 400 million whites on the European and American continents; from this base the white races have started out to swallow up other races. The American red aborigines are gone, the African blacks will soon be exterminated, the brown race of India is in the process of dissolution, the yellow races of Asia are now being subjected to the white man's oppression and may, before long, be wiped out. But the 150 million Russians, when their revolution succeeded, broke with the other white races and condemned the white man's imperialistic behaviour; now they are thinking of throwing in their lot with the weaker, smaller peoples of Asia in a struggle against the tyrannical races. So only 250 million of the tyrannical races are left, but they are still trying by inhuman methods and military force to subjugate the other 1, 250 million. So hereafter mankind will be divided into two camps: on one hand will be the 1, 250 million; on the other side, the 250 million. . . . Now we want to revive ['s] lost nationalism and use the strength of our millions to fight for mankind against injustice; this is our divine mission. The Powers are afraid that we will have such thoughts and are setting forth a specious doctrine. They are now advocating cosmopolitanism to inflame us, declaring that, as the civilization of the world advances and as mankind's vision enlarges, nationalism becomes too narrow, unsuited to the present age, and hence that we should espouse cosmopolitanism. In recent years some of ['s] youth, devotees of the new culture, have been opposing nationalism, led astray by this doctrine. But it is not a doctrine which wronged races should talk about. We, the wronged races, must first recover our position of national freedom and equality before we are fit to discuss cosmopolitanism.

For a contemporary readership, especially one unfamiliar with the history of colonialism and anticolonial struggles, this passage will, I suggest, be quite startling in its matter-of-factly *racialist* framework of analysis. The author takes for granted, in a way that clearly indicates he does not see it as likely to be controversial for his audience, that he and his readers are living in a world characterized by white racial domination and exterminist policy. Whites dominate the planet and are seeking to extend their rule indefinitely, if necessary through the genocide of the remaining races. (The reference to Africa is probably due to the depredations of King Leopold II in the Belgian Congo from the late 19th to the early 20th centuries, largely forgotten in the West until Adam Hochschild's *King Leopold's Ghost* refreshed official memory 15 years ago.[1] Hochschild estimates the death toll under the regime at about 10 million people.) So white supremacy is global, and a united, transnational struggle of the nonwhite races against it is necessary for their survival. Races are not at all merely abstract sociological categories, but active social agents.

The editor of the collection from which I took this excerpt characterizes the author's views as "Social Darwinist." But if Social Darwinism is committed to natural racial hierarchy, unavoidable interracial struggle, a biologistic dynamic, and the evolutionary goal of the triumph of the "superior" races, this judgment (at least on the basis of the passage here) seems to me to be questionable.[2] The author's interpretation of the Bolshevik Revolution as constituting a massive white defection from the ranks of the "tyrannical races"—politically naïve as it may appear to us a century later—shows that what is presumed to be at work is not an ineluctable, biologically driven racial determinism. Options are open and moral choice is possible. A class-based Marxism is clearly not taken to be incongruent with a "racial" struggle against global white supremacy; whites may change sides (becoming, in a contemporary vocabulary, "race traitors") and adopt a politics of anti-imperialism instead of a politics of conquest. Note also that this resistance is not being represented as the struggle to achieve a racial dictatorship of nonwhites over their oppressors, nor to prosecute a retaliatory exterminism. Rather, what is being sought is global justice for the "wronged races" of "mankind," a mission with divine sanction. In the writer's opinion, however, it would be a mistake at this stage to endorse a cosmopolitan ideal. Instead, a racial nationalism to restore the "freedom and equality" of the author's oppressed co-nationals is what is called for.

---

1 Adam Hochschild, *King Leopold's Ghost: A Story of Greed, Terror, and Heroism in Colonial Africa* (New York: Houghton Mifflin, 1998).

2 For a general discussion, see Mike Hawkins, *Social Darwinism in European and American Thought, 1860–1945: Nature as Model and Nature as Threat* (New York: Cambridge University Press, 1997), esp. ch. 8.

Only after that has been achieved will it be appropriate to discuss the issue of cosmopolitanism.

I want to use this passage, with all its obvious problems, as a stalking horse to challenge the conventional frameworks in which global domination and global justice are discussed. (The author, I will now reveal, is Sun Yat-sen, standardly viewed as "the father of modern China"; the population figure, which I omitted since it would have given the game away, was 400 million.[3] You might have guessed Marcus Garvey, though imminent African extinction would certainly not have been so off-handedly mentioned by him.) For what it does is bring home both how routinely racial categories were employed in the analysis of European colonial domination only a few decades ago, and how absent they are today from contemporary debates on the problems of globalization.

The philosophical literature on global justice has dramatically expanded in recent years, a manifestation both of the contraction of the planet through ease of communication and travel (so that the longtime cliché of the global village is on the verge of literal realization) and the worsening in many respects of issues of poverty and relative underdevelopment. What might once have been the subject of an occasional article in the conscientious editor's ethics anthology is now routinely the exclusive topic of entire courses. But though a wide range of normative approaches (modified Rawlsian, egalitarian, utilitarian, sufficientarian, cosmopolitan) will typically be canvassed in such readings, a commonality of this literature is the virtual absence of any discussion of race and racism. For those from the former third world (such as myself) familiar with any of the anticolonial writings of the 19th and 20th centuries, this silence is remarkable, since the global injustice of imperialism and colonialism was classically seen (as the Sun Yat-sen excerpt makes clear) precisely *as* a matter of white domination over people of color. This racial dimension was not at all taken to be a merely contingent correlation, accidental and theoretically irrelevant, but causally central and deeply consequential.

Consider the black radical political tradition, which, though it has sometimes degenerated into chauvinism and racism, has at its best been both internationalist and anti-racist, seeking racial equality rather than racial revenge, and advocating a global elimination of racial hierarchy and privilege.[4] Here we can find former slave Quobna Cugoano condemning in 1787 the "Christian nations" not merely for their enslavement of Africans

---

[3] Sun Yat-sen, "San Min Chu I (The Three Principles of the People)" [1927; selections from lecture 4], trans. Frank W. Price, excerpted in *Decolonization: Perspectives from Now and Then*, ed. Prasenjit Duara (New York: Routledge, 2004), 25.

[4] See Anthony Bogues, *Black Heretics, Black Prophets: Radical Political Intellectuals* (New York: Routledge, 2003), for an illuminating overview of some key figures from this international tradition.

but also for their treatment of "the various Indian nations," thereby violating "the universal natural rights and privileges of all men," among whom "there are no inferior species, but all of one blood and of one nature"; David Walker directing his 1829 *Appeal* not just to his fellow black Americans but to "the coloured citizens of the world"; Pan-Africanist Martin Delany complaining in 1852 that "there are two colored to one white person throughout the earth, and yet . . . the white race predominates the colored"; W.E.B. Du Bois describing at the 1900 Pan-African Conference the global problem of "the color line, the question as to how far differences of race . . . are going to be made, hereafter, the basis of denying to over half the world the right of sharing to their utmost ability the opportunities and privileges of modern civilization," and in his famous 1903 *The Souls of Black Folk* predicting that "The problem of the twentieth century is the problem of the color-line, the relation of the darker to the lighter races of men in Asia and Africa, in America and the islands of the sea," a judgment still being echoed more than half a century later by Frantz Fanon's 1961 *The Wretched of the Earth*: "It is evident that what parcels out the world is to begin with the fact of belonging to or not belonging to a given race."[5]

Admittedly, because blacks had to suffer racial slavery and its stigmatizing legacy, as well as colonization, and because anti-black racism has historically been more virulent and more systematically and elaborately developed than any of the other varieties of colonial white racism (as against anti-Semitism), racial theorization has been more salient here than in any other anticolonial/anti-imperialist tradition. A forced black diaspora, largely to the Americas but also to Europe, generated an oppositional body of political theory for which race was the central organizing prism. But it was not at all unique for the period, which is why I made a point of beginning with the Chinese nationalist rather than a black writer. The question then is whether it is worth trying to recuperate the insights of such a racially informed internationalism in a contemporary context. Would the formal thematic introduction of race add anything of value to the current debate, if so how, and by what means do we successfully negotiate the various conceptual and methodological hurdles on such a path?

---

[5] Quobna Ottobah Cugoano, *Thoughts and Sentiments on the Evil of Slavery and Other Writings*, ed. Vincent Carretta (New York: Penguin, 1999), 22, 28–29, 61; David Walker, *David Walker's Appeal: To the Colored Citizens of the World*, ed. Peter P. Hinks (University Park: Pennsylvania State University Press, 2000); Martin Robinson Delany, *The Condition, Elevation, Emigration and Destiny of the Colored People of the United States, Politically Considered* (Philadelphia: 1852), 37; W.E.B. Du Bois, "To the Nations of the World" [1900], *W.E.B. Du Bois: A Reader*, ed. David Levering Lewis (New York: Henry Holt, 1995), 639; W.E.B. Du Bois, *The Souls of Black Folk* [1903], (New York: Penguin, 1996), 13; Frantz Fanon, *The Wretched of the Earth* [1961], trans. Constance Farrington (New York: Grove Press, 1968), 40.

1 RACE (AND WHITENESS) AS A GLOBAL INSTITUTION

The natural starting point is a clarification of the racial metaphysics presupposed by this framework. While skeptics may concede that racism was central to the ideological rationale for imperialism and colonialism, this concession will not generally be intended to imply the same for race. One is ideational, the other material. The understandable fear is that this vocabulary, this kind of discourse, cannot in fact be retrieved without a resurrection of Social Darwinist assumptions, or something similarly dubious. After all, it will be pointed out, it is no accident that these terms have disappeared from mainstream theory. Why try to revive a language which is surely no more than an "oppositional" version of classic racial theory, an "anti-racist racism" in Sartre's famous characterization of Negritude—motivationally perhaps perfectly understandable, but theoretically deficient, a stage to be sublated and transcended? Moreover, how in any case could this vocabulary be applied on a global scale? So a series of refutations is constructed, what could be seen as concentric fallback positions: either race does not exist at all, or it does not exist globally, or it does not exist in the way necessary to sustain any generalizations and theorizations, descriptive and normative, of the desired kind.

Consider the first claim. In the (small) philosophical circles where race is discussed, the key umbrella metaphysical positions are eliminativism and anti-eliminativism. Eliminativists, as the word implies, want to eliminate "race" from our vocabulary, as a non-referring term like "witch" or "phlogiston."[6] They argue that science has disproved the reality of race and we should stop using a concept that is not only evidentially discredited, but one that has caused great harm historically. Anti-eliminativists disagree. Some contend that there is by no means a scientific consensus yet, and that research in forensic anthropology and medical biology shows that we need to retain the concept, even if we reject the idea of racial hierarchy that is, of course, its most famous and pernicious accompaniment. So for them, reports of the demise of the concept of biological race are greatly exaggerated. However, the most important version of anti-eliminativism agrees with eliminativism that race does not exist biologically, but insists that it exists as a social construct. So from this perspective, we need to retain the term to track social realities, both descriptive/explanatory (how particular social groups, "races," come into being and how a racialized society then works) and normative (issues of racial injustice).

---

6 The most prominent eliminativist among philosophers who have worked on race would probably be Kwame Anthony Appiah (from whom the comparison to witches comes). See, for example, *In My Father's House: Africa in the Philosophy of Culture* (New York: Oxford University Press, 1992): "The truth is that there are no races" (40).

In this framework, to say that race is constructed means that it is brought into existence as a social convention established by social mores, legal decisions, opportunity structures, discriminatory practices, the internalization of these norms and concepts, and the corresponding habits of "self" and "other" categorization developed in everyday cognition and everyday interaction.[7] As this listing should have made clear, such a reconceptualization of race is quite anti-biologistic in its assumptions, so that it would be denied that the specter of classic racial theory is necessarily invoked by it. Indeed, the point of the "critical" in "critical race theory," apart from linking it with "critical theory" in the left tradition, is in part precisely to distinguish it from classic "[*uncritical*] race theory," which usually just meant racist theory. So critical race theory is explicitly anti-racist in its mission and in its assumptions, and should not at all be seen as potentially assimilable to a nonwhite version of *Rassenwissenschaft*.[8]

Now, for the past few hundred years, whiteness has been the central racial category—the normative reference point, the default mode.[9] This is illustrated by the simple fact that it comes "naturally" to us (a social naturalness, to be sure) to speak of whites and nonwhites, and not, say, of blacks and nonblacks, or to speak of whites and people of color, and not, say, of people of color and people of noncolor. Whiteness is not natural, but, as with race in general, a social construct: hence such literature of recent years as *The History of White People*, *The Invention of the White Race*, *Whiteness of a Different Color*, *How the Irish Became White*, *How Jews Became White Folks and What That Says about Race in America*, *White on Arrival*, *White by Law*, and many others.[10] These books make it clear that whiteness as a social category is invented (it did not exist in the pre-modern world) and its boundaries and content are conventionally determined. But this invention does not mean that it is *not* real; it is quite real in its social effects of privileging whites, disadvantaging people of color, shaping social opportunities, affecting public policy, determining life chances, impacting how nominally

[7] See Paul Taylor, *Race: A Philosophical Introduction*, 2nd ed. (Malden, MA: Polity, 2013).

[8] For critical race theory in legal theory specifically, see Kimberlé Crenshaw et al., eds., *Critical Race Theory: The Key Writings That Formed the Movement* (New York: New Press, 1995).

[9] Richard Dyer, *White* (New York: Routledge, 1997).

[10] Nell Irvin Painter, *The History of White People* (New York: Norton, 2010); Theodore W. Allen, *The Invention of the White Race*, 2nd ed. (New York: Verso, 2012); Matthew Frye Jacobson, *Whiteness of a Different Color: European Immigrants and the Alchemy of Race* (Cambridge, MA: Harvard University Press, 1998); Noel Ignatiev, *How the Irish Became White* (New York: Routledge, 1995); Karen Brodkin, *How Jews Became White Folks and What That Says about Race in America* (New Brunswick, NJ: Rutgers University Press, 1998); Thomas Guglielmo, *White on Arrival: Italians, Race, Color, and Power in Chicago, 1890–1945* (New York: Oxford University Press, 2003); Ian Haney López, *White by Law: The Legal Construction of Race*, revised ed. (New York: New York University Press, 2006).

inclusive rights and freedoms are actually differentially operationalized, structuring moral consciousness and one's sense of identity, and so forth. As such, race could be seen not merely as *an* institution, but as an institution so important that it would arguably count as part of John Rawls's "basic structure" in its multidimensional social impact on the modern state.[11] The modern state in general, as David Theo Goldberg contends—and certainly the US state—is in fact a racial state.[12]

So that would be the first hurdle cleared. The second is the objection that even if race is real, it could not be global in the appropriate way. After all, the texts above are all American, written by Americans, and referring primarily to the United States. Michael Root has famously said that "Race does not travel." If race is a social construct, an artifact of convention, then surely there is going to be variation in the construction and the conventions from nation to nation, including the possibility that in some countries race will not exist at all. I am classified as black in the United States, for example, and duly fill in the appropriate box on bureaucratic forms, thereby counting as "African-American" for the census and Northwestern University's faculty statistics. But in my native Jamaica, I count as "brown" rather than black, not being dark enough, and as such I am fitted into the middle stratum of what was once, post-Emancipation, a three-tiered pyramid (white/brown/black).[13] So could it not be argued that even if race is global (and there might be exceptions), it is a global patchwork of diverse and competing local systems rather than a planetarily uniform set of norms? And as such, it would be claimed, it cannot play the kind of role this analysis is trying to impute to it.

But though Root's aphorism does capture a constructionist truth, the reality of national variation, it is misleading insofar as it implies that there are *no* overarching commonalities. In both Jamaica and the United States, I will still be categorized as a person of color, someone not white, and as such on the "wrong" side of what is the central and most important global racial divide. And though the borders of whiteness vary, white is a transnational category for the simple reason that it is established by European expansionism—European imperialism and European colonialism. As Howard Winant writes, the result of this process is an "immense planetary metamorphosis" that leads to the creation of a "world racial

---

[11] John Rawls, *A Theory of Justice* (Cambridge, MA: Harvard University Press, 1971).

[12] David Theo Goldberg, *The Racial State* (Malden, MA: Blackwell, 2002); Anthony W. Marx, *Making Race and Nation: A Comparison of the United States, South Africa, and Brazil* (New York: Cambridge University Press, 1998); Moon-Kie Jung, João H. Costa Vargas, and Eduardo Bonilla-Silva, eds., *State of White Supremacy* (Stanford: Stanford University Press, 2011).

[13] M. G. Smith, *The Plural Society in the British West Indies* [1965] (Berkeley: University of California Press, 1984).

system."[14] So though some people counted as white in some countries will not count as (fully?) white in others,[15] it is generally the case across the planet that Europeans and their descendants are dominant, and that there is a "core" (roughly, northwestern Europeans) whiteness of people who are counted as whites pretty well everywhere. Recently, theorists have begun trying to extend critical race theory beyond US borders—see, for example, the British sociologist Steve Garner's *Whiteness: An Introduction*[16]—and as the body of such literature expands, we may expect more detailed and fine-grained case studies of race and whiteness across the world that both address such variations and point out the commonalities.

Finally, to the objection that a global whiteness, even if it existed, could have no explanatory power, bear in mind that in the modern period this category becomes, as emphasized, one of the most central markers of social privilege. It is a matter neither of an accidental and causally otiose correlation, like foot size, nor of a biologically driven *Rassenkampf*, with all the unhappy historical associations such a term will evoke. It is a matter of people being categorized in a certain way, internalizing that categorization, growing up in a world structured around such categories, *and leading lives in the light of that ascribed empowering identity* (with its distinctive motivational and belief sets).

In my own work, I have used the phrase "global white supremacy," which to many will seem like a clearly extremist and indefensible concept.[17] But imagine we jump in the time machine and set the controls for a trip of a century backward. Emerging in early 1914, what will we find? We will find a world on the eve of World War I, which is completely dominated by the colonial empires: British, French, Dutch, Belgian, German, Portuguese, Russian. By Edward Said's estimate, 85% of the earth at the time is under some kind of control by the European powers, white European nations ruling over nonwhite nations.[18] (China is not formally colonized, but it is under European hegemony.) Moreover, in independent countries like the white settler states—the United States, Canada, South Africa, Australia, and New Zealand—it is again whites who are the dominant group, with widespread formal and informal discrimination against Aboriginal peoples and (where

[14] Howard Winant, *The World is a Ghetto: Race and Democracy since World War II* (New York: Basic Books, 2001), 21, 3.
[15] However, with specific reference to the United States, though perhaps with more general applicability, Thomas Guglielmo has argued that the "ethnic" European immigrants (Jews, Irish, Italians) some have claimed to be originally (late 19th century/early 20th century) nonwhite in the United States *were* actually categorized as whites, but inferior ones. In other words, "whiteness" in the period was not a monolith but itself a hierarchically structured category. Nonetheless, even inferior whites were superior to people of color. Guglielmo, *White on Arrival*.
[16] Steve Garner, *Whiteness: An Introduction* (New York: Routledge, 2007).
[17] Charles W. Mills, *The Racial Contract* (Ithaca, NY: Cornell University Press, 1997).
[18] Edward W. Said, *Culture and Imperialism* (New York: Alfred A. Knopf, 1993), 8.

they exist) the descendants of black slaves being the norm. In the Latin American nations, which gained their independence in the 19th century, whites and the light-skinned are, *contra* the myths of "racial democracy" and an all-inclusive *mestizaje*, economically, socially, politically, and culturally privileged over the darker and the indigenous.[19] In sum, across most of the globe, whites are the rulers, both internationally and nationally. The few independent nations of color—black nations like Haiti and Ethiopia, the Asian nation of Japan—all have to operate within a white-dominated world, and are all constrained by its norms and power relationships.

None of these facts is novel; they can be found in any objective history book. What is lacking is the theoretical will to recognize their implications, the refusal to put them together into a composite picture. It might also be objected that "global white supremacy" implies a single coordinating and governing body, say a White House that is not American but globally empowered and authoritative. But a planet dominated by subplanetary political entities that are themselves white-ruled is still, though polycentric, white-ruled overall, even if there is no white world state as such. For though there is no centralized planetary seat of formal white governing power, though whites the world over are divided by national membership, citizens of countries sometimes in conflict with each other, and internally divided by class and gender, there are nonetheless binding transoceanic and transsocial links. Racial ideologies circulate globally, assumptions of nonwhite inferiority and the legitimacy of white rule are taken for granted, a shared colonial history of pacts, treaties, international jurisprudence, and a racial-religious self-conception of being the bearers and preservers of civilization provide common norms and reference points. Across the world, whites coordinate and share information on particular racial issues and follow prescriptions of international law predicated on differential white entitlements. So their "whiteness" is not at all causally irrelevant, but shapes their conception of themselves and others, their view of their group interests, their collective and individual identities, the political and moral framework within which they understand the world. As Branwen Gruffydd Jones comments, "The belief in a hierarchy of peoples—in the superiority of Europeans or people with European ancestry and the inferiority of non-Europeans or 'people of color'—was widespread and routine, a generally unquestioned assumption embedded both in the public and personal European imagination and in the formal institutions of European and international order."[20]

So I would suggest that the concept implicit or explicit in the excerpts cited from Sun Yat-sen, Walker, Delany, Du Bois, and Fanon—the concept of

---

[19] George Reid Andrews, *Afro-Latin America, 1800–2000* (New York: Oxford University Press, 2004).

[20] Branwen Gruffydd Jones, "Introduction: International Relations, Eurocentrism, and Imperialism," in *Decolonizing International Relations*, ed. Gruffydd Jones (Lanham, MD: Rowman & Littlefield, 2006), 2.

a white supremacy that is global—which when first encountered may seem obviously problematic, is actually theoretically quite defensible. And in fact it *is* now being used by some historians to characterize the period. Thus historian Martin Borstelmann refers to "the era of global white supremacy," "the international character of white rule over people of color:" "Continuing differences in the racial distribution of power and wealth confirm the ongoing relevance of this theme to contemporary international history."[21] Similarly, two Australian historians, Marilyn Lake and Henry Reynolds, have published a book whose title pays tribute to Du Bois: *Drawing the Global Colour Line: White Men's Countries and the International Challenge of Racial Equality*. They describe "the spread of 'whiteness' as a transnational form of racial identification," "the basis of geo-political alliances and a subjective sense of self," and comment critically on Benedict Anderson's well-known *Imagined Communities*: "Paradoxically, one outcome of Anderson's argument has been to naturalize the nation as *the* imagined community of modern times, an effect that has obscured the ascendancy of transnational racial identifications and their potency in shaping both personal identity and global politics."[22] Likewise, one chapter of the Italian philosopher Domenico Losurdo's recently translated *Liberalism: A Counter-History* is titled "The West and the Barbarians: A 'Master-Race Democracy' on a Planetary Scale."[23]

In effect, then, these contemporary scholars are *recovering* a concept that was quite obvious and uncontroversial to theorists and activists of color of the period, but which seems strange to us *now* because of the efficiency of the postwar West's erasure of the centrality of race to its rule. Writing specifically about the "Anglosphere" (which for me would be a subsystem, even if the most important one, of the larger global racial system), Srdjan Vucetic points out that in "an effort to forget its racist past, IR [international relations] turned race into a 'taboo.'"[24] But the reality is that "the origins of [the] Anglosphere are racial," "a hierarchy made up of the core and mostly white Self on the one hand and on the other the peripheral and overwhelmingly nonwhite Other."[25] Similarly, Sankaran Krishna argues that "the discipline of International Relations (IR) was and is predicated on a systematic politics of forgetting, a willful amnesia, on the question of race."[26]

---

[21] Martin Borstelmann, *The Cold War and the Color Line: American Race Relations in the Global Arena* (Cambridge, MA: Harvard University Press, 2001), 15, 6.
[22] Marilyn Lake and Henry Reynolds, *Drawing the Global Colour Line: White Men's Countries and the International Challenge of Racial Equality* (New York: Cambridge University Press, 2008), 3, 6.
[23] Domenico Losurdo, *Liberalism: A Counter-History* [2006], trans. Gregory Elliott (New York: Verso, 2011), ch. 7.
[24] Srdjan Vucetic, *The Anglosphere: A Genealogy of a Racialized Indentity in International Relations* (Stanford: Stanford University Press, 2011), 7.
[25] Vucetic, *The Anglosphere*, 3, 6.
[26] Sankaran Krishna, "Race, Amnesia, and the Education of International Relations," in *Decolonizing International Relations*, ed. Gruffydd Jones (Lanham, MD: Rowman & Littlefield, 2006), 89.

Embarrassed both by the death camps' demonstration of where the logic of racism leads—even Europeans could be subjected to mass murder—and by a colonial discourse no longer appropriate for a postcolonial world (if only nominally), the West has sought to white-out the multiple ways race and racial ideology underpinned its global domination. But we need to recover this past both so as better to understand it and to enable us to dismantle the legacy it has left behind. Suitably reconceptualized, race is necessary for such a revisionist theorization and intended egalitarian transformation.

2 LIBERALISM AND RACE

Facing rather than evading this history thus requires that we confront how liberalism has been shaped by race. For with the seeming demise of Marxism, liberalism is now the globally dominant ideology. As such, it constitutes an ethico-juridical set of concepts, norms and principles, underlying assumptions and overarching narratives, which will necessarily be a central reference point for debate, whether as an accepted framework or one to be challenged, modified, and built upon. And at least until recent decades, liberalism has sanitized its racial past. Even now, the accounts standardly given in political philosophy textbooks and encyclopedia summaries are whitewashed versions of the reality. (I emphasize political *philosophy* because far greater progress has been made in political theory.) These accounts usually center on Europe and focus on the white male population, telling an inspirational Whig narrative of the triumph of moral egalitarianism over ascriptive hierarchy, of John Locke vs. Sir Robert Filmer. But once this tale is set in a global context, and the focus broadened to include white women and people of color (i.e., the majority of the world's population), it will be appreciated that the actual story is very different. As Duncan Ivison, Paul Patton, and Will Sanders pointed out more than a decade ago:

> Contemporary political theory has much to learn from the encounter with its colonial past. . . . [D]ifferent strands of western political thought have not only been complicit with, but helped to justify, colonial expansion and imperial control over indigenous peoples and their territories. As much as modern political theory, especially in its liberal and social democratic variants, has emphasized universal human rights, equality before the law and individual and collective freedom, it has also explicitly denied such entitlements to indigenous peoples. . . . As a result, egalitarian political theory has often ended up justifying explicitly inegalitarian institutions and practices.[27]

[27] Duncan Ivison, Paul Patton, and Will Sanders, "Introduction," in *Political Theory and the Rights of Indigenous Peoples*, ed. Duncan Ivison, Paul Patton, and Will Sanders (New York: Cambridge University Press, 2000), 1–2.

And race has provided the theoretical and normative rationale for reconciling egalitarianism and inegalitarianism, differentiating the human population into those deserving and those undeserving of equal treatment. In such works as Barbara Arneil's *John Locke and America*, Uday Singh Mehta's *Liberalism and Empire*, Jennifer Pitts's *A Turn to Empire*, James Tully's *Imperialism and Civic Freedom*, Thomas McCarthy's *Race, Empire, and the Idea of Human Development*, John Hobson's *The Eurocentric Conception of World Politics*, and others, we have traced for us the contours of what Pitts usefully calls an "imperial liberalism," in which it is not merely that pejorative characterizations of Native Americans and Native Australians, Africans and Asians are routine, but in which the key concepts of liberalism *as a theory* are shaped by this imperial logic.[28] The latter is, of course, the really interesting theoretical point, since obviously contemporary white liberals will be emphatic about their repudiation of any demeaning representations of non-European peoples in the tradition's classic writings. But the question is whether such excisions are sufficient to address possibly deeper structural biases in terms of crucial assumptions, framings, norms, and narratives. If liberalism is to be salvaged, if we want to develop an anti-imperial liberalism, such as Pitts claims can be found in many theorists in the tradition before the development of empire, an *Enlightenment against Empire*,[29] in Sankar Muthu's titular phrase, how can this best be done? In political theory, as noted above, there is already a significant body of work seeking to address this question by engaging nuts-and-bolts issues of constitutional reform and indigenous autonomy. But what might the distinctive contribution at the more abstract level of political philosophy be, in terms of the kind of descriptive and normative theory that is its specialization?

I suggest that the feminist example on gender could be illuminating as a model for race. Second-wave feminist philosophers, faced with the task of advancing a feminist agenda in a theoretical and conceptual universe dominated by male frameworks, took various approaches. One was to repudiate liberalism (and Marxism, at a time when Marxism was still seen as a viable contender) in the name of a distinctive, radically new theory that (putatively)

---

[28] Barbara Arneil, *John Locke and America: The Defence of English Colonialism* (Oxford: Clarendon Press, 1996); Uday Singh Mehta, *Liberalism and Empire: A Study in Nineteenth-Century British Liberal Thought* (Chicago: University of Chicago Press, 1999); Jennifer Pitts, *A Turn to Empire: The Rise of Imperial Liberalism in Britain and France* (Princeton, NJ: Princeton University Press, 2005); James Tully, *Public Philosophy in a New Key*, vol. 2, in *Imperialism and Civic Freedom* (New York: Cambridge University Press, 2008); John M. Hobson, *The Eurocentric Conception of World Politics: Western International Theory, 1760–2010* (New York: Cambridge University Press, 2012); Thomas McCarthy, *Race, Empire, and the Idea of Human Development* (New York: Cambridge University Press, 2009); McCarthy, "Liberalism and the Dilemma of Development" (this volume).

[29] Sankar Muthu, *Enlightenment against Empire* (Princeton, NJ: Princeton University Press, 2003).

owed nothing to "masculinist" thought in any form. But another approach was to argue that liberalism's key assumptions and values were not intrinsically problematic, but needed to be rethought in the light of its sexist exclusions. So as Susan Moller Okin pointed out long ago, it was not just a matter of conscientiously using "person," or sometimes even "woman," as the generic human representative, but of reconceptualizing the theory from the ground up.[30] One asked oneself the question: how, counterfactually, would liberalism have developed had its leading thinkers not taken female subordination for granted? What kind of liberalism would one get if the public/private divide had not been drawn in such a way as to exclude women from political life and social justice? How would a theory nominally predicated on the need to safeguard the rights and freedoms of all individuals have to be reconstructed if half of those individuals had not been positioned, by virtue of their sex, as superior to the other half, and had this not been embedded in conceptual framings, normative orientation, value development?

So rather than regarding this body of thought as *liberalism* simpliciter, one framed it self-consciously as *patriarchal liberalism*, and then tried to go beyond its epistemic horizon, in keeping with the critical theory tradition (originally applied just to class society), that the ideological effects of systems of domination are best analyzed and corrected for by reconstructing how the material functioning of the system produces and reproduces them. Thomas McCarthy writes in general of critical theory's strategy that it

> contains elements of immanent, transcendent, and genealogical critique: "immanent" in that it starts from values, ideas, and principles embedded in the cultures and societies it analyzes; (context-) "transcendent" in that it reconstructs these values, ideals, and principles in terms of a general, discourse-ethical account of practical reasoning; and "genealogical" in that it is self-reflectively metacritical of the historical and contemporary forms of existing reason that it seeks to reconstruct as critical resources.[31]

The key point, then, is that one examines hegemonic concepts and norms from a critical perspective predicated on the assumption that they will have been shaped by social domination, and so need either to be reconstructed in more acceptable forms, or rejected outright, by the standards of the superior social-mapping and egalitarian norms of an order without such domination. Class society and class theory historically played this role for Marxism and subsequent critical theory; patriarchy and gender theory have more recently played this role for feminism. And what I am suggesting is that global white supremacy and critical race theory can and should play a similar role for

---

30 Susan Moller Okin, *Justice, Gender, and the Family* (New York: Basic Books, 1989).

31 McCarthy, *Race, Empire*, 14n26.

anti-racism. Pitts's "imperial liberalism" can, I suggest, be more broadly formulated as "racial liberalism"[32] (thereby conceptually uniting inter- and intranational racial domination). Reconceptualizing liberalism this way would, I believe, have several virtues:

(i) It would make clear what I have suggested has tended to be buried in postwar political philosophy, the intimate historical connection between liberalism and race. The study of the racial shaping of the thought of many, if not most, of the central figures of the modern Western canon could thus become a legitimate research area within the field rather than an offhand concession marginalized to the realm (if that much) of occasional footnotes. We would then have a more comprehensive and holistic picture of the tradition, one not sanitized for reasons of political expediency. In addition, it would highlight the link between imperial expansion and the creation of racial polities[33] both in the former first world and the former third world nations, preempting the psychologizing of racism which has been the liberal norm since the aftermath of World War II. Continuing racial subordination would be conceptualized, as it should be, as a matter of political economy, with racism as its ideology. Whether as one strain of (in Rogers Smith's formulation)[34] "multiple traditions" in American national political culture (and elsewhere too, I would claim) or as "symbiotic" with liberalism (my own preferred analysis), racial discourse would be given the theoretical centrality to moral and political philosophy it deserves.

(ii) Correspondingly, it would open the conceptual door for the admission to the canon of thinkers in the black, anticolonial, and third world traditions of political philosophy, whose central focus historically was, of course, white racism and European domination. In other words, the construction of "Western" political philosophy as raceless has the ideological consequence not merely of misrepresenting its own actual past, but of erecting a convenient *cordon sanitaire* between it and the oppositional anti-racist tradition of people of color. A political theorist of the stature of W.E.B. Du Bois, for example, can be excluded from the canon because his work is preoccupied with the issue of racial subordination and how to overcome it. And since racial subordination is not recognized *as* political (or even as existent), his writings—"Afro-modern political thought"[35]—cannot be political philosophy. Thus we get the absurd situation of a white tradition representing itself as colorless and separate from the black tradition when it is *precisely because*

---

32 Charles W. Mills, "Racial Liberalism," *PMLA (Publications of the Modern Language Association of America)* 123, no. 5 (2008): 1380–97.

33 Charles W. Mills, "The Racial Polity," in *Blackness Visible: Essays on Philosophy and Race* (Ithaca, NY: Cornell University Press, 1998).

34 Rogers M. Smith, *Civic Ideals: Conflicting Visions of Citizenship in US History* (New Haven, CT: Yale University Press, 1997).

35 See Robert Gooding-Williams, *In the Shadow of Du Bois: Afro-Modern Political Thought in America* (Cambridge, MA: Harvard University Press, 2009).

of its exclusionary racist whiteness that the oppositional black tradition has had to come into existence in the first place! And given the planetary reach of the West, a case can obviously be made that globalization *avant la lettre* suggests the need for a redrawing of how the political thought of the nationals of non-Western nations should be categorized also, when we seek to demarcate the boundaries of "Western" political philosophy.

(iii) Finally, it would help end the ghettoization of contemporary political philosophers who work on race, who are currently regarded as pursuing an idiosyncratic agenda, marginal to the mainstream of the profession. Critical race theory would not be viewed as a field unto itself, a self-created intellectual ghetto conceptually separated from both the (by implication raceless) mainstream political philosophy literature and the global justice literature, but as offering a distinct perspective on that subject matter that needs to be engaged with. Through such a desegregation of intellectual worlds—a desegregation of both key thinkers and key themes—the conceptual space would then be opened up for a rethinking of descriptive and normative political philosophy in the light of this unacknowledged history: Locke's self-owning appropriators confronted with the non-self-owning Frederick Douglass; Kant's cosmopolitanism in critical dialogue with Edward Said's; Hegel's World-Spirit challenged by Du Bois's indictment of global whiteness. Personhood, rights, freedoms, democracy, recognition, autonomy, property, self-ownership, respect for self and others, civilization, the nation-state, the social contract, the ambit of justice—how might all of these have to be rethought once the history of imperialism and colonialism is taken into account, and its influence on the shaping of all of these concepts made the subject of philosophical investigation?

3 RACE AND THE RETHINKING OF JUSTICE

Let us turn now to justice, and racial justice. There is a remarkable disjuncture—indeed a chasm—between the *professional* literature on justice produced by philosophers and the *popular* discussions of the subject, both in the United States and—at least historically (as pointed out in my opening pages)—globally. *Racial justice* is one of the main banners under which the American civil rights movement and to a significant extent the global anticolonial movement (which Martin Borstelmann characterizes as "the international civil rights movement")[36] marched. Yet in the tremendous revival of Anglo-American political philosophy over the past 40 years, stimulated by John Rawls's 1971 *A Theory of Justice*, it is a phrase and a topic that is virtually completely absent. Whether directed at national or planetary justice, this huge body of work has almost nothing to say about racial justice. In such authoritative reference works of the last decade as Samuel

[36] Borstelmann, *Cold War*, 46.

Freeman's edited *Cambridge Companion to Rawls* (2003), his own exhaustively expository *Rawls* (2007), Jon Mandle's *Rawls's* A Theory of Justice: *An Introduction* (2009), Percy B. Lehning's *John Rawls: An Introduction* (2009), and Sebastiano Maffettone's *Rawls: An Introduction* (2010), for example, one finds at best isolated sentences or paragraphs referring to racial discrimination, and never any detailed exploration of its implications for racial justice.[37]

What explains this silence? In my opinion, a confluence of factors is at work. First, there is the demographic whiteness of the profession: about 98% in the United States. Insofar as, even within a subject as abstract as philosophy, group experience and group privilege play a role in influencing concerns and interests, we would expect that those who have historically been the beneficiaries of racial injustice would tend to have less interest in exploring the topic than those who have been its victims. (Again, the feminist analogy is illuminating: compare the non-discussion of gender justice as a topic in philosophy before the relative influx of women into the profession from the 1970s onward.) Second, there is the whiteness of the tradition itself—the fact that race has not generally been an issue critically examined within white philosophy (as against uncritically endorsed in racist statements by white philosophers).[38] Third, as mentioned at the start, it might be felt (now) that race is not really a respectable category, and that racial justice can be subsumed into other kinds of justice, so that in any case it is really redundant. Fourth, we have the problem—not peculiar to philosophy, but exacerbated here because of its disciplinary abstraction away from the empirical—of the general sanitization of the racist historical record, at least until comparatively recently, by the academies of the European colonial powers and their offshoots, such as the United States. With a few honorable exceptions, it has been a history of whitewash, a past of racial atrocity now embarrassing, that needs to be denied or downplayed. Finally, I would suggest that the overwhelming orientation of the field towards what Rawls famously called "ideal theory," the theory of distributive justice appropriate for a "perfectly just society," has itself been a major contributor to this outcome. Not only did it postpone matters of non-ideal theory, preeminently matters of compensatory justice, to such time (ever receding over the horizon) as ideal theory would have been properly worked out, but it marginalized as a peripheral concern the historically accurate mapping of the past with which compensatory justice is definitionally concerned. Ideal theory would

---

[37] Samuel Freeman, ed., *The Cambridge Companion to Rawls* (New York: Cambridge University Press, 2003); Samuel Freeman, *Rawls* (New York: Routledge, 2007); Jon Mandle, *Rawls's* A Theory of Justice: *An Introduction* (New York: Cambridge University Press, 2009); Percy B. Lehning, *John Rawls: An Introduction* (New York: Cambridge University Press, 2009); Sebastiano Maffettone, *Rawls: An Introduction* (Malden, MA: Polity, 2010).

[38] See Andrew Valls, ed., *Race and Racism in Modern Philosophy* (Ithaca, NY: Cornell University Press, 2005).

turn out to have deleterious effects not merely normatively but, as Onora O'Neill has pointed out, descriptively, in terms of the conceptualizations typically deployed of society and the polity, which have generally abstracted away from real-life, non-ideal structures of oppression.[39]

How do we redress this situation? In her recent *Scales of Justice*, Nancy Fraser argues that the "framing" of justice needs to be self-consciously rethought in a world where "transnational social movements contest the national frame within which justice conflicts have historically been situated and seek to re-map the bounds of justice on a broader scale," one that challenges "the Westphalian mapping of political space"; that is, "political communities as geographically bounded units, demarcated by sharply drawn borders and arrayed side by side."[40] As indicated at the start of the essay, such a mapping was always put into question by the international anticolonial movement, which saw European domination and white racial hegemony as global. More recently, the question of what justice demands to repair the legacy of the colonial past has explicitly been raised by nations of the Global South. The marginality of such concerns in the mainstream justice literature can illuminatingly be thought of as manifestations of a particular frame, what Joe Feagin calls the "white racial frame," which has been so influential in shaping white cognition over the past few hundred years that even normative theory is affected by it.[41] As feminist liberals trying to reclaim rather than repudiate liberalism have sought to rethink patriarchal liberalism so as to purge it of a masculinist bias that runs far deeper than overtly stigmatizing representations of women, so too, I would suggest, we need to rethink imperial liberalism, racial liberalism, so as to eliminate its distinctive white bias.

(i) The first step, in my opinion, should be explicitly to shift from ideal to non-ideal theory. While a growing body of recent work has questioned the utility of Rawlsian ideal theory, the specific problems posed by race have still not been addressed.[42] But racial justice is, almost by definition, a matter of non-ideal theory. This follows because *races would not even exist in an ideal society*. We would still have human beings of different skin colors, hair textures, and facial morphologies, but they would not constitute *races*. As argued in the opening section, race is socially constructed, and in the absence

---

39 Onora O'Neill, "Justice, Gender, and International Boundaries," in *The Quality of Life*, eds. Martha C. Nussbaum and Amartya Sen (New York: The Clarendon Press, 1993).

40 Nancy Fraser, *Scales of Justice: Reimagining Political Space in a Globalizing World* (New York: Columbia University Press, 2009), 1, 4.

41 Joe R. Feagin, *The White Racial Frame: Centuries of Racial Framing and Counter-Framing* (New York: Routledge, 2010).

42 Ingrid Robeyns and Adam Swift, eds., "Social Justice: Ideal Theory, Nonideal Circumstances" [Special Issue], *Social Theory and Practice* 34, no. 3 (2008); A. John Simmons, "Ideal and Nonideal Theory," *Philosophy & Public Affairs* 38, no. 1 (2010): 5–36.

of racially discriminatory (non-ideal) social practices and institutions, race would never have come into existence in the first place. So the "whiteness" of ideal theory is manifest not merely in an epistemology that draws a curtain over the past and focuses instead on the depiction of an ideally just order that supposedly has the potential for addressing everybody's concerns, transracially, but in its very metaphysics, in that a Rawlsian, well-ordered society would be raceless. And even if racelessness can arguably constitute a normative target for us, an ideal to be aimed at, a society where race has been created and then dismantled through the appropriate public policy measures is not the moral equivalent of a society where race never came into existence in the first place. So the principles of justice necessary for bringing about the former will in key respects be different from Rawlsian principles, since they will be predicated on the need to correct past oppression, whereas Rawls's principles are not.

Racial justice should then be thought of as a concept for the realm of non-ideal theory, meant to complement rather than substitute for work such as Thomas Pogge's moral targeting of past Western colonialism and imperialism, and present Western global institutional domination.[43] *Racial justice* is a heuristically useful category because, to a high degree, it tracks the legacy of the unfair global racial structure, established by colonialism and imperialism, white settlement and African slavery, that tendentially privileges whites globally, and that needs to be "repaired." As Thomas McCarthy writes:

> [S]ince the most developed countries are disproportionately former colonial powers, and the least developed are former colonies, the neo-imperial system of domination and exploitation appears to be, in some considerable measure, a legacy of the five preceding centuries of colonialism and imperialism in their classical modern forms. If this is so, the present requirements of global justice include not only establishing relations of non-domination and fair terms of exchange but also, and interdependently, repairing the harmful effects of past injustice. . . . Coming to terms with this past of racial and imperial injustice, and seeking to remedy the continuing harms that resulted from it are demands of reparative justice.[44]

"Race," in other words, tracks unfair advantage and disadvantage. Whites as a group have more wealth, more status, and more political and cultural influence. This edge is not the result of differential innate ability, or a greater degree of industriousness, but is the outcome of several hundred years of transnational, as well as intranational (in the white settler states, for example), exploitation, manifest both in greater resources for

---

[43] See, for example, Thomas Pogge, *World Poverty and Human Rights*, 2nd ed. (Malden, MA: Polity, 2008).
[44] McCarthy, *Race, Empire*, 4, 17.

whites as a racial group (which would advantage them in itself) and national and transnational structures which favor whites locally and the European and Euro-settler states globally. This is not a claim about individual racism, though it would also be naïve to think we are living in a post-racial epoch. Rather, it is a claim about *the social-systemic reproduction of unfair white advantage*. Race cannot subsume other categories of justice because other metrics of social oppression exist also (class, gender). But neither is it the case that these other metrics can subsume race without theoretical residue, because of racial differentiation in the causal chains accounting for poverty among whites and nonwhites, distinct dimensions to racial injustice that are absent from class injustice, and a radically divergent history that violates the norms even of right-wing liberalism, thus making possible a normative strategy that need not rely on social-democratic values.

(ii) The conceptual shift from distributive to corrective justice, from the distributive norms of a well-ordered society to the rectificatory norms of an ill-ordered society, is thus crucial and can, in my opinion, be seen as roughly the equivalent for race theory of the feminist challenge to the drawing of the public/private demarcation for gender theory. The key insight of second-wave feminism was that the way the private sphere was demarcated from the public sphere was theoretically pivotal, since gender justice as a normative issue was then conceptually obfuscated. Injustice happened in the public sphere, the state, and the marketplace, not in the family and the household, which were beyond justice.[45] Here the approximate homologue is the realization that what Rawls calls "compensatory justice" cannot, for race, be achieved within his conceptual framework, and that ideal theory, rather than providing the best theoretical foundation upon which to do non-ideal theory adequately, as Rawls claimed, actually obstructs its mission. So the very orientation towards ideal theory has not merely left these issues *contingently* unaddressed (that is, white philosophers have not as a matter-of-fact chosen to address them), but *structurally unaddressable* (that is, the apparatus itself is inimical to carrying out this normative agenda).

The introduction of racial justice as a theme and imperative in both the domestic and the global justice literature would thus have the virtue of making clear that what is demanded is a correction of past wrongs, thereby forcing onto the table an accounting of those wrongs. Moreover, a reparative normative project has traditionally been seen as more urgent in ethical theory, since it is obligatory for all liberals to correct violations of negative rights, whereas poverty relief is too easily pushed over the moral border into the realm of the supererogatory, praiseworthy but not (for right-liberals) required of us. Rectificatory justice might thus generate a higher degree of convergence between rival theoretical positions than distributive justice—think of the huge differences between egalitarians, modified Rawlsians, libertarians, utilitarians, adequacy theorists, and cosmopolitans on what the

[45] Okin, *Justice, Gender, and the Family.*

latter requires of us. As Daniel Butt points out in his recent book, *Rectifying International Injustice*,

> It is hard to maintain that there is a great deal of real world support for redistributive cosmopolitanism. . . . Given the apparent lack of public support for global egalitarianism . . . it may well be that the best political strategy for those who support extensive redistribution is not to seek to challenge the deeply held foundational principles of real world political actors, but to maintain that these very principles, if properly understood, call for a substantial [global] redistribution of resources. . . . [Accordingly, the] account of harm given in this book . . . draws upon paradigm cases of unjust international interaction.[46]

Insofar as even right-wing liberals presumably oppose (as good liberals) racism and unjust enrichment, they should be able to agree that the victims of racial injustice deserve compensation for the past. (Of course, the picture is more complicated than I am representing it here, since there can be value-convergence across the spectrum of views on anti-discrimination principles, but radical *factual* divergence on what that history is, and whether it can truly be claimed that the situation of the less-developed nations today, or of, say, blacks in the United States, results from this history. The political right will have competing narratives of their own to offer.)

But apart from this strategic point, there is also, more importantly, a principled point. Simply put, justice, and morality in general, requires that moral actions be carried out under a certain description for them to have the appropriate identity. This is not, of course, peculiar to ethics but a general feature of all actions. In this context, the relevant point is that all redistribution is not the same. If I give you 20 dollars because I am feeling sorry for you, it is not the same as if I were to give you 20 dollars to repay the money I borrowed last month. In both cases, 20 dollars has gone from me to you, but the first is an act of charity while the second is the repayment of a debt. So the answer to the question of what the nature of the transaction is depends not merely on the ("objective") material transfer of a 20 dollar bill between us but the ("subjective"/"intersubjective") description under which it is carried out, and our respective understandings of what is going on.

More seriously, and on a global scale, suppose that government or international bodies were won over by egalitarian arguments or a Rawlsian commitment to remedying the situation of the worst-off, and transferred resources to black Americans who are the descendants of slaves, or to Australian Aborigines suffering from their ancestors' expropriation, or to third world peoples impoverished because of the colonization of their

[46] Daniel Butt, *Rectifying International Injustice: Principles of Compensation and Restitution Between Nations* (New York: Oxford University Press, 2009), 13, 14, 16.

country. Still, they would have arguably not gotten their due. For reparations to be made, for the wrong against them and their ancestors to be corrected—repaired, made good, rectified—what is required is not merely a physical transfer of resources but a transfer taking place under a description and on a normative foundation that makes it a certain kind of action and not another kind of action. If the narrative that philosophers such as McCarthy and myself believe is roughly true (and obviously this is a hugely controversial and contested topic), then distributive justice approaches, Rawlsian or otherwise, are failing to target the actual wrong involved.

Relatedly, rectificatory justice, resting on a different normative justification than distributive justice, has additional prerequisites for it to be fully achieved. There are symbolic aspects to rectification—an official apology, moral condemnation of perpetrators, rewriting of governing narratives, memorialization—that simply do not arise if it is just a matter of redistributing assets and resources. The ideal of rectification is healing, and the recognition of the wrongs of the past *as* wrongs. If the wrong has involved the systematic denial of personhood to the group in question, as racial wrongs typically do, then correction requires that this denial be retracted through a reaffirmation of racial personhood (or an affirmation, if personhood was never conceded in the first place). Moreover, this applies not just to the living but the dead also. The dead cannot be brought back, but one can choose to respect or continue to disrespect them. This is, of course, one of the central aims of memorialization, which justified the postwar creation of Holocaust Memorial Museums. But the question to be asked is: where are the memorials for all of Europe's other dead? The Third Reich is universally condemned, but what about the Weiss Reich? Where are the memorials for Spain's Amerindian Holocaust, or the Congolese who died under Belgian rule, or the Nama and Herero people exterminated by the *Vernichtungsbefehl* in German Southwest Africa, or the Ethiopians and Libyans gassed in Italy's colonial wars, or the Kikuyu slaughtered in the British counterinsurgency campaign in Kenya, or the Algerians subjected to torture and massacre by French troops, or the millions of Africans who perished in the Atlantic Slave Trade? What is required is a global Truth and Reconciliation Commission that would bring to light these suppressed histories, and pay the appropriate respect to this huge, unmarked and unacknowledged nonwhite necropolis.

CONCLUSION

I want to close by returning to the issue raised at the start of this essay. Against this background, we should now better be able to appreciate Sun Yat-sen's wariness about what could be termed a premature cosmopolitanism, and understand why a racially informed cosmopolitanism is neither a contradiction in terms nor incompatible with liberal universalism. In the final chapter of her book on Du Bois, *Democracy's Reconstruction*, Lawrie Balfour warns that in "a modern world order begotten through racial slavery and colonial conquest," a putatively color-blind and race-transcendent cosmopolitanism is likely to be bogus, evading rather than confronting "the racialized forms of power that have defined modern experience."[47] In the context of the times—and even today, nearly a century later—the cosmopolitanism being excoriated by Sun Yat-sen was, I would suggest, the global conceptual equivalent of the "color-blindness" and "post-raciality" now hegemonic among the white population in the United States—a verbal, rather than substantive, dissolving of continuing hierarchies of white racial privilege in a spuriously attractive ideal that, by its failure to name, confront, and address the past will only guarantee its perpetuation. Race can only be transcended by facing and working through it, not by evading and pretending to have sublated it. A liberalism and a cosmopolitanism that fail to deal with race will continue to be a racial liberalism and cosmopolitanism, incapable of prescribing the measures of rectificatory racial justice necessary not just for dismantling the long-established structures of racial domination, but also for transforming white moral psychology and consciousness, thereby laying the foundations for a new, genuinely post-racial world.[48]

---

[47] Lawrie Balfour, *Democracy's Reconstruction: Thinking Politically with W.E.B. Du Bois* (New York: Oxford University Press, 2011), 116, 129.

[48] An earlier version of this chapter was presented at the conference, "Domination Across Borders," in Bad Homburg, Germany on July 4–5, 2011. I would like to thank Barbara Buckinx, Jonathan Trejo-Mathys, and Timothy Waligore for the invitation, Justitia Amplificata for the funding, and the attendees for their comments and criticisms.

BIBLIOGRAPHY

Allen, Theodore W. *The Invention of the White Race*, 2nd ed. New York: Verso, 2012.

Andrews, George Reid. *Afro-Latin America, 1800–2000*. New York: Oxford University Press, 2000.

Appiah, Kwame Anthony. *In My Father's House: Africa in the Philosophy of Culture*. New York: Oxford University Press, 1992.

Arneil, Barbara. *John Locke and America: The Defence of English Colonialism*. Oxford: Clarendon Press, 1996.

Balfour, Lawrie. *Democracy's Reconstruction: Thinking Politically with W.E.B. Du Bois*. New York: Oxford University Press, 2011.

Bogues, Anthony. *Black Heretics, Black Prophets: Radical Political Intellectuals*. New York: Routledge, 2003.

Borstelmann, Thomas. *The Cold War and the Color Line: American Race Relations in the Global Arena*. Cambridge, MA: Harvard University Press, 2001.

Brodkin, Karen. *How Jews Became White Folks and What That Says about Race in America*. New Brunswick, NJ: Rutgers University Press, 1998.
Butt, Daniel. *Rectifying International Injustice: Principles of Compensation and Restitution Between Nations*. New York: Oxford University Press, 2009.
Crenshaw, Kimberlé, Neil Gotanda, Gary Peller, and Kendall Thomas, eds. *Critical Race Theory: The Key Writings That Formed the Movement*. New York: New Press, 1995.
Cugoano, Quobna Ottobah. *Thoughts and Sentiments on the Evil of Slavery and Other Writings*. Edited by Vincent Carretta. New York: Penguin Books, 1999.
Delany, Martin Robinson. *The Condition, Elevation, Emigration and Destiny of the Colored People of the United States, Politically Considered*. Philadelphia: 1852.
Du Bois, W.E.B. *The Souls of Black Folk* [1903]. New York: Penguin, 1996.
Du Bois, W.E.B. "To the Nations of the World" [1900]. In *W.E.B. Du Bois: A Reader*, edited by David Levering Lewis, 639–641. New York: Henry Holt, 1995.
Dyer, Richard. *White*. New York: Routledge, 1997.
Fanon, Frantz. *The Wretched of the Earth* [1961]. Translated by Constance Farrington. New York: Grove Press, 1968.
Feagin, Joe R. *The White Racial Frame: Centuries of Racial Framing and Counter-Framing*. New York: Routledge, 2010.
Fraser, Nancy. *Scales of Justice: Reimagining Political Space in a Globalizing World*. New York: Columbia University Press, 2009.
Freeman, Samuel, ed. *The Cambridge Companion to Rawls*. New York: Cambridge University Press, 2003.
Freeman, Samuel. *Rawls*. New York: Routledge, 2007.
Garner, Steve. *Whiteness: An Introduction*. New York: Routledge, 2007.
Goldberg, David Theo. *The Racial State*. Malden, MA: Blackwell, 2002.
Gooding-Williams, Robert. *In the Shadow of Du Bois: Afro-Modern Political Thought in America*. Cambridge, MA: Harvard University Press, 2009.
Guglielmo, Thomas. *White on Arrival: Italians, Race, Color, and Power in Chicago, 1890–1945*. New York: Oxford University Press, 2003.
Haney López, Ian. *White by Law: The Legal Construction of Race*, revised ed. New York: New York University Press, 2006.
Hawkins, Mike. *Social Darwinism in European and American Thought, 1860–1945: Nature as Model and Nature as Threat*. New York: Cambridge University Press, 1997.
Hobson, John M. *The Eurocentric Conception of World Politics: Western International Theory, 1760–2010*. New York: Cambridge University Press, 2012.
Hochschild, Adam. *King Leopold's Ghost: A Story of Greed, Terror, and Heroism in Colonial Africa*. New York: Houghton Mifflin, 1998.
Ignatiev, Noel. *How the Irish Became White*. New York: Routledge, 1995.
Ivison, Duncan, Paul Patton, and Will Sanders. "Introduction." In *Political Theory and the Rights of Indigenous Peoples*, edited by Duncan Ivison, Paul Patton, and Will Sanders. New York: Cambridge University Press, 2000.
Jacobson, Matthew Frye. *Whiteness of a Different Color: European Immigrants and the Alchemy of Race*. Cambridge, MA: Harvard University Press, 1998.
Jones, Branwen Gruffydd. "Introduction: International Relations, Eurocentrism, and Imperialism." In *Decolonizing International Relations*, edited by Gruffydd Jones. Lanham, MD: Rowman & Littlefield, 2006.
Jung, Moon-Kie, João H. Costa Vargas, and Eduardo Bonilla-Silva, eds. *State of White Supremacy*. Stanford: Stanford University Press, 2011.
Krishna, Sankaran. "Race, Amnesia, and the Education of International Relations." In *Decolonizing International Relations*, edited by Gruffydd Jones. Lanham, MD: Rowman & Littlefield, 2006.

Lake, Marilyn, and Henry Reynolds. *Drawing the Global Colour Line: White Men's Countries and the International Challenge of Racial Equality*. New York: Cambridge University Press, 2008.
Lehning, Percy B. *John Rawls: An Introduction*. New York: Cambridge University Press, 2009.
Losurdo, Domenico. *Liberalism: A Counter-History* [2006]. Translated by Gregory Elliott. New York: Verso, 2011.
Maffettone, Sebastiano. *Rawls: An Introduction*. Malden, MA: Polity, 2010.
Mandle, Jon. *Rawls's* A Theory of Justice: *An Introduction*. New York: Cambridge University Press, 2009.
Marx, Anthony W. *Making Race and Nation: A Comparison of the United States, South Africa, and Brazil*. New York: Cambridge University Press, 1998.
McCarthy, Thomas. "Liberalism and the Dilemma of Development." In *Domination and Global Political Justice: Conceptual, Historical, and Institutional Perspectives*, edited by Barbara Buckinx, Jonathan Trejo-Mathys, and Timothy Waligore. New York: Routledge, 2015.
McCarthy, Thomas. *Race, Empire, and the Idea of Human Development*. New York: Cambridge University Press, 2009.
Mehta, Uday Singh. *Liberalism and Empire: A Study in Nineteenth-Century British Liberal Thought*. Chicago: University of Chicago Press, 1999.
Mills, Charles W. *The Racial Contract*. Ithaca, NY: Cornell University Press, 1997.
Mills, Charles W. "Racial Liberalism." *PMLA (Publications of the Modern Language Association of America)* 123, no. 5 (2008): 1380–97.
Mills, Charles W. "The Racial Polity." In *Blackness Visible: Essays on Philosophy and Race*. Ithaca, NY: Cornell University Press, 1998.
Muthu, Sankar. *Enlightenment against Empire*. Princeton, NJ: Princeton University Press, 2003.
Okin, Susan Moller. *Justice, Gender, and the Family*. New York: Basic Books, 1989.
O'Neill, Onora. "Justice, Gender, and International Boundaries." In *The Quality of Life*, edited by Martha C. Nussbaum and Amartya Sen. New York: The Clarendon Press, 1993.
Painter, Nell Irvin. *The History of White People*. New York: Norton, 2010.
Pitts, Jennifer. *A Turn to Empire: The Rise of Imperial Liberalism in Britain and France*. Princeton, NJ: Princeton University Press, 2005.
Pogge, Thomas. *World Poverty and Human Rights*, 2nd ed. Malden, MA: Polity, 2008.
Rawls, John. *A Theory of Justice*. Cambridge, MA: Harvard University Press, 1971.
Robeyns, Ingrid, and Adam Swift, eds. "Social Justice: Ideal Theory, Nonideal Circumstances" [Special Issue]. *Social Theory and Practice* 34, no. 3 (2008).
Said, Edward W. *Culture and Imperialism*. New York: Alfred A. Knopf, 1993.
Simmons, A. John. "Ideal and Nonideal Theory." *Philosophy & Public Affairs* 38, no. 1 (2010): 5–36.
Smith, M. G. *The Plural Society in the British West Indies* [1965]. Berkeley: University of California Press, 1984.
Smith, Rogers M. *Civic Ideals: Conflicting Visions of Citizenship in US History*. New Haven, CT: Yale University Press, 1997.
Taylor, Paul. *Race: A Philosophical Introduction*, 2nd ed. Malden, MA: Polity, 2013.
Tully, James. *Imperialism and Civic Freedom*, vol. II of *Public Philosophy in a New Key*. New York: Cambridge University Press, 2008.
Valls, Andrew, ed. *Race and Racism in Modern Philosophy*. Ithaca, NY: Cornell University Press, 2005.
Vucetic, Srdjan. *The Anglosphere: A Genealogy of a Racialized Identity in International Relations*. Stanford: Stanford University Press, 2011.

Walker, David. *David Walker's Appeal: To the Colored Citizens of the World*. Edited by Peter P. Hinks. University Park: Pennsylvania State University Press, 2000.
Winant, Howard. *The World is a Ghetto: Race and Democracy since World War II*. New York: Basic Books, 2001.
Yat-sen, Sun. "San Min Chu I (The Three Principles of the People)" [1927; selections from lecture 4]. Translated by Frank W. Price. Excerpted in *Decolonization: Perspectives from Now and Then*, edited by Prasenjit Duara. New York: Routledge, 2004.

9 Indigenous Peoples, Injustice, and Global Politics

Duncan Ivison

1

In what remains one of the more intriguing discussions of injustice in recent Anglo-American political theory, Judith Shklar identifies a number of crucial features of what she calls the "faces of injustice."[1] One part of her argument is to distinguish between misfortune and injustice and explore what lies at the heart of claims of injustice in Western political thought. Another is to track our indifference to the cruelty inherent in injustice, at least from the perspective of its victims. But one of her deep claims is also that injustice should not be understood as merely the absence of justice—at least, if by justice we mean an essentially procedural and distributive concept. Her point is not that the absence of normal justice does not matter, but that the "normal" model's approach is "complacent" and overestimates the extent to which the institutions it underwrites can really cope with the kind of harm human beings can do to each other.[2]

There are two striking aspects to her argument. The first is her insistence about really getting to grips with the nature of injustice; that is, about the ability of our theories of justice to actually do justice to injustice—to give injustice its due. Part of her answer is to insist that victims of injustice need to be heard, especially by theorists of justice. This complicates any easy distinction between "mere" misfortune and "active" injustice. The second interesting aspect of her argument is the way she goes about it. She does not begin with a general theory, or attempt to subsume the explanation of injustice to a timeless set of principles, but attempts to wrestle with it in all of its complexity and in a range of different contexts. Thus in the course of her book, *The Faces of Injustice*, we hear not only from political theorists (including Plato, Augustine, Montaigne, and Rousseau), but also from novelists (such as Dickens, Hardy, and E. L. Doctorow), which complicates and contextualizes her analysis.

---

[1] Judith N. Shklar, *The Faces of Injustice* (Cambridge, MA: Harvard University Press, 1990).
[2] Ibid., 18.

Theorizing about injustice is not in itself problematic. But there is something to Shklar's idea that we seem to have more immediate access to what constitutes injustice, as opposed to what is just. Political movements often seem to acquire their motivational force in rallying around what is perceived to be wrong, as opposed to ideal theories about what is just. Indeed, Amartya Sen has recently argued that we do not need an ideal theory of justice in order to identify what is unjust in the world, or even to develop means of addressing that injustice.[3]

In this chapter I want to explore the relation between injustice and domination with regard to our broader theories of domestic and global justice. Can our dominant theories and approaches to justice give injustice its due? I will begin with my own example, which over the course of the chapter will point towards a conception of global political justice.

2

In June 2007, the Australian government announced the creation of the *Northern Territory Emergency Response* (NTER), otherwise known as the "Intervention." The several statutes that made up the response, passed with bipartisan support in the Parliament, were developed in light of a devastating report on the social conditions of Aboriginal communities in the Northern Territory, and especially the situation faced by young children and women.[4] This was not news. There have been plenty of similar reports and similar howls of outrage. But this report struck a powerful chord among the general public, due to the timing of its release (close to a federal election), and especially the deeply disturbing accounts of child abuse and social dysfunction. The measures introduced in the legislation included improving community healthcare and taking immediate steps to improve housing, sanitation, and school facilities. But it also included a range of other things: mandatory income management for Aboriginal welfare recipients, the banning of alcohol and pornography from Aboriginal communities, the suspension of a permit system that controlled access to Aboriginal territories, and the compulsory acquisition of some Aboriginal lands on five-year leases.[5]

For the purposes of this chapter, two other things are important to note. First is the scale of the measures: the "prescribed areas" defined under the legislation include over 600,000 square kilometers and over 70% of the Aboriginal people who live in the Northern Territory. Second is the way the legislation was introduced. In order to pass the legislation, the government

---

[3] Amartya Sen, *The Idea of Justice* (Cambridge MA: Harvard University Press, 2009).
[4] Australian Government, *Northern Territory Emergency Response: Report of the NTER Review Board*, October 2008, www.nterreview.gov.au/docs/report_nter_review.PDF, 9.
[5] See ibid., 24, 41, 46, 99.

suspended the operation of the *Racial Discrimination Act* (1975)—passed when Australia became a signatory to the International Convention on the Elimination of all Forms of Racial Discrimination—and the Northern Territory anti-discrimination legislation.[6] The government justified these moves on the basis of there being a national emergency. And yet, six years later, although there has been severe criticism of particular aspects of the government's response, many of the measures remain in place, and the Intervention continues to have supporters, including some prominent Aboriginal leaders.[7]

This bears all the hallmarks, of course, of the classic Schmittian paradox of the "legal exception" lying at the heart of liberal conceptions of sovereignty: the ability of the sovereign to declare an emergency that enables the suspension of the rule of law on the grounds of being necessary, ultimately, to save it.[8] One might be tempted to see the Intervention as confirmation of the Schmittian critique of the impossibility (and bad faith) of liberal constitutional orders—though, of course, not drawing the same conclusions about alternatives as Carl Schmitt does.[9] However, that is not my purpose here. Instead, in this chapter, I am interested in exploring the relation between injustice and domination and the extent to which our dominant theories of social justice (both domestic and global) are able to give injustice its due.

What is the fundamental injustice that the "Intervention" is seeking to address and yet also, arguably, itself manifesting? It provides an undoubtedly perverse extension of the distributive paradigm of justice: we call in the army to ensure people enjoy an equal distribution of primary goods or equal basic capabilities. But what does the example tell us, more generally, about the nature of injustice and the relation between injustice and domination?

The relations between justice and domination are multiple and overlapping. The social and economic "disadvantages" suffered by indigenous peoples, especially in remote Australia, are severe. They cry out for distributional redress. And yet they are also connected to deep and pervasive historical, cultural, and political features of the polity—to colonialism, to embedded racism, to failed policy experiments over many years, and to the challenges indigenous peoples themselves face in dealing with deep social and cultural change. These failings are systematic; they did not just happen, like a flood or a snowstorm.

---

[6] Ibid., 9.

[7] Ibid., 10.

[8] Carl Schmitt, *Political Theology: Four Chapters on the Concept of Sovereignty*, trans. George Schwab (Chicago: University of Chicago Press, 2005). For Schmitt, of course, this power was necessary in order to overcome the inherent indeterminacy of liberal jurisprudence, as opposed to something that should be guarded against.

[9] For a trenchant critique of both Schmitt and those who see such possibilities in his work, see William E. Scheuerman, *Carl Schmitt: The End of Law* (New York: Rowan & Littlefield, 1999).

3

What has characterized the dominant debates about justice in contemporary political theory in recent years has been their relative abstractness. This is not a criticism in itself. Abstraction is an unavoidable and often desirable feature of philosophical argument. But what this has meant is that by far the most attention has been paid to identifying the goals of distributive justice and the principles that should govern distribution in a just society, as opposed to *how* these distributions came about and *who* decides *what* matters for allocation. Having said that, there are still clear outlines of how liberal theorists might answer these questions in very general terms. One of the most important debates has been around the dimensions in relation to which individuals should be compared in determining whether or not they are being treated justly. If almost all recent liberal theories of justice have been egalitarian, the obvious next question is equality in relation to what—welfare, resources, or capabilities? Answering that question helps identify what counts as injustice.

Another key question at the heart of recent debates about justice has been the criteria according to which the distributions should then be assessed. Should we be aiming for strict equality of welfare, for example, or rather an equal distribution of rights and basic liberties? John Rawls, and others inspired by him, have focused instead on an equal distribution of resources (including liberties, material resources, and opportunities) such that the background conditions against which people make their choices can be equalized.[10]

Still, it is clear that even the Rawlsian framework remains highly abstract. It does not provide clear answers for what it means for the distribution of particular goods, such as health or education, which Rawls himself foreswears from spelling out. Nor is it clear how it deals with the different ways in which individuals and groups can make use of the resources available to them. These concerns have informed the development of the "capabilities approach to justice," led by Amartya Sen and others.[11] In essence, although the capabilities approach accepts the focus on resources, it argues that justice needs to be reframed in terms of an equal or sufficient distribution of capabilities: the capacity of individuals to make use of the resources they have (given different personal and social circumstances) and that are required for living a decent life. A just society is thus one that ensures a fair distribution of the means for an individual to conceive of and then actually live a decent life—one defined in relation to a set of overarching capabilities and "functionings" that Martha

---

10 John Rawls, *A Theory of Justice* (Cambridge, MA: Harvard University Press, 1971). See also Ronald Dworkin, *Sovereign Equality* (Cambridge, MA: Harvard University Press, 2000).
11 Sen, *The Idea of Justice.*

Nussbaum, in particular, has developed through a quasi-Aristotelian framework.[12]

In one way, normative conceptions of social and distributive justice can certainly help us to identify and evaluate those forms of power that are "dominating" or oppressive, at least when defined in terms of the lack of access to equal resources or welfare. Rawls refers to justice as the "first virtue of social institutions" and perhaps by extension it becomes a kind of primary virtue of politics in general, providing the analytical grid through which to map unjust social relations.[13]

On the other hand, it might also be the case that our conceptions of justice are insufficiently robust or fine-grained to capture the harms of significant forms of domination. Or indeed, our conceptions might—in a Marxian vein—leave them untouched, and worse, reify them. Looking to domination (or oppression) first—rather than justice—might therefore not only help us to identify the blind spots in our theories and approaches to justice, but also their inherent limits.

Consider Rawls's conception of "justice as fairness." Justice, he argues, is "a standard whereby the distributive aspects of the basic structure of society [i.e., rights and duties, benefits and burdens] are to be assessed."[14] The focus is on procedural and distributive unfairness or disadvantage: the problem is one of individuals lacking the "fair value" of the equal basic liberties owed to them through the first of Rawls's two principles of justice, as well as equal access to those "primary goods" required to live a decent life. To suffer injustice is therefore to lack a certain standing and to lack equal access to certain key resources. A theory of social justice is meant to provide a vision of how both of these disadvantages can be addressed. Justice is thus primarily a matter of the allocation of goods (tangible and intangible) on grounds that could not reasonably be rejected by those conceived as "free and equal."

A familiar but important set of criticisms of this way of thinking about justice (and thus injustice) is not so much that it is wrong, but radically incomplete. The crucial claim of this critique is what we might call the critique from *power*. Goods do not simply spring forth from the world. People do not simply find themselves disadvantaged. To become unemployed is not akin to finding one's house flooded by heavy rains, despite the fact that both are forms of disadvantage. Bad luck is something we need to mitigate, to be sure, but it is not the paradigmatic case of what injustice consists in, or what the point of equality is.[15]

---

[12] Martha Nussbaum, *Creating Capabilities: The Human Development Approach* (Cambridge, MA: Harvard University Press, 2011).

[13] Rawls, *A Theory of Justice*, 3.

[14] Ibid., 9.

[15] Elizabeth Anderson, "What is the Point of Equality?" *Ethics* 109, no. 2 (1999): 287–337.

At this point, conceptions and theories of domination (and non-domination) come to the fore as possible alternatives—or at least supplements—to contemporary theories of justice. Consider, for example, the now classic work of Iris Marion Young.[16] She argues that what she called the "distributive paradigm" needs to be supplemented by attention to both oppression and domination. Oppression consists in systematic "institutional processes which inhibit people's ability to play and communicate with others or to express their feelings and perspectives on social life in contexts where others can listen."[17] Domination, however, "consists in institutional conditions which inhibit or prevent people from participating or determining their actions."[18]

Another variation of this critique is the republican conception of non-domination, developed by Quentin Skinner and Philip Pettit. For Pettit, a relationship of domination exists just to the extent that A has "alienating control"—i.e., arbitrary power—over certain of B's choices.[19] And what "alienating control" means is that A can obstruct, coerce, deceive, or manipulate B's choices in ways that B cannot meaningfully check in some manner, or which are not "reasoned" in the appropriate sense; that is, involving reasonable, refusable, "non-mesmerizing" rewards for B to consider in addition to the ones he already has.[20] B enjoys non-domination in relation to A when it can be said that A cannot exercise alienating control over him; or that if A has the capacity to do so, the costs of exercising such control are prohibitive. To the extent that someone else (whether a private or public person) exercises exclusive, non-accountable control over resources and opportunities I need to realize certain of my most important interests, I am in a relation of domination vis-à-vis their control. Where A does not exercise such control over me, I enjoy non-domination. It follows from this analysis then that I can be restricted in my options in various ways—interfered with, in other words—but not, by definition, un-free. Equally, I am not free simply because no one *actually* interferes with me. According to this republican conception of liberty, the bare potential for interference threatens my liberty, not only the likelihood or probability of its exercise, and that means as long as it is counterfactually the case that someone could arbitrarily interfere with me, I am un-free.

For Pettit, non-domination is in many ways an alternative ideal to Rawls's conception of "justice as fairness." This has to do with the distinction

---

16 See Iris Marion Young, *Justice and the Politics of Difference* (Princeton, NJ: Princeton University Press, 1990); Young, *Inclusion and Democracy* (Oxford: Oxford University Press, 2000).

17 Young, *Justice and the Politics of Difference*, 38.

18 Ibid.

19 Philip Pettit, "A Republican Law of Peoples," *European Journal of Political Theory* 9, no. 1 (2010): 70–94; cf. Pettit, "The Republican Law of Peoples: A Restatement" (this volume); Pettit, *On the People's Terms: A Republican Theory and Model of Democracy* (Cambridge: Cambridge University Press, 2012).

20 Pettit, "A Republican Law of Peoples," 75.

between social justice and political legitimacy. For Rawls, social justice is an inherently comprehensive ideal: the question is how to establish a just, "basic structure" that satisfies a mutual justification test. That test, from the perspective of the "original position," generates two basic principles of justice, the first of which provides for certain "basic liberties" for citizens, made up of both substantive and procedural liberties. However, for Pettit, the emphasis provided by the first principle concerning the basic liberties is insufficiently robust, especially with regard to the procedural liberties associated with democratic control.[21] If we are investing the state with significant powers to help realize social justice, then we also require the means to ensure we are not subject to its arbitrary domination. He claims the Rawlsian tradition is insufficiently attentive to the demands of political legitimacy, subsuming it all too quickly to that of justice.

Social justice, for Pettit, bears ultimately on the nature of the order imposed by the state as the determinant of people's relationships with one another, whether as individuals or members of groups. It is fundamentally about the nature of the social order as it shapes people's relationships with one another. Political legitimacy, however, pertains to the manner in which the state imposes that order—how satisfactory that order is as a procedural order, and how it shapes people's relationship with the state itself.[22] And so, on the republican conception, "justice" requires that people enjoy freedom as non-domination in their relationships with one another—along the lines explored above—which is also another way of treating those citizens as equals. As Pettit describes it, in a just republican order "free persons can walk tall, and look others in the eye. They do not depend on anyone's grace or favour for being able to choose their mode of life. And they relate to one another in a shared, mutually reinforcing consciousness of enjoying this independence."[23] Citizens thus enjoy equal, free status, one that is determined in part by their entitlement to certain goods, but also a relational equality in their interactions with others. A political order is legitimate when the power it exercises over people—and thus potential domination—is controlled by the will of those over whom it is exercised.[24] And by "control" Pettit means that you have both some influence over the process to which you are subject, and are also able to influence that process in ways that ensure certain results occur. "Control" without influence is empty, but it must also enable "designed difference," whether active, virtual, or reserved.[25] I must be able to shape the process to which I am subject in specific ways. Note that my exercising control over power acting on me might well still involve my being

---

[21] Pettit, *On the People's Terms*, 184–86.
[22] Ibid., 76–77.
[23] Ibid., 82.
[24] Ibid., 153.
[25] Ibid., 153–56; cf. Pettit, "The Republican Law of Peoples: A Restatement," 51ff.

interfered with in various ways. The measure of non-domination is not the degree of interference to which I am subject, but rather the degree of control I exercise over it. It follows, therefore, that a political order can be legitimate even if it involves all manner of interference in people's freedom. But insofar as this interference does not reflect the exclusive will of the ruler—his *arbitrium*—but rather our own, as an individual and/or as a people, we enjoy freedom as non-domination.

4

Let us return to the problem of injustice. Does a focus on domination and non-domination help refine our understanding of the nature of injustice? Recall the concern expressed in the critiques summarized above: the primary focus on the appropriate distribution and allocation of goods to individuals as a means of evaluating the justness of a political order misses the structure within which goods are produced and the contexts within which they circulate—whether social, economic, political, or "affective." These critiques point to a more political conception of justice (and thus injustice), where the focus is as much on non-humiliation and non-domination as it is on distributional questions. The difference, therefore, is that injustice, in these cases, is tied much more closely to questions of not only the *standing* of those making claims, but also to the context of the *uptake* of those claims. What forms of social power are being exercised in ways that shape the agency of those subject to various institutional arrangements, both formal and informal? To what extent can our theories of justice (and freedom) account for those forms of social power?

There are at least two paths one could take at this point. According to the first, you might think that we should simply bite the bullet and limit considerations of justice to essentially those of a distributive kind. Although it is tempting to extend the concept to apply to a whole range of political phenomena, the more we try to shoehorn into the concept the less real work, arguably, it is able to do. There is a range of other conceptual resources available to us to analyze and evaluate the badness of things in the world. Domination (or oppression) might best be conceived independently of injustice, just because of the way it captures something distinctive about our practices—methodologically and substantively—that our best theories of justice cannot. Also, there might well be inherent limits to what *liberal* theories of justice can do to address the kind of concerns identified in these critiques. In a slightly different vein, it might also be the case that that distributive justice is not—despite what Rawls claims—the "first virtue of social institutions," and although undoubtedly important, is therefore not the most important question in political theory and practice.

A second path, however, might be to head in the opposite direction. This would put domination (and hence non-domination) at the center of our concerns about justice and injustice, just insofar as it represents the denial of a person's fundamental standing—their "right to have rights" in Hannah Arendt's evocative phrase—in the process of establishing the conditions for social and political cooperation in the first place. In other words, that the first question of justice is not about the "distributive aspects of the basic structure," but the capacity—or "justificatory power," as Rainer Forst has put it—of persons to demand justifications for and participation in the processes that identify the various goods and modes of distribution to be considered in the first place.[26] Of course, there are institutional and material preconditions for *these* capacities too, and so even here we need a kind of distributive principle. However, this approach tips our thinking about justice in a more democratic direction and away from a priori and teleological ones. If we are not simply concerned with fairness and non-arbitrariness, but also with systematic and institutionalized forms of domination, then we should have an orientation where we take our lead from those closest to the action, so to speak, and thus to the particular contexts within which goods emerge, gain meaning, and circulate. Both Forst and Pettit recognize this critical dimension of a more political approach to justice, although they draw on different theoretical frameworks to elaborate this aspect of justice. And both also draw on the language of equal respect to cash out their respective "pictures" of justice. Of course there are important differences too: one critical difference lies at the metaethical level, between the consequentialist promotion of non-domination as a political ideal, on the one hand, and the Kantian instantiation of a certain pattern or set of principles, on the other. But what is attractive and important in both approaches is the extent to which the focus of critical attention shifts to the conditions required for the effective exercise of agency and freedom by those subject to the "basic structure" of the social and political order, as much as to the principles intended to regulate them.

Does freedom as non-domination allow us to capture and address the kinds of social power that critics of liberal approaches to justice are concerned about? One obvious concern is the extent to which non-arbitrary power is conceived and exercised over individuals and groups in a republican political order. For Pettit, I can be interfered with—my freedom constrained or curtailed—if the exercise of power tracks my "avowable interests," or is required to secure my freedom as non-domination.[27] Insofar as it actually does track my interests in this way, it is not arbitrary and therefore not

---

[26] Rainer Forst, *The Right to Justification: Elements of a Constructivist Theory of Justice*, trans. Jeffrey Flynn (New York: Columbia University Press, 2011); Forst, *Justification and Critique: Towards a Critical Theory of Politics*, trans. Ciaran Cronin (Cambridge: Polity Press, 2013). Cf. Forst, "Transnational Justice and Non-Domination: A Discourse-Theoretical Approach" (this volume).

[27] Pettit, "The Determinacy of Republican Policy: A Reply to McMahon," *Philosophy & Public Affairs* 34, no. 3 (2006): 275–83, 280.

illegitimate. But what is the nature of this exercise of power and does the republican conception of domination fill the crucial gaps to which critics of liberal justice are alluding?

For example, is Pettit's approach sufficiently attuned to the lurking elements of arbitrariness remaining in his account of a legitimate (non-arbitrary) republican political order? This harks back to older critiques of republican conceptions of positive freedom and the paradoxical notion of being "forced to be free." Has Pettit provided a sufficiently robust account of the extent to which the relations of power acting on republican citizens is sufficiently under their control? For example, Patchen Markell has suggested that Pettit's account needs to be supplemented by the notion of freedom from "usurpation"—the extent to which individuals and groups are not only interfered with "arbitrarily," but displaced from active participation in political life in ways that express their effective agency as individuals or groups.[28] Pettit is (rightly) skeptical of over-romanticizing the extent to which popular "control" rests entirely on the practice of citizenly virtue. But he is equally skeptical of relying entirely on electoral competition as the main means of ensuring popular control and influence. His solution is to argue for the pluralization of the institutional sites for challenge and contestation, and discussion and decision-making in a polity. This entails mixing elements from the republican tradition that are often kept separate. In particular, he embraces the need for a "mixed constitution," an ideal (rejected by classic theorists of sovereignty like Bodin and Hobbes, but also republicans like Rousseau) that pluralizes the sites of sovereign control and the exercise of political power—especially the powers of legislation, which ought to be dispersed and shared between different elements in the polity.[29] But such a mixed regime then requires a "contestatory citizenry"—a contestatory culture amongst the citizens that disposes people to resist government abuse.[30] What makes for such a culture? Aside from citizens possessing the appropriate rights and liberties—both procedural and substantive—and having the ability to exercise those liberties, it requires a division of labor in the "exercise of civic vigilance."[31] There must be the space for and energy to organize and support a plethora of extra-governmental and non-governmental organizations agitating across a range of issues. John Keane has referred to this as the rise of "monitory democracy:" the rapid growth of extra-parliamentary, power-scrutinizing mechanisms, both domestic and global.[32]

---

[28] Patchen Markell, "The Insufficiency of Non-Domination," *Political Theory* 36, no. 1 (2008): 9–36, 25–26. See generally similar concerns, albeit from a different perspective, in John P. McCormick, *Machiavellian Democracy* (Cambridge: Cambridge University Press, 2011).
[29] Pettit, *On the People's Terms*, 220–25.
[30] Ibid., 225–29; McCormick, *Machiavellian Democracy*.
[31] Pettit, *On the People's Terms*, 226.
[32] John Keane, *The Life and Death of Democracy* (London: Simon & Schuster, 2009).

It breaks from traditional conceptions of republican citizenship in that it does not require a singular commitment to the public good on the part of citizens, but rather the opportunity for the articulation and pursuit of a suite of common concerns—whether to do with civil liberties, environmental activism, or racial equality, among other issues.

5

What happens when we turn our analysis of domination and justice to the global sphere and to accounts of global justice? Can our cosmopolitan or global theories of justice give injustice its due?[33]

In her Tanner Lectures, Seyla Benhabib uses the example of the presence of "others"—legal and illegal immigrants—in liberal democracies to explore the lineaments of what she calls "another cosmopolitanism"—one in which the project is about "mediations" and democratic "reiterations," as opposed to reductions or totalizations.[34] Her answer, in short, involves drawing on the idea of the "co-originality" of popular sovereignty and human rights norms, and the way in which over time, through democratic reiteration—through "repetitions-in-transformation" that occur when democratic publics appeal to and domesticate cosmopolitan norms—they come to be mediated, if never reconciled.[35] The basic idea is that norms are reiterated via democratic will-formation such that they come to be seen as valid from the perspective of the *demos*, though also often transformed in the process.

I want to use Benhabib's line of thought in a different way—that is, to use the example of indigenous peoples' claims within the overarching structure of liberal international law to tease out the possibilities of perhaps *another* "another cosmopolitanism." The basic thought is that if rights claims always point beyond themselves—given the underlying tension between what Arendt famously called the unconditional "right to have rights" and their actual instantiation in concrete legal and political orders—what do the claims of indigenous people point towards and prefigure? One way of answering this question is to explore the extent to which contemporary theories of justice or non-domination are capable of capturing the wrong or harm to which indigenous peoples are referring in criticizing both domestic and global political arrangements.

---

33 I draw in this section on Duncan Ivison, "Justice and Imperialism: On the Very Idea of a Universal Standard," in *Law and Politics in British Colonial Thought: Transpositions of Empire*, eds. Shaunnagh Dorsett and Ian Hunter (New York, NY: Palgrave Macmillan, 2010).
34 Seyla Benhabib, *Another Cosmopolitanism*, ed. Robert Post (Oxford: Oxford University Press, 2006), 20, 32, 34–35, 46, 59.
35 Ibid., 48–49, 58–60, 70–71.

I use the case of indigenous peoples as a way of thinking about both the sources of domination within and across states, but also potential remedies and responses to domination as well. It is also useful as a way of stepping outside the dominant Kantian tendencies of much contemporary global justice theorizing, as important and rich as that tradition is. Could there be a form of "emergent" cosmopolitanism or universalism that was not teleological in the Kantian sense, but nevertheless genuinely transnational? "Emergence" is a notoriously slippery philosophical concept and so I use it here with caution. But the general point is this: a property is emergent insofar as it arises out of some lower level properties in place, but is not merely those lower level ones differently described. It arises out of them and yet is novel or irreducible with respect to them. The interaction amongst the parts produces a whole, but also changes the parts in the process. The analogy here is intended as a rough one: could there be a form of cosmopolitanism or universalism that was emergent in this sense, emerging from the complex interactions of individuals, states, and non-state actors, but not simply reducible to them, nor the expression of some externally derived rule or *telos*? Could there, in other words, be a form of cosmopolitanism or universalism that is aimed at constructing a kind of normative reality, but not necessarily one captured by either "ideal theory" or "political realism?"[36]

One of the most important reasons for turning to the case of indigenous peoples in relation to cosmopolitanism and universalism has to do precisely with a key theme of this volume—domination—and with what we might call the *imperialism objection* to cosmopolitanism. Imperialism, in the modern era, tends to refer to relations between states and peoples in which one party is able to effectively impose, constrain, dominate, and exploit others in ways affecting their most important interests but leaving little room for maneuver. This can occur either directly or indirectly, formally or informally. Of course, it is never complete. Those subject to these relations of power always have some room to move, though this can still be severely limited. The imposition of "metropolitan law" within an imperial political order, for example, was defined in terms of its inherently hierarchical structure. The independence of any other legal order was therefore, by definition, contingent and shifting, depending on the interests of the imperial power. Recall here Pettit's analysis of the harm of domination, from a republican perspective. If domination is harmful for individual human beings—defined as being subject to arbitrary power in the terms outlined above—then it applies to collective persons as well, such as states or nations. The domination of corporate agencies matter insofar as they are agencies made up of individual human beings who have incorporated them. A collective agent—a representative state, say—is

[36] I have explored this issue at greater length in "Emergent Cosmopolitanism: Indigenous Peoples and International Law," in *Between Cosmopolitan Ideals and State Sovereignty: Studies in Global Justice*, ed. Ronald Tinnevelt and Gert Verschraegen (New York: Palgrave Macmillan, 2006), 120–31.

therefore dominated when it is subject to the alien control of others and lacks the ability to exercise reasonable influence and direction over that control. This kind of alien control can be exercised by other states, but also by international agencies and private corporations of one kind or another.[37]

So how does empire become transposed onto justice? There are historical questions and conceptual questions here, though they are often entwined. With the first kind of question, we may ask whether there are particular arguments about justice that were subsequently used in the justification of empire or colonialism. Or, we may seek to trace the conceptual structure of arguments justifying imperialism to their roots in particular philosophical views, debunking their supposed universalism. With the second kind of question, we may ask about the very nature of the concept of global justice and the values it expresses in relation to other important values. Is the very notion of global justice imperialistic, simply because it claims there are universal values applicable to everyone everywhere, whatever their particular ways of life or worldviews? Is it possible to hold all societies to a common standard that is thick enough to protect important human interests, and yet not grounded in a particular set of cultural values that would mean essentially imposing one way of life on another? Or put another way, do suitably "thin" conceptions of cosmopolitanism motivated by compassion for the vulnerable actually end up leaving thick asymmetries of power, inequality, and wealth intact, given either their abstraction from power, or their inability to penetrate it?

A crucial question here is whether the very idea of global justice is invalidated by the debunking of supposedly universal political forms—such as Immanuel Kant's republican constitutional state system, or the idea of a philosophical history having "cosmopolitan intent."[38] Claiming that a *particular* constitutional form is or is not universal is distinct from denying that any universals exist. Every argument has its origins in some particular cultural form, but does that mean there are not any claims or values that can be vindicated across cultures?

As I mentioned above, if we are concerned to give injustice its due then we should be concerned to understand the relation between power and justice as best we can. Therefore, in the case of non-state actors (such as indigenous peoples) it is important to pay attention to the extent to which both domestic and global structures of justification are often deeply shaped by assumptions about the relation between claims of justice and the role of the state.

Thomas Nagel, for example, has drawn a distinction between a "political" and "cosmopolitan" approach to global justice.[39] The former suggests

[37] Pettit, "A Republican Law of Peoples"; cf. Pettit, "A Restatement."
[38] Kant, Immanuel. "Idea for a Universal History from a Cosmopolitan Perspective," in *Toward Perpetual Peace and Other Writings on Politics, Peace, and History*, ed. Pauline Kleingeld (New Haven, CT: Yale University Press, 2006). See also Thomas McCarthy, "Liberal Imperialism and the Dilemma of Development" (this volume).
[39] Thomas Nagel, "The Problem of Global Justice," *Philosophy & Public Affairs* 33, no. 2 (2005): 113–47.

that states give "the value of justice its application, by putting the fellow citizens of a sovereign state into a relation they do not have with the rest of humanity, an institutional relation which must then be evaluated by the special standards of fairness and equality that fill out the content of justice."[40] The critical aspect of this institutional relation is that it is a coercive one: coercive institutions are required for large-scale social and economic cooperation, and justice is that moral value linked tightly to the claims we can make on each other in light of that coercive regime. We have moral obligations to non-citizens to prevent the worst kind of harms occurring to them, but since we do not stand in the same institutional relation to them as we do with our fellow citizens, they lack claims of distributive justice on us—or so Nagel argues.

Nagel's argument forms part of a lively debate in the global justice literature on the scope of egalitarian justice. What I want to focus on here, for now, is the suggestion of justice being an institution-dependent or practice-dependent concept. Perhaps a better way of making sense of this idea is to say that principles of justice hold only among individuals who stand in certain "practice-mediated" relations with each other.[41] A practice-independent approach to thinking about the nature of justice would be one in which the contingent, practice-mediated relations in which we find ourselves do not affect or change the justifying reasons and premises underpinning the content and scope of justice. The intuition that justice should be grounded on the premise that we should seek to mitigate the effects of brute bad luck—or people's "circumstances" (as opposed to their choices)—on their life prospects is practice-independent in this sense. The appeal is to moral value alone. The institutions and practices to which they are meant to apply play no role in the content, scope, and justification of the principles.

Practice-dependent theorists, however, think that our living under certain institutions (whatever their origins), or our sharing specific kinds of practice-mediated relations, does have bearing on our thinking about justice. It creates the context in which questions around the standing of the participants and the distributions of power and opportunity between them come to matter. A practice-dependent theorist is committed, therefore, to saying a conception of justice rests at least as much on an interpretation of actually existing practices and institutional systems as it does on common values: the content, scope, and justification of the conception will be determined, in part, by the role it is meant to play given those institutions and practices, including the history of and impact those institutions have had in particular circumstances. While this approach might entail principles of justice with

---

[40] Ibid., 120.

[41] Bernard Williams, *In the Beginning was the Deed: Realism and Moralism in Political Argument* (Princeton, NJ: Princeton University Press, 2005); Andrea Sangiovanni, "Justice and the Priority of Politics to Morality," *The Journal of Political Philosophy* 16, no. 2 (2008): 137–64; Sen, *The Idea of Justice*.

less than global scope, it would not be limited to *only* such principles: justice ought to track those practices and relations that implicate individuals and groups in structures of cooperation and domination. *Pace* Nagel, this surely entails taking into consideration both domestic *and* transnational relations of cooperation and domination: the international sphere is, arguably, a coercive system in a myriad of ways, especially when considering the historical and practical situation of non-state actors such as indigenous peoples. In particular, the very shape and form of the international system is itself the product of imperial domination and coercion that has rendered non-state actors outside or on the margins of theoretical concern.[42] It seems clear then that the institutional or practice-mediated approach to justice requires thinking beyond the domestic case.[43]

Considering the claims of indigenous peoples in debates over global justice returns us to the question of how historical injustices structure contemporary institutions and the extent to which these are "enduring injustices."[44] Enduring injustices shape the structures of justification linked to democratic legitimation. In particular, enduring injustices can mean that citizens continue to experience forms of domination and oppression even when the state is considered in some sense "generally" legitimate. In this scenario, rights protection seems to come apart from the realization of justice. To put it another way: Rawls argued that we do not have an obligation to submit to unjust institutions—to institutions that "exceed the limits of tolerable injustice."[45] But how do we determine where to draw the line beyond which injustice becomes intolerable?[46]

The risk is that the justificatory scheme itself becomes dominating in various ways. Of course, any particular institutional manifestation of a justificatory scheme can be said to be recursively subject to the very demand of justification itself, as Forst has argued.[47] But this seems a slightly too easy separation between theory and practice, at least from the perspective of the agent for whom the institutional manifestation can come to suffuse everything to do with the principle being justified. The danger is that

---

42 David Armitage, *Foundations of Modern International Thought* (Cambridge: Cambridge University Press, 2013).

43 This claim deserves more elaboration than I can provide here. A familiar critique of the practice-dependent approach is that it seems to entail that where there are no shared practices or institutions, obligations of justice do not apply. This would seem to rule out the possibility of any kind of substantive conception of global justice, or render its validity dependent on highly contestable empirical claims. My view is that there are global practices that raise problems of both distributional, and especially relational, justice.

44 Jeff Spinner-Halev, *Enduring Injustice* (Cambridge: Cambridge University Press, 2012).

45 John Rawls, *A Theory of Justice*, 112.

46 Thomas Shelby, "Justice, Deviance, and the Dark Ghetto," *Philosophy & Public Affairs* 35, no. 2 (2007): 126–60.

47 Forst, *The Right to Justification*.

the claim that someone subject to a norm or rule must be offered justifications for it that she can accept (or not reasonably reject) begins to sound hollow if you are part of a conversation to which you are constantly invited to participate, but in which you struggle to be heard.

Where does this leave the prospects for cosmopolitan political theory in light of the historical and conceptual issues raised above? The difference between cosmopolitan and non-cosmopolitan global justice is often taken to hinge on differing interpretations of the role, legitimacy, and normative distinctiveness of the state. There is a risk, however, that if cosmopolitanism is taken to be the inverse of a focus on states and peoples, it can end up (perhaps unwittingly) reifying a standard against which any alternative way of conceptualizing normative orders—including global ones—is always compared. The choice becomes to project forward to a world without states, or one in which they are ever present—between utopianism and ideal theory, on the one hand, and "non-ideal" theory or realism, on the other. But this is a false choice and leaves uncontested the very conceptual frame within which we grasp the problem of legitimacy and global justice in the first place. Considering the case of indigenous peoples in the context of the emergence of our domestic and global political orders helps us see this.

One thing the situation of indigenous peoples in domestic and global politics makes clear is that we need multiple modes of political membership in order to realize the goods of citizenship. And this returns us to some of Pettit's conditions for securing non-domination. Recall that in the domestic case, non-domination is best secured when we pluralize and disperse the sites where political power is exercised, as well as encourage a division of labor in the exercise of citizenly civic virtue, expressed through various forms of "monitory democracy." Something similar can be extended to the international case. But the challenges are daunting. Powerful states continue to dominate and shape both the international legal and economic order and those transnational agencies and forums that might be able to provide countervailing checks to dominating power. Still, the proliferation of international forums that brings different alliances of states and non-governmental organizations together in debate and deliberation over common global challenges (such as the environment, weapons control, human rights, and other issues) provides a source for promoting and highlighting emerging global public norms. And the ability of weaker states or non-state actors to appeal to these norms—weak as they often are—provides at least one possible mechanism for asserting, if not control, then some direction of the control being exercised over them.

Once again, the case of indigenous peoples' claims is interesting in this respect. They have sought to negotiate the terms of their membership within the states in which they currently reside, and yet also secure international standing as "peoples"—all the while helping to challenge and retheorize what a "people" refers to in international law and practice. They are territorially rooted and yet also non-statist in orientation, just insofar as they see the protection and promotion of their fundamental interests in various forms of shared jurisdiction and overlapping political membership within and across borders. Of course, their experience of existing in between national and transnational citizenship has more often than not been one of frustration and disadvantage. And their push for recognition of overlapping political membership is still viewed skeptically, and often resentfully, by many of their fellow citizens and other international actors, including states and private corporations.[48] But as I see it, they are claiming the conceptual space between nationalism and cosmopolitanism, at times transcending, but still anchored in, particular communities. We need a more nuanced theoretical framework with which to grasp these conceptual spaces between the local and global. The focus on the nature of domination and non-domination helps us evaluate the extent to which our theories of domestic and global justice are genuinely up to the task of addressing injustice today.

---

48 See Ivison, "Emergent Cosmopolitanism: Indigenous Peoples and International Law."

BIBLIOGRAPHY

Anderson, Elizabeth. "What Is the Point of Equality?" *Ethics* 109, no. 2 (1999): 287–337.

Armitage, David. *Foundations of Modern International Thought*. Cambridge: Cambridge University Press, 2013.

Australian Government. *Northern Territory Emergency Response: Report of the NTER Review Board*. October 2008. www.nterreview.gov.au/docs/report_nter_review.PDF.

Benhabib, Seyla. *Another Cosmopolitanism*. Edited by Robert Post. Oxford: Oxford University Press, 2006.

Dworkin, Ronald. *Sovereign Equality*. Cambridge, MA: Harvard University Press, 2000.

Forst, Rainer. *Justification and Critique: Towards a Critical Theory of Politics*. Translated by Ciaran Cronin. Cambridge: Polity Press, 2013.

Forst, Rainer. *The Right to Justification: Elements of a Constructivist Theory of Justice*. Translated by Jeffrey Flynn. New York: Columbia University Press, 2011.

Forst, Rainer. "Transnational Justice and Non-Domination: A Discourse-Theoretical Approach." In *Domination and Global Political Justice: Conceptual, Historical, and Institutional Perspectives*, edited by Barbara Buckinx, Jonathan Trejo-Mathys, and Timothy Waligore. New York: Routledge, 2015.

Ivison, Duncan. "Emergent Cosmopolitanism: Indigenous Peoples and International Law." In *Between Cosmopolitan Ideals and State Sovereignty: Studies in Global Justice*, edited by Ronald Tinnevelt and Gert Verschraegen, 120–31. New York: Palgrave Macmillan, 2006.

Ivison, Duncan. "Justice and Imperialism: On the Very Idea of a Universal Standard." In *Law and Politics in British Colonial Thought: Transpositions of Empire*, edited by Shaunnagh Dorsett and Ian Hunter. New York, NY: Palgrave Macmillan, 2010.

Ivison, Duncan. "Multiculturalism and Resentment." In *Political Theory and Australian Multiculturalism*, edited by Geoffrey Brahm Levey, 129–48. New York: Berghnan Books, 2008.

Ivison, Duncan. *Rights*. Stocksfield: Acumen Publishing, 2008.

Kant, Immanuel. "Idea for a Universal History from a Cosmopolitan Perspective." In *Toward Perpetual Peace and Other Writings on Politics, Peace, and History*, edited by Pauline Kleingeld. New Haven, CT: Yale University Press, 2006.

Keane, John. *The Life and Death of Democracy*. London: Simon & Schuster, 2009.

Markell, Patchen. "The Insufficiency of Non-Domination." *Political Theory* 36, no. 1 (2008): 9–36.

McCarthy, Thomas. "Liberal Imperialism and the Dilemma of Development." In *Domination and Global Political Justice: Conceptual, Historical, and Institutional Perspectives*, edited by Barbara Buckinx, Jonathan Trejo-Mathys, and Timothy Waligore. New York: Routledge, 2015.

McCormick, John P. *Machiavellian Democracy*. Cambridge: Cambridge University Press, 2011.

Nagel, Thomas. "The Problem of Global Justice." *Philosophy & Public Affairs* 33, no. 2 (2005): 113–47.

Nussbaum, Martha. *Creating Capabilities: The Human Development Approach*. Cambridge, MA: Harvard University Press, 2011.

Pettit, Philip. "The Determinacy of Republican Policy: A Reply to McMahon." *Philosophy & Public Affairs* 34, no. 3 (2006): 275–83.

Pettit, Philip. *On the People's Terms: A Republican Theory and Model of Democracy*. Cambridge: Cambridge University Press, 2012.

Pettit, Philip. "A Republican Law of Peoples." *European Journal of Political Theory* 9, no. 1 (2010): 70–94.

Pettit, Philip. "The Republican Law of Peoples: A Restatement." In *Domination and Global Political Justice: Conceptual, Historical, and Institutional Perspectives*, edited by Barbara Buckinx, Jonathan Trejo-Mathys, and Timothy Waligore. New York: Routledge, 2015.

Rawls, John. *A Theory of Justice*. Cambridge, MA: Harvard University Press, 1971.

Sangiovanni, Andrea. "Justice and the Priority of Politics to Morality." *The Journal of Political Philosophy* 16, no. 2 (2008): 137–64.

Scheuerman, William E. *Carl Schmitt: The End of Law*. New York: Rowan & Littlefield, 1999.

Schmitt, Carl. *Political Theology: Four Chapters on the Concept of Sovereignty*. Translated by George Schwab. Chicago: University of Chicago Press, 2005.

Sen, Amartya. *The Idea of Justice*. Cambridge, MA: Harvard University Press, 2009.

Shelby, Thomas. "Justice, Deviance, and the Dark Ghetto." *Philosophy & Public Affairs* 35, no. 2 (2007): 126–60.

Shklar, Judith N. *The Faces of Injustice*. Cambridge, MA: Harvard University Press, 1990.

Spinner-Halev, Jeff. *Enduring Injustice*. Cambridge: Cambridge University Press, 2012.

Williams, Bernard. *In the Beginning was the Deed: Realism and Moralism in Political Argument*. Princeton, NJ: Princeton University Press, 2005.

Young, Iris Marion. *Inclusion and Democracy*. Oxford: Oxford University Press, 2000.

Young, Iris Marion. *Justice and the Politics of Difference*. Princeton, NJ: Princeton University Press, 1990.

Part III

Global Governance, Institutions, and Normative Theory

10 Should Republican Liberty as Non-Domination Be Outsourced?

John W. Maynor

INTRODUCTION

Politics, along with economic and cultural ideals and institutions, seems no longer bound by the traditional borders of the nation-state.[1] Individuals, citizens, nation-states, multinational corporations, and other parties have been forced to respond to what James Bohman has called "new global 'circumstances of politics.'"[2] As a result, many individuals have become increasingly exposed to forms of interference and potential instances of domination arising from sources of foreign origin, but which they have no capability to counter. In response to this challenge, many republican writers have turned to cosmopolitan thinking to begin to chart a way forward. On the one hand, since contemporary republicanism is primarily concerned with minimizing and combating domination, republican cosmopolitan thinking seems to be a positive way forward. On the other hand, these moves appear to cut against conventional wisdom that holds that since republicanism is primarily rooted in the past and tied to the existence of classical notions of sovereignty, construction of a cosmopolitan version of it may prove difficult. This seeming inconsistency raises two related questions. First, is it really possible to detach republican ideals and institutions from the nation-state and outsource them to transnational institutions? If it is possible, then the second question focuses on whether or not moving to a more globally oriented republican political theory is an attractive and positive step forward. The goal of this chapter is to address these two questions.

The chapter proceeds like this. First I sketch out two related, but distinct strands of republican political theory. I then go on to outline a contemporary version of republicanism built around an alternative conception of

---

[1] An early draft of this chapter was presented to a panel at the Midwest Political Science Association Annual Meeting in 2011 and I am grateful to the participants for their helpful comments. I am also very grateful to the editors of this volume for their many useful comments.

[2] James Bohman, "Republican Cosmopolitanism," *The Journal of Political Philosophy* 12, no. 3 (2004): 336–52, 337.

liberty as non-domination. Next I examine how globalization has increased the amount of domination individuals experience before critically exploring two recent attempts to show how the only way to remedy this is to detach republican institutions and ideals from the nation-state and instead vest them in transnational institutions and a global civic society. Finally, I offer an alternate approach to these that focuses less on the construction of robust, transnational political institutions and more on using the existing structures of the nation-state to lead the charge against domination. In this section I also consider some of the recent developments in the European Union (EU) from a republican perspective to offer a preliminary analysis of the prospects of developing republican cosmopolitanism. As a first line of defense against domination I will argue that a nation-state's political institutions and ideals should reflect civic republican priorities. To be sure, I will not argue that real and meaningful cosmopolitan, transnational political institutions cannot ever develop or that we should necessarily dismiss them because they have not developed yet. Rather, I will counter that a key to their development firmly lies within the domestic efforts of nation-states to ensure that their citizenry have the necessary democratic institutions and ideals to control and constrain political power, including from institutions that reside outside of a nation-state's borders.

1 REPUBLICANISMS: ANCIENT, MODERN, AND CONTEMPORARY

While the republican tradition as a whole was primarily concerned with the themes of freedom, political participation, civic virtue, and corruption, two distinct strands can be discerned.[3] The first, often referred to as neo-Athenian republicanism, is inspired by the civic humanism of the ancient Greeks such as Aristotle. Such a view endorses the Aristotelian concern for the good life and holds that individuals can best realize their essential social or political nature in a democratic society characterized by active participation in political life. From an institutional perspective, democratic participation, fostered by a rich sense of civic virtue and strong versions of citizenship and patriotism, is thought to be the primary means of maintaining the freedom of the state. In contemporary terms, this strand of civic republicanism is often associated with communitarianism and writers such as Michael Sandel and Charles Taylor.[4]

---

[3] Cécile Laborde and John Maynor, eds., *Republicanism and Political Theory* (Oxford: Blackwell, 2008), 3.

[4] Michael J. Sandel, *Democracy's Discontent: America in Search of a Public Philosophy* (Cambridge, MA: Belknap Press of Harvard University Press, 1996), 24–25; Charles Taylor, *Philosophical Arguments* (Cambridge, MA: Harvard University Press, 1995), 192.

For these writers, being a good citizen of a self-governing democratic polity contributes to a rich formative project of identity that can only be realized within a particular kind of specific community.[5] The thought is that the act of participation itself helps to constitute certain ultimate goods, such as civility, solidarity, and trust, which contribute to an individual's well-being while at the same time allowing him control over the content and direction of his community.[6] Such moves unify the good and offer a political and ethical system that is singular and indivisible.[7] Thus, feelings of patriotism become firmly fused within specific cultural or ethnic contexts, which in turn feed into rich notions of solidarity and are necessary components of civic virtue and citizenship. It follows, then, that these neo-Athenian republican citizens are loyal to the shared morality epitomized by the values that constitute their community or nation's ideals and norms.[8]

Writers such as John Rawls, Will Kymlicka, and Jürgen Habermas have decried the particularism inherent in this "communitarian" view of neo-Athenian republicanism, and declared it inconsistent with the realities of modern political life.[9] For Habermas, the "fundamental republican idea of the self-conscious political integration of a 'community' of free and equal persons is obviously too concrete and simple for modern conditions. . . . the republican idea is still more problematic if one's model is an ethnically homogeneous 'community of shared destiny' held together by common traditions."[10] Likewise, as Maurizio Viroli has pointed out, it is widespread within international political theory to think that this kind of republican thinking necessarily ties a citizen's membership in this or that particular self-governmental, ethnic, and/or cultural community. Thus, this form of republicanism "considers citizens parts of the community that can develop and express their own identity and moral excellence only within a shared tradition and culture that includes a conception of moral goodness."[11] These

---

[5] John Maynor, *Republicanism in the Modern World* (Cambridge: Polity Press, 2003), 11; see also Maynor, "Constitutional Patriotism or Neo-Republican Citizenship: A Way Forward for the EU?," in *Constituting Communities: Political Solutions to Cultural Difference*, eds. Per Mouritsen and Kund Erik Jørgensen (London: Palgrave Macmillan, 2008), 187–209.

[6] Adrian Oldfield, *Citizenship and Community: Civic Republicanism and the Modern World* (London: Routledge, 1990), 6; Will Kymlicka, *Contemporary Political Philosophy*, 2nd ed. (Oxford: Oxford University Press, 2002), 295.

[7] Chantal Mouffe, *The Return of the Political* (London: Verso, 1993), 36.

[8] Maurizio Viroli, *For Love of Country: An Essay on Patriotism and Nationalism* (Oxford: Clarendon Press, 1995), 170–76.

[9] John Rawls, *Political Liberalism*, paperback ed. (New York: Columbia University Press, 1996), 205; Will Kymlicka, *Liberalism, Community, and Culture* (Oxford: Oxford University Press, 1989); Jürgen Habermas, *Between Facts and Norms: Contributions to a Discourse Theory of Law and Democracy*, trans. William Rehg (Cambridge, MA: MIT Press, 1996).

[10] Habermas, *Between Facts and Norms*, 505.

[11] Maurizio Viroli, *Republicanism*, trans. Anthony Shugaar (New York: Farrar Straus and Giroux, 2002), 65.

sentiments are similar to Ryoa Chung's argument that these kinds of rich versions of republican citizenship and civic virtues are necessarily vested in overly thick communal and patriotic attachments that render them fundamentally inconsistent with cosmopolitanism.[12] It would seem, then, that the neo-Athenian strand of republicanism is incompatible with the "cosmopolitan turn" in contemporary political theory. Can the same be said of the other strand of republicanism? I turn to this next.

While the second civic republican approach, often referred to as neo-Roman republicanism, stresses many of the same principles as its neo-Athenian counterpart, it represents a decisive shift away from overly rich and thick versions of citizenship and civic virtue being tied to particular notions of certain moral goods. Quentin Skinner, in a number of influential writings, has argued that neo-Roman republicans held a distinctive conception of liberty.[13] Unlike their neo-Athenian counterparts, these republican writers did not maintain the Aristotelian view that ties freedom to self-mastery or self-realization in a community with others. Instead, within this approach, the central concern was *libertas*— the ideal of the freedom of individuals under the rule of law. These citizens did not want to rule, rather they wanted to not be ruled by living in what they termed a free state, a state where individuals do not live subjugated under the arbitrary power, or domination, of a ruler. Among neo-Roman republican writers, the ancient republics were viewed as unstable and susceptible to mob rule, factions, and tyrants. To counter this threat to freedom, the republic's constitutional focus should be on creating the institutional arrangements that preserve individual freedom by stressing, in addition to traditional republican ideals, more modern principles, such as certain anti-majoritarian devices like judicial review, representative government, and a strong sense of the rule of law. The thought behind these principles is to ensure that the government does not exercise any arbitrary power over the citizenry.

Building on Skinner's more historically focused work, Philip Pettit's work in this area has brought this alternative conception of liberty out of the history of ideas.[14] Pettit argues that freedom consists neither in the non-interference of others, as in negative liberty, nor is it equated with self-mastery, as in positive liberty. Instead, individuals are thought to be free to the extent that they are not subject to any interference that arises apart from

[12] Ryoa Chung, "The Cosmopolitan Scope of Republican Citizenship," in *Republicanism: History, Theory and Practice*, eds. Daniel Weinstock and Christian Nadeau (London: Frank Cass, 2004), 141–42.

[13] Quentin Skinner, *Reason and Rhetoric in the Philosophy of Hobbes* (Cambridge: Cambridge University Press, 1996); Skinner, *Liberty Before Liberalism* (Cambridge: Cambridge University Press, 1998); Skinner, "A Third Concept of Liberty," *Proceedings of the British Academy* 117 (2002): 237–68.

[14] Philip Pettit, *Republicanism: A Theory of Freedom and Government* (Oxford: Oxford University Press, 1997); Pettit, *A Theory of Freedom: From the Psychology to the Politics of Agency* (Cambridge: Polity Press, 2001).

their own *arbitrium*, or will. Thus, individuals are free to the extent that they live under the conditions where they count as "a 'freeman' rather than a 'bondsman', a *liber* rather than a *servus*."[15] This formulation stands in contrast to classical liberal approaches where interference, or the absence of it, is the primary measure of freedom. Alternatively, individuals are considered to be at liberty when they are free from interferences that do not track their common avowed interests.[16] For Pettit, republican liberty is defined as the absence of alien or alienating control on the part of other persons that negatively affects an individual's freedom of choice.[17]

One attractive aspect of the republican approach is that it identifies arbitrary power as the nemesis of freedom, whether that power arises from the state (*imperium*) or among the people (*dominium*). As Pettit points out, for many liberal writers, whether or not an individual is free often boils down to whether or not he/she experiences any actual interference.[18] Thus, on the one hand, in this way of thinking, any actual interference is seen as a restriction of liberty. On the other hand, this way of looking at liberty is impoverished since often what really matters is not necessarily whether one is able to rid oneself of all interferences, if that were even possible. Rather, what matters is if one rids oneself of a particular kind of interference, namely arbitrary or uncontrolled interference. This sentiment is born out of an interpretation of the classic master/slave metaphor utilized by many republican theorists. What makes slaves un-free is that even if they are not interfered with by their master, say one of a benevolent or kind nature, the mere fact that they remain enslaved means that they are not free regardless of whether or not they suffer any actual interferences. Thus, even a slave of a benevolent master has no effective power to shape, constrain, or fight back against the interference he experiences because his status precludes it. So, being dominated or un-free in this manner is a function of unequal power relations between persons, groups, or agencies of the state. The same unequal power relation would exist if an individual lived as a subject of a benevolent despot, regardless of the amount of liberty that existed within the state.

For republicans, it is not the quantity of liberty present, it is the quality of that liberty relative to the power of individuals to shape and determine the restrictions and limitations of that liberty. This is because thinking of liberty in this manner opens up the possibility that some forms of interference, namely

---

15 Pettit, "Freedom in the Market," *Politics, Philosophy & Economics* 5, no. 2 (2006): 131–49, 134.

16 Hereafter I will simply refer to this as an individual's interest. See Pettit, *Republicanism*, 156.

17 Pettit, "Republican Freedom: Three Axioms, Four Theorems," in *Republicanism and Political Theory*, eds. Cécile Laborde and John Maynor (Oxford: Blackwell, 2008), 102–31, 106–8.

18 José Louis Martí and Philip Pettit, *A Political Philosophy in Public Life: Civic Republicanism in Zapatero's Spain* (Princeton: Princeton University Press, 2010), 34–35.

those that are not arbitrary, do not restrict an individual's freedom. What this means is that certain interferences which are forced to track an individual's interests, and that are not imposed in an arbitrary fashion, are not restrictive of freedom. Central to this idea is the relationship between interference and domination. Interference is thought to be when an individual's activities or choices are subject to some form of intentional intervention by another agent, whereas domination is understood to occur when an individual's activities or choices are subject to arbitrary interference by others. Seen this way, an act can be said to be arbitrary if it is chosen or not chosen at an individual's pleasure and does not track his/her interests. Thus, interference is considered to be arbitrary when it does not track the interests of the people, both individually and collectively.[19] This points to another distinction between republican liberty and those that view liberty in the traditional negative sense. This difference centers on the thought that it is possible to view certain interferences as not necessarily being an infringement on freedom if individuals can shape or direct these interferences. In Pettit's way of thinking, these individuals do not confront these interferences as something arising from alien control. Rather, they confront them as powerful agents able to exercise a level of democratic control capable of influencing and directing.

In operationalizing this way of thinking, republicans maintain that there is a constitutive relationship between non-domination and the citizenry, institutions, laws, and values of the state. Thus, as Lena Halldenius has argued, "republican freedom makes sense only in an institutional setting; it is institution-dependent."[20] For republicans, another consequence of seeing liberty in this manner is that being free is seen as a kind of status, one that is recognized by others and receives institutional support. This in turn means that individuals are shielded or immunized from arbitrary interference.[21] Thus, republican institutional design, the rule of law, and the political virtues that support them all point to a robust form of liberty that seeks to secure citizens from arbitrary interference.[22] Understood this way, an individual is free in the republican sense only if she is recognized by others as enjoying a kind of status that resiliently serves to protect her from any interference that does not track her interests and promote her equal status as citizen.[23]

So, from a constitutional standpoint, republican institutions, guided by principles such as checks and balances and the dispersion of power across a

---

[19] Pettit, *Republicanism*, 52–53; Pettit, *A Theory of Freedom,* 154–56.

[20] Lena Halldenius, "Building Blocks of a Republican Cosmopolitanism: The Modality of Being Free," *European Journal of Political Theory* 9, no. 1 (2010): 12–30, 12–13.

[21] Pettit, "Freedom in the Market," 133; Iseult Honohan, *Civic Republicanism* (London: Routledge, 2002), 184.

[22] Christian List, "Republican Freedom and the Rule of Law," *Politics, Philosophy & Economics* 5, no. 2 (2006): 201–20, 218.

[23] Cécile Laborde and John Maynor, eds., *Republicanism and Political Theory* (Oxford: Blackwell, 2008), 9.

range of legislative, administrative, and judicial levels, seek to minimize arbitrary interference through inclusivity, democratic contestation, and active civic engagement.[24] It is important to note here the important role that democracy plays in republican political theory. In minimizing arbitrary interference, democratic institutional structures allow individuals to bring their interests out into political forums so they can be accounted for and tracked by others and the state. What this points to is a kind of constitutional power that utilizes democratic institutions and practices to transform potentially dominating policies so they are not considered alien to the many individuals and groups that make up society.[25] Moreover, what this also points to is that, for neo-Roman republicans, an individual's liberty was inherently linked to governing institutions that resided within their sphere of influence. Republican citizens knew these institutions, how they worked, and could engage with them in a positive manner to help shape the policies that emerged from them. In other words, they were in close proximity to these institutions—they could see them operate and, importantly, influence them to help minimize arbitrary interference.

However, relying on institutions and on constitutionalism may, in an age of globalization, present republicans with a significant challenge. This is because it appears that globalization has weakened the very institutions and mechanisms republicans rely on to minimize domination. The result is that republican institutions and constitutional mechanisms may have a diminished ability to shield individuals from sources of domination that arise outside of their nation-state. I turn to this issue next.

2 GLOBALIZATION AND DOMINATION

There is a growing consensus among many writers that states can no longer protect their citizens from the external effects of certain decisions or actions taken by other actors, or from "the causal chain of decision-making processes originating beyond the national borders."[26] The result is that

---

[24] Maynor, *Republicanism in the Modern World*; Maynor, "Modern Republican Democratic Contestation: A Model of Deliberative Democracy," in *Republicanism in Theory and Practice*, eds. Iseult Honohan and Jeremy Jennings (London: Routledge, 2005).

[25] I have argued elsewhere that this form of power connects to another form of power, one that is more intimate and personal and associated with the civic virtues of reciprocity and democratic practices. This power reinforces the equal status that agents have toward one another and builds on the thought that not being dominated by others is in part dependent on treating others in a non-dominating manner. For more on this form of power, see Maynor, "Fighting Back Against Domination: Republican Citizenship and Unbounded Reciprocity," *Diacrítica* 24, no. 2 (2010): 73–90.

[26] Jürgen Habermas, "Making Sense of the EU: Toward a Cosmopolitan Europe," *Journal of Democracy* 14, no. 4 (2003): 86–100, 89–90.

the nation-state's capacity to enact an increasing range of public policies has been severely affected by the forces of globalization, due to the interconnected and interdependent nature of global markets.[27] As a result, it is thought that many states have lost a significant portion of their autonomy as their boundaries have become increasingly porous. José Luis Martí puts it more bleakly when he speaks of governments that have lost the ability to make their own decisions, resulting in a loss of at least part of their sovereignty.[28] Because states have a diminished power to act against interference arising from outside of their borders, individuals in turn are exposed to increasing instances of domination. The problem, it seems, is that under the present national and global order, for many individuals there are no effective means of countering these forms of domination. Put simply, the disempowerment of the nation-state has left individuals at a distinct disadvantage with respect to the control of their lives and the liberty that they enjoy (or would like to enjoy).

For Cécile Laborde, these "complex new forms of unchecked arbitrary power" flow across national borders and are exercised by distant and usually anonymous agents and agencies against vulnerable individuals who have little capacity to counter this kind of arbitrary interference. Moreover, "instead of relationships of cooperation or interdependence, which would imply reciprocity and mutual benefit, the current international order is marked by one-sided and largely coerced domination and dependency."[29] What we are left with is an image of seemingly powerless individuals who are subjected to real and sustained instances of arbitrary interference without any means of effectively countering it. These individuals live at the mercy of others—others who do not track their interests and who exercise their power at will and with impunity—all without any effective means of fighting back and regaining their freedom. What this points to is a legitimization deficit in certain decision-making processes in instances where individuals are exposed to certain actions or decisions in which they have no capacity to influence through the existing networks and norms of democratic participation. Not surprisingly, these deficits represent a serious problem for the liberty of individuals since, as I have pointed out, these interferences are often arbitrary in nature and thus are indicative of domination and dependency.

If individuals will inevitably be exposed to the kind of interference described above, the next thing to consider is what, if anything, can be done to not only empower them to cope with it, but also give them meaningful and effective democratic institutions in which they can use that power. Thus,

---

[27] Ibid., 90.

[28] José Luis Martí, "A Global Republic to Prevent Global Domination," *Diacrítica* 24, no. 2 (2010): 31–72, 37.

[29] Cécile Laborde, "Republicanism and Global Justice: A Sketch," *European Journal of Political Theory* 9, no. 1 (2010): 48–69, 50; Rainer Forst, "Towards a Critical Theory of Transnational Justice," *Metaphilosophy* 32, no. 1/2 (2001): 160–79.

it is not surprising that there is a growing body of literature that advocates a cosmopolitan approach. Stripped down to its essence, cosmopolitans believe that in light of our common humanity, individuals are members of a shared global community and that rights and obligations are owed to all equally. As Gillian Brock and Harry Brighouse point out, cosmopolitanism involves a thesis about identity—seeing oneself as a "citizen of the world"—and it involves a thesis about responsibility—acknowledging certain universal obligations owed equally to others both near and far.[30] It follows, then, that in order for these rights and obligations to be realized effectively there is a need for some kind of political institutional structure that reflects this global orientation with some degree of sovereignty over traditional nation-states.[31] For their part, contemporary republicans have only recently begun to think along these lines. This may be because, as I pointed out, there are serious questions about whether it is possible to adapt the classical republican approach in this manner. However, there are good reasons to think that these impediments do not apply to the neo-Roman republican strand and its contemporary version outlined above. This is because these approaches do not prioritize the bounded political community, with shared values, of its neo-Athenian counterpart. Instead, as I have pointed out above, they promote a particular conception of liberty, vested in certain republican institutions and ideals that, as some argue, can be detached from the bounded nature of the nation-state. I turn to this issue now.

3 COSMOPOLITAN REPUBLICANISM

As with all labels of philosophical approaches, cosmopolitanism is a contested concept and not one that can be viewed in a monolithic manner. Indeed, as I will argue below, within republican political theory, there are at least two main varieties of cosmopolitanism ranging from calls for a global republic to thinner, more abstract notions that build on existing networks of transnational political institutions. To help clarify these, in this section, I will briefly sketch out how some see republican institutions and ideals emerging in a global context before I critically evaluate them. As a starting point, echoing Brock and Brighouse's definition above, Bohman has stated that political cosmopolitanism is the normative claim that there is an obligation to form a political community beyond the nation-state.[32] Halldenius notes that there are commonly three main features of contemporary cosmopolitan theories: a global community, moral universalism, and support

[30] Gillian Brock and Harry Brighouse, *The Political Philosophy of Cosmopolitanism* (Cambridge: Cambridge University Press, 2005), 2–3.
[31] Halldenius, "Building Blocks of a Republican Cosmopolitanism," 23.
[32] Bohman, "Republican Cosmopolitanism," 336.

for transnational regulatory institutions with a priority over national or regional ones.[33]

Where cosmopolitan theories seem to diverge centers on the level of intensity and the scope of institutional structures within these three points. There is not only little agreement over just what the terms of universal morality are, if indeed such a concept exists. There are also important, and some would say intractable, questions about the implied obligations and practices of a global community and how this in turn relates to global institutional political structures. While there are a few cosmopolitans that argue for a world state, there is considerable debate surrounding the kinds of transnational institutions that serve to globalize the obligations that correspond with rights that kick in when national institutions fail.[34] What we are left with is a great variety of cosmopolitan-inspired approaches, including republican-inspired ones, that vary considerably on each of these issues.

A Global Republic

While many consider a world state overly utopian, for José Luis Martí there are several conceptual reasons why such a polity might prove to be the most effective institution to combat global forms of domination. Martí maintains that it is only through the successful creation of a global polity in the form of a global republic that global forms of domination can be effectively minimized. For Martí, the global republic must be guided by three main principles.[35] The first is that it must contain a centralized set of properly constituted republican institutions, such as those characterized by mixed government, separation of powers, the rule of law, checks, and balances, democratic representation, and public invigilation. These essential republican technologies, as was pointed out above, serve to help minimize domination through various institutions, methods, and means. Essentially what Martí is arguing for is to take the institutional mechanisms of traditional republican theory and apply them to some kind of global political structure. Thus, those kinds of republican structures currently vested within the more narrow confines of the nation-state would be outsourced and transported to a new, global entity constituted by existing states and peoples.

Not surprisingly, the second principle of Martí's global republic is that it must also be constrained and its power checked. This manifests itself in two main ways. First, he suggests that there must be some kind of robust constitutional and legal system aimed at checking the power of the state. This reflects a long republican concern with state power and the dangers that arise out of *imperium*. As was pointed out above, republicans view the state as both a means to minimize domination, and also a source of domination.

33 Halldenius, "Building Blocks of a Republican Cosmopolitanism," 23–24.
34 Ibid., 24.
35 Martí, "A Global Republic to Prevent Global Domination," 33.

In other words, governmental institutions must be constantly checked to ensure that they themselves do not become a source of domination. And, as Martí rightly points out, one way to combat this threat is to have a constitutional and legal system that serves to disperse power and prevent the rise of factions. The other means is through the development of innovative methods of political representation and popular control. For republicans, the people themselves represent an important check on the power of the republic and, combined with the constitutional and legal constraints, help guard against the state becoming a source of domination. Martí describes this institutional set up as a kind of

> bottom up strategy (or combined ones) for which international and street level politics is carried out by engaged citizens. These citizens need to be organized in transnational networks and organizations to create a dynamic global public sphere. These citizens need to be organized in transnational networks and organizations and to extend common channels of communication and coordination through a dynamic global public sphere—or through a number of transnational, distributed public spheres.[36]

Martí maintains that these institutions will have to be guided by deliberative procedures and be reason-giving and responsive to citizens in the global public sphere. The thought is that everyday citizens, ones that are not necessarily experts on this or that global political issue, should have an easy and effective means of expressing their interests. However, perhaps not surprisingly, Martí is vague on how this kind of mechanism would actually come into being or function. What makes this important, for republicans at least, is that without the mechanisms or access points for meaning and genuine deliberation to occur, it would be impossible for any kind of republic—global or nation-state—to track the interests of the citizenry. This point ties into one I made earlier about the proximity of republican institutions to individuals: if such institutions are too far removed from them it seems unlikely that individuals will have ready access to influence and control the policy outputs—a key requirement for ensuring that domination is eliminated.

The third part of Martí's argument, perhaps anticipating a statist critique against his position, is that the creation of a global republic must be compatible with the preservation of a nation-state's sovereignty on some, but importantly not all, issues. The thought here is that any kind of global republic would, by necessity, have to utilize a nation-state's political infrastructure and competencies in order to effectively function. Seen in this way, it is perhaps more accurate to characterize Martí's ideal polity as made up of smaller, quasi-sovereign nation-states feeding into a larger, more globally oriented institution that would be the final arbiter of global policy.

[36] Ibid., 57.

Within this way of thinking, there are shades of the kind of relationship that the European Union has to its member states. This, however, again raises important questions surrounding the complexity of this relationship and the availability for real and meaningful citizen input. I will more fully deal with this issue below, but I first want to turn to a similar, but less robust, version of cosmopolitan republicanism.

Transnational Republicanism

The second main cosmopolitan republican approach is less comprehensive than Martí's, namely because it does not envisage the creation of a global republic, and is perhaps best articulated by James Bohman through a series of writings.[37] This approach is mainly characterized by its reliance on the development of effective and meaningful transnational institutions combined with a reliance on some kind of loosely unified global civic society under the banner of universal human rights. Bohman argues that "without appealing to either an *ethnos* or clearly bounded *demos*, republican cosmopolitanism offers a pluralistic association within the framework of transnational civil society, global public spheres, and formal institutions for allowing those who are subject to supranational authority to collectively authorize it."[38] The jumping-off point of Bohman's analysis is that humanity itself constitutes a specific kind of republic through the reification and normalization of the international human rights regime. Dubbing this the Republic of Humanity, Bohman argues that included in normative human rights is a claim that everyone must have the right to membership in a political community, a manifestation of Arendt's famous phrase, "the right to have rights." Moreover, Bohman sees the establishment of certain transnational agencies such as the International Criminal Court (ICC) as the "addressee of such rights claims in which individuals have the legal status of *citizens* of the world."[39] The thought is that if human rights are violated, it is an attack on all of humanity and a mark against the fundamental status of being a human endowed with certain basic rights, such as those found in the Universal Declaration of Human Rights and subsequent international conventions and agreements. Thus, an affront against human rights ends up having a dual consequence. On the one hand, it is an affront

---

[37] Because of its succinctness, I will mostly concentrate on Bohman, "Republican Cosmopolitanism." For more of Bohman's work in this area see Bohman, "Domination, Global Harms and the Priority of Injustice" (this volume); Bohman, "Cosmopolitan Republicanism: Citizenship, Freedom and Global Political Authority," *The Monist* 84, no. 1 (2001): 3–21; Bohman, *Democracy across Borders: From Dêmos to Dêmoi* (Cambridge, MA: MIT Press, 2007); Bohman, "Non-Domination and Transnational Democracy," in *Republicanism and Political Theory*, eds. Cécile Laborde and John Maynor (Oxford: Blackwell, 2008), 190–216.

[38] Bohman, "Cosmopolitan Republicanism," 7 (emphasis in original).

[39] Bohman, "Republican Cosmopolitanism," 343–45 (emphasis in original).

on the actual person whose rights were violated, whereas on the other hand, it is an affront against all of humanity—hence the phrase "crimes against humanity."

While having this kind of transnational juridical institution is consistent with Bohman's approach, it is not sufficient on its own to root out global domination. What is needed, argues Bohman, in addition to these kinds of transnational institutions are alternative forms of political space populated by all citizens who are seen as bearers of human rights and members of the larger, global, human political community.[40] What this points to is other kinds of transnational institutions, ones that operate alongside juridical institutions like the ICC that are more democratic in nature and more responsive to the people. The thought is that these institutions, like the ones advocated by Martí, would serve to gain citizen input so that domination can be minimized through public accountability. This kind of accountability has two dimensions, one horizontal and the other vertical.[41] The horizontal dimension focuses on relations within institutions such as the World Bank and the International Monetary Fund. The vertical dimension centers on relations between these institutional actors and the general public to provide accountability down to the street level through mechanisms like public forums, either real or virtual.

What Bohman is highlighting here is that in his view what really plagues cosmopolitan approaches is not a democratic deficit but rather an accountability deficit. This is something that I will address more fully in the next section, but for now it is important to note that this sentiment is consistent with broader republican approaches. This is because more generally, as pointed out above, republicans have always believed that multiple levels of inquiry and accountability, coupled with deliberative institutions, provide important checks on the power of state. What Bohman hopes is that these processes and mechanisms can be detached from the nation-state and vested within transnational entities.[42] Having these kinds of institutions and structures in place will allow for an increase in the number of eyes watching policy makers. According to Bohman, "a large and diverse body of citizens is better able to test whether or not the common good or universal interest is actually being pursued and to engage in the multi-perspectival form of social inquiry necessary for cooperative institutions."[43] Put in a more modern context, what Bohman is suggesting is that having multiple and multifaceted layers and opportunities to participate will lead to a kind of crowdsourcing effort aimed at rooting out domination by increasing access to public forums, and to other mechanisms to increase levels of accountability.

---

[40] Ibid., 342.
[41] Ibid., 346–47.
[42] Ibid., 348–50.
[43] Ibid., 350.

There are three main takeaways from Bohman's approach. The first is his contention that it is possible to discern a global community predicated on an understanding of universal human rights. This would, in turn, be vested in transnational structures aimed at protecting everyone's rights and providing an important focal point for a particular kind of global political community. It follows, then, that the second takeaway is the creation of juridical institutions that both constitute the international political community as an addressee of legal claims and establish enforceable universal rights of political membership. The final takeaway is that there must be an effort to establish a wide-ranging democratic political community that promotes non-domination through traditional republican mechanisms of cooperation, deliberation, and inquiry. While the precise details of Bohman and Martí's cosmopolitan republicanism differ, not surprisingly, there is quite a bit of overlap. The main differences revolve around questions of centralization and the role of traditional national sovereignty.[44] Where Martí argues for a centralized global republic that supersedes traditional notions of national sovereignty, Bohman prefers a decentralized approach where transnational entities are dispersed and mutually independent authorities are not subordinate to any kind of global sovereign. While these two approaches differ in scope and intensity, they are to various degrees subjected to the same kinds of critique. In the next section, I want to tease out these areas and argue that there is another way to see republicanism's contribution to these debates.

4 THE NATION-STATE IS DEAD: LONG LIVE THE NATION-STATE

In their most basic formulations, the most obvious potential weaknesses of these kinds of cosmopolitan republican approaches center on questions of both scope and means. Regarding the means, tough questions must be asked of these kinds of republicans regarding the effectiveness and functionality of the kinds of republican institutions they advocate. Both of these theorists suggest that because it is possible to discern some kind of global public sphere, transnational republican institutions will be able to process the interests of the people while at the same time ensuring that the people have the ability to provide a check on the power of these institutions. Insofar as the scope is concerned, cosmopolitan republicans believe that the only way to root out global domination is through transnational institutions, since average individuals are inevitably exposed to sources of domination that arise from outside of their nation-state. In other words, since the sources of some forms of domination are often external to the nation-state, the thought is that

[44] Martí, "A Global Republic to Prevent Global Domination," 54–55.

only political entities that reside outside of and above the nation-state can effectively work to minimize it. But this way of thinking raises an obvious question regarding something that republicans have always been concerned about. This is the possibility that political institutions may well become a source of domination themselves. It follows that the same fear must also be present in any kind of transnational institutional arrangement. This gives rise to another problem, one of proximity, since these kinds of institutions will reside far from the reach of average individuals. The upshot is that there is a real danger that they may become an overly powerful source of domination, uncheckable because of their sheer size and complexity. While both Martí and Bohman seem to be aware of the problem, it is not clear that their hope for a singular, global deliberative public sphere is realistic, or even desirable.

We can see echoes of this challenge in some of the difficulties engulfing the European Union with respect to what is often referred to as its democratic deficit. In what follows below, I want to explore these issues in greater detail, since many point to the EU as an example of how cosmopolitan transnational institutions have become a reality. Moreover, this case seems to be a particularly pertinent one since there seems to be a growing chorus of writers who argue that republican values and technologies can be employed at the EU level, especially to remedy some of the democratic and structural challenges it currently faces.[45]

There seem to be two overarching commonalities why Euro-republicans believe the EU can be usefully analyzed through the lens of republican political theory. The first is that some writers believe that recent developments in the EU reflect essential republican ideals and institutions such as mixed constitutions, the dispersion of power across a range of government institutions, popular input through representation and in vibrant, deliberative structures,

[45] For a broad sample of Euro-republican approaches, see Richard Bellamy, "The 'Right to Have Rights': Citizenship Practice and the Political Constitution of the EU," in *Citizenship and Governance in the European Union*, eds. Richard Bellamy and Alex Warleigh (London: Continuum, 2001), 41–70; Bellamy, *Political Constitutionalism: A Republican Defense of the Constitutionality of Democracy* (Cambridge: Cambridge University Press, 2007); Heidrun Friese and Peter Wagner, "Survey Article: The Nascent Political Philosophy of the European Polity," *The Journal of Political Philosophy* 10, no. 3 (2002), 342–64; Jürgen Habermas, *Between Facts and Norms*; Habermas, "Making Sense of the EU"; Kōstas A. Lavdas and Dimitris N. Chryssochoou, "Public Spheres in the European Polity," in *Republicanism in Theory and Practice*, eds. Iseult Honohan and Jeremy Jennings (London: Routledge, 2005); David Miller, "Republicanism, National Identity, and Europe," in *Republicanism and Political Theory*, eds. Cécile Laborde and John Maynor (Oxford: Blackwell, 2008), 133–58; Maynor, "Constitutional Patriotism or Neo-Republican Citizenship"; Christopher Bickerton, "Europe's Neo-Madisonians: Rethinking the Legitimacy of Limited Power in a Multi-Level Polity," *Political Studies* 59, no. 3 (2011): 659–73.

the rule of law, and certain counter-majoritarian elements such as judicial review bodies. Lavdas and Chryssochoou put it this way:

> A 'balanced constitution' is reflected in the Commission's exclusive right to initiate legislation and its interaction with civil society; the co-decision rights of the European Parliament (EP) in fostering more deliberative outcomes; the political activism of the [European Court of Justice] in interpreting EU law; and the relation between the indirect democratic mandate of the Council of Ministers and the fact that Europe's political constitution rests on an international treaty.[46]

The thought is that the structures of the EU have the potential to, on the one hand, strike a proper institutional balance to prevent the rise of domination and tyranny within its larger geopolitical footprint. On the other hand, many of these writers point to an emerging political *demos* featuring a vibrant range of deliberative forums within an EU-wide single civil society.[47]

The second is that Euro-republican theorists seem to more or less adopt a neo-Madisonian approach that holds that a republican form of government is best realized in a large and diverse political community such as the EU. The thought is that the size and diversity of the EU is advantageous to the development of republican politics. This contention is built upon a reading of republicanism that argues that large polities made up of smaller self-governing units can develop overarching policies that serve the common good through the judicious use of certain republican ideals and institutions, like the ones mentioned above. As David Miller has pointed out, these republicans believe that "the political community should be large, it should be divided into numerous subunits (cities, provinces or states), it should rely on constitutional checks and balances to create stability and protect liberty, and popular rule should be mediated by representative institutions."[48] However, there is one important caveat to the establishment and maintenance of large-scale republics, namely the threat brought about by factions. Seen in this way, factions are those political cleavages that give rise to allegiances that displace allegiance to the whole of the political community. For large-scale republics to survive, an essential ingredient is a robust and vibrant political community that can hold the allegiance of the people so that smaller, vertically organized groups do not cleave off into factions, promoting their own interests above that of the common good.[49] This is an issue I will come back to below, but taking these points together, there seem to be two requirements for republican politics to obtain in this manner.

---

[46] Lavdas and Chryssochoou, "Public Spheres in the European Polity," 159.
[47] Paul P. Craig, "Democracy and Rule-Making within the EC: An Empirical and Normative Assessment," *European Law Journal* 3, no. 2 (1997): 103–30, 114.
[48] Miller, "Republicanism, National Identity, and Europe," 136.
[49] Maynor, *Republicanism in the Modern World*, ch. 5.

The first is some form of a political constitution that features certain properly constituted republican institutions so that power is dispersed and domination can be dislodged not only from the structures of government, but also within civil society. The second is the need for a particular kind of political community, one that is intimate and vibrant enough to resist the threat of factions. If this kind of political community can become a reality, then it is certainly feasible that at least from an institutional perspective, republican technologies can be useful in helping to counter interference that may arise from outside of the narrower confines of the nation-state. However, the key part of the challenge of realizing these possibilities is contingent on the ability of transnational entities like the EU to develop meaningful democratic practices and institutions that reside in close proximity to individuals so that they can both check its power and meaningfully influence its policy outputs.

And therein lies one of the central problems of trying to develop any kind of transnational republic. So far, at least, it is not clear that the EU has been able to achieve this. As Føllesdal and Hix point out, there are at least five main claims that the EU suffers from a democratic deficit.[50] The first is the thought that European integration has resulted in an increase in executive power and a decrease in individual state's parliamentary power. This is because policy-making at the EU level is dominated by executive actors who often reside beyond the reach of national parliaments, one of the main mechanisms of democratic engagement for individuals. The second is that although the power of the European Parliament has increased over time, its power still does not rival the European Council, the non-elected executive. Related, the third is that even though there is a European Parliament, there are no Europe-wide elections. Instead, these elections operate through the national structures of member states and often reflect the domestic agendas of their domestic political parties. It follows, then, that the fourth is the perception, either real or imagined, that the EU is too distant from voters. Many believe that EU policies are made by distant Euro-elites who only serve their own agenda with little input from or accountability to average

[50] Andreas Føllesdal and Simon Hix, "Why There is a Democratic Deficit in the EU: A Response to Majone and Moravcsik," *JCMS: Journal of Common Market Studies* 44, no. 3 (2006): 533–62. For an alternative view, see Andrew Moravcsik, "In Defense of the 'Democratic Deficit': Reassessing the Legitimacy of the European Union," *Journal of Common Market Studies* 40, no. 4 (2002): 603–634; Moravcsik "Is there a 'Democratic Deficit' in World Politics? A Framework for Analysis," *Government and Opposition* 39, no. 2 (2004): 336–63. Moravcsik's overarching position is that it is best to view the EU as more or less the appointed agents of the democratically elected governments of its member states. Moreover, he believes that the interplay and bargaining that occurs between these centers of power minimizes the risk that EU policy goes against the interests of the people. The upshot is that, for Moravcsik, there is no democratic deficit, because ultimately the EU is under the control of its member states, who look after the interests of their citizenry at the transnational level.

citizens. This point ties into one I made above about the proximity of institutions to citizens and the likelihood that the farther they are removed from them the greater the risk of domination. So, if this is the case, republicans would surely identify this as a source of the kind of domination they abhor. Finally, the collective weight of the democratic deficit results in a "policy drift" that sees the EU adopting measures that are not supported by a majority of citizens in many of its member states. In other words, there is a real disconnect between the interests of European citizens on an individual level and the policies that emerge from the institutions of the EU.

Chris Bickerton has recently argued that the neo-Madisonian turn in the normative phase of the EU ignores the realities and limitations of this kind of "mixed government approach."[51] Bickerton's charge is that the kind of mixed government favored by Madison was trying to accomplish a fundamentally different conceptual task than those multilevel forms and overlapping frameworks found within the EU. In contemporary politics, mixed governments need to be legitimated through some kind of representative function that stresses unity through the "normative agreement between various parties" and not through authoritative command.[52] Thus, the actors involved in making EU politics need to utilize the neo-Madisonian mixed government elements not as ends themselves, but rather as a means to make and modify policies. The problem, at least for Bickerton, is that neo-Madisonians within the EU have argued for a system of checks and balances and separation of powers, but in doing so they have attempted to separate sovereignty from legitimacy. The result, then, is an underpoliticization within the EU that finds national legislatures, the European Parliament, and the EU's other institutions all struggling to gain popular legitimacy.[53] Thus, EU institutions and policies lack the crucial positive relationship with their collective political subjects. What is needed, Bickerton argues, is a renewed focus on building a European *demos* that will reconcile democracy with pan-European governance.

In more general terms, what these problems highlight is that there are real questions as to whether real and meaningful transnational institutions can develop that serve to minimize the arbitrary interference that individuals experience. In fact, there is a real danger that these kinds of efforts may well increase levels of domination.[54] Insofar as the EU is concerned, as Miller points out, its workings are quite opaque, even to the most politically informed.[55] The fact that the EU is a highly complex political system with

---

[51] Bickerton, "Europe's Neo-Madisonians," 668.
[52] Bellamy, "Sovereignty, Post-Sovereignty and Pre-Sovereignty: Three Models of The State, Democracy and Rights Within the EU," in *Sovereignty in Transition*, ed. Neil Walker (Hart Publishing, 2003), 167–90, 184.
[53] Bickerton, "Europe's Neo-Madisonians," 669–70.
[54] Maynor, "Constitutional Patriotism or Neo-Republican Citizenship."
[55] Miller, "Republicanism, National Identity, and Europe."

many agencies of overlapping competences might seem to point to the kind of mixed constitution favored by republicans. However, there is a danger that these agencies are overly complex and unintelligible to average citizens. The result is that not only do these kinds of institutions reside far away from individuals, there is a real disconnect between the institutions of power and those individuals who are on the receiving end of that power. Thus, there is considerable danger that the EU or any other transnational polity may end up not minimizing domination, but rather increasing it. In other words, instead of decreasing the amount of arbitrary interference that individuals experience, it is possible that transnational institutions may end up being a considerable source of domination due to the disconnect and distance between the institutions themselves and the citizens they claim to serve.

So what are we left with? If transnational institutions cannot provide the kind of constitutional democratic polity necessary to minimize domination and arbitrary interference, it seems as if republicanism cannot be successfully deployed in a cosmopolitan manner. But this conclusion may be too quick. It ignores the fact that although perhaps diminished, the nation-state may not be as politically irrelevant and powerless as some maintain. There does seem to be another way to look at these challenges that involves not only moving to create and develop meaningful transnational political institutions where possible that contain sufficient democratic elements and are guided by republican ideals and values. It also involves working to ensure that republican political institutions and ideals continue to become more prevalent within nation-states, since, as Kymlicka has pointed out, at the moment the "only forum in which genuine democracy occurs is within national boundaries."[56] Moreover, as Pettit has pointed out in his chapter in this volume, since states will remain a permanent feature of our world, it makes sense to work within the present system to create structures, both of a domestic and transnational sort, to fight back against domination.[57] This sentiment is close to one put forward by Steven Slaughter, who maintains that the nation-state is the most effective, if flawed, "location of governance aimed directly at the expression of popular sovereignty and the construction of liberty."[58] And as such, for Slaughter, a republican nation-state is the institution best suited to minimize domination, since its citizenry are able to exercise, observe, and discipline its public power.[59] It follows, then, as a first line of defense against domination, a nation-state's political institutions and

[56] Kymlicka, "Citizenship in an Era of Globalization: Commentary on Held," ch. 17 in *Politics in the Vernacular* (Oxford: Oxford University Press, 2001), 325.
[57] Pettit, "A Republican Law of Peoples," 70; Pettit, "The Republican Law of Peoples: A Restatement," 37.
[58] Steven Slaughter, *Liberty Beyond Neo-Liberalism: A Republican Critique of Liberal Governance in a Globalising Age* (Basingstoke: Palgrave Macmillan, 2005), 202.
[59] For a more comprehensive account of Slaughter's argument, see his *Liberty Beyond Neo-Liberalism*, esp. ch. 7: "Global Civic Republicanism; Retrieving the State."

ideals should reflect republican priorities. This is not to say that real and meaningful transnational political institutions that minimize domination cannot ever develop, but rather that a key to their development firmly lies within the domestic efforts of nation-states to ensure that the citizenry have the necessary democratic institutions and ideals to check arbitrary power. If individuals can democratically work through properly constituted, domestic political structures that reduce arbitrary interference, their influence can extend to matters of a global nature. Moreover, these kinds of domestic republican structures will be better placed to make positive contributions to transnational entities, which is likely to increase the legitimacy of these kinds of institutions and policies.

For example, take the recent Euro crisis in Greece. The austerity demands placed on Greece by the other members of the Euro, and Germany and France in particular, were for the most part not seen as legitimate by the Greek people. It was only after this issue was debated and subsequently litigated by the Greek political community that the policies keeping Greece in the Euro gained a degree of legitimacy for many of the Greek people. Seen through a republican lens, many viewed these measures as something being forced from the outside and, likely, as domination, since they lacked legitimacy and did not track the interest of the Greek people. However, some of these measures, having been a key issue in the Greek parliamentary elections of June 2012, subsequently became legitimized and non-arbitrary in nature because, through democratic self-government, they became policies that the people chose themselves.[60] What this points to is the importance of domestic, democratic political institutions that work to resolve and legitimize policy issues so that they are non-arbitrary. Outsourcing republican ideals and institutions to transnational entities runs the risk that the policy outputs of those institutions fail to gain the necessary input from the individuals that those policies most directly affect. If individuals on the receiving end of those policies view them as alien or having originated from beyond their reach, they will most likely view them as arbitrary interference and domination.

Perhaps the best that we can hope for is a kind of dual trajectory that sees meaningful, democratic-republican practices and institutions developed at both the national and transnational level. To be sure, there is a complex relationship between these two levels of governance. However, this sentiment ties into a similar argument along these lines that moving in this direction may well help *increase* the democratic nature of both transnational

---

60 Rachel Donadio, "Supporters of Bailout Claim Victory in Greek Election," *New York Times*, June 17, 2012, www.nytimes.com/2012/06/18/world/europe/greek-elections.html?smid=pl-share. For a more in-depth study of the austerity crisis in Europe and democratic legitimacy, see Vassilis K. Fouskas and Constantine Dimoulas, *Greece, Financialization and the EU: The Political Economy of Debt and Destruction* (Basingstoke: Palgrave Macmillan, 2013); Huw Macartney, *The Debt Crisis and European Democratic Legitimacy* (Basingstoke: Palgrave Macmillan, 2013).

and national political structures. Robert Keohane, Stephen Macedo, and Andrew Moravcsik suggest that multilateral institutions—international organizations, regimes, and networks governed by formal international agreements—can lead to an increase in the quality of domestic democracy. For these writers, multilateralism can

> enhance domestic democracy in a number of important ways. Involvement with multilateral institutions often helps domestic democratic institutions restrict the power of special interest factions, protect individual rights, and improve the quality of democratic deliberation, while also increasing capacities to achieve important public purposes. Under some plausible circumstances international cooperation can thus enhance the quality of democracy in reasonably well-functioning democratic polities.[61]

The trick to pulling this off lies in two key areas consistent with what I have argued above. First, on a domestic level, there must be some kind of democratic, legal/constitutional structures in place that are responsive to the interests of the citizenry and protect individuals from domination. These structures must help to minimize factions, promote individual and minority rights, and help citizens see how their actions are intimately tied to others who lie outside of their immediate sphere. Second, there must be vibrant deliberative forums and opportunities for citizen input into the structures of both national and transnational institutions. In other words, citizens must not only practice deliberation and contestation about both domestic and foreign issues within their states, they must also be willing to engage in the nascent civil society currently emerging that to date has not, but may become, a global political community.

CONCLUSION

I have made two main arguments in this chapter. First I have argued that it is possible to think in cosmopolitan terms when thinking about republican political theory. However, I have also argued that this is only possible when thinking about the neo-Roman strand of republican thinking, since the neo-Athenian version is too closely tied to the development of certain political virtues in some kind of specific, bounded political community. Beyond this conclusion, I have also argued that while it may be possible to think of republicanism in a cosmopolitan manner, outsourcing republican liberty as non-domination away from nation-states to transnational institutions and

---

[61] Robert Keohane, Stephen Macedo, and Andrew Moravcsik, "Democracy-Enhancing Multilateralism," *International Organization* 63, no. 1 (2009): 1–31, 1–2.

entities may not be the best way forward. This conclusion is based on the thought that the two main varieties of republican cosmopolitanism have failed to demonstrate adequately how they will overcome the real and significant challenges of scope and means in trying to root out domination in a global context. In fact, I have argued that outsourcing the effort to curtail domination to transnational institutions may well lead to an increase in arbitrary interference. Instead, as an alternative, I have argued that while thinking in cosmopolitan terms for some republicans may be at least theoretically sound, a more practical and immediate means of combatting domination must begin within the existing structures of the nation-state. This is not to preclude the creation of a vibrant set of transnational institutional networks and norms consistent with republicanism. But this effort must come from within and be controled by nation-states, and not from some kind of forced global political entity that is far removed from the influence of average individuals.

BIBLIOGRAPHY

Bellamy, Richard. *Political Constitutionalism: A Republican Defense of the Constitutionality of Democracy*. Cambridge: Cambridge University Press, 2007.

Bellamy, Richard. "The 'Right to Have Rights': Citizenship Practice and the Political Constitution of the EU." In *Citizenship and Governance in the European Union*, edited by Richard Bellamy and Alex Warleigh. London: Continuum, 2001.

Bellamy, Richard. "Sovereignty, Post-Sovereignty and Pre-Sovereignty: Three Models of The State, Democracy and Rights Within the EU." In *Sovereignty in Transition*, edited by Neil Walker, 167–90. Portland, OR: Hart Publishing, 2003.

Bickerton, Christopher. "Europe's Neo-Madisonians: Rethinking the Legitimacy of Limited Power in a Multi-Level Polity." *Political Studies* 59, no. 3 (2011): 659–73.

Bohman, James. "Cosmopolitan Republicanism: Citizenship, Freedom and Global Political Authority." *The Monist* 84, no. 1 (2001): 3–21.

Bohman, James. *Democracy across Borders: From Dêmos to Dêmoi*. Cambridge, MA: MIT Press, 2007.

Bohman, James. "Domination, Global Harms and the Priority of Injustice: Expanding Transnational Republicanism." In *Domination and Global Political Justice: Conceptual, Historical, and Institutional Perspectives*, edited by Barbara Buckinx, Jonathan Trejo-Mathys, and Timothy Waligore. New York: Routledge, 2015.

Bohman, James. "Non-Domination and Transnational Democracy." In *Republicanism and Political Theory*, edited by Cécile Laborde and John Maynor, 190–216. Oxford: Blackwell, 2008.

Bohman, James. "Republican Cosmopolitanism." *The Journal of Political Philosophy* 12, no. 3 (2004): 336–52.

Brock, Gillian, and Harry Brighouse. *The Political Philosophy of Cosmopolitanism*. Cambridge: Cambridge University Press, 2005.

Chung, Ryoa. "The Cosmopolitan Scope of Republican Citizenship." In *Republicanism: History, Theory and Practice*, edited by Daniel Weinstock and Christian Nadeau. London: Frank Cass, 2004.

Craig, Paul P. "Democracy and Rule-Making within the EC: An Empirical and Normative Assessment." *European Law Journal* 3, no. 2 (1997): 105–30.

Donadio, Rachel. "Supporters of Bailout Claim Victory in Greek Election." *New York Times*, June 17, 2012. http://www.nytimes.com/2012/06/18/world/europe/greek-elections.html?smid=pl-share.
Føllesdal, Andreas, and Simon Hix. "Why There is a Democratic Deficit in the EU: A Response to Majone and Moravcsik." *JCMS: Journal of Common Market Studies* 44, no. 3 (2006): 533–62.
Forst, Rainer. "Towards a Critical Theory of Transnational Justice." *Metaphilosophy* 32, no. 1/2 (2001): 160–79.
Fouskas, Vassilis K., and Constantine Dimoulas. *Greece, Financialization and the EU: The Political Economy of Debt and Destruction*. Basingstoke: Palgrave Macmillian, 2013.
Friese, Heidrun, and Peter Wagner. "Survey Article: The Nascent Political Philosophy of the European Polity." *The Journal of Political Philosophy* 10, no. 3 (2002): 342–64.
Habermas, Jürgen. *Between Facts and Norms: Contributions to a Discourse Theory of Law and Democracy*. Translated by William Rehg. Cambridge, MA: MIT Press, 1996.
Habermas, Jürgen. "Making Sense of the EU: Toward a Cosmopolitan Europe." *Journal of Democracy* 14, no. 4 (2003): 86–100.
Halldenius, Lena. "Building Blocks of a Republican Cosmopolitanism: The Modality of Being Free." *European Journal of Political Theory* 9, no. 1 (2010): 12–30.
Honohan, Iseult. *Civic Republicanism*. London: Routledge, 2002.
Keohane, Robert, Stephen Macedo, and Andrew Moravcsik. "Democracy-Enhancing Multilateralism." *International Organization* 63, no. 1 (2009): 1–31.
Kymlicka, Will. "Citizenship in an Era of Globalization: Commentary on Held." Ch. 17 in *Politics in the Vernacular*. Oxford: Oxford University Press, 2001.
Kymlicka, Will. *Contemporary Political Philosophy*, 2nd ed. Oxford: Oxford University Press, 2002.
Kymlicka, Will. *Liberalism, Community, and Culture*. Oxford: Oxford University Press, 1989.
Laborde, Cécile. *Critical Republicanism*. Oxford: Oxford University Press, 2008.
Laborde, Cécile. "Republicanism and Global Justice: A Sketch." *European Journal of Political Theory* 9, no. 1 (2010): 48–69.
Laborde, Cécile, and John Maynor, eds. *Republicanism and Political Theory*. Oxford: Blackwell, 2008.
Lavdas, Kōstas A., and Dimitris N. Chryssochoou. "Public Spheres in the European Polity." In *Republicanism in Theory and Practice*, edited by Iseult Honohan and Jeremy Jennings, 154–69. London: Routledge, 2005.
List, Christian. "Republican Freedom and the Rule of Law." *Politics, Philosophy & Economics* 5, no. 2 (2006): 201–20.
Macartney, Huw. *The Debt Crisis and European Democratic Legitimacy*. Basingstoke: Palgrave Macmillan, 2013.
Martí, José Louis. "A Global Republic to Prevent Global Domination." *Diacrítica* 24, no. 2 (2010): 31–72.
Martí, José Louis, and Philip Pettit. *A Political Philosophy in Public Life: Civic Republicanism in Zapatero's Spain*. Princeton: Princeton University Press, 2010.
Maynor, John. "Constitutional Patriotism or Neo-Republican Citizenship: A Way Forward for the EU?" In *Constituting Communities: Political Solutions to Cultural Difference*, edited by Per Mouritsen and Kund Erik Jørgensen, 187–209. London: Palgrave Macmillan, 2008.
Maynor, John. "Fighting Back Against Domination: Republican Citizenship and Unbounded Reciprocity." *Diacrítica* 24, no. 2 (2010): 73–90.

Maynor, John. "Modern Republican Democratic Contestation: A Model of Deliberative Democracy." In *Republicanism in Theory and Practice*, edited by Iseult Honohan and Jeremy Jennings. London: Routledge, 2005.
Maynor, John. *Republicanism in the Modern World*. Cambridge: Polity Press, 2003.
Miller, David. "Republicanism, National Identity, and Europe." In *Republicanism and Political Theory*, edited by Cécile Laborde and John Maynor. Oxford: Blackwell, 2008.
Moravcsik, Andrew. "In Defense of the 'Democratic Deficit': Reassessing the Legitimacy of the European Union." *Journal of Common Market Studies* 40, no. 4 (2002): 603–34.
Moravcsik, Andrew. "Is There a 'Democratic Deficit' in World Politics? A Framework for Analysis." *Government and Opposition* 39, no. 2 (2004): 336–63.
Mouffe, Chantal. *The Return of the Political*. London: Verso, 1993.
Oldfield, Adrian. *Citizenship and Community: Civic Republicanism and the Modern World*. London: Routledge, 1990.
Pettit, Philip. "Freedom in the Market." *Politics, Philosophy & Economics* 5, no. 2 (2006): 131–49.
Pettit, Philip. "Republican Freedom: Three Axioms, Four Theorems." In *Republicanism and Political Theory*, edited by Cécile Laborde and John Maynor. Oxford: Blackwell, 2008.
Pettit, Philip. "A Republican Law of Peoples." *European Journal of Political Theory* 9, no. 1 (2010): 70–94.
Pettit, Philip. "The Republican Law of Peoples: A Restatement." In *Domination and Global Political Justice: Conceptual, Historical, and Institutional Perspectives*, edited by Barbara Buckinx, Jonathan Trejo-Mathys, and Timothy Waligore. New York: Routledge, 2015.
Pettit, Philip. *Republicanism: A Theory of Freedom and Government*. Oxford: Oxford University Press, 1997.
Pettit, Philip. *A Theory of Freedom: From the Psychology to the Politics of Agency*. Cambridge: Polity Press, 2001.
Rawls, John. *Political Liberalism*, paperback ed. New York: Columbia University Press, 1996.
Sandel, Michael J. *Democracy's Discontent: America in Search of a Public Philosophy*. Cambridge, MA: Belknap Press of Harvard University Press, 1996.
Skinner, Quentin. *Liberty Before Liberalism*. Cambridge: Cambridge University Press, 1998.
Skinner, Quentin. *Reason and Rhetoric in the Philosophy of Hobbes*. Cambridge: Cambridge University Press, 1996.
Skinner, Quentin. "A Third Concept of Liberty." *Proceedings of the British Academy* 117 (2002): 237–68.
Slaughter, Steven. *Liberty Beyond Neo-Liberalism: A Republican Critique of Liberal Governance in a Globalising Age*. Basingstoke: Palgrave Macmillan, 2005.
Taylor, Charles. *Philosophical Arguments*. Cambridge, MA: Harvard University Press, 1995.
Viroli, Maurizio. *For Love of Country: An Essay on Patriotism and Nationalism*. Oxford: Clarendon Press, 1995.
Viroli, Maurizio. *Republicanism*. Translated by Anthony Shugaar. New York: Farrar Straus and Giroux, 2002.

11 Deprivation and Institutionally Based Duties to Aid

Stefan Gosepath

THE PROBLEM: DEPRIVATION

In this world, it is all too often the case that people exist in misery: not just misery relative to others, but absolute misery. Large parts of the earth's population live in poverty; they suffer from diseases; they are victims of natural disasters or cruel wars and the ensuing displacement and depredation; they die in famines, or are deprived of food, of access to basic health care, water, housing, and basic sanitary facilities; or they find themselves subjected to other forms of hardship. These kinds of deprivation threaten the very existence of those people. As a rule, such deprivation constitutes a disadvantage that entitles these people to compensation if the following conditions are met: these persons must have entered into these circumstances through no fault of their own, and they must be unable to extricate themselves from them without extraordinary sacrifices of their own and external aid. The persons in question must be unable to deliberately influence these circumstances, or at least only be able to influence them to an insignificant degree. The restraints circumstances place upon these people must objectively stop them from achieving things that are universally regarded as essential to their lives, including first and foremost the realization of basic human rights.[1] Under such conditions, people are threatened with the violation of basic rights, including physical integrity, security, and subsistence. People who cannot (freely) access a combination of the various goods and abilities sufficient to enjoy these basic rights and to achieve the things we regard as essential to their lives are said to be deprived.

Some scholars who have spearheaded the contemporary revival of the concept of non-domination present non-domination as a first-order principle of (global) justice. They contend that non-domination can capture what is problematic about extreme poverty, destitution, and misery. They argue that the political question, *Who decides about the injustice or justice of*

[1] Cf. Wilfried Hinsch, *Gerechtfertigte Ungleichheiten* (Berlin: de Gruyter, 2002), chap. V; Stefan Gosepath, *Gleiche Gerechtigkeit. Grundlagen eines Liberalen Egalitarismus* (Frankfurt: Suhrkamp, 2004), chap. V.1.5.

a distribution of goods? takes philosophical precedence over the distributive question, *What is a just or unjust distribution of goods?* This paper argues that this approach is mistaken. A focus on preventing arbitrary and pernicious forms of power is too minimalistic. The alleviation of global deprivation is prior to politics and gives rise to the requirement to create and reform global political institutions.

It is not merely arbitrariness with regard to power that matters, but other forms of arbitrariness as well. Circumstances that are generally and reciprocally accepted to be depriving entitle those requiring aid through no fault of their own to support. When confronted with poverty, destitution, and misery—except perhaps for self-inflicted poverty—we have a very clear intuition as to what we should do. Deprived persons are prima facie entitled to help from those who are already well provided for.

Even if one agrees that all "decent" people share the idea that deprivation justifies a claim to support, it is still difficult to give a plausible concept of aid in case of need—difficult not just for a random "man on the street," but also for philosophical conceptions of morality. The answers to the following questions are especially unclear and contentious: 1. Who should help in case of need? Who is responsible for putting a stop to deprivation? 2. Who exactly should one help—just the people nearby or all members of a society, or even those living far away? 3. To what extent should we provide aid to the needy? What should we deny ourselves in order to help others? 4. Are we at all *obligated* to help and if so, in what sense? At one extreme, we might think our aiding the deprived is a morally valuable and desirable action (or motivation to act), but is not a strict obligation. At the other extreme, we might think it constitutes a broad universal obligation owed by everyone to everyone. Between these two poles lies the entire range of interpretations offered by moral philosophy regarding the problem of helping the needy. So those who feel they should help often have no clear idea of whether, why, and to which extent they are obligated to do what. This constitutes the problem of *moral clarity* in aiding the deprived.[2] We see this lack of clarity as a problem because most people (at least if they are intellectually informed and candid and motivated to do right) seek a clear understanding of what they are required to do when confronted with people in need. Furthermore, as long as the problem is not resolved, there is the danger that people lament the fact that others exist in a state of deprivation but that possibly no one will provide (effective) remedies. In this way, moral ambiguity induces practical apathy, thus increasing the misery of the needy.

In order to at least begin addressing this extensive problem to some degree, I will first argue that the duty to aid the deprived is not merely a charitable one, dependent on the discretion, or the arbitrary will, of the giver (1). Then, before further analyzing the individual duty to aid, I will critically examine

---

[2] In addition to this, there are vexatious empirical and practical problems, most of which will not be addressed in this chapter.

whether deprivation is better alleviated or remedied through the duties of corrective justice. I will argue that the perspective of corrective justice is important, but not sufficient when it comes to dealing with deprivation (2). I will then argue that non-domination cannot serve as a first-order principle of justice. It is too minimalistic, since it would not require duties of justice where deprivation exists, but dominating relations and institutions do not (3). Going back to the individual duty to help, I argue that the duties to aid the needy must be assessed according to the situation at hand (4). In order to avoid meaninglessness and morality's excessive demands, one should be able to identify the responsible agents by constructing a shared and, in the last resort, institution-based duty to help (5). The institutional approach in this paper argues that we should create and reform institutions in order to realize the preexisting requirement to alleviate global deprivation. This is a form of "global political justice" that does not start with politics, but ends with global political institutions.

1 CHARITY OR DUTY TO HELP?

The simplest form of moral aid is the kind of poor relief we know from history, practiced by religious institutions and also occasionally by members of the aristocracy. The traditional line of moral justification in this context was based solely on the apparent neediness of those who found themselves in such a situation through no fault of their own. In the West, this idea was related to the (often ecclesiastical) organization of voluntary aid, which in turn rested on the Christian commandment of mercy. This form of moral aid is thus benevolently granted without any kind of claim on the part of the needy. Because the aid is purely voluntary, it can be either bestowed or not, depending on the wealthy's moral sense of responsibility. In its simplest form, one person, the giver, gives something to another person, the recipient, although the giver has no strict duty to do so, and the recipient has no corresponding right and cannot lay a justified claim to whatever it is that is given to them.[3] In this way, they resemble someone receiving a present. This kind of giving is motivated neither by a self-interested anticipation of some kind of reward, nor is it motivated (unlike a gift)[4] by the expectation that

[3] A has a claim toward B that B does X if and only if B has a corresponding duty toward A to do X. Cf. Wesley Hohfeld, *Fundamental Legal Conceptions* (New Haven: Yale University Press, 1923).

[4] Theories of the gift and of reciprocity in the tradition of Marcel Mauss claim that one is better able to explain the voluntary sacrifice of time and money as a social initiator of mutual exchange than theories of rational agency that rely on egotism or theories that explain altruism and the underlying norms and values in terms of tradition or socialization. See Mauss, *The Gift: Forms and Functions of Exchange in Archaic Societies* [1923/1924] (London: Routledge, 1990). Cf. Frank Adloff and Steffan Mau, eds., *Vom Geben und Nehmen. Zur Soziologie der Reziprozität* (Frankfurt: Campus, 2005).

the act will be reciprocated. A present is morally valuable because the giver acts altruistically—i.e., primarily for the good of the receiver—and because the receiver is dependent on the present, since his poverty is such that he cannot work himself out of it. The unsolicited present thus assumes the trait of a benevolent donation.

According to mainstream western (deontological) ethics, charity as individual philanthropy is not seen as a duty, but as something that supererogatorily goes beyond what is strictly required. It is deemed morally good and desirable but cannot be demanded from anyone. Just as we are not required to do everything we could do that is morally desirable, charity is not, according to this conception, a duty, even for all its moral value. Willingness to help those in need as an expression of sympathy with the plight of strangers is indeed considered to be a morally desirable attitude, but is at the same time an entirely voluntary effort, clearly distinguished from the actual duties we owe. According to this conception, then:

> The morality of philanthropy in fact requires us to add to justice the salt of love and to engage, out of sympathy with the plight of others, in charity: helpfulness, even generosity. But charity is not owed. As a commendable surplus effort, it deserves a place in the community, since it contributes to the community's wellbeing, but as an entirely voluntary effort, charity cannot be enforced.[5]

There are, however, strong objections to be made against the idea that helping the needy is an entirely optional affair: First, voluntary aid is not, according to that conception, an obligation and thus cannot really be relied upon where deprivation takes place. Second, the criteria of distribution must appear arbitrary to the needy, since the extent of aid depends on the individual's discretion. The benefactor must decide how much to give, when, and to whom. Third, those benefactors feeling responsible may find that the burden of aiding the deprived is quite unevenly distributed. Fourth, finally and most importantly, helping the needy should morally not be regarded as a voluntary affair, but as a duty. In the *locus classicus* of deontological ethics, in Kant's writings on moral philosophy, helping the needy is expressly mentioned as a commandment of the categorical imperative.[6] The duty to help, alongside the duty not to injure anyone (*neminem laede*), is one of the most important commandments of those modern moral theories that stipulate that certain principles and duties be obeyed for their own sake. The universal duty to aid obliges everyone who has the capacity to do so to use a part of their income and time, which is determined according to their individual capacities, for charitable activities. It demands that we help every

---

[5] Otfried Höffe, *Demokratie im Zeitalter der Globalisierung* (München: C. H. Beck, 1999), 89.

[6] Cf. Immanuel Kant, *Grundlegung zur Metaphysik der Sitten* [1785], edited by Karl Vorländer (Hamburg: Felix Meiner, 1965), 45, 8:423.

needy person, not just the one closest to ourselves, even where we are sure that they will never repay our efforts. This duty to help must be carried out for the purpose of alleviating the misery of those affected, that is to say disinterestedly and exclusively towards this end.

It is true that we usually differentiate between positive duties demanding action and negative duties requiring us to refrain from doing something. We do not feel that the duty to support and assist others entails the same kind of compulsion as the duty not to hurt our fellow human beings. If, however, they are vitally threatened and may be saved through our intervention, the difference between acting and refraining from acting is morally irrelevant. Negative duties, and particularly the corresponding negative rights, demand at least in certain extreme conditions not just to refrain from acting, but to act. Thus the proscription on killing demands more than not killing someone; it requires us to protect people attacked by a third party, where we can do so without a disproportionate sacrifice.[7]

Similarly, we distinguish between perfect and imperfect duties. In the modern age (from Pufendorf to Kant) those duties are termed "strict" or "perfect," which implies the kind of prohibition where subjective desires and ends are disregarded and where it is only demanded that we refrain from actions that would harm others and that would be morally wrong. Those duties, however, are termed "imperfect" which promote the good by constraining subjective ends and desires so as to embody virtues such as mercifulness, charity, and benevolence. In addition, such virtuous actions are considered to be only supererogatory.[8] The duty to aid is the prototype of an imperfect duty. What distinguishes an imperfect duty (such as the duty to aid) from a perfect duty (such as the duty not to kill, to lie, or to break promises) is, according to a common conception, its incompleteness. While an incomplete, negative duty such as the proscription to kill, prescribes exactly what to do at all times, this is apparently not the case where incomplete, positive duties are concerned: their formulation must necessarily leave open who owes how much and when to whom. Imperfect duties merely establish a normative framework. The interpretation of this framework is left to the non-moral preferences of the actors. Where the duty to aid is concerned, only its application in a specific case will allow one to determine with reference to the specific context who owes what kind of help to whom. But the distinction between perfect and imperfect duties has repeatedly proven to be a difficult one. As the example of the duty to keep promises shows, it is not really possible to maintain the correlation of proscriptions and perfect duties. Moreover, all duties, including the perfect ones, are incomplete, since

---

7 Cf. Henry Shue, *Basic Rights: Subsistence, Affluence and U.S. Foreign Policy*, 1st ed. (Princeton, NJ: Princeton University Press, 1980). Shue claims that almost all moral rights, at least all basic rights, have three corresponding types of duties: "I. Duties to avoid depriving. II. Duties to protect from deprivation. III. Duties to aid the deprived" (52). Cf. Ernst Tugendhat, *Vorlesungen über Ethik* (Frankfurt: Suhrkamp, 1993), 351, who follows Shue.

8 For a critique of this account, see below.

even they are not (or cannot be) sufficiently specific when prescribing what to do. This too can be demonstrated with reference to the multiple interpretations of the duty to keep promises. For all duties couched in terms of general principles, positive as well as negative, require for their application a capacity of judgment as an additional element which cannot be further specified in terms of rules.[9]

Perfect duties in the sense of indispensable commandments are therefore usually regarded as enforceable duties which do not reward the performance of a duty but sanction its violation. They may be codified as statutory duties as they contain objective criteria that can be phrased as juridical rules and do not saliently require interpretation based on subjective preferences. They are valid independent of whether those subjected to it recognize what is commanded of their own accord. For Kant, however, there are no rights corresponding to those duties to help. Thus, help is neither owed nor enforceable; instead, it is the individual's moral responsibility that is appealed to. Moral duties depending on an unenforceable inner attitude, such as the duty to aid, are not inferior but are nevertheless rated lower because it is not possible to accurately determine exactly what they require. Viewed from the outside, a non-enforceable act of assistance constitutes a merit. From the perspective of the agent, however, Kant considers it as obligatory and claims the agent should feel "duty-bound" to act. Duty in the Kantian framework, however, necessarily entails coercion, either self-inflicted coercion where the motivation to act is concerned (duty of virtue), or external coercion where the consequences are concerned (duty of right). It is moreover by no means clear or even mandatory that perfect duties as opposed to imperfect duties are, or should be, legally enforceable. Thus, there are negative duties that are not usually legally enforced, such as, for example, the prohibition of breaking promises. There are also positive duties that can be legally sanctioned, such as the duty to help, which in some countries is laid down in law. For example, in Germany, the § 323c of the German criminal code ("failure to render assistance") stipulates that every person is obligated to render assistance if the situation so requires. According to this law, assistance is owed in cases of emergency, danger, or distress where this is necessary, can reasonably be expected in the circumstances, and, especially, is possible without significant personal danger or neglect of other important duties.

A specific characteristic of incomplete duties is that they are not owed to anyone in particular. Because they contain no implicit instruction as to whom to offer help, the individual has much greater freedom to decide on this matter. They do not explicitly or implicitly indicate with regard to whom the obligation must be met. To an incomplete duty, there is therefore no corresponding legal claim. Every person capable of helping those in need

---

[9] Cf. Onora O'Neill, "The Great Maxims of Justice and Charity," in *Constructions of Reason: Explorations of Kant's Practical Philosophy* (Cambridge: Cambridge University Press, 2001), 219–233, 224f.

has the duty to do so, but because he cannot help all of them he does not owe this duty to each and every one of them. As long as the claimant cannot be identified, there can thus be no corresponding claim to the duty to help. This is where the inherent deficiencies of a purely moral consideration of duties become apparent; it fails to take into account the necessary political institutionalization. The legal and political institutionalization of the duty to aid enables us to attribute to positive duties corresponding claims of certain legal entities. (I will return to this further below.)

Be that as it may, all these distinctions do not alter the character of the moral duty of aiding the deprived; it is neither a personal preference nor supererogatory. Helping is a duty and by no means optional. Despite the Kantian distinction between strict (*unnachlassliche*) duties and wide or meritorious duties of virtue, aiding the deprived is, according to Kant, a moral duty, albeit one of virtue. This goes particularly for those whose affluence enables them to forego certain things in order to help the needy without having to significantly modify their own ambitions in life. Thus, aiding the deprived is a duty and not merely an act of benevolence. This conception is nowadays widely agreed upon.

Moral duties are not all negative duties requiring us to refrain from doing something immoral or unjust. They also comprise the positive duty of helping to bring about moral or just conditions while rectifying existing wrongs—even where no one in particular may be blamed for them. Thus a widely shared intuition stipulates (certain particular differences notwithstanding) that there exists not only a primary and negative duty not to commit a moral wrong, but also a secondary and positive duty to prevent or rectify a morally deficient state of affairs. One may systematically distinguish between two types of reasons for action, no matter what terms are used to denote them, namely primary and secondary moral reasons. Primary moral reasons are those an individual must oblige with since otherwise, they would be behaving immorally. Thus it is not permissible, for example, to steal someone's property (save in exceptional cases); this would be immoral. If a person's voluntary actions predictably lead to certain wrongs, he should be held responsible for them and ought to compensate for them or to see to their removal. Primary reasons commit an individual to preventing or to removing any moral wrongs that are the result of one's own immoral individual or collective actions. A subject is first and foremost morally accountable, i.e., prospectively responsible for the foreseeable consequences of its own voluntary actions. These primary reasons are relatively related to the agent. They imply responsibility if the individual was free, causally responsible for the action in question, accountable, and in a sane state of mind. Unlike primary reasons of morality, secondary reasons are those every person has for helping to bring about a morally superior state of affairs or to eliminate neediness or moral wrongs. These reasons do not pertain to the individual agent but are valid for all those capable of helping to prevent or remove a moral wrong for whose existence they cannot be held directly responsible.

These should be people who are effectively and competently capable of changing institutional structures, practices, or actions based on principles of morality. Thus, where persons find themselves deprived through no fault of their own, and cannot put an end to this without undue sacrifices or outside assistance, this constitutes, according to a generally shared intuition, a secondary moral reason for ameliorating this situation. Every person capable of helping and of (re)establishing a moral situation has such a secondary moral reason—at least where no significant personal costs are involved. This definition of the shared intuition by "reasons of morality" does not answer the question of whether there are any rights of the victims or duties on the part of the potential helpers that would correspond to these primary and secondary reasons of morality. Primary and secondary reasons of morality may differ in significance. In general, personal responsibility for one's own actions will carry greater weight than the (individual and collective) duty of transforming morally deficient into morally desirable situations, since in the former case the responsibility is a more direct one whereas in the latter case it is of a graded kind. Nevertheless, certain primary moral reasons (such as not stealing chocolate or not being late) can be less urgent than secondary ones (such as saving someone dying of thirst).

The moral requirement of helping the needy demands more from us than we would be prepared to do in the absence of such a requirement. Although we are not motivated exclusively by self-interest, we normally help those most willingly who are closest to us (friends, relatives, and so forth). As far as our immediate environment is concerned, willingness to help may be considered a natural duty commonly displayed by humans.[10] Moreover, we are generally willing to help where we can expect that those requiring our help would in turn help us should the need arise.[11] For a specific, confined group, the compliance with the duty to help could increase the total shared welfare. Where the members of a group assume a certain reciprocity in their behavior towards each other and where they may expect compensation in the form of group prosperity, it is likely that the person providing aid in one situation will be at the receiving end in another. Thus, it is a social fact that the duty to aid is nowadays recognized as a moral commandment. Nevertheless, compliance with this duty does not always occur and can even be

[10] According to Hume, this natural virtue derives from the human constitution of sympathy, feeling with the feelings of others. Under conditions of peace and security, sympathy leads us naturally and without consideration of our own advantage to appreciate all those characteristics we normally appreciate in ourselves or our friends. We therefore practice charity as an end in itself, and coercion as a means of furthering it would be counterproductive. Cf. David Hume, *A Treatise of Human Nature* [1739] (Oxford: Clarendon Press, 1978), book 3, part 2, para. 1, and part 3, para. 1.

[11] Cf. Claus Offe, "Pflichten versus Kosten: Typen und Kontexte solidarischen Handelns," in *Transnationale Solidarität. Chancen und Grenzen*, eds. Jens Beckert, Julia Eckert, Martin Kohli, and Wolfgang Streeck (Frankfurt: Campus, 2004), 35–50.

rare. So from a normative standpoint, this commandment is seen as justified and aid is judged to be morally right and required, whereas in practice, this insight does not usually translate into an actual motivation. In terms of action, the commandment is rather ineffective. We are therefore faced with a motivational deficit which arises because we humans are quite cunning when it comes to finding and constructing concrete reasons that purport to exempt us from what we have recognized as being justified in principle, and because the laws rarely require aid or sanction a failure to provide it. To wit, the moral character of the duty to help thus becomes particularly evident where we are not motivated by sympathy or the expectation of a reward, but where we believe that we must comply with the duty to aid for its own sake, and thus also extend it to all those requiring aid, regardless of time, place, and their relationship to the person potentially administering aid. The belief that we must comply points to its characteristic as a moral duty, and this requires a specific justification in terms of moral philosophy.

From the point of view of moral philosophy, both types of moral reasons follow from the principle of justification characteristic of Kantian deontological ethics. Thus, actions or omissions are moral only if, under conditions of liberty and equality, they can be generally and reciprocally justified to those concerned. According to this principle, all circumstances capable of being changed require justification insofar as they (potentially) affect the interests or well-being of others. This is the central argument against the frequently encountered notion that while there are no strong reasons why the status quo (for example, a certain distribution of resources) is just, things are the way they are and therefore they are good because nobody intentionally made them that way. Nobody acted immorally since nobody treated anyone unjustly. The response to this notion is that all existing circumstances require justification in any case, because, and as long as, they may be altered. Moral principles can be applied to all circumstances that are capable of being changed. Consequently, immoral circumstances must be transformed into moral ones where this is possible. The notion that conditions that are capable of being changed are morally relevant means that moral considerations provide us with secondary reasons for transforming immoral conditions into moral ones. This is because moral judgments are prescriptive and not just descriptive. A moral judgment that something is immoral or unjust prompts us to act; simply to leave things as they are would be unjust or immoral. This is why the criterion of changeability is such a far-reaching (and contested) condition of morality.

Before further exploring the justification and organization of the duty to aid, I will, in the two following sections, digress somewhat in order to analyze two different strategies of justification that attempt to circumvent the use of the concept of incomplete positive duties and the problems related to it. These may be strategically useful in arguing for the alleviation of some need, but they do not go far enough.

2 CORRECTIVE AND COMMUTATIVE JUSTICE

Instead of appealing to the universal mutual duty to aid the deprived and consequently finding oneself embroiled in the philosophical and motivational predicaments I have just described, it seems promising to define the group of those obligated to aid in terms of the responsibility for the fact that there is deprivation in the first place. If it can be traced back to unjust conditions or actions, we are not dealing with a positive duty to help, but with a case of corrective and commutative justice. In such a case, the persons primarily responsible for improving conditions are those responsible for their existence, perpetuation, and exploitation. If we are not simply dealing with deprivation but with deficient conditions brought about by unjust actions, then we need not appeal to any positive duties, but simply to the demands of compensatory justice. Their legitimacy is rather uncontroversial and can be generally agreed upon.

One may, for example, plausibly assume that the poverty of the "third world" was brought about by the "first world" via colonialism, imperialism, and the organizational structure of world trade (think of patents, custom duties, credits, market access, monopolies, and so forth). Alternatively (or in addition to that), one may be forced to recognize that the first world continues to cause and to exploit the neediness of the third world. From this would follow that we, as members of the first world, must compensate for this injustice, because we share at least part of the blame.

In order to identify deprivation as being unjust, we would first require an empirical proof as to what caused it. Second, to highlight the unfairness of our dealings with the third world that are responsible for the poor condition it is in, we would be required to define a standard of justice for fair dealings and transactions. This would allow us to determine where and to what extent existing conditions deviate from this normative standard. Most often, this standard is defined in terms of equivalence, meaning that what is given and what is taken in a transaction (of goods) must form a certain equilibrium.[12] For a transaction is fair only where certain initial conditions are given, which must be determined prior to, and independent of, the transaction itself. Thus transactional justice is possible only where every participant already has his fair share of goods and burdens, which he may then trade with those of other participants. A transaction cannot create fair conditions if one of the participants had no legitimate claim to the object of a present or past transaction. Transactional justice thus presupposes a fair distribution of goods. This distribution may in turn be the result of a transaction, but every transactional sequence must be

---

[12] Cf. Otfried Höffe, "Transzendentaler Tausch—eine Legitimationsfigur für Menschenrechte?," in *Philosophie der Menschenrechte*, eds. Stefan Gosepath and Georg Lohmann (Frankfurt: Suhrkamp, 1998), 29–48; Höffe, "Soziale Gerechtigkeit als Tausch: ein neues Paradigma," in *Politik und Ethik*, ed. Kurt Bayertz (Stuttgart: Reclam, 1996), 229–48.

based on a fair initial distribution, which itself cannot be justified in terms of transactional justice, but only in terms of distributive justice. This is why distributive justice takes logical and chronological precedence over transactional justice. Commutative justice is thus secondary to distributive justice.[13]

If the injustice of a situation has been established, commutative and corrective justice require first that those processes that caused it (at least in part) be either terminated immediately or turned into just ones; i.e., others must at least not be actively harmed, and where this does happen, it must be stopped or changed. This prohibition on harming others applies to individuals as well as to states and institutions. Second, from this prohibition there follows the strict, universal, and negative duty not to contribute to the prolongation of these unjust structures.[14] Third, it follows that there is a duty to change them. This duty is neither purely negative, nor can it be performed by individuals alone; it requires collective action. Fourth and finally, the commandment of distributive justice requires that any injury be corrected or, should that not be possible, that those harmed be compensated in one way or another.

The consequences that follow from the prohibition on inflicting harm and from the further requirements of corrective justice are very far-reaching indeed. Much could be gained if we were to apply them conscientiously. Thus, we would, for example, have to put a stop to any dealings with corrupt elites, and we would have to correct any unfair distortions of competition in the world market and adjust them in accordance with the principles of free cooperation.[15]

At first, then, the argument in terms of corrective and commutative justice seems advantageous from a strategic point of view, as it promises to lend argumentative support to a far-reaching and valuable goal, namely the alleviation or elimination of poverty in developing countries, without burdening us with the problems of moral philosophy we encounter when arguing in terms of a duty to aid.

But contrary to such appearances, this argument in terms of commutative and corrective justice also comes with a significant burden of justification. For the empirical causes of deprivation are often unclear or controversial. The counterfactual conditional along the lines of "had it not been for colonialism, poor countries would now be better off" may seem plausible in its generality. Concrete causal relationships, however, are much more difficult to prove. The opposite may even seem just about as plausible. Thus in practical terms, it is hardly possible to prove the first empirical premise of this

---

[13] Cf. Gosepath, *Gleiche Gerechtigkeit*, chap. I.5.2.

[14] This point is emphasized by Thomas Pogge. See especially Pogge, *World Poverty and Human Rights: Cosmopolitan Responsibilities and Reforms*, 1st ed. (Cambridge: Polity, 2002).

[15] Pogge, in *World Poverty and Human Rights*, has made several convincing suggestions to this end.

line of argument with absolute certainty. The criteria for what constitutes a fair transaction between developed and developing countries are similarly subject to controversy. While the criteria and duties of corrective justice may be beyond dispute, this is certainly not true of the underlying standards of transactional equivalence and of initial distributive justice. Here, the burden of justification is similar to the one we encounter when arguing for a positive duty to aid. Moreover, the argument in terms of commutative and corrective justice does specify the type and scope of compensation due. A duty to compensate depends on who caused what to happen to whom; this, I have stressed, is hard to determine. Furthermore, there is the problem of historical justice: victims and perpetrators are not identical to their descendants and therefore it is questionable exactly what the perpetrators' descendants owe to the victims' descendants. For in principle, the demands of corrective justice only apply to injustice committed by oneself. Finally, the demands of corrective and commutative justice must be met regardless of whether the victims are deprived or not. As a matter of fact, it is injustice rather than actual deprivation that gives rise to such demands. Accordingly, corrective and commutative justice does not specifically require anyone to support people in need where their situation is not the result of outside interference (as is the case with natural disasters). In the case of the duty to help, however, the underlying intuition is analytically independent of unfair conditions or historical injustice. Duties of corrective justice differ from duties to aid the deprived not only in terms of justification, but also in terms of where they apply. Furthermore, the intuitions underlying these principles may in fact be at odds with each other. Thus, corrective justice may, for example, require that those who are already better off be awarded some form of compensation, or that their property be protected even though those who are worse off may, as a result, find themselves in absolute poverty. Therefore, principles of corrective and commutative justice cannot, in all circumstances, serve as a replacement for the duty of aiding the deprived.

3 DUTY TO AID – OR DUTY NOT TO DOMINATE?

The claim that it is our universal and mutual duty to aid the deprived is the object of accusations which I shall attempt to repudiate below. The objections are connected with the assumption that the duty to aid the deprived implies an exclusively distributive and resource-oriented understanding of (duties of) justice. Neo-republican[16] conceptions of justice as non-domination, amongst others, argue against this distributive paradigm of justice. These objectors regard justice as a primarily relational, practice-dependent duty not to dominate others arbitrarily. But in my opinion, this

[16] I will speak of neo-republicans as exemplars of this approach, even if that term is too narrow for the wide range of critics I aim to capture.

approach has its own weaknesses, as I shall demonstrate in this section. Above all, it is too minimalistic, which is why it is not a better alternative to the approach taken here.

One of the objections to the universal and mutual duty to aid the deprived is that it is conceived of as part of a distributive paradigm of justice. According to the distributive paradigm, it is the material requirement of justice to ensure a just distribution of those goods which grant all members of society the status of a free and equal person, and which allow them to pursue their autonomously chosen projects within this framework, as long as it does not interfere with another person's freedom. Here, resources, construed as all-purpose goods, constitute the object of distribution. Resources (or "goods") is a general term that encompasses material goods (money, jobs, property), social goods (chances, privileges, prestige), and political goods (rights, authority, liberties). The opponents[17] of the distributive paradigm claim that it presents a misleading "picture" of justice, and that we are trapped in this picture and cannot free ourselves from it, or at least not easily. Instead, they argue for a concept of justice that is primarily concerned with the social status of persons. Here, the mutual recognition of individuals as equals and an adequate power structure are regarded as the foundation of a just order. Distributive justice is held to be an aspect of justice, but not one that is fundamental. Some of the critics agree with theorists of global distributive justice that the duty to aid the deprived is, at least in our world, a requirement of *justice*, as opposed to a mere requirement of *humanity*. Yet they also reject the view that the moral rationale for the duty to aid the deprived is to further realize an ideal of global distributive justice. According to the critics, a perspective centering on the recipient and concentrating on goods and their distribution should not be considered the be-all and end-all; such a perspective would necessarily miss central aspects of justice.[18] By concentrating on goods, we would ignore the essential political element of justice. The critics worry that if the concept of distributive justice were expanded to include non-material things as "goods" in some metaphorical sense, these things would then be treated as if they were static objects rather than as functions of social relations and processes. This in turn would cause us to lose sight of the social structures and institutional contexts that

---

[17] I am thinking here of various theorists, including Elizabeth Anderson, "What Is the Point of Equality?," *Ethics* 109, no. 2 (1999): 287–337; Rainer Forst, "Two Pictures of Justice," in *Justification and Critique*, trans. Ciaran Cronin (Cambridge: Polity Press, 2013), 17–37; Jürgen Habermas, *Between Facts and Norms: Contributions to a Discourse Theory of Law and Democracy*, trans. William Rehg (Cambridge, MA: MIT Press, 1992); Axel Honneth, "Das Gewebe der Gerechtigkeit," in *Das Ich im Wir. Studien zur Anerkennungstheorie*, ed. Axel Honneth (Berlin: Suhrkamp, 2010), 51–79; Samuel Scheffler, "What is Egalitarianism?," *Philosophy & Public Affairs* 31, no. 1 (2003): 5–39; Iris Marion Young, *Justice and the Politics of Difference* (Princeton: Princeton University Press, 1990).

[18] Cf. Rainer Forst, "Two Pictures of Justice."

often determine the patterns of distribution. According to the critics, it is difficult to link these structures and contexts to the distributive paradigm, because the patterns of distribution (such as cultural and symbolic injustice, social rules, procedures, influences, classes, conditions of production and institutions, e.g., the state, the family, and civil society) are not material goods. Consequently, the institutional context in which distribution occurs is neglected or ignored, even though it is often one of the factors determining distributive patterns. In this way, the key political question of who determines the structures of production and distribution—i.e., the question of power—is not sufficiently taken into account, or may even be ignored altogether.[19] In other words, the logic of distribution misrepresents these dimensions by producing a false account of the justice issues in question. Again, it reifies aspects of social life that are better understood as functions of social rules and relations. Moreover, social justice is mainly conceptualized as the structure of a final state of affairs, rather than being related to social processes.[20] In this way, subjects are regarded as passive recipients.[21]

The republican idea of non-domination, or more precisely the moral and political imperative not to interfere with others arbitrarily, is an especially good candidate for an alternative approach to justice. As a result of its apparent minimalism, it seems at present to be in the process of becoming a widely accepted ideal for the global political order—i.e., the standard according to which interactions among global actors, and between global and domestic actors, are judged.[22]

Two senses of non-domination should be distinguished. I have no quarrel with the first, only with the second. Non-domination in the first, wider sense can be used to characterize the moral point of view in general. As the concept which is opposed to arbitrariness, justice requires a counterfactual and non-dominated discourse as an idealized constructivist and procedural idea to determine what it requires. Non-domination is however often used in a second, narrower sense as a first-order principle of justice. It is often claimed that the principle of non-domination (in this second sense) is what justice requires in the first place (as opposed to distributive justice). The safeguarding of non-domination as a first-order principle of justice has certain implications, above all institutional ones. These theories argue that the political question, *Who decides about the (in)justice of a distribution of goods?* takes philosophical precedence over the distributive question, *What is a(n) (un)just distribution of goods?* They argue that this requires us to rethink things, so that we regard power relations, rather than the distribution of goods, as the fundamental concern of a theory of justice.

---

[19] Cf. Forst, "Two Pictures," 20.

[20] A similar objection can be found in Robert Nozick, *Anarchy, State, and Utopia* (New York: Basic Books, 1974), ch. 7.

[21] Cf. Forst, "Two Pictures," 20.

[22] Cf. the other papers of this volume.

However, in this second, narrower sense, non-domination is only the weak, diminished form of justice. As such, it is, at most, the absolute minimum of what we can mutually demand of one another; but it does not nearly suffice to express the full sense and range of the charge of injustice.

Proponents of non-domination usually regard it as the basic principle of justice, since they hold a relational view of justice. Relational views hold that obligations of social justice are only triggered in the presence of relevant forms of social interaction or relationship. Non-relational views, however, hold that these obligations apply to human beings as such, and hence independently of whether they are engaged in any form of social relationship or interaction.[23] Since a relational view holds that justice depends on certain factually and contingently existing circumstances, empirical facts about the factually and contingently existing human relations have an irreducible function in the justification of justice.[24]

Non-moral facts provide an empirical indication of where the fundamental moral principle of the duty of non-maleficence was violated, how it was violated, and by whom. The harm relation explains where and through what form of social interaction a reparable harm has resulted. However, the duty to repair the harm is based not on empirical facts or relations, but on moral principles. The content, scope, and justification of a political value, duty, or principle of justice depend on the structure and form of the practices (or social interactions) that the value, duty, or principle is intended to govern.[25] Accordingly, the relevant relations do not merely consist in factually contingent circumstances, but in man-made social relations, actual modes of interaction, and forms of the regulation of collective issues between people. Examples of relevant relations would be institutional practices such as social cooperation, state coercion, or the existence of a basic institutional structure, as well as cultural practices and relations.

However, non-relational approaches challenge this relational, practice-dependent conception. According to a non-relational view, the existence of problems of justice and the origins of duties of justice (such as the duty to aid the deprived) do *not* depend on existing interpersonal actions or institutional background conditions. For according to a non-relational view, problems of justice exist wherever there are morally advantageous and disadvantageous situations.

As regards these two conceptions of justice, namely the relational and the non-relational approaches, there seem to be two different intuitions, ultimately resulting in two different conceptual explications of justice. According

---

23 For the most prominent relational view, cf. Andrea Sangiovanni, "Global Justice, Reciprocity, and the State," *Philosophy & Public Affairs* 35, no. 1 (2007): 3–39; Sangiovanni, "Justice and the Priority of Politics to Morality," *Journal of Political Philosophy* 16, no. 2 (2008): 137–64.

24 Cf. Sangiovanni, "Global Justice"; Sangiovanni, "Justice and the Priority."

25 This is the practice-dependent thesis, cf. Sangiovanni, "Justice and the Priority."

to these two opposed conceptions of justice, we can either understand justice as meaning that one does not suffer from ill, or that one does not suffer from a lack of freedom as a result of domination. Since it is almost certainly impossible to defuse this debate between two partially competing conceptions of justice with a terminological fiat, I should like to take a brief look at the possible reasons for preferring one alternative or the other, and to try to show why non-domination does not suffice as a basic principle of justice.

i) Non-domination as a relational principle of justice only applies to those with whom we are in a relation of domination. According to this principle then, justice would be limited to a situation of domination, where some people already dominate others. Thus, any cases that were free from domination would not require justice. That is counterintuitive. Most of us would hold that we have duties of justice that are independent of, and take precedence over, all social relationships. We also need justice in situations of negative cooperation. A thought experiment often invoked in this context in various forms can help us to grasp intuitively that instances of injustice serious enough to need rectifying may arise even in the absence of social structures or relations.[26] We only have to imagine people living on different islands. The islands offer the inhabitants varying living conditions and varying standards of quality of life, and the individuals are variously endowed with capacities such as physical strength, physical talents, or intelligence. Interaction and cooperation between the islands are impossible, but the inhabitants possess precise knowledge about the situation of the inhabitants of the other islands. By chance, it is possible to send boats from certain islands to other islands at high tide; they are carried alone to the shores of the other islands by the wind and the waves. Do instances of deep-seated inequality pose a problem of justice in a scenario such as this? If we follow our reasoned judgments, we probably have to answer in the affirmative. The unequal human and natural resources of the island inhabitants, which they have simply taken on along with the circumstances, without having done anything to obtain them and without being able to do anything about them, present us with instances of serious but alterable inequality. These instances of inequality must therefore be corrected as far as possible. Anyone who intuitively feels that this is going too far should imagine that the inhabitants of one of the islands are threatened with starvation. Is it not a duty of justice to help them, if help is possible? This is the case, even though there exists no social relationship, no cooperation, and no society with common institutions and practices.

---

26 This thought experiment can be found in Richard J. Arneson, "Egalitarianism and Responsibility," *The Journal of Ethics* 3, no. 3 (1999): 225–47, 226. Cf. Nozick, *Anarchy*, 185, and David Gauthier, *Morals by Agreement* (Oxford: Oxford University Press, 1986). Nozick and Gauthier make use of similar island scenarios in order to illustrate (i) that no one has an obligation to help anyone, if everyone lives separately, and (ii) that the introduction of voluntary trade and other forms of social cooperation cannot generate obligations to help the needy if there are no obligations to give help outside society.

The restriction of considerations of justice to existing relations is therefore, although common, intuitively implausible. It only constitutes a special case of distributive justice, for the just distribution of non-produced resources must also be taken into account. In addition, claims can be made on goods, claims which seem to be legitimated not on the strength of relational dependence, but on the strength of needs. Even within a society, justice is not restricted to justice within cooperative associations. As well as the relational justice within a society, there is also the non-relational justice based on the solidarity among humans.[27] Since emergencies are instances of moral harm at least as serious as cases of domination, restricting the grounds for the validity of justice to the sole or central ground of human-made domination is to my mind utterly reductive.

ii) Neo-republicans and other critics see it as an advantage of their approach that they take power seriously as the central aspect of justice. Accordingly, their objection to recipient-oriented theories of justice is that, being non-relational conceptions, they fail to recognize the human-made causes of injustice. By assuming an objective purpose of justice, non-relational theories often lay more stress on the side of those receiving justice. But non-relational conceptions do not by any means have to fail to recognize the causes of injustice. In other words, recipient-oriented and non-relational aspects of theories of justice are not necessarily connected. When criticizing purely outcome-oriented conceptions of justice, it is worth stressing the fact that the causes of injustice should be taken into account, for they can detract from the severity of the injustice. This objection only applies to theories that are exclusively concerned with the end result of distribution. However, there are moral reasons for rejecting such an approach. As it is argued in section 4, it is not only the result of individual actions that is morally relevant; we must also take into account how the result was achieved. The moral quality of the way in which it was achieved plays a role in the moral assessment of the result.[28] What is true of individual actions also goes—*mutatis mutandis*—for social distribution. A judgment of justice must take into account the relationship between social institutions and certain social facts (such as distribution).[29]

---

[27] In contrast, Forst thinks it is not a duty of justice, but of moral solidarity ("Two Pictures," 19).

[28] This objection to purely recipient-oriented theories of justice is given particular emphasis by Pogge, *World Poverty*, ch. 1.4. See also Pogge, "Relational Concepts of Justice: Responsibilities for Health Outcomes," in *Public Health, Ethics, and Equity*, eds. Sudhir Anand, Fabienne Peter, and Amartya Sen (Oxford: Oxford University Press, 2004), 135–62, esp. 146f.

[29] My view could perhaps be called "relational" in the sense that it can take into account these relationships. I call my view "non-relational" in part because it is not *limited* to human-caused injustice. See below. Compare this to the terminology adopted by Pogge in work after *World Poverty*, such as in his "Relational Concepts of Justice," and contrast it to the terminology adopted by Sangiovanni in his "Global Justice, Reciprocity, and the State."

Many problems of justice are concerned not merely with the patterns or end results of distribution at a certain point in time, but also with the (re)production of an established pattern of distribution over time. The important considerations of the causation and the structural injustices of particular situations can and must be included in a distributive theory of justice. Thus, the distributive paradigm need not be "oblivious to power" (even though it has frequently displayed such tendencies in the past).[30] It can and must conceive of justice from a different perspective than that of the "recipient" by following through the political question of which structures determine the production and distribution of goods, and by demanding restructuring as opposed to mere redistribution. However, the distributive paradigm will construe this restructuring as a redistribution of rights, liberties, and opportunities. Including the context of social formation in the evaluation of a particular state of affairs is surely not enough. Rather, as a number of critics have stressed, it is crucial to inquire into the justice of the social processes themselves.

However, non-relational conceptions can, and in my opinion also should, insist that man-made injustice is "only" one possible cause of injustice. Justice reacts to injustice between people,[31] it is said, and rightly so. But that does not mean that it *only* reacts to man-made injustice. Potential harm, which people could have prevented without excessive morally relevant costs, but in fact failed to prevent, represents a different case of injustice—that at least is my theory. Natural harm that people could not have prevented or eliminated is in any case irrelevant from the point of view of a theory of justice. The responsibilities and the distribution of corresponding duties for the elimination of the injustice differ according to the cause of the injustice. Thus, it is crucial to take into consideration the sources of the injustice to be dealt with and to distinguish between them. But this is not to speak out unequivocally in favor of relational approaches, even if it is true that some non-relational approaches, namely the purely outcome-oriented approaches, make the mistake of overlooking the distinction between the sources of injustice.

iii) Neo-republicans do not deny that we may also have some moral obligations (namely, duties of humanity) towards all human beings over and above the obligations we have towards those with whom we are in a relation of domination. But, they claim, justice is triggered by circumstances of justice (sometimes called grounds of justice) that are different from circumstances of morality. The circumstances of justice are defined by structures of domination that postulate that justice has to start *ex negativo* from an existing malfunctioning practice. Thus, on this account, principles of justice serve as

---

30 This is the objection of, among others, Forst, "Two Pictures," 34–35.

31 "The circumstances of justice are in the first place . . . the circumstances of injustice: they are circumstances which generate the problems for whose resolution justice is needed" (Onora O'Neill, *Towards Justice and Virtue* [Cambridge: Cambridge University Press, 1996], 98–99).

principles of rectifying or corrective justice, principles that put wrongful acts and structures right. Such principles of rectifying or corrective justice are, however, only derivative. As I argued in the previous section, the principle of corrective justice is of secondary significance, because it ultimately serves only the maintenance or reestablishment of a situation, whose original creation was a precept of the principle of distributive justice. It is in principle necessary to possess a positive formulation of the correct principle or ideal of justice in order to be able to judge where injustice lies, on the one hand, and on the other hand, how it could be made good.

iv) Neo-republican theories stipulate non-domination as the only real principle of justice, regarding the others as mere principles of morality or humanity; since duties of justice have a particular strength and urgency which are not granted to all other moral duties, the principle of non-domination is also regarded as stronger than, for example, the principle of aid. It is, however, debatable how the strength and urgency of the principle of non-domination is to be conceptualized as compared with that of the principle of aiding the deprived. Relational views attempt to conceive of duties of justice as perfect or specific duties, which only hold with respect to those with whom we share a common practice. However, this aspect only arises if we conceive of them as negative duties to prevent or make good any injustice for which we are responsible. As negative duties, their validity is strict and perfect. However, reducing justice to negative duties in this way seems to be objectively inappropriate. The non-relational views seem to me more plausible in this respect; from a non-relational point of view, duties of justice, just like moral duties, can instead be general and imperfect duties, which we owe only to unspecified others.

v) It sometimes seems that the non-domination approach does not distinguish sharply enough between justice (or freedom), on the one hand, and legitimacy on the other. From my perspective, the "primary question" has to be one of legitimacy rather than of justice. The fundamental, and in that sense primary, question is concerned with the justification (i.e., legitimation) of any power relation: when and where is the exercise of any kind of political, economic, and other forms of power legitimate? The basic requirement to justify any power relation[32] is in itself a moral duty and concerns all types of actions, even those we would not usually place in the context of justice, such as humanitarian aid. Power not only constitutes a problem within the context of justice, but also beyond the sphere of justice. Thus, power is not a specific ground of justice but a ground of morality in general. That is why it cannot be the first question of justice[33] but is the fundamental question of morality of which freedom and justice are only parts, albeit central ones.

vi) While a critical theory of justice will always take as its point of departure a factual political order in which the oppressed demand a justification

[32] See Forst, "Two Pictures," 34.
[33] As Forst claims in "Two Pictures," 34.

of their situation, such a theory must still rely to some degree on idealization. For if factual relations cannot be justified reciprocally and universally, the theorist must demand that the political order (i.e., the distribution of power) be changed. This in turn leads to the abstract question (one that is often unjustly frowned upon) of how the social world should be organized if justice is to prevail, and how the status quo must be altered to achieve this. Thus, the critique of actual justifications will always necessarily rely on a concept of true, or at least better, relations of justification. An elaborate theory of justice cannot then be avoided if one wishes to retain a critical standard for evaluating existing social and political deficiencies.

vii) Like liberal autonomy, non-domination speaks to the equal capacity of individuals to command the attention and respect of others. Since neo-republicans prioritize freedom as their central political ideal, they are tempted to forget that liberty alone most certainly cannot be the highest value, but must be considered in the context of justice. "Natural" liberty is curtailed in the name of equality and justice. A right to adequate, subjective realms of freedom cannot be stipulated without recourse to distributive equality, because freedom and its corresponding rights constitute an application of the concept of distributive equality. The characteristic feature of liberty is concerned with the question of what is valuable. A (certain) concept of liberty thus constitutes (part of) the content of equality. Furthermore, the decision to address the destitution of people primarily as an afterthought to the freedom of citizens is inappropriate, since we ought to presume that other individuals care as much about their lives, needs, and freedom as we do about ours.

viii) Non-domination as a central concept of political theory has—at least in the eyes of neo-republicans—the advantage of being closely connected with the idea of democratic self-determination. But we must "mind the gap!" It seems self-evident, if problematic, to derive an argument in favor of self-government from the principle of justification. From these premises of autonomy and consensus, one could be tempted to conclude that to be self-governing in the political realm entails participation in democratic discussions and enables decision-making under certain conditions. The main difficulty with this schematic argument should, however, be clear: it is strongly dependent on the possibility of consensus. Constructed in this way, the argument neglects the crucial phenomenon of disagreement or dissent. This is no accident. There is, in fact, considerable tension in this theory between the idea that an individual must be free to govern autonomously the world he or she shares with others and the claim that he or she must also grant every other citizen the same freedom. Democracy would thus seem to be incompatible with individual self-government. The argument fails to provide a philosophical justification for democracy as it is practiced in real societies, which make widespread use of majority rule.

I do agree with the neo-republican theorists in this important way: institutions and practices matter. However, the neo-republican theorists would not generally demand the creation of institutions where dominating relations and institutions do not already exist. Later in this chapter, I outline an institutional approach that is not based on the prior *presence* of power, but on the creation of institutions (or "power," if you like) to fulfill preexisting duties. This comes from the need to clarify and specify the duty of aid.

4 DEGREES OF OBLIGATION

Let us first return once more to the obligation to aid the deprived. How can this duty be justified and specified in the context of moral philosophy?

Peter Singer has made the best-known argument in favor of an obligation to help, an argument that is nevertheless controversial.[34] Singer's position is a rather distinctive one in that he forcefully argues for significantly more individual aid for those in need than we are ordinarily prepared to give.

Without assuming a consequentialist approach, Singer's argument in favor of an obligation to aid proceeds as follows:[35] (1) If we can prevent something bad without sacrificing anything of comparable moral significance, we ought do it. (2) Absolute poverty is bad. (3) There is some absolute poverty we can prevent without sacrificing anything of comparable moral significance. (4) We ought to prevent some absolute poverty.

Intuitively, the greatest problem with Singer's conclusion has to be the excessive moral demands and the instrumentalization of the helper's life it entails. If, according to the argument, you must give as much as you can possibly give without becoming helpless yourself, and if this continues until the problem of worldwide poverty is solved, then it follows that you must devote your life to helping others, and there is hardly any room left for living a good life. This seems to be an excessive moral demand—the expectation is simply too high. This is not a problem when it comes to saving a single child drowning in a nearby pond, because that help is limited. To avoid the danger of excessive moral demands and instrumentalization, as well as to avoid stretching the duty to aid beyond what is reasonable, it must be possible to assign limits and/or threshold levels for obligations beyond which no more help is owed.

Arguments like the ones of Singer and others focus solely on the ability of the potential helper and the need of the people suffering. They thus lose sight of other morally relevant aspects of their situation. The victims' own

---

[34] Cf. Peter Singer, *Practical Ethics*, 2nd ed. (Cambridge: Cambridge University Press, 1999); Singer, "The Singer Solution to World Poverty," in *Writings on an Ethical Life* (New York: Harper Perennial, 2000), 118–24. A similar argument is made in Peter Unger, *Living High and Letting Die: Our Illusion of Innocence* (New York: Oxford University Press, 1996). Another piece in support of Singer is Garrett Cullity, "International Aid and the Scope of Kindness," *Ethics* 105, no. 1 (1994): 99–127. See also, on a more general level, Garrett Cullity, *The Moral Demands of Affluence* (Oxford: Oxford University Press, 2004).

[35] Cf. Singer, *Practical Ethics*, 294.

personal responsibility is not adequately considered. There is, primarily, an obligation to aid the deprived if they bear no responsibility for their situation and if they cannot extricate themselves from their situation without external help or excessive personal sacrifices. Both limitations of the duty to aid are neglected in this argument, although they are of essential importance to our moral intuition about this obligation.[36] If a person is in need, then this circumstance justifies demands for external help, unless the situation is a consequence of their own free decision. Every person has a right to decide what happens to him. This, however, means that people also have a responsibility to bear the consequences of their self-determination. We ascribe to each other responsibility for our actions and our lives and we prevent each other from evading responsibility for the consequences of our decisions, from burdening others with the costs, or from blaming the circumstances. Within a "regime of justice" that guarantees universally valid, liberal, and equal rights for every citizen, every individual has the right and the duty to live a life of personal responsibility and self-determination. Justice ensures among other things conditions of personal autonomy, political freedom, and democratic self-determination. It follows that individuals have the duty to help themselves. A duty to help others who can help themselves without any great sacrifices cannot be justified. Such extensive demands expect too much. Autonomy and freedom are at once a right and an obligation. Agents must bear the consequences of their autonomous actions, if the starting conditions of all those concerned are fair. The individual capable of changing them is primarily responsible for the correction of unjust circumstances, no matter how they came about. However, this duty to help oneself only exists within otherwise just and fair conditions.

Similarly lacking is a consideration of the role of institutions as a framework for morality and justice. The question of a structural relation between wealth and poverty is relevant for the moral evaluation of deprivation. As we have seen in the second part, the moral situation changes if it can be traced back to unjust conditions or actions. In cases such as these, whoever is responsible for establishing, maintaining, and exploiting conditions of deprivation is also primarily responsible for improving them. This moral demand follows from corrective justice, not from the obligation to aid. Only when the primary obligations of corrective justice are not (or cannot be) met, must others (ultimately the global civil society) subsidiarily step into the breach.[37] At the same time, not enough attention is paid to structures and institutions as conditions for a sensible implementation of aid.[38] For

[36] Cf. Gosepath, *Gleiche Gerechtigkeit*, V.1.2.

[37] Cf. Ibid.

[38] Cf. Andrew Kuper, "Global Poverty Relief: More Than Charity," in *Global Responsibilities: Who Must Deliver on Human Rights?*, ed. Andrew Kuper (London: Routledge, 2005), 135–72; Peter Singer, "Poverty, Facts, and Political Philosophies: A Debate with Andrew Kuper," in *Global Responsibilities: Who Must Deliver on Human Rights?*, ed. Andrew Kuper (New York: Routledge, 2005), 173–81.

instance, the monetary aid can trickle away because it is misappropriated due to social and political local structures that are lacking or corrupt. This is why, in some cases, aid should take the form of building structures and institutions rather than assistance for singular cases.

By suggesting that rich individuals ought to transfer some of their resources to the deprived, this approach accepts the existing (global and/or local) distribution of holdings. This is because the moral considerations of an individual duty to aid concern what one ought to do with one's *own* resources in order to relieve human suffering. This, in turn, means that any claim about what is owed to the deprived makes an assumption about the just distribution of entitlements. Determining what and how much someone should give someone else in need assumes a baseline set by justice. For only when it has been settled what is ours by right, can it be determined what we are allowed to do with our goods, or what we ought to do with them.[39]

Thus, the Singerian individual obligation to help is badly formulated, especially regarding the questions of who is addressed, what can reasonably be expected, and how the aid for those in need is grounded in institutions. I will now attempt to answer at least some of these objections and to modify the constitution of the obligation to help in a way that results in a more plausible and reasonable duty to collectively construct political institutions to meet a shared obligation to help.

A person's obligation to aid the deprived varies in degree depending on the situation. One should bear in mind at least five considerations that determine who is obligated to aid and which kind of specific obligation is at stake. *First*, one must judge a given situation to be either good or bad. Let us assume that there are self-evident criteria for morally evaluating situations and that according to these criteria, we are dealing with a bad situation, e.g., with deprivation. If the situation can be changed, then the state of affairs is not simply bad, but also morally wrong in the sense that it has to be corrected. Assuming that we are confronted with such a moral wrong, the following considerations are important for a moral evaluation, such as praise or criticism, as well as for assigning responsibility and moral reasons for action. Although all changeable states of affairs provide secondary moral reasons for action, assigning responsibility for such action requires that we ask how the moral wrong came about, what kind of influence the individual in question can bring to bear on the situation, which social relations connect those in need to the potential helpers, and which abilities and possibilities are available to the potential helpers. While the first consideration concerns the moral evaluation of the situation itself, a *second* consideration would be to ask whether the morally wrong situation was or is caused by someone, and if so, by whom and how. A *third* consideration would be the question

39 Brian Barry, "Humanity and Justice in Global Perspective," in *Global Justice: Seminal Essays*, eds. Thomas Pogge and Darrell Moellendorf (St. Paul, MN: Paragon House), 179–209, 206f.

to what extent the wrong could or can be corrected by the individual in question, and which agents possess the best abilities or possibilities to help. A *fourth* consideration must be included in this evaluation: what are the social circumstances and do those who are capable of correcting the wrong benefit from these circumstances? The circumstances then suggest a *fifth* consideration, namely the relationship between the potential helpers and the potential receivers of aid. The following example should illustrate this point:

There are children in this world who go hungry. Their hunger is a moral wrong and amounts to deprivation, because it is a bad, but correctable, situation which is unfairly inflicted on the children. A natural disaster, such as a tsunami, which causes misery and hunger, cannot be morally wrong or unjust, since it was not directly or indirectly caused by man and it could not have been prevented. However, the consequences of such a disaster, such as poverty or hunger, can be morally wrong—depending on whether they could have been avoided through better prevention (for example, through an early warning system or safe houses) or alleviated through relief efforts. To evaluate actions, it is not enough to judge the moral quality of their outcomes. One must also always pay attention to the way these events or states of affairs came about. If the hunger was caused by the parents' neglect of their child, then primary moral reasons were violated and it is the moral duty and responsibility of the parents, who should not have allowed this to happen in the first place, to at least at this point help their child.

However, deprivation is more reprehensible if those present fail to prevent it, although they could have done so. Hunger is even more objectionable if the society in question allows it—for example, if parents cannot be prosecuted for neglecting their children's needs—and yet more so if a society demands it. Thus, the action's outcome (the perspective of the ethics of responsibility) is not the only relevant consideration for a moral evaluation; the intention of the agent is also crucial (the perspective of the ethics of conviction).[40] The type of source and its moral quality play a role for the moral evaluation of the result. This holds true not only for primary but also for secondary moral reasons. When evaluating secondary moral reasons, one must therefore ask why those capable of acting actually do so or why they choose not to.

What is true for individual actions (or their omission) must *mutatis mutandis* apply to social institutions and social circumstances that are the result of social actions or their omission. Thus, the influence a social institution has on the quality of life of the persons in question cannot be the sole basis for the evaluation of said institution. If, in a given society, the risk of dying in

---

[40] However, purely consequentialist ethical theories deny or implicitly ignore this deep-seated intuition. They evaluate actions only according to their results, just as purely contractarian moral theories, which understand social institutions from the perspective of rational future members of society, focus exclusively on the quality of life in the regime they want to assess.

a car crash is about the same as the risk of dying due to a violent incident, an exclusive focus on this result might suggest that the consequences of traffic and violence are of the same moral quality; this, however, would be absurd.[41] A high risk of dying due to a violent attack is generally thought to be a graver deficiency of justice, and more deserving of an institutional solution, than the equally high (or even much higher) probability of dying in a car crash. Evidently, the various ways in which social institutions can influence a person's quality of life need to be considered. Another consideration for the moral evaluation of avoidable deficiencies in the quality of life is the type of institutional influence, regardless of its size.[42]

If the way a wrong came about and the reasons for individual or social action or non-action constitute the second evaluative consideration, the extent to which one might individually or collectively influence this result constitutes a third consideration. The allocation of positive obligations to help also depends on the agent's corresponding abilities and his potential to actually help the deprived. Stronger, secondary moral reasons to help in cases of need exist, depending on the extent to which, and the ease with which, the wrong can be avoided or corrected (for example, hungry children can be fed)—and the same is true for moral censure where aid is withheld. The more potential and abilities an agent has, the more likely he is to be a potential helper. After all, only this consideration can ensure that aid is as effective as possible, and one can generally assume that aiding the deprived will be less taxing for someone with more abilities and potential. The cost to such a person is less than it would be to someone who is equipped with fewer abilities and less potential.[43] The less influence an individual person has, the weaker the secondary moral reasons are. Thus, they are generally

---

41 Pogge stresses this repeatedly; cf., for example, Pogge, *World Poverty*, ch. 1.4. However, the question whether there obtains background injustice plays a role here. There can for example be blameworthy actions lying behind traffic accidents. There is a very high rate of roadside accidents in Africa because there are no sidewalks and because so many people are so poor that they must walk.

42 Pogge ("Relational Conceptions of Justice," 156–57, italics in original) distinguishes six scenarios that are arranged in order of the deficiency of justice, using the specific example of a deficiency of nutritional foodstuffs. (1) The deficit is "*officially mandated*, paradigmatically by the law." (2) The deficit results from "*legally authorised* conduct of private subjects." (3) The deficit arises when "social institutions *foreseeably and avoidably engender* (but do not specifically require or authorise)" the deficit through the conduct they stimulate. (4) The deficit arises "from private conduct that is *legally prohibited but barely deterred*." (5) The deficit arises from "social institutions *avoidably leaving unmitigated the effects of a natural defect*," such as when persons with a treatable genetic defect avoidably lack access to treatment that would correct this. (6) The deficit arises from "social institutions *avoidably leaving unmitigated the effects of a self-caused defect*."

43 It is possible that one of these two reasons, efficiency and cost, points to one group or person and the other to another: they do not always suggest the same group or person as the best possible helper, as David Miller has remarked. See Miller, "Distributing Responsibilities," *The Journal of Political Philosophy* 9, no. 4 (2001): 453–71, 461.

weaker in complex social situations than in less complex ones, because the former are harder to influence.

A fourth element to consider is the kind of social circumstances that determine which secondary moral reasons we need to take into account when establishing a scale of priority of responsibility for a given situation. If we find ourselves in the kind of situation in which someone's deprivation is indirectly caused by the better circumstances of others, this makes a difference for the evaluation of our reason for acting. If the situation is embedded in social or intersubjective circumstances that cause the deprivation, or at least maintain it, because those better off benefit from it, then this constitutes a context of power or unjust distribution that in itself requires special justification. If circumstances are unjust, someone ought to change them. Those who create such a situation, support it, or benefit from it are primarily responsible for correcting the wrongs arising from it. If someone is in need because she suffers under structures of unjust rule or distribution, exploitation and unfairness, which benefit—possibly very indirectly—those who, for example, obtain cheap goods because of conditions on the world market, then there is clearly a duty of justice and a corresponding responsibility to establish just institutions for rulers as well as for subjects, and for those who benefit, as well as for those who are disadvantaged. This is a question of justice, which means that one person or persons owe it to others to end these injustices. Those who benefit from existing, unjust social conditions violate the negative duty not to harm anyone by not improving the conditions according to their possibilities.[44] Because of their context, the reasons and the obligation to aid address all those who benefit, and they are weightier than the general moral obligations to aid the deprived. In some cases, such as natural disasters or displacements, in which a group of people neither created the existing injustice nor benefits from it, but simply coexists with it and would be able to help, those who can help have secondary moral reasons to do so. (The exact nature of these reasons still needs to be explored.) However, in this case the responsibility to help is not based on practice-dependent reasons of justice, but on practice-independent reasons of justice. We are dealing with a morally wrong situation and thus one that ought to be corrected. It is not a situation of unjust dominion or distribution; rather, it is a question of accidentally passing by and being able to help. However, the morally wrong failure to help in such a situation can quickly bring about advantages that lead to a situation of unjust dominion or distribution. If this happens, the situation rapidly becomes a wrong in which one is somehow involved, which in turn changes the type of obligation to help, since most persons either benefit from the existing situation or suffer under it. When evaluating and weighting the secondary moral reasons one must therefore also consider the type of causal connection between social institutions and the consequences for the individual. And the question which type

[44] See Pogge, *World Poverty*.

of causal connection it is naturally has consequences for the responsibility of the individual.

A fifth consideration states that while all those concerned are equally obligated to comply with the negative obligations, the obligation to aid the deprived addresses (justifiably) primarily those who share a community and ties of solidarity with the victims in some broad sense, be it a shared tradition, religion, identity, conviction, love, friendship, or family relation, or those who are somehow "closer" to the victims, thus more immediately experiencing their need, which leads to them feeling more strongly obligated to help these concrete others. This "closeness" and the common ties create a special obligation of those linked to the victims, which explains why they (ought to) feel particularly obligated to help. The "closeness" and the common ties are thus an amplifier of the general, secondary moral reasons to help those in need.

Thus, we are responsible both for our actions and our omissions. The extent of our responsibility depends on how good or bad the situation is; on who created the situation in question, how and why; on the extent to which someone can help, as well as who and how; and on the question of whether we are dealing with a shared, institutionally complex situation. In an ideal case, all five considerations point to the same person or persons as being most responsible for help, but if they should diverge they must be balanced against each other in the context of the action in question.[45]

5 CONCERTED AID EFFORTS THROUGH COLLECTIVE CONSTRUCTION OF POLITICAL INSTITUTIONS

According to the above, moral agents are generally responsible in a weak sense and to varying degrees for all things they can influence (or could have influenced) with their actions. If one accepts this position, one must turn to the question of attributing this general responsibility for correcting wrongs to certain persons (or groups). If persons as members of groups are also responsible for the correction of wrongs they did not cause, who exactly should be the one to act? The principles of morality or justice must always refer to identifiable individual subjects who must be specified in the moral principle in question.[46] The difficulty lies in the identification of the persons who are concretely required to correct what is found to be morally wrong or unjust. In some cases there are a number of persons who would be able to act accordingly, and to some of them a special responsibility must be attributed; in other cases, the task of tackling deprivation places excessive demands on individual persons. In both cases, the obligation is in

---

45 For this account, cf. Miller, *Distributing Responsibilities*.

46 Cf. Onora O'Neill, "Agents of Justice," in *Metaphilosophy* 32, no. 1–2 (1989): 180–95.

danger of eroding, because nobody actually acts, although everybody agrees that action is needed. It is morally unacceptable to be confronted with real, massive deprivation and misery that could be eradicated and then to simply allow it to continue and implausibly claim that no one is responsible for helping. Instead, one must ensure that at least in extreme cases of emergency the responsibility to help can always be attributed to someone. It is not a question of rights: they are always empty if no actual addressees for the obligation to implement them are named. Rather, the question is how to identify the right responsible agents out of the large contingent of persons who, according to secondary moral reasons, are able to meet the obligation and have the duty to aid.

Now, who should be the one to help? Who specifically is obligated? The addressees of moral obligations are first of all us as members of the comprehensive community of all human beings, and this means us as individuals and all of us together; and as such, we are primarily required to respect the subjective moral rights of others and to act accordingly. According to the classic model of personal responsibility, the individual human being is the subject of responsibility.[47] Individuals have the responsibility and the obligation to establish just conditions. Individuals are primarily the subjects of responsibility, first and foremost for their own actions and omissions. As individual persons, we must accept responsibility for our individual actions and their results insofar as we can change them to the best of our knowledge through our actions or inactions. This is required by the moral principle of subsidiarity, according to which individuals are primarily responsible for achieving what is in their power, instead of relying on the community.[48] The individual has an obligation, as well as a right, to personal responsibility and self-help.

Clearly, individual attributions of responsibility are not sufficient for all cases of responsibility for morally deficient circumstances that are capable of change. To demand that individuals by themselves establish just conditions (everywhere and at once) is often excessive. The individual moral responsibility for the correction of wrongs must be restricted.[49] For practical reasons alone a general individual obligation to help could not be met—after all, no one can correct all that is amiss by themselves. This holds for institutionally unregulated contexts, such as large parts of the world order, as well as for those specifically political spheres of justice that concern the basic orders of society; that is to say, their most fundamental institutions, in particular their constitutions guaranteeing fundamental rights and their

---

[47] See Stefan Gosepath, "Verantwortung für die Beseitigung von Übeln," in *Verantwortung in der Zivilgesellschaft. Zur Konjunktur eines widersprüchlichen Prinzips*, eds. Ludger Heibrink and Alfred Hirsch (Frankfurt: Campus, 2006), 387–408, 388f.
[48] See Gosepath, *Gleiche Gerechtigkeit*, ch. III.6.1.
[49] See Stephan Schlothfeld, *Individuelle oder gemeinsame Verpflichtung? Das Problem der Zuständigkeit bei der Behebung gravierender Übel* (Paderborn, DE: Mentis, 2008).

most important social and economic relations.[50] In the context of such a basic order, the boundaries of the individual's personal sphere of influence are dependent on what others do. An individual obligation to help in case of need would also be an excessive moral demand for individuals who should be able to organize their lives autonomously according to their "basic projects" and in accordance with equal chances and liberties for everyone. After all, the autonomous organization of the agents' lives is a moral value that is important enough that we have a legitimate interest in affording them the (necessary) space. This is another reason why the individual moral responsibility for removing unjust grievances must be less extensive.

Therefore, individuals by themselves cannot be completely responsible for correcting everything that is amiss; they may however contribute something towards improving things. This duty to help those in need addresses all members of the moral community of human beings and demands of them in their capacity as "citizens of the world" to create institutions which may effectively put a stop to such violations of rights, for (all) individuals collectively share a common moral responsibility.[51] Because such deprivation can be remedied only through the (coordinated) actions of many, this is a communal task. Thus, in such a case, a collective of individuals is responsible, although it is dependent on the individual members and their shared or partial responsibility.

But the responsible collective in question is not necessarily one of perpetrators or of culprits. It is not only those causing injustice who have the duty to alleviate or correct it. Because in many cases injustice is not brought about through culpable causation and because individuals are often not up to the task of rectifying an injustice, those who are capable of doing so at an acceptable cost have the duty to aid. This position allocates the responsibility to help in a crisis to individuals as a collective, even though these individuals do not have a "causal responsibility."[52]

Ideally, this shared responsibility is one that responsible citizens and individuals impose upon themselves; i.e., they accept responsibility wherever they can (already) be held accountable for moral reasons.[53] Where there is no straightforward answer to the question of moral accountability, citizens will come to realize the complexities of assessing responsibility for

---

[50] Cf. John Rawls, *A Theory of Justice* (Cambridge: Harvard University Press, 1971), §2.
[51] For the argument that there are "mediated" positive duties that correspond to the moral duty to help the needy, cf. Henry Shue, "Mediating Duties," *Ethics* 98, no. 4 (1988): 687–704; Shue, *Basic Rights: Subsistence, Affluence and U.S. Foreign Policy*, 1st ed. (Princeton, NJ: Princeton University Press, 1980).
[52] For this somewhat ill-chosen term for a certain type of responsibility, cf. H.L.A. Hart, "Postscript: Responsibility and Retribution," in *Punishment and Responsibility* (Oxford: Oxford University Press, 1968), 211–30.
[53] Cf. Klaus Günther, "Verantwortlichkeit in der Zivilgesellschaft," in *Das Interesse der Vernunft*, ed. Stefan Müller-Dohm (Frankfurt: Suhrkamp, 2000), 465–85.

deprivation, and will solve the problem of excessive demands, on the one hand, and a lack of specific content, on the other, by reflecting on the concept of responsibility, as well as on the corresponding criteria and the rules of their application. In a social procedure of decision-making and reflection, citizens may then formulate different context-sensitive criteria for cases where the attribution of responsibility is problematic. Such criteria may not be construed completely arbitrarily if there are primary moral reasons pointing to a specific responsibility. If, for example, certain persons were involved in creating injustice, it is their responsibility to correct it. In many countries, however, it has now become common to construe legal concepts of accountability that may be applied to cases where the condition of responsibility is met only in a weak sense or not at all.

The two most important examples are probably, first, the attribution of liability, where a society decides who is liable for possible damages on the basis of moral considerations and criteria of efficiency, and second, the attribution of blanket responsibility for certain spheres of life, regardless of any actual culpable behavior.[54]

One could, I maintain, structure this collective responsibility for the correction of injustice along the lines of the concept of liability. We all have a considerable interest in mechanisms designed to prevent damages (preemptive effect of liability regulations) and to correct them or compensate for them in case damages do arise. This is why we together as a society should agree on such mechanisms (i.e., we should do so for moral reasons). In this scenario, a group may be held collectively responsible even though not all of its members share the blame.[55] This is a case of vicarious liability without partial responsibility. Collective liability for risk or absolute liability (instead of tortious liability) means to be held responsible for the actions of others. In the case of responsibility or liability for injustices it is often not possible to assign distributive blame to a group; i.e., the blame cannot be allocated among its individual members. Thus, the group should be held responsible for correcting such wrongs, precisely because they cannot be imputed to the individual members. There is only one possible way of fulfilling this duty, and that is through effective cooperation. This is why collective liability in the last resort

[54] In the second case, we may think of a certain kind of liability (in German called '*Zustandshaftung*') where the proprietor of an object is responsible for averting any danger that might stem from it by virtue of his power of disposal, or of a minister's political responsibility for his department within the sphere of his competence and duties ('ministerial responsibility'). Cf. Werner Krawietz, "Theorie der Verantwortung—neu oder alt? Zur normativen Verantwortlichkeitsattribution mit Mitteln des Rechts," in *Verantwortung—Prinzip oder Problem?*, ed. Kurt Bayertz (Darmstadt, DE: Wissenschaftliche Buchgesellschaft, 1995), 184–216, 202f.; Reinhold Zippelius, "Varianten und Gründe rechtlicher Verantwortung," in *Verantwortlichkeit und Recht*, Jahrbuch für Rechtssoziologie und Rechtstheorie 14, ed. E. J. Lampe (Opladen, DE: Westdeutscher Verlag, 1989), 257–66, 261f.

[55] Cf. Joel Feinberg, "Collective Responsibility," *The Journal of Philosophy* 65, no. 21 (1968): 674–88.

creates a duty to cooperate (prospectively to provide for possible risks and retrospectively to cope with the shared responsibility for man-made wrongs and injustices), a duty to come together to engage in collective action, and a duty to create institutions to collectively manage common responsibility.[56]

In order to account for the individual distributive (joint) responsibility in an initially randomly composed group, a responsibility which at the same time opens up the possibility of effectively putting an end to injustices without overly burdening the individuals, it is necessary to institute a coordinated collective based on principles of fairness. If a randomly composed group can transform itself into a collective which is capable of acting and of developing procedures of decision-making in a situation in which rational human beings should have a clear understanding of the moral nature of the action required, then such a group can be said to be responsible.[57]

A group organized according to these principles meets the criteria for moral responsibility we routinely apply to individuals.[58] (i) The group is formed on the basis of a general consensus of all participants. In order for them to act collectively, the group must first make a concerted decision about its aims and intentions. The ensuing consensus constructs the plural subject of action. (ii) A group may act voluntarily, on the basis of a free agreement of its members, or it may act under duress. Where the group's action follows a collective decision, taken without external constraint, it may be considered voluntary. (iii) Knowledge of the group's moral norms may be assumed since the group members' joint definition of the shared aims presupposes their moral values and constitutes the group's moral framework. (iv) By creating an internal organization and a decision-making procedure, the collective enables itself to reach communal decisions and coordinate the actions of its members, to implement effective measures correcting any existing wrongs, and to allocate individual duties that do not overburden the individual members. If in this way a group can meet the criteria for moral responsibility, there exists the possibility of genuine collective responsibility. With its structure of organization and decision-making, the group may be seen more as a kind of corporation which is treated, according to legal and everyday principles, as a responsible corporative agent with "corporative intentionality" analogous to natural persons.[59]

---

[56] Gunter Teubner, "Die unsichtbare, 'Cupola'. Kausalitätskrise und kollektive Zurechnung," in *Kausalität und Zurechnung. Über Verantwortung in komplexen kulturellen Prozessen*, ed. Weyma Lübbe (Berlin: de Gruyter, 1994), 91–143, 118.

[57] Cf. Virginia Held, "Can a Random Collection of Individuals be Morally Responsible?," in *Collective Responsibility*, eds. Larry May and Stacey Hoffmann (Lanham, MD: Rowman & Littlefield, 1991), 89–100.

[58] Cf. Margaret Gilbert, "The Idea of Collective Guilt," in *Sociality and Responsibility: New Essays in Plural Subject Theory* (Lanham, MD: Rowman & Littlefield, 2000), 141–52.

[59] Cf. Peter A. French, *Collective and Corporate Responsibility* (New York: Columbia University Press, 1984). Peter A. French, "The Corporation as a Moral Person," *American Philosophical Quarterly* 16, no. 3 (1979): 207–15.

Neo-republicans also speak of the construction of corporative agents.[60] However, the neo-republicans see the question of politics, of "who" decides, as the problem; they see politics as both the question and the answer. My institutional approach sees the political construction of a corporative agent—a *who*, so to speak—as an answer for how to apportion responsibility for alleviating need.

The collective does not necessarily need to be an established and institutional entity to be able to engage in responsible action. Loose aggregates of people may be considered as candidates for assuming collective responsibility if they meet the above conditions. This is particularly relevant where deficiencies requiring collective action exist, but where responsible institutional collectives have not yet been firmly established, such as in the case of world poverty. In order to account for the particular individual (joint) responsibility, a collective must be established according to principles of fairness which can, in a continuous and steady manner, effectively put an end to the existing wrongs. Based on previous experience, we can say that a state-like structure would best meet the requirements for a solution of the problem of coordinating shared responsibility. Various alternatives are however presently emerging and are being discussed as part of the concept of "global governance."

Once an effective collective is established, possibly taking the shape of a state-like organization, one would expect it, as a rule, to guarantee the individual adherence to primary moral reasons by means of legal sanctions, as well as to regulate the individuals' commonly shared responsibility with the purpose of bringing about justice. Thus, one advantage of collective liability is that the compensation for deficiencies is made easier. The second advantage is that responsibility and liability become internalized. For, legal rules of liability aside, we wish to achieve, and should achieve, a situation where certain individuals feel responsible,[61] accept, and, if possible, internalize the arrangement. Only then can we achieve a viable social practice effectively regulating responsibility. A third advantage is that, ideally, agents begin adjusting their risk calculation and thus improve the level of foresight.

A more precise definition of the individuals' duties is, however, required if we are to know exactly who is responsible for what. Furthermore, because the group members together defined their goal, the group is responsible for the actions undertaken in achieving it. The collective responsibility is thus distributed among members in the form of subtasks. Therefore, collective responsibility is not a substitute for individual responsibility; instead, the former complements the latter with an additional element; i.e., that amount of joint responsibility assigned by the community of responsibility. The group members meet their shared responsibility by reasonably allocating

[60] See Philip Pettit, "The Republican Law of Peoples: A Restatement" (this volume), and various works cited there.
[61] Cf. Miller, "Distributing Responsibilities," 469.

their duties in the form of a social and moral division of labor, whereby individuals are either evenly taxed or only a few people are assigned tasks for which they are adequately compensated. Thus, when specifying individual responsibilities, a certain degree of reindividualization of collective liability is involved by which the group determines the internal measure for the distribution of burdens. We have thus, as indicated above, a situation where a cooperative agent is created through a conscious social effort.[62] Finally, the creation of collective responsibility presents itself as follows: In a first step, actions, rights, and obligations are ascribed to the collective agent as such. In a second step, profits and losses (metaphorically speaking) are individually allocated among the members according to their causal, moral, and functional responsibility, as well as to criteria of effectiveness and personal bonds. It is here that different criteria can be combined and weighed against each other. It thus makes sense from a moral point of view to maintain that causing injustice is the most important measure for the attribution of responsibility.[63] Only where this cannot be applied exclusively because the moral demands on the culpable individual become excessive should different criteria be applied, such as how much individuals contribute to the risk of exacerbating injustices, or how far they tolerate injustice or profit from it. The criterion of ability may also be applied. Where even this is impossible, all members should assume an equal share of responsibility. A two-step procedure such as ours is attractive because it combines the advantages of collective liability with the incentives of an individualized approach. Collective liability ensures that the victims of moral wrongs receive compensation even where no individual causation can be determined; the individual distribution of this approach generates an individually assignable share of the duty to alleviate injustices. Third, in recognition of the joint responsibility, a system of insurances should be introduced along with a statutory duty to insure. This generates a reasonable and fair allocation of individuals' rights to protection from moral wrongs. Where people are generally willing to participate in such a scheme, the burden for the individual member can be kept to a relative minimum, and no excessive moral demands are made. Where people are not prepared to enter into this scheme voluntarily, the coordinated collective must resort to sanctions in order to ensure that all members satisfy their fair share of the collectively shared responsibility for fair conditions.

The starting point of our inquiry was a problem of *moral* philosophy concerning the duty of correcting global deprivation. It was argued that charity

---

[62] Cf. Teubner, "Die unsichtbare," 127.

[63] For this principle, cf. Christian Barry, "Understanding and Evaluating the Contribution Principle," in *Real World Justice: Grounds, Principles, Human Rights, and Social Institutions*, eds. Andreas Føllesdal and Thomas Pogge (Dordrecht, NL: Springer, 2005), 100–35; Christian Barry, "Applying the Contribution Principle," *Metaphilosophy* 36, no. 1–2 (2005): 210–27.

is not sufficient; rather, there is a basic duty to help those in need. The problem of global deprivation cannot be adequately addressed in terms of moral philosophy without drawing on this idea of a basic duty; even principles of corrective justice do not solve the underlying problem. Instead of holding, as Singer does, that every relatively well-off individual is globally responsible for aiding the deprived until he/she would have to sacrifice something of similar moral significance, we must consider the individual situation and differentiate the individual duty accordingly. Like Singer, and unlike the neo-republicans discussed in section 3, I *start* with the requirement to alleviate need. However, like the neo-republicans, and unlike Singer, my approach does have an important focus on politics and institutions. In my approach, what is fundamental to justice is not the *question of politics*, but the duty to alleviate need. However, this duty cannot be realized without the *political construction* of shared responsibility. The addressees of the duty to help are all relatively well-off individuals who share a duty of aiding the deprived. In order to live up to this responsibility, they must come together and create shared political institutions that will allow them to help as part of a concerted effort that will nevertheless accord each individual his/her fair share of what is due, and that will also have the means of enforcing such demands. This political construction of shared responsibility enables us to specify the addressees of the duty to aid, as well as to solve problems of coordination and of excessive demands. We may therefore hope that global deprivation will actually be eliminated, or at least significantly alleviated.

6 CONCLUSION: IDEAL THEORY, POLITICS, AND GLOBAL REFORM

In ideal, just, institutional circumstances, the criteria of responsibility, reasonableness, permissibility, and a chance of succeeding are all fulfilled. In ideal institutional circumstances, human rights protection would be guaranteed as well as feasible. Human beings would be equipped with basic goods, and this state of affairs would also be institutionally secured.

But as good as this may sound, there still seems to be a serious problem for this institutional approach.[64] According to my proposal, the indeterminate positive duty to aid needs to be converted into a determinate role, which the responsible institutional collective assigns as a subtask to each group member within the scope of a collective liability. In this approach, the individual positive duty to aid is transformed into the joint responsibility to create and maintain suitable institutions for the common joint responsibility to eliminate serious need on the principle of the division of labor. The

[64] Cf. Elizabeth Ashford, "Global Poverty and Human Rights: The Case for Positive Duties," in *Freedom from Poverty as a Human Right: Who Owes What to the Very Poor?*, ed. Thomas Pogge (New York: Oxford University Press, 2007).

important intuition behind the institutional approach defended here is that duties to help, which precede any institutions, cannot be properly implemented without institutions identifying, in legitimate and efficient ways, duty-bearers and right-holders instantiating their demands. The institutions should be created precisely in order to articulate the specific implementation of the otherwise imperfect duties in non-ideal circumstances.

The general institutional setup makes a difference to the individual degree of duty. Thus an efficient institutional allocation of duties can contribute to the fact that individual contributions to help support people in need are determinate rather than indeterminate. Furthermore, the individual reasonableness of the fulfilment of duties can change dramatically when duties are allocated by an institution and it is guaranteed that everyone's duties are fulfilled and all burdens are fairly distributed. In ideal institutional circumstances our duties towards the poor could be both reasonable and clearly determined.

In the ideal institutional circumstances of just institutions it is first of all our natural duty to comply with whatever the institutions may ask of us. Second, we should support the institutions. For the purposes of these natural duties of justice we must also support the institutions even when we ourselves have not profited from them and are not in any other way involved in them. Third, we should further the realization of just regulations not yet in existence. This means that in non-ideal institutional circumstances it is our natural duty "to further just arrangements not yet established," as far as is reasonable.[65]

Now it is possible to object to this approach on the grounds that it merely transforms the imperfect moral duty to help individually into an imperfect moral duty to construct and support political institutions collectively. As an incomplete duty it must necessarily leave open who owes how much when and to whom. After attempting to solve the indeterminacy of duties to aid by collective institution-building, the institutional approach would then find itself faced with a further collective action problem: who is to do what to create the necessary institutions capable of effectively organizing common aid?

But the situation for the institutional approach is not quite as bad as the above objection makes it seem. In the institutional approach to duties to aid we have three duties: a) If an institutional scheme fulfilling the collective responsibility is in place, everyone should support it. b) If that scheme is absent, everyone has a natural duty to help create it. There are then two duties depending on the circumstances: we should support institutional schemes implementing collective responsibility to aid the deprived if they exist, and help create them if they do not. c) Only if no institutional solution is possible is it necessary for everyone to fulfill individually his/her moral duty to help in states of need.

65 Cf. Rawls, *Theory of Justice*, 119.

The first question to be answered then is whether the necessary institutions that could effectively organize aid exist. The question requires of course more detailed analysis than I can provide here. But let it suffice for the moment to point out that these kinds of institutions of organized, collective responsibility do of course exist on a national level, namely states. It is true to say that they tend to carry out their responsibilities rather inadequately, or, worse still, do not even regard their common moral responsibility to provide aid in cases of need as one of their primary tasks. It is however clear what we as citizens are to do in this instance, which on a national level is in effect a typical one: for moral reasons we should use our political, democratic powers of influence to make our states and their governments do justice to our common responsibility to provide aid. If we live in a tolerably functioning, sufficiently democratic state, as most citizens in the "Global North" do, this task is feasible. Since the politico-democratic influence exerted in these countries is organized by political institutions, elections, and political groupings such as parties, non-governmental organizations (NGOs), and so forth, the possibility that some citizens remain apathetic does not necessarily diminish the powers of influence of those who are willing to fulfill their moral duty to reorganize the existing political system. The complacency problem typical of non-ideal circumstances can therefore be passably surmountable, if halfway functioning political institutions are in place. It is enough if a sufficiently large number of citizens (think of the morally elite, of charismatic politicians with a moral conscience, or of ethical revolutionaries) are adequately motivated to exert their influence on political organizations and make them fulfill their common moral responsibility to provide aid in cases of need. Once more it becomes clear that the nature and degree of our moral duty to reorganize the political system varies (like the duties to aid) according to the powers of influence of the individuals concerned.

At this point, it may seem that I have reached the conclusion that influence and power are key to justice—something I earlier disavowed. But this mischaracterizes my position. I have said that politics—the *question* of who *decides politically*—is not the basic question of justice. There are other, more fundamental questions of justice. One such problem is how to realize the requirement of the basic duty of aid. Further, there is the lack of clarity regarding what these duties entail. To specify this, we need to have political institutions that allocate duties. The further problem, just mentioned, is that (at least some) actors then have a duty to form and reorganize such political institutions. The actors' power to have political influence changes the character of one's duty to engage in political reform. But, *pace* the neo-republicans, it is not only the presence of arbitrary power and influence that begins the question of justice. The duty of aid would be relevant if political institutions or domination did not exist. Political influence and power are relevant to characterizing individuals' duties of justice. But what matters is the presence of political possibility, not domination.

On an international level matters are more complex. It is true that there is for the most part still a lack of robust, state-like, international institutions capable of securing the fulfilment of our collective duties to help. Equally, though, global economics is largely controlled by the international organizations, such as the World Trade Organization, the International Monetary Fund, the World Bank, and the United Nations. These international institutions depend, if they are to function, on the authorization and enforcement provided by nation-states. The structure of our cooperative global economy was created by our states as a complex hierarchical system of global governance, which is maintained up to this day to the advantage of the citizens of the first world. This can be seen in the globally coordinated operations to save the world's financial and banking system. If this account is even roughly correct, it should be clear that even in the international sphere the new establishment of institutions matters less than the absolutely essential reconstruction of the already existing system. Such institutions seem to many of us illegitimate if they are not reformed in such a way that their procedures involve more democratic accountability and their outcomes become more equitable. A reform of the global economic system towards a system that would recognize and guarantee socioeconomic human rights seems feasible insofar as it is in principle politically doable, if only for the reason that the present morally corrupt system could be created by the will of powerful political agents. However, even if they could be stable once created, it may be unrealistic to expect that political agents with the right kinds of moral motives pursuing their reform will succeed in doing so. For on an international level the powers of influence are considerably more limited, because there is only a very indirect kind of controlled exertion of influence along the established political channels. However, where there is a will, institutional reform on an international political and economic level is possible. It is in principle also possible for us to put the fight against poverty on the agenda and prevail through protest, critical publicity, blaming and shaming, pressure on our national governments, etc. This hardly needs emphasis. This moral duty to exert political influence on the reform of international organizations is, however, unfortunately accompanied by the complacency problem.

Even if this and other questions have yet to be answered, I hope that it has become clear that the institutional approach to duties to aid in cases of need which I have proposed here is not ideal theory in a bad sense, but offers instead viable recommendations—recommendations, that is, that are both achievable and desirable, as far as we can judge in the circumstances we find ourselves in at present, or are likely to find ourselves in the not-too-distant future.

BIBLIOGRAPHY

Adloff, Frank, and Steffan Mau, eds. *Vom Geben und Nehmen. Zur Soziologie der Reziprozität*. Frankfurt: Campus, 2005.

Anderson, Elizabeth. "What Is the Point of Equality?" *Ethics* 109, no. 2 (1999): 287–337.

Arneson, Richard J. "Egalitarianism and Responsibility." *The Journal of Ethics* 3, no. 3 (1999): 225–47.

Ashford, Elizabeth. "Global Poverty and Human Rights: The Case for Positive Duties." In *Freedom from Poverty as a Human Right: Who Owes What to the Very Poor?*, edited by Thomas Pogge. New York: Oxford University Press, 2007.

Barry, Brian. "Humanity and Justice in Global Perspective." In *Global Justice: Seminal Essays*, edited by Thomas Pogge and Darrell Moellendorf, 179–209. St. Paul, MN: Paragon House, 2008. Originally printed in Nomos XXIV: *Ethics, Economics and the Law*, edited by J. Roland Pennock and John W. Chapman, 219–52. New York: New York University Press, 1982.

Barry, Christian. "Applying the Contribution Principle." *Metaphilosophy* 36, no. 1–2 (2005): 210–27; also in *Global Responsibilities: Who Must Deliver on Human Rights?*, edited by Andrew Kuper, 210–27. London: Routledge, 2005.

Barry, Christian. "Understanding and Evaluating the Contribution Principle." In *Real World Justice: Grounds, Principles, Human Rights, and Social Institutions*, edited by Andreas Føllesdal and Thomas Pogge, 100–35. Dordrecht: Springer, 2005.

Cullity, Garrett. "International Aid and the Scope of Kindness." *Ethics* 105, no. 1 (1994): 99–127.

Cullity, Garrett. *The Moral Demands of Affluence*. Oxford: Oxford University Press, 2004.

Feinberg, Joel. "Collective Responsibility." *The Journal of Philosophy* 65, no. 21 (1968): 674–88.

Forst, Rainer. "Two Pictures of Justice." In *Justification and Critique*, translated by Ciaran Cronin, 17–37. Cambridge: Polity Press, 2013.

French, Peter A. *Collective and Corporate Responsibility*. New York: Columbia University Press, 1984.

French, Peter A. "The Corporation as a Moral Person." *American Philosophical Quarterly* 16, no. 3 (1979): 207–15.

Gauthier, David. *Morals by Agreement*. Oxford: Oxford University Press, 1986.

Gilbert, Margaret. "The Idea of Collective Guilt." In *Sociality and Responsibility: New Essays in Plural Subject Theory*, 141–52. Lanham: Rowman & Littlefield, 2000.

Gosepath, Stefan. *Gleiche Gerechtigkeit. Grundlagen eines liberalen Egalitarismus*. Frankfurt: Suhrkamp, 2004.

Gosepath, Stefan. "The Principle of Subsidiarity." In *Real World Justice: Grounds, Principles, Human Rights and Institutions,* edited by Andreas Føllesdal and Thomas Pogge, 153–66. Dordrecht: Springer, 2000.

Gosepath, Stefan. "Verantwortung für die Beseitigung von Übeln." In *Verantwortung in der Zivilgesellschaft. Zur Konjunktur eines widersprüchlichen Prinzips*, edited by Ludger Heibrink and Alfred Hirsch, 387–408. Frankfurt: Campus, 2006.

Günther, Klaus. "Verantwortlichkeit in der Zivilgesellschaft." In *Das Interesse der Vernunft*, edited by Stefan Müller-Dohm, 465–85. Frankfurt: Suhrkamp, 2000.

Habermas, Jürgen. *Between Facts and Norms: Contributions to a Discourse Theory of Law and Democracy*. Translated by William Rehg. Cambridge, MA: MIT Press, 1992.

Hart, H.L.A. "Postscript: Responsibility and Retribution." In *Punishment and Responsibility*, 211–30. Oxford: Oxford University Press, 1968.

Held, Virginia. "Can a Random Collection of Individuals be Morally Responsible?" In *Collective Responsibility*, edited by Larry May and Stacey Hoffmann, 89–100. Lanham: Rowman & Littlefield, 1991.

Hinsch, Wilfried. *Gerechtfertigte Ungleichheiten*. Berlin/New York: de Gruyter, 2002.

Höffe, Otfried. *Demokratie im Zeitalter der Globalisierung*. München: C.H. Beck, 1999.

Höffe, Otfried. "Soziale Gerechtigkeit als Tausch: ein neues Paradigma." In *Politik und Ethik*, edited by Kurt Bayertz, 229–48. Stuttgart: Reclam, 1996.
Höffe, Otfried. "Transzendentaler Tausch – eine Legitimationsfigur für Menschenrechte?" In *Philosophie der Menschenrechte*, edited by Stefan Gosepath and Georg Lohmann, 29–48. Frankfurt: Suhrkamp, 1998.
Hohfeld, Wesley. *Fundamental Legal Conceptions*. New Haven: Yale University Press, 1923.
Honneth, Axel. "Das Gewebe der Gerechtigkeit." In *Das Ich im Wir. Studien zur Anerkennungstheorie*, edited by Axel Honneth, 51–79. Berlin: Suhrkamp 2010.
Hume, David. *A Treatise of Human Nature* [1739]. Oxford: Clarendon Press, 1978.
Kant, Immanuel. *Grundlegung zur Metaphysik der Sitten* [1785]. Edited by Karl Vorländer. Hamburg: Felix Meiner, 1965.
Krawietz, Werner. "Theorie der Verantwortung – neu oder alt? Zur normativen Verantwortlichkeitsattribution mit Mitteln des Rechts." In *Verantwortung – Prinzip oder Problem?*, edited by Kurt Bayertz, 184–216. Darmstadt: Wissenschaftliche Buchgesellschaft, 1995.
Kuper, Andrew. "Global Poverty Relief: More Than Charity." In *Global Responsibilities: Who Must Deliver on Human Rights?*, edited by Andrew Kuper, 135–72. London: Routledge, 2005.
Mauss, Marcel. *The Gift: Forms and Functions of Exchange in Archaic Societies* [1923/1924]. London: Routledge, 1990.
Mieth, Corinna. "Hilfspflichten im Kontext globaler Gerechtigkeitstheorien." In *Zwischen Sicherheitskalkül, Interesse und Moral*, edited by Klaus Hirsch and Klaus Seitz, 83–104. Frankfurt: Verlag für Interkulturelle Kommunikation, 2005.
Miller, David. "Distributing Responsibilities." *The Journal of Political Philosophy* 9, no. 4 (2001): 453–71. Reprinted in *Global Responsibilities: Who Must Deliver on Human Rights?*, edited by Andrew Kuper, 95–116. New York: Routledge, 2005.
Nozick, Robert. *Anarchy, State, and Utopia*. New York: Basic Books, 1974.
Offe, Claus. "Pflichten versus Kosten: Typen und Kontexte solidarischen Handelns." In *Transnationale Solidarität. Chancen und Grenzen*, edited by Jens Beckert, Julia Eckert, Martin Kohli, and Wolfgang Streeck, 35–50. Frankfurt: Campus, 2004.
O'Neill, Onora. "Agents of Justice." In *Metaphilosophy* 32, no. 1–2 (1989): 180–95; also in *Global Justice*, edited by Thomas Pogge, 188–203. Malden, MA: Blackwell, 2001; and also in *Global Responsibilities: Who Must Deliver on Human Rights?*, edited by Andrew Kuper, 37–52. New York: Routledge, 2005.
O'Neill, Onora. "The Great Maxims of Justice and Charity." In *Constructions of Reason: Explorations of Kant's Practical Philosophy*, 219–33. Cambridge: Cambridge University Press, 2001.
O'Neill, Onora. *Towards Justice and Virtue*. Cambridge: Cambridge University Press, 1996.
Pogge, Thomas, ed. *Global Justice*. Oxford: Wiley Blackwell, 2001.
Pogge, Thomas, ed. "Relational Concepts of Justice: Responsibilities for Health Outcomes." In *Public Health, Ethics, and Equity*, edited by Sudhir Anand, Fabienne Peter, and Amartya Sen, 135–62. Oxford: Oxford University Press, 2004.
Pogge, Thomas, ed. *World Poverty and Human Rights: Cosmopolitan Responsibilities and Reforms*, 1st ed. Cambridge: Polity, 2002.
Rawls, John. *A Theory of Justice*. Cambridge, MA: Harvard University Press, 1971.
Sangiovanni, Andrea. "Global Justice, Reciprocity, and the State." *Philosophy & Public Affairs* 35, no. 1 (2007): 3–39.
Sangiovanni, Andrea. "Justice and the Priority of Politics to Morality." *Journal of Political Philosophy* 16, no. 2 (2008): 137–64.
Scheffler, Samuel. "What is Egalitarianism?" *Philosophy and Public Affairs* 31 (2003): 5–39.

Schlothfeld, Stephan. *Individuelle oder gemeinsame Verpflichtung? Das Problem der Zuständigkeit bei der Behebung gravierender Übel*. Paderborn: Mentis, 2008.
Shue, Henry. *Basic Rights: Subsistence, Affluence and U.S. Foreign Policy*, 1st ed. Princeton, NJ: Princeton University Press, 1980.
Shue, Henry. "Mediating Duties." *Ethics* 98, no. 4 (1988): 687–704.
Singer, Peter. "Poverty, Facts, and Political Philosophies: A Debate with Andrew Kuper." In *Global Responsibilities: Who Must Deliver on Human Rights?*, edited by Andrew Kuper, 173–81. New York: Routledge, 2005.
Singer, Peter. *Practical Ethics*, 2nd ed. Cambridge: Cambridge University Press, 1999.
Singer, Peter. "The Singer Solution to World Poverty." In *Writings on an Ethical Life*, 118–24. New York: Harper Perennial, 2000.
Teubner, Gunter. "Die unsichtbare ‚Cupola'. Kausalitätskrise und kollektive Zurechnung." In *Kausalität und Zurechnung. Über Verantwortung in komplexen kulturellen Prozessen*, edited by Weyma Lübbe, 91–143. Berlin: de Gruyter, 1994.
Tugendhat, Ernst. *Vorlesungen über Ethik*. Frankfurt: Suhrkamp, 1993.
Unger, Peter. *Living High and Letting Die: Our Illusion of Innocence*. New York: Oxford University Press, 1996.
Young, Iris Marion. *Justice and the Politics of Difference*. Princeton: Princeton University Press, 1990.
Zippelius, Reinhold. "Varianten und Gründe rechtlicher Verantwortung." In *Verantwortlichkeit und Recht, Jahrbuch für Rechtssoziologie und Rechtstheorie 14*, edited by E. J. Lampe, 257–66. Opladen: Westdeutscher Verlag, 1989.

12 Antipower, Agency, and the Republican Case for Global Institutional Pluralism

Terry Macdonald

INTRODUCTION

One notable contribution made by recent work in republican theory has been its push to shift the focus of normative political analysis away from *the structure of institutions that distribute social goods*, and towards *the structure of power relationships* among individuals and groups within a social order. The republican political ideal prescribes combating power within social relationships that takes a particular pernicious form—generally called "arbitrary," or "alien"—in which control is exercised by one actor over another without appropriate political endorsement or contestability.[1] This focus on power within republican theory equips it well to contribute to contemporary debates about institution-building in the global domain, where dynamics of power relationships are prominent features of the political landscape.

Republican theory's contribution to debates about international institutions has been constrained, however, by the fact that its normative institutional principles have mostly been applied to structures and policies of constitutional sovereign *states*. Few are persuaded that the same institutional models that enact republican ideals at the level of the state could effectively or legitimately be replicated straightforwardly on a global scale. Yet there is no straightforward way to apply republican institutional principles to some global institutional subject—analogous, say, to the application of some established principles of socioeconomic justice to a global, rather than a statist, "basic structure" or "institutional scheme."[2] A key reason for this is that republican state institutions are often characterized as themselves *constitutive of* the normative ideal of non-domination, as

---

[1] See Philip Pettit, *Republicanism: A Theory of Freedom and Government* (Oxford: Oxford University Press, 1999); Pettit, "A Republican Law of Peoples," *European Journal of Political Theory* 9, no. 1 (2010): 70–94. Cf. Pettit, "The Republican Law of Peoples: A Restatement" (this volume).

[2] See for example Thomas Pogge, *Realizing Rawls* (Ithaca: Cornell University Press, 1989).

distinct from being merely subjects to which its principles can be applied.[3] As such, it is not altogether clear how normative standards can be drawn out from republican thought to critique statist institutional models, or to guide the development of alternative institutions more suitable for the global political sphere.

Before the republican political ideal can be extended systematically to the global domain, it is therefore necessary to reformulate our conception of the ideal itself, in order to open it to a wider range of institutional applications across varying political contexts. Reformulating the republican ideal in this way directs us to undertake a twofold theoretical analysis. First, we can formulate the ideal in terms that are abstracted from state-level institutional models, so that we have some critical tools with which to devise and evaluate institutional alternatives to statism. Second, with these theoretical tools in hand, we can then consider how this ideal could be institutionally constituted or promoted under the particular empirical circumstances of contemporary global politics. These are the two central tasks that I undertake in this chapter.

A promising starting point for such a theoretical reformulation of the ideal of non-domination is Philip Pettit's concept of "antipower,"[4] understood as a set of active social forces that serve to counteract, contain, and regulate "public" political power. This concept is promising for these purposes, since it is abstracted from any specific statist institutional forms. This idea of antipower is prominent only in one of Pettit's early essays on republicanism, and there its sociological character is a little mysterious; it is unclear whether it is best understood as a type of *institution*, a kind of institutional *function*, or a form of social *agency*. In Pettit's subsequent writing on the republican ideal, talk of antipower is largely abandoned in favor of talk of non-domination as an institutionally constituted political good.

In my analysis here, however, I proceed with the view that the earlier concept of antipower is in fact a very useful one for thinking about the problems of republican institution-building, if it is put to work in the right kind of way. More specifically, I propose that antipower can be most helpfully understood as *a form of social agency with a special political function* (partially, but not wholly, constituted by the right kind of political institutions)—and that, alongside the partner concept of *public power*, can form the basis of a functional conception of non-domination that can usefully guide prescriptions for institution-building within the global political domain.

In what follows, I develop this general idea about antipower by presenting a functional account of group agency, followed by a functional conception of non-domination in which functional agencies of antipower—alongside those of public power—play constitutive roles. With these

[3] Pettit characterizes non-domination as "institutionally constituted" in *Republicanism*, 106–7.

[4] Pettit, "Freedom as Antipower," *Ethics* 106, no. 3 (1996): 576–604.

theoretical tools in hand, I then consider the implications of this functional and agency-based account of the republican ideal for practical questions about the design and development of global institutions. I argue that antipower, on the functional agency account, is not wholly institutionally constituted; rather, its agency is constituted in part through background material and cultural structures. In order for political institutions to foster non-domination, they must therefore be designed in a way that reflects and accommodates background material and cultural structures, so that the functional agency of "antipower" can develop and flourish within them. Given present "pluralist," global background structures, I argue that republican political institutions must also adopt a loose and pluralist character—with important implications for some contemporary institutional dilemmas concerning practices of global governance, accountability, and democracy.

1 A FUNCTIONAL ACCOUNT OF GROUP AGENCY

My account of the ideal of non-domination as constituted by the interplay of special functional forms of social agency depends upon accepting a more general, functional conception of *group agency* itself. I conceive of group agents as functionally constituted, in the sense that we can see certain kinds of groups to function as agents somewhat autonomously from the agency of their individual members. It is therefore important to begin by sketching the key elements of this conception of group agency.

There is now a wide (and growing) philosophical literature on the topics of both collective action and collective agency. For the present purposes I draw my account of group agents directly from the recent work of Christian List and Philip Pettit—which articulates a conception of group agency that highlights characteristics most salient to the kind of normative political analysis I wish to undertake here.[5] This salience is to some degree by design, since this work on group agency is very closely aligned and has been developed in conjunction with Pettit's work on the political philosophy of republicanism, as well as List's work on the philosophy of democracy; their theoretical model of group agency has important applications in research on both of these political ideals.

I cannot rehearse here in full all salient details of this sophisticated philosophical account of group agency, but for the present purposes it is sufficient to note some features of the account that provide grounds for understanding the functional roles I want to attribute to group agents (of public power and

[5] List and Pettit have both published widely on problems of group decision and agency, but here I draw most directly on their recent, book-length treatment of the topic: Christian List and Philip Pettit, *Group Agency: The Possibility, Design, and Status of Corporate Agents* (Oxford: Oxford University Press, 2011).

antipower, respectively) within my reading of the republican political ideal. The central point to emphasize, in doing so, is that group agents share in common with individual agents the same basic characteristics that together constitute the goal-seeking function of agency in general. In simple terms, the three features constitutive of an agent are: *beliefs* about what its environment is like; *desires* regarding how it would like things in that environment to be; and the capacity to *process* these beliefs and desires, leading it to intervene in the environment to better satisfy its desires.[6] In order for an agent to intervene successfully in its environment in pursuit of its desires (or as we often say more plainly, to advance its goals), it must also meet some adequate standards of functioning, which are commonly called "standards of rationality," in each of the three dimensions: formation of beliefs in accordance with reality, coherence and viability of desires, and the efficacy of interventions (through action) with respect to these beliefs and desires.[7] As List and Pettit put it, a group agent

> is organized so as to seek the realization of certain motivations in the world and to do so on the basis of certain representations about what that world is like. When action is taken in the group's name—say, by its members or deputies—this is done for the satisfaction of the group's desires, and according to the group's beliefs.[8]

It is important to emphasize that this account of group agency is a *functional* one. Although group agents *function* analogously to individual agents, there is no claim that they *exist* in any way independently from their individual members; that is, they are not any kind of metaphysically mysterious entities, incompatible with methodological individualism in social science. Rather, they are constituted by a collection of individual agents organized in such a way as to meet these conditions and standards of functioning that are definitive of agency. The manner in which groups of individuals can meet these conditions and standards is complex and contextually variable, and is dependent on various kinds of "joint intentions" being in place among members of the group—often including the joint intention to act as a group—as well as other institutional and non-institutional conditions being met. It is beyond the scope of this chapter to elaborate on or address the various philosophical difficulties with explaining how groups of individuals can

---

[6] To put these three features more technically, agents are systems that incorporate: "representational states that depict how things are in the environment"; "motivational states that specify how it requires things to be in the environment"; and "the capacity to process its representational and motivational states, leading it to intervene suitably in the environment whenever that environment fails to match a motivating specification" (ibid., 20).

[7] List and Pettit call these standards "attitude-to-fact," "attitude-to-attitude," and "attitude-to-action" standards of rationality (ibid., 24).

[8] Ibid., 32.

meet these conditions and standards (though in the next section I consider some aspects of these difficulties as they bear upon the question of the limits of institutional design in constituting group agents). In general, though, I assume in what follows here that these difficulties can be overcome, and that there are robust philosophical grounds for viewing group agents as real, functional entities in the social world.[9]

This functional understanding of what group agents are helps us to grasp why it is important to recognize group agents as distinct social entities within the conceptual frameworks of our political ideals, even though such group agents do not *exist* independently from the individuals that make them up—that is, even though the ontological relationship of group attitudes and actions to those of their individual members is one of *supervenience* rather than independence. The importance of recognizing group agents as autonomous from individuals arises from the fact that—from the perspective of the individuals who encounter group agents in social life—they *appear to those who interact with them* to function more or less autonomously from these individuals, and can be most effectively engaged with if they are understood and treated as such.[10] As List and Pettit put this point:

> [t]he agency of the group relates in such a complex way to the agency of individuals that we have little chance of tracking the dispositions of the group agent, and of interacting with it as an agent to contest or interrogate, persuade or coerce, if we conceptualize its doings at the individual level. . . . [W]e will be unable to recognize the kind of group agent we have in mind as an agent, and to predict how it is likely to perform and what we can do to affect it, if we keep our gaze fixed at the level of individuals. We will fail to see the wood for the trees.[11]

As List and Pettit emphasize, the sense in which group agents are functionally autonomous from their individual members is epistemological rather than ontological, but the claim of functional autonomy is no less important for that. The features of social reality that should be incorporated within our political ideals are those that the actors whose relationships the ideal aims to regulate can *perceive and engage with* at a political level; political ideals, in this sense, need to be formulated in terms of political rather than metaphysical conceptions of social ontology. And for this purpose, the conception of group agents as functionally constituted autonomous actors within the social world clearly fits the bill.

---

9 List and Pettit provide some detailed arguments for the validity of this assumption in ibid., chs. 2–3.

10 By "effective" here I am referring to effectiveness relative to the goals of individual agents.

11 List and Pettit, *Group Agency*, 76.

2 PUBLIC POWER, ANTIPOWER, AND THE FUNCTIONAL CONCEPTION OF NON-DOMINATION

With this general functional account of group agency in hand, we can move now to an elaboration of the ideas of *public power and antipower* as denoting special functional forms of group agency within a political order. We can understand these as performing not only the general functions characteristic of agency, but also the more specialized functions of advancing common goods (in the case of public power) and counteracting the choice-constraining effects of public power with participatory and countervailing, collective political action (in the case of antipower). When operating appropriately in conjunction, it is my claim that these together perform the overarching function that constitutes the political good of non-domination.

To explain these claims in more detail, it will help to begin by characterizing the political good of non-domination—and the functions of public power and antipower that together constitute it—in pragmatic terms: as a good in virtue of serving as a *functional remedy* for a particular (characteristically "political") *social problem*. This problem arises from the parallel operation of two basic roles in which individuals encounter and engage with powerful group agents in the course of their social lives. The first of these roles is that of *participants*, or "members," in group agencies.[12] The participation characteristic of membership here can take the form either of participation in the creation and authorization of a group agent with specified functions and powers, or direct participation in the decision-making and action of the group agent at an operational level—or both. Here, individuals encounter group agency from the "inside," so to speak, via involvement in the formation of collective intentions and actions—that is, the channeling of individual interests into the articulation and pursuit of common goals.[13]

The second of these roles is that of *subjects* of group agents. In this capacity individuals are affected and constrained by the power of a group agent, whose intentions and actions, as previously established, will have some degree of autonomy from those of individuals—including individual members, as well as non-members. While the autonomy of the intentions and actions of group agents from those of non-member individuals is straightforwardly evident, the sense in which they are autonomous from those of member individuals is more complex, and depends on the fuller philosophical account of how a group agent can come to acquire its functional autonomy from its

---

[12] I talk about "members" and "participants" here in roughly the senses in which List and Pettit describe group membership, in ibid., 35–36.

[13] Viewing non-domination as a political ideal in this pragmatic sense is distinct from the consequentialist sense in which Pettit characterizes it as a political ideal—namely, as "a value that the state ought to try and advance" (Pettit, *Republicanism*, 92).

individual members. Leaving aside complex philosophical problems of preference aggregation and group rationality,[14] I simply assume this autonomy for the present purposes. What is important to emphasize here is that when in the role of subjects, individuals encounter group agents from the outside, so to speak—in the sense that they find themselves affected by decisions and actions that they have not as individuals intended.

In some political contexts an individual will engage with a powerful group agent in both roles at once. To illustrate this with the familiar example of a closed and ideally constituted democratic state, an individual will engage with the agency of the state in both roles: as participant, in the role of democratic citizen participating in the authorization and, to a lesser extent, the collective decision-making of the group agent of the state, and as subject to the significant powers the state possesses to execute its decisions. In other contexts, the roles of participant and subject can come apart. To take again the example of the group agency of the state, an individual can be, and often is, *subject* to state power without also being incorporated as a participant in the collective decision-making and action of the state as group agent. This can be the case either for legal citizens or non-citizens, depending on the forms of political participation in state decision-making that are available, and the extent to which the interests of either are represented in state decision-making, in a particular context. Individuals can also encounter powerful group agents of other non-state types—such as economic corporations, and nonprofit "civil society" actors of various kinds—in roles of either participant or subject, and these relationships also form an important part of the social order in which individuals live.

The basic political problem that results from the parallel operation of these two kinds of roles is the following. On the one hand, participation in the creation, authorization, and operation of functionally effective group agencies can produce many benefits for the individuals involved. The goods that can be produced for individuals by acting collectively to authorize or directly operate group agents can vary according to individuals' preferences and circumstances, but important examples of such goods are the provision of physical security, the production and distribution of new social goods, or—as in the case of an ideal republican state agency—the promotion of the political good of non-domination itself. As a result, there are good reasons for individuals to continue to choose to create and enable group agents to advance their goals, and thus there are good reasons too for rejecting any political ideal that recommends forms of political "non-intervention" that are incompatible with the persistence of robust forms of collective action and agency within the social order.

On the other hand, however, the creation and maintenance of powerful agencies brings the persistent risk that the group agents which individuals have constituted to advance their common goals will become alienated

[14] An account of this is elaborated in List, *Group Agency*, chs. 2–3.

from, and fail to act effectively in pursuit of, the common goals that motivated their creation. When this happens, individual members will interact with group agents less in the role of active participants, and more in the role of affected subjects. Moreover, creating group agents with significant powers also increases the degree of affectedness and constraint to which *non-members*, along with members, risk subjection.

The political problem, then, is how to achieve two goals in conjunction: first, enabling groups of individuals to act collectively in order to more effectively pursue the goods that they share and strive for in common with others, while second, minimizing the extent to which individuals will need to interact with and relate to these group agents in the capacity of affected subjects, as distinct from active participants.[15] The political purpose to which the republican ideal of non-domination is directed is that of preserving the functions of effective collective agencies within a social order, while enabling individuals to participate in these collective agencies as far as possible *as insiders rather than outsiders*—that is, as participants whose individual goals are channeled in some way into the articulation and pursuit of the goals of powerful groups.

This view of the political problem to which the republican ideal is offered as a remedy provides the basis for the specific functional account of non-domination that I want to present here, in which non-domination is constituted by the *functions of public power and antipower*, performed in conjunction by distinct political agencies within a social order. Here public power and antipower are conceived as *distinct functional types of political agency*, defined in terms of the differentiated functions that they perform in instantiating the republican ideal of non-domination.

Public power, on this republican conception, is that which functions to advance goals shared in common by a group's participants, through the creation of agencies with some special set of powers and competencies. When they are fully developed, agencies of public power will incorporate some mechanisms for the authorization (by group members) of some specialized set of individuals to act on behalf of the wider group as representatives. They will also generally incorporate some accompanying set of material and organizational structures, which function to support and facilitate the effective action in pursuit of collective goals by the group's representatives.

[15] There are many ways of formulating moral arguments in favor of the view that this kind of function constitutes a moral "good." Pettit articulates a sophisticated consequentialist defense of his conception of non-domination in *Republicanism*. I also believe that a robust defense of my conception of non-domination can be mounted on the basis of a commitment to an appropriately formulated conception of individual autonomy (which incorporates a recognition of the ways in which individual autonomy can be exercised not only independently but also collectively). I cannot here present or defend a full account of the moral value attached to this political function; instead, I just note that I assume that the moral attractiveness of the republican ideal depends upon a successful account of this kind being available.

The character of such mechanisms and structures will vary according to the scale, complexity, and content of the goals being advanced in a given case. But examples of such structures include: material infrastructures such as those for processing and communicating complex forms of information, or for transporting products and people; organizational systems for strategically cultivating, coordinating, and deploying relevant individual skills and expertise; and underlying both of these, strategic distributions of material resources across the locations and populations where these structures are embedded, to enable the individuals occupying roles and performing tasks within these structures to do so effectively. Republicans have conventionally viewed the state as the paradigmatically "public" political agent, since the state most straightforwardly fits the picture of this general functional account (though, as I will discuss later in this chapter, the state may not be the only kind of agent that qualifies as public in contemporary global politics).

The special political powers constituted through such mechanisms and structures enable public political agencies to advance participants' goals more effectively than the set of individual group members could achieve acting independently. But these special powers also possess a special capacity to threaten individuals—both members and non-members—with arbitrary or alien forms of control. It is in response to this feature of public power that the functional demand for agencies of antipower arises. Agencies of *antipower* function as a kind of countervailing political force within the social order—balancing against the force of public power, and countering the threat of its dominating control.

Since agencies of antipower are not burdened with the functional demand to supply any concrete social goods to the group (as are agencies of public power), they do not need to be constituted (as do agencies of public power) as specialized and structurally empowered elites acting merely "on behalf," or "in the name," of a group with shared goals. Instead, agencies of antipower are constituted to perform quite different functions: *formulating and articulating the content of the group's common goods*, through facilitating group dialogue, reasoning, and public communication, and *channeling these understandings into the decision-making processes of agents of public power* through some effective and public means.[16] As Pettit puts it, "[t]he promotion of freedom as non-domination requires . . . that something be done to ensure that public decision-making tracks the interests and the ideas of those citizens

[16] By "channeling" here, I mean to allow for means that involve both collaboration with and contestation of public power, and also for varying forms and degrees of institutionalization. Pettit emphasizes the importance of contestation in elaborating his account of what it means for power to be non-arbitrary (*Republicanism*, 184), but it is important to recognize that in some cases agents of public power might in fact be welcoming of this input, and in such cases collaborative rather than contestatory means for channeling ideas and interests into public decision-making processes may play an important role in discharging the general function of antipower.

whom it affects."[17] In response to this demand, antipower is comprised of the various social agencies that function to ensure, to the greatest possible degree, that the interests and ideas of those subjected by public power remain alive and active in the formulation of public political decisions.

Although strongly empowered individual agents may in some circumstances function as important agents of antipower, in most cases *collective* forms of political agency will be required to perform the functions of antipower effectively—in counteracting the threat of domination emanating from large-scale, complex, and well-resourced agencies of public power. Democratic "publics" or *dêmoi*[18] will be among the strongest sources of antipower, where such agencies can be successfully constituted through the establishment of mechanisms for democratic deliberation and social choice. Democratic agencies have particular strength because they are—in virtue of the democratic norms that shape their constitution—strongly participatory and egalitarian. But other kinds of social agencies can also perform the functions of antipower, albeit in more partial ways.

Of particular importance in this latter category are publicly oriented (albeit not fully participatory or egalitarian) group agencies constituted within what is often called the sphere of "civil society"—in particular those advocacy groups that contribute to collective social dialogues in which common goals are explored and articulated, as well as engaged with directly, through contestatory or collaborative processes, with agents of public power to channel these goals into public decision-making. Less publicly oriented groups within "civil society"—what are now often called "interest groups," and which are linked to what James Madison called "factions"[19]—can also perform some more limited functions of antipower, in particular in situations where conflicting interest groups or factions are sufficiently evenly matched in social power that they can counter each other's attempts to capture public political agencies as instruments for their factional interests.[20]

3 STRENGTHENING AGENTS OF ANTIPOWER IN SUPPORT OF NON-DOMINATION: THE ROLE AND LIMITS OF INSTITUTIONAL DESIGN

So far I have described the political functions that must be performed by agencies of public power and antipower operating in conjunction within

[17] Pettit, *Republicanism*, 184.
[18] For an important republican discussion of the pluralism of democratic *dêmoi* in contemporary global politics, see James Bohman, *Democracy across Borders: From Dêmos to Dêmoi* (Cambridge, MA: MIT Press, 2007).
[19] Alexander Hamilton, John Jay, and James Madison, *The Federalist Papers*, ed. Clinton Lawrence Rossiter (New York: New American Library, 1961).
[20] A Madisonian separation of powers is a familiar institutional means of harnessing and augmenting this more general social function of antipower that can be discharged through interactions among competing interest groups. See ibid.

the social order, in order for the ideal of non-domination to be instantiated. With an understanding of these functions in hand, we can begin to tackle the crucial institutional question of interest to republicans aiming to reduce domination within the global order: what can be done, via global institution-building, to create and strengthen the functions of antipower, in its relationship with public power at the global level?

Before getting to a discussion of concrete and specific institutional design problems raised by this question, it is helpful to raise a more general question about *the role and limits of institutions* in constituting the functional agencies of public power and antipower. This question is important since any practical project aimed at building institutions must begin with a clear understanding of the scope of what such institutions can be expected to achieve and transform within the global social order, and conversely the range of non-institutional facts that must be accommodated and adjusted for in the construction of concrete institutional proposals. If it is the case, as I will argue, that the social agencies functioning as antipower cannot be wholly constituted through the structures of political institutions, but rather are constituted also in part by some set of independent, *non-institutional* social facts, then the character of these independent facts must be clearly identified and adjusted for in the formulation of republican institutional proposals.

It is my claim that, although agencies of public power and antipower cannot function effectively without institutions of the right kinds in place to enable and promote their functioning, we cannot regard public power or antipower as *wholly* institutionally constituted. Rather, they are constituted in part also by contextually variable, *non-institutional* facts, of kinds that I will specify, which lie beyond the scope of effective strategic institutional control, and to which republican institution builders must be responsive if they are to succeed in creating functionally effective agencies of antipower in a given context.

Let us consider first the dimensions in which agencies of public power and antipower *are* institutionally constituted. First, in the constitution of a group agent in general, the roles played by individuals can be variable, depending very much on the particular goals that the group agent is pursuing, and the relevant features of the environment in which it acts. List and Pettit note this variability:

> When a group of individuals form an agent, they may relate to one another in a more or less coordinate manner, with each playing a similar role. Alternatively, they may be divided up into different subgroups, each with its distinctive tasks. In either case their relations with one another may involve a hierarchy or a more or less egalitarian arrangement.[21]

[21] List, *Group Agency,* 32.

When the goals being pursued, or the environment(s) in which they are being pursued, are complex, then group agents will usually need to be constituted with correspondingly complex divisions of labor among individuals—to develop expert understandings of various different elements of the goals being pursued and of the environment of action, and to perform different specialized tasks in the overall complex processes of pursuing strategies to pursue goals, and carrying these strategies out. Institutions are often crucial to constituting group agents, insofar as they operate to define these differentiated roles within the group, and to allocate such roles to different individuals through suitable rules and procedures. Institutions can also play a crucial role in constituting group agents insofar as they embody structures through which various social resources are distributed, and as such they can operate to help allocate the necessary resources to individuals in different roles to enable them to perform their specialized functions effectively.

For agencies of public power, institutions articulate the complex webs of *organizational norms and rules* that are required to facilitate the production, distribution, and mobilization of resources, as well as the cultivation and deployment of expertise, that are necessary to perform functions of governance in particular environments and issue areas. In the case of states, these constitute the various roles and institutional powers within the functional domains of legislative, executive, and judicial public power. In the case of non-state forms of public power—those engaged in forms of what is commonly called "governance" activity—the range of institutionally constituted roles and rules is more contextually variable, but the role of institutions in constituting their functions is no less significant for that.

For agencies of antipower, institutions articulate a different set of norms and rules for participants, commensurate with the distinct functions that individuals are required to perform as participants in these group agencies. Most importantly, they articulate the norms and rules that constitute practices of collective reasoning and deliberation, through which collective goals can emerge and receive clear articulation. Institutional norms and rules can also help create clear procedures for the formation of decisive, collective intentions (about what should be done by agencies of public power). Examples of these include the aggregative procedures through which democratic group decisions are sometimes produced, or procedures for authorizing certain individuals or smaller groups to make decisive judgments on behalf of the group and in the group's name, in light of the various reasons emerging as salient through collective reasoning and deliberation. Some kinds of procedures for authorizing decision-making may count as democratic—when compliant with appropriate representative norms—while others may fall short of democratic standards, but still be sufficient to enable effective functioning of the group as a collective agent.

Although the functions of antipower will mainly need to be performed by collective agents, if they are successfully to rival and create a balance with the often significant powers of public political agencies, individuals can also—albeit in more limited ways—serve to engage directly with agencies of public power to counteract the force of their power, and to channel wider interests into their decision-making processes. Institutions can play a role here too in helping empower individuals to act as important agents of antipower, through allocating resources to individuals that help foster their political skills and capacities, and by creating rules and roles that offer them protections against the arbitrary exercise of power by others.[22]

But there are also significant limits to the work that institutions can do to constitute group agencies with capacities to perform functions of public power and antipower effectively. To understand the character of these limits, it is important first to understand that agencies of public power and antipower are constituted not only by structures of rules, of the kind that are put in place by institutions, but also by certain kinds of *material structures and cultural artifacts*, which help ensure that actors in given roles have the requisite knowledge, capacities, and resources to discharge their designated functions as part of the function of the whole group agent.

Important material structures in the case of public power include resources and infrastructures such as government buildings, information systems and technologies, and technologies, equipment, and other resources for performing the myriad specialized tasks assigned to different agencies within governance structures. In the case of antipower, the most material structures are the material dimensions of communicative infrastructures that enable groups of individuals to reason and deliberate together. Certain basic cultural artifacts will also need to be available to enable the functioning of group agencies of both kinds—most importantly shared languages, but also some wider set of shared meanings and understandings that are prerequisites for the recognition of common interests and goals among members of the group, and for coordinated social action in support of institutions with specified social goals.

Institutions can certainly support the development of these requisite material structures and cultural artifacts to some degree by strategically creating and resourcing new roles and rules that are likely to encourage their development and production over time. But institutions cannot ever be expected to produce, or steer the production of, *all or even most* of the important material structures and cultural artifacts within a social order that shape the capacities of particular groups of individuals to join together as agents with particular, specified functions. The simple reason for this is that a certain set of non-institutional material structures and cultural artifacts must already be in place to constitute the shared understandings of common interests and goals, and the basic capacities for collaborative and cooperative action, which are required to establish institutions in the first place.

Institutions can serve to reinforce, develop, and systematize these shared understandings and structures, and in doing so to generate the more rational and functionally effective forms of collective behavior that meet the criteria

[22] Pettit emphasizes the importance of institutions that he describes as protective, regulatory, and empowering, in this connection (*Republicanism*, 589–90).

for what we can call group agency. And the causal effects of these institutions upon their social environment can also alter, over time, the character of the material structures and cultural understandings that initially gave rise to earlier instantiations of the institutions. In doing so, they can create impetus for the groups acting through the institutions to adjust institutional goals, and accordingly reform the structure of roles and rules to function more effectively in support of the new goals. (Though the causal relationships involved in producing these effects will generally be so complex that the level of strategic control over the effects, by institutional designers, will often be low.)

But despite the undoubtedly significant and transformative effects that institutions can have on social orders, one very plain constraint will always remain: institutions cannot have goals that are independent from those held by the agents that establish them. As such, the content of those goals, and the elements of collective agency that are necessary to articulate and to pursue them through institutions, embody those elements of the social order that institutions cannot aim to transform, but rather must take as givens—starting points—for any institution-building project.

These general arguments have significant implications for our understandings of what can and cannot be done, via global institution-building, to create and strengthen the functions of antipower, in its relationship with public power, at the global level. What is called for in the design of republican political institutions for global politics is a strong responsiveness to material structures and cultural artifacts of relevant kinds that shape and limit the potentialities for agencies of public power and antipower to develop and function effectively. Republican institutions can be built with the aim of nurturing and strengthening embryonic agencies of public power and antipower, by creating roles and rules and allocating resources in helpful ways. But they cannot aim to design institutions to constitute agencies of public power and antipower with the expectation that the project of institution-building is one of devising blueprints for social order—as though starting, like the design project of an architect or engineer may sometimes do, with a blank page and an empty lot.

4 REPUBLICAN INSTITUTION-BUILDING IN THE CONTEXT OF GLOBAL POLITICAL PLURALISM

With the general approach to republican institution-building that is recommended by the arguments I have presented so far in hand, we are now in a position to consider what prescriptions follow for more concrete, contemporary dilemmas of global institutional development and design. The basic institutional problem for republicans is that of identifying what strategies can best steer global institutional development in ways that are likely to strengthen agencies of antipower in their domination-combating functions. In order to identify these strategies, we must address the following two questions.

First, what agencies of public power and antipower currently exist at the level of global politics, in fully developed or embryonic functional forms, of the kind that could provide the sociological materials for republican institutions to go to work on, with the goal of strengthening functions of antipower in its relationship with public power? Second, what kinds of institutions will be effective in strengthening the functions of agencies of antipower in relation to public power in these existing structural forms, in different contexts within the contemporary global social order? These are both very large questions, and it is not possible within the constraints of this chapter to answer them in anything approaching a comprehensive way; but some general and illustrative observations can be presented in relation to each.

To begin, let us consider the present structure of global public power. Traditionally, republicans have linked the concept of public power to the specific institutional structures associated with statehood. State institutions have been thought of as uniquely—sometimes even by definition—"political" and "public." In parallel to this, other institutional forms—such as markets, corporations, processes of economic "production," institutionalized "supply chains," "civil associations," "social movements," non-governmental organizations (NGOs), and so on—have been presumed to be "private." But once we adopt a *functional rather than an institutional* understanding of republican public power—as I have argued here that we should do—it becomes clear that states are no longer the only kind of agencies that perform the functions characteristic of public power. More specifically, states are no longer the only agencies that possess significant powers to advance important shared goals within those groups in the name of which they act, as well as to constrain the choices of affected populations.

Under existing conditions of globalization, the reality now is that non-state actors such as multinational corporations, NGOs, and hybrid institutional actors constituted by both state and non-state actors now wield many of these forms of decision-making power (in fields of law-making, economic development, public service provision, and so on), alongside a plurality of states.[23] As I have discussed in more depth elsewhere, the structure of public power within the existing global order can be characterized as *pluralist*—by which I mean that public power is exercised by myriad, separate state,

[23] For more detailed accounts of the various and significant accounts of non-state power, please see Susan Strange, "The Declining Authority of States," in *The Global Transformations Reader: An Introduction to the Globalization Debate*, eds. David Held and Anthony McGrew (Malden, MA: Blackwell, 2000); David Held, *Democracy and the Global Order: From the Modern State to Cosmopolitan Governance* (Cambridge: Polity Press, 1995); A. Claire Cutler and Virginia Haufler, *Private Authority and International Affairs* (Albany: State University of New York Press, 1999); Nico Krisch, *Beyond Constitutionalism: The Pluralist Structure of Postnational Law* (Oxford: Oxford University Press, 2011); Terry Macdonald, *Global Stakeholder Democracy: Power and Representation Beyond Liberal States* (Oxford: Oxford University Press, 2008).

intergovernmental, and non-state agents operating at multiple and overlapping jurisdictional levels, rather than unified through any one supreme global political authority or hierarchy of constitutional principles.[24]

As I argued above, a crucial question for republican institution builders confronted with these plural agencies of public power must be: how malleable are these configurations of public power—and to what extent, and over what kind of timeframe, are we likely to be stuck with them in roughly this form? It will certainly be possible to reconfigure the structure and functions of these agencies of public power to some degree—through various strategies of public institution-building and reform. However, the sheer complexity of the causal relationships that combine to generate the functions of public power that are discharged through these agencies is so high that strategic interventions to alter the structure of these agencies can only realistically be achieved partially, incrementally, and over very long timeframes. Recall that agencies of public power are constituted not only by institutions, but also by complex configurations of functionally effective material technologies and infrastructures, structural resource distributions, concentrations of relevant information and expertise, and the shared background of cultural understandings that enable the many individuals that participate in these complex group agencies to recognize shared interests and goals and coordinate their communication and action in pursuit of such goals.

Effective strategic interventions to change the structure and functions of agencies of public power can only occur to the extent that is possible for political actors to grasp the complex empirical detail of how the various constitutive elements interact to create the relevant functions, as well as what interventions would be effective in bringing about the relevant changes. Performing these feats would require the capacity not only to acquire and analyze vast quantities of information, but also to undertake enormous creative and imaginative leaps of strategic innovation, at the levels of both technological and organizational design, of a kind that I assume it is unrealistic to expect either of affected populations, mobilizing to transform public power via organized agencies of antipower, or of "expert" republican institutional designers, working with philosophical and social-scientific tools. If this assumption is a reasonable one, then it follows that republican institution builders should limit their ambitions with respect to the extent to which

---

[24] Kate Macdonald and Terry Macdonald, "Democracy in a Pluralist Global Order: Corporate Power and Stakeholder Representation," *Ethics & International Affairs* 24, no. 1 (2010); Macdonald, *Global Stakeholder Democracy*; Philip Cerny, "Plurality, Pluralism and Power: Elements of Pluralist Analysis in an Age of Globalization," in *Pluralism: Developments in the Theory and Practice of Democracy*, ed. Rainer Eisfeld (Opladen, DE: Barbara Budrich Publishers, on behalf of the International Political Science Association, Research Committee No. 16 [Socio-Political Pluralism], 2006); Philip Cerny, "Globalization and the Erosion of Democracy," *European Journal of Political Research* 36, no. 1 (1999): 1–26.

the global order can be transformed through the development of republican political institutions.[25]

Let us turn next, then, to examine the character of agencies of antipower within the existing global political order. The existing configuration of such agencies is—just like the configuration of agencies of public power—pluralist in character. Parallel to the idea of pluralism in relation to public power, this pluralism means that the functions of antipower are performed by myriad, separate social agencies comprised of distinct, though sometimes overlapping, population groups, operating within multiple distinct, though sometimes overlapping, issue areas, and engaging with various, sometimes overlapping, sets of public political agencies.[26] The social agencies that work to challenge and counteract public political power—and to channel wider and shared social interests into their decision-making processes—include the following.

Most straightforwardly, democratically constituted groups within established states (traditional democratic *dêmoi*), or other national or subnational groups constituted as group agents through the requisite (albeit not fully democratic) communicative and decision-making structures, can function as sources of antipower in relation to global, as well as domestic, agencies of public power. They can do so when they mobilize in direct political engagement with agents of public power operating in the global domain—whether corporations, other states, or international or nongovernmental public actors. Sometimes—in states where public agencies are strongly representative—these nationally bounded and subnational group agents can channel their goals and apply pressure on external public actors through delegating state agencies to do so on their behalf through instruments of foreign policy. But where states are less representative, or when domestic constituencies are more divided, these groups sometimes find or create alternative conduits for channeling their goals into public global decision-making—such as delegations of individual parliamentarians, representatives of political parties, or representatives of domestically constituted advocacy groups.

Myriad transnational advocacy groups—most prominently international NGOs, but also looser campaign coalition groups, and more specialized transnational agencies such as international trade unions—also operate alongside these domestically constituted groups. These perform functions

[25] This modesty of transformative ambition that I am advocating is, I believe, shared by Pettit in his "Republican Law of Peoples," insofar as he begins by accepting as given the prominence of states as public political actors within the international system. I depart from him only in insisting that a proper responsiveness to existing social facts requires us to recognize a range of non-state actors, also, as agents of public power within a contemporary republican order.

[26] Pluralism in the domain of antipower is contrasted with the kind of unified *demos* that is tasked with performing these functions within some variants of democratic thought.

of antipower by channeling a wide range of goals and interests shared in common by populations across state boundaries into the decision-making processes of powerful public actors such as corporations and international organizations. Their strength and success in doing so is widely variable across different issue areas, and across different relationships and cases of political engagement. But the general character of their functions as agencies of antipower within the global political order is nonetheless readily recognizable.

As in the case of public power, a crucial question for republican institution builders confronted with these existing plural agencies is: how will attempts to reconfigure and strengthen these agencies of antipower via republican institution-building projects be constrained by the background material and cultural structures that partially constitute them? The character of these constraints can be inferred from the highly uneven patterns by which existing agencies of public power have developed. Functionally effective agencies of antipower do not match or track the configurations of objective interests that groups within the global order may share in common. Rather, their development has tended to track the various preexisting material and cultural structures (communicative and other social infrastructures, resource distributions, shared cultural understandings, and so on) that are required to enable groups with common interests to recognize and articulate shared goals, and to advance them collectively through political action.

More concretely, this means that antipower has tended to develop in ways that build on existing, established infrastructures within civil society—established trade unions, community associations, domestic political parties and lobby groups, etc. And it tends to be stronger within issue areas, and in relation to interest groups, that have better access to the relevant resources, infrastructures, and so on. The uneven development of public power against these varying background conditions can thus be adduced in support of the more general claim that the constraints on institution-building projects are real and significant, and must be adequately accommodated in the development of republican institutional prescriptions.

These constraints do not mean, however, that the development of republican institutions cannot serve to reconfigure and strengthen existing global agencies of antipower in any significant ways. Rather, what follows is that institution-building projects must proceed with a clear understanding of these constraints, so that these can be suitably adjusted for within institutional models—thus enabling these institutions to be strategically targeted and designed to strengthen the functions of antipower as effectively as possible under prevailing background conditions. How, then, can this be done? At the most general level, we can say that the constraints on how far and how readily existing configurations of public power and antipower can be altered through strategic institutional interventions are sufficient to conclude that—at least in the foreseeable future—both public power and antipower are likely to retain a broadly *pluralist* structure. As a result, republican institutional interventions must begin with an acceptance of this political pluralism, and tailor institutional proposals to this reality.

The concrete implications of these arguments for the kinds of institutions that republicans should support and promote will be highly contextually variable. As such, a fully satisfying elaboration of the practical implications of the theoretical arguments I have presented here would require detailed examination of specific institutional problems and cases, of a kind that is beyond the scope of the present chapter. For the present purposes, it will have to suffice to present some cursory and illustrative observations about the implications of these arguments, focusing on some familiar and prominent controversies about global institutional design concerning the appropriate interpretation and application of norms of democracy and accountability.

One significant application of these arguments is to dilemmas concerning the design and development of democratic institutions beyond the level of the state—in particular, how the "boundaries" of democratic, decision-making institutions should be delineated. While many powerful and important arguments have been advanced in favor of developing certain "cosmopolitan," democratic institutions,[27] adapting many institutional features of state-based democratic practices to a global context, the arguments presented here suggest that at least some institutional features of an emerging global democratic order should be developed to reflect the pluralism of the existing structures of public power and antipower. The pluralist model requires that democratic boundaries should be determined by locating existing agencies of political power within the global social order, and then working towards their incremental, democratic co-optation and control by strengthening and expanding their functions—in accordance with democratic norms of inclusion, representation, and so on.[28]

The arguments presented here about the limits of institutional design in constituting agencies of public power and antipower have some further implications for dilemmas about appropriate policies of democracy promotion and democratic interventionism in international politics. The dilemmas here concern the extent to which policy interventions to promote democracy—ranging from military intervention to promote "regime change" and the establishment of democratic institutions, through to less coercive, but similarly "top-down" and strongly "institutional" approaches to democracy promotion, focused on establishing and strengthening the operation of democratic constitutions—are likely to be successful.

Since agencies of antipower are constituted not only by the right institutions, but also by congenial background material structures and cultural

---

[27] David Held, *Democracy and the Global Order*; Daniele Archibugi, *The Global Commonwealth of Citizens: Towards Cosmopolitan Democracy* (Princeton: Princeton University Press, 2008).

[28] Macdonald, *Global Stakeholder Democracy*; Macdonald, "Democracy in a Pluralist Global Order"; Bohman, *Democracy across Borders*.

artifacts which cannot in turn be wholly reconfigured through strategic institutional interventions, projects to bring about democratic "regime change" or to strengthen democratic practices in areas of weakness cannot disregard these structures but must find ways to build institutions that can function within the constraints that they impose in particular contexts. Once we recognize democratic antipower as a form of social agency—not a mere institutional structure—it is easier to see why democracy can rarely be imposed from outside a social order, through external institution-building interventions. Policies for the promotion of democracy, then, should aim instead at locating existing agencies of antipower, and nourishing and cultivating their growth, through strategies that are more developmental and incrementalist in character.

A final set of institutional dilemmas on which these theoretical arguments may have some bearing is concerned with the broader question: what responsibilities should powerful non-state actors, such as powerful, international NGOs and multinational corporations, have for promoting non-domination? And how should their responsibilities be differentiated from the responsibilities of this kind accorded to states? This general question translates into a range of more specific dilemmas concerning the public status and political responsibilities of powerful non-state actors. These include current and ongoing debates about whether and how international law should accord any responsibilities for upholding human rights standards,[29] and familiar debates about the forms of social and political "accountability" and "legitimacy" that should be demanded from powerful corporations and NGOs.[30] Whereas it has been traditional to argue that public responsibilities for promoting non-domination (through human rights protections, the establishment of accountability practices, and so on) fall exclusively to states, the arguments that I have presented here about the status of powerful non-state actors as agencies of public power lends support to the view that they too should be accorded strong public responsibilities and held firmly to account in discharging them.

CONCLUSIONS

In this chapter I have elaborated an account of non-domination as a political ideal that combines normative individualism with a recognition of the functional reality and political significance of group agents within the social

---

[29] John Ruggie, "Interim Report of the Special Representative of the Secretary-General on the Issue of Human Rights and Transnational Corporations and Other Business Enterprises," *UN Coc E/CN.4/2006/97*.

[30] Macdonald, *Global Stakeholder Democracy*; Michael Edwards, David Hulme, and Save the Children Fund (Great Britain), *Non-Governmental Organisations: Performance and Accountability: Beyond the Magic Bullet* (London: Earthscan, 1995).

world inhabited by individuals. On this reading of the republican ideal, non-domination is *valued for* the goods that individuals enjoy in virtue of it, but *consists in* a particular functional configuration of the relationships of power between individuals and group agencies within the social order. It is constituted by the dual functions of public power and antipower, operating together to combat the alien or arbitrary control of individuals by agents (sometimes individuals, but most importantly powerful groups) within the social order.

This has important implications for our understandings of the concrete institutional projects that republicans should aim to advance. Strategically formulated republican institutional projects can do a certain amount to make existing agencies of public power more effective and to expand and reform some of their functions. They can also contribute to strengthening agencies of antipower, by allocating resources, creating institutional channels for communication, establishing procedures for joint decision-making, and so on. But institution-building projects must always be structured around, and engaged with, the contextual particularities of the agencies of public power and antipower that already exist within the global social order, and are embedded in those background material and cultural structures that are beyond the scope of strategically rational institutional control.

On this agent-centric formulation of the ideal of non-domination, we may think then that the appropriate metaphor for republican institution-building is not the objectifying one of institutional *design*—which implies a practical focus on institutional engineering and architecture; rather, it is the organic one of *cultivating institutional growth*. Overall, this should be taken to encourage a republican approach towards institution-building that is characterized by an attitude of developmental nurturing rather than one of interventionist control.

BIBLIOGRAPHY

Archibugi, Daniele. *The Global Commonwealth of Citizens: Towards Cosmopolitan Democracy*. Princeton: Princeton University Press, 2008.

Bohman, James. *Democracy across Borders: From Dêmos to Dêmoi*. Cambridge, MA: MIT Press, 2007.

Cerny, Philip. "Globalization and the Erosion of Democracy." *European Journal of Political Research* 36, no. 1 (1999): 1–26.

Cerny, Philip. "Plurality, Pluralism and Power: Elements of Pluralist Analysis in an Age of Globalization." In *Pluralism: Developments in the Theory and Practice of Democracy*, edited by Rainer Eisfeld, 81–111. Opladen, DE: Barbara Budrich Publishers, on behalf of the International Political Science Association, Research Committee No. 16 [Socio-Political Pluralism], 2006.

Cutler, A. Claire, and Virginia Haufler. *Private Authority and International Affairs* [Suny Series in Global Politics]. Albany: State University of New York Press, 1999.

Edwards, Michael, David Hulme, and Save the Children Fund (Great Britain). *Non-Governmental Organisations: Performance and Accountability: Beyond the Magic Bullet*. London: Earthscan, 1995.

Hamilton, Alexander, James Madison, and John Jay. *The Federalist Papers*. Edited by Clinton Lawrence Rossiter. New York: New American Library, 1961.

Held, David. *Democracy and the Global Order: From the Modern State to Cosmopolitan Governance*. Cambridge: Polity Press, 1995.

Krisch, Nico. *Beyond Constitutionalism: The Pluralist Structure of Postnational Law*. Oxford: Oxford University Press, 2011.

List, Christian, and Philip Pettit. *Group Agency: The Possibility, Design, and Status of Corporate Agents*. Oxford: Oxford University Press, 2011.

Macdonald, Kate, and Terry Macdonald. "Democracy in a Pluralist Global Order: Corporate Power and Stakeholder Representation." *Ethics & International Affairs* 24, no. 1 (2010): 19–43.

Macdonald, Terry. *Global Stakeholder Democracy: Power and Representation Beyond Liberal States*. Oxford: Oxford University Press, 2008.

Pettit, Philip. "Freedom as Antipower." *Ethics* 106, no. 3 (1996): 576–604.

Pettit, Philip. "A Republican Law of Peoples." *European Journal of Political Theory* 9, no. 1 (2010): 70–94.

Pettit, Philip. "The Republican Law of Peoples: A Restatement." In *Domination and Global Political Justice: Conceptual, Historical and Institutional Perspectives*, edited by Barbara Buckinx, Jonathan Trejo-Mathys, and Timothy Waligore. New York: Routledge, 2015.

Pettit, Philip. *Republicanism: A Theory of Freedom and Government*. Oxford: Oxford University Press, 1999.

Pogge, Thomas. *Realizing Rawls*. Ithaca: Cornell University Press, 1989.

Ruggie, John. "Interim Report of the Special Representative of the Secretary-General on the Issue of Human Rights and Transnational Corporations and Other Business Enterprises." *UN Coc E/CN.4/2006/97*.

Strange, Susan. "The Declining Authority of States." In *The Global Transformations Reader: An Introduction to the Globalization Debate*, edited by David Held and Anthony McGrew. Malden, MA: Blackwell, 2000.

13 Democracy and World Law
On the Problem of Global Constitutionalism

Hauke Brunkhorst

The storms of globalization have torn loose the most important functional systems of society and related spheres of value from their anchor in the national state, and thus largely placed them beyond the control of democratic legislation. At the same time, a process of legalization and constitutionalization has led to the structural coupling of world politics, world law, and the world economy (a "functional" constitution). All politics has become world domestic politics. So far, however, there has not been any post-national compensation for the ever more threatening endangerment of the democratic rule of law. Legislation tends rather to favor the stabilization and enhancement of post-democratic hegemonic power and the emergence of new forms of transnational class rule. Even world domestic politics has a Janus face. But legalization and constitutionalization are not just the newest clothes of the same old emperor, who always throws them away and has recourse to the symbiotic mechanism of violence whenever it pleases him. The new world law also discloses new spaces of public affairs and constitutes a global *res publica* without a global state, one in which hegemonic and counterhegemonic movements, agitators and moderates, hardened realists and zealous human rights activists, globalization apologists and globalization critics, conservatives and reformers can and must organize and articulate their claims globally.[1] Of course, it remains an open question whether the institutional framework of world law is already strong enough or can be further strengthened in such a way as to not merely stabilize undemocratic rule, but also minimize violence and enable the "struggle for law" (*Kampf ums Recht*) to take place *within* the law.

In what follows, I will first recall the evolutionary achievements of the national state (1). Then I will discuss the most important results of

[1] For a reconstruction of political self-organization in the world public sphere in terms of constitutional law, see Kolja Möller, "Subalterne Konstitutionalisierung. Zur Verfassung von Evolution und Revolution in der Weltgesellschaft," in *Kritische Systemtheorie? Zur Evolution einer normativen Theorie*, eds. Marc Amstutz and Andreas Fischer-Lescano (Frankfurt am Main: Suhrkamp, 2012).

the revolutionary upheavals in world law in the 20th century (2) as well as their consequences for society as a whole (3), in order to show in conclusion that the democracy problem of world society is not solved by legalization and constitutionalization, but rather posed by it in the first place (4).

1 THE EVOLUTIONARY ACHIEVEMENTS OF THE NATIONAL STATE

When a form of life has grown old, one knows what its true significance was. The Western national state, using its formidable administrative apparatuses and means of violence, successfully transformed the destructive energy of the productive force of communication into still risky, but controlled, chain reactions. Since the 16th century that force had been unleashed by technological innovations, new ideas, and the breaking up of social stratification into innumerable value spheres and subsystems. Only this state succeeded in subjecting the three most productive, but also most destructive, powers of modern life to democratic rule: *disembedded capitalism*, with its boundless *markets for land, labor, and money*;[2] *autonomous religion*, with its destructive *fundamentalism*;[3] and finally a *public authority* (*Gewalt*) that had become reflexive and wielded all-penetrating forms of administrative power, disciplinary power, and bio-power.[4]

It was precisely the administrative power of the state, constantly growing and with every growth spurt more autonomous, that was needed in order to finally *constitutionalize* capitalism, religion, and public authority in such a way that the productivity of their unfettered communication could be preserved while its destructiveness was held down to a tolerable level. Without the ambivalent effects of a reflexively closed and highly concentrated executive power that was at once beneficial and repressive, the communicative energies of capitalism, religion, and power that had been unleashed since the 16th century would have immediately destroyed the new society. At the very least, it was true that in the first phase of modernity (*vergangenen Moderne*) there could be no rational capitalism without a strong state, no

---

2 Karl Polanyi, *The Great Transformation* (Boston: Beacon Press, 1957).

3 Max Weber, *The Protestant Ethic and the Spirit of Capitalism*, trans. Talcott Parsons (New York: Routledge, 1992); Harold Berman, *Law and Revolution II: The Impact of the Protestant Reformation on the Western Legal Tradition* (Cambridge, MA: Harvard University Press, 2006); John Witte, *Law and Protestantism: The Legal Teachings of the Lutheran Reformation* (Cambridge: Cambridge University Press, 2002).

4 Alf Lüdtke, "Genesis und Durchsetzung des modernen Staates," *Archiv für Sozialgeschichte* 20 (1980): 470–91; Michel Foucault, *The History of Sexuality*, vol. 1: *An Introduction* [1976] (London: Allen Lane, 1979); Foucault, *Discipline and Punish: the Birth of the Prison* (New York: Random House, 1975).

freedom of speech without a thick net of legally sanctioned norms, no peace among religious sects without repressive administrative machinery, and no taming of public power without a simultaneous taming and heightening of this power through the division of power.

Out of all the national state regimes with which social evolution has experimented, only the *democratic* constitutional state (*Rechtsstaat*) was capable of solving the unavoidable structural problems of modern society *through a simultaneous* heightening and expansion of egalitarian, collective, and individual freedom, something it managed better and more effectively than any other authoritarian or even mixed authoritarian-constitutional regime. *Modern* democracy has been more successful in *simultaneously preserving and reconciling*[5] the sharply drawn oppositions between social classes, religious and non-religious communities, fragmented powers, cultural value spheres and single-minded discourses, rationalities and functional systems than any of the constitutional regimes experimented with in the framework of the Western legal tradition.[6] No longer resting on the rule of one (the majority) over the other (the minority),[7] it has fractured and broken up domination by discovering the peculiar and paradoxical *rule of the ruled*.[8] Constitutions make it possible to institutionalize the antagonistic interests (class conflicts) and opposed convictions (value conflicts) that collide irreconcilably in revolutions in such a way that *after* the revolution *they are maintained in their opposition*, so that their productivity—the productivity of antinomies[9]—is preserved and the struggle *for* legal rights takes place *within* a legal framework; in other words, the struggle for law is waged by means of law.[10] Democratically constituted law does not only function as

---

[5] For a historical perspective on the Western legal tradition as a whole, see Berman, *Law and Revolution II*, 5f.

[6] Harold Berman, *Recht und Revolution* (Frankfurt: Suhrkamp, 1991), originally published in English as Berman, *Law and Revolution: The Formation of the Western Legal Tradition* (Cambridge, MA: Harvard University Press, 1983).

[7] Aristotle, *Politics*, trans. C.D.C. Reeve (Indianapolis: Hackett, 1998).

[8] Ingeborg Maus, *Zur Aufklärung der Demokratietheorie* (Frankfurt: Suhrkamp, 1992); Hauke Brunkhorst, *Solidarität. Von der Bürgerfreundschaft zur globalen Rechtsgenossenschaft* (Frankfurt: Suhrkamp, 2002), 96ff, translated into English as Hauke Brunkhorst, *Solidarity: From Civic Friendship to Global Legal Community*, trans. Jeffrey Flynn (Boston, MA: MIT Press, 2014). For the formulation and the thesis that democratic rule can only be justified as "rule of the ruled," see Christoph Möllers, "Der parlamentarische Bundesstaat—Das vergessene Spannungsverhältnis von Parlament, Demokratie und Bundesstaat," in *Föderalismus—Auflösung oder Zukunft der Staatlichkeit?*, eds. Josef Aulehner, Andreas Dengler, and Karlheinz Konrad (Stuttgart: Boorberg: 1997), 97.

[9] Thomas Kesselring, *Die Produktivität der Antinomie. Hegels Dialektik im Lichte der genetischen Erkenntnistheorie und der formalen Logik* (Frankfurt: Suhrkamp, 1993).

[10] On the struggle in and for the law, see Sonja Buckel, *Subjektivierung und Kohäsion. Zur Rekonstruktion einer materialistischen Theorie des Rechts* (Weilerwist, DE: Velbrück Wissenschaft, 2007). On the way modern democracy is characterized by enduring conflicts, see Chantal Mouffe, *The Democratic Paradox* (London: Verso, 2000).

the "immune system of society,"[11] stabilizing behavioral expectations. At least since the French Revolution and Immanuel Kant, it is also, as a law of freedom, the very medium for *transforming the world.*[12]

It was only in the wake of *democratic* constitutionalization and under the increasingly juridified pressure of intense social struggles that the modern state was able to solve the three great structural problems of modern society that first became manifest in the *motivational crises* of the religious civil wars and the Protestant revolutions of the 16th and 17th centuries, the *legitimation crises* of the constitutional revolutions of the 18th and 19th centuries, and the *rationality crises* of the social revolutions and class struggles of the 19th and 20th centuries.[13] Its successful resolution of these crises, in each case on condition of including the entire population, ran as follows:

- The *religious crisis of motivation* was solved via the simultaneous institutionalization of freedom *of* religion and freedom *from* religion in the form of *political rights*. In this way, enlightenment and religion were both shown to be sources of solidarity.[14]
- The *political crisis of legitimation* was solved by bringing freedom *from* public power into equilibrium with the freedom *of* public life and subjecting the administrative and executive state to *democratic legal organization* (*Staatsorganisationsrecht*).
- The *socioeconomic crisis of rationality* was solved by securing the freedom *of* markets together with freedom *from* their negative externalities via *legal programming* (political planning and steering of the economy, social reforms, and rights of participation).

In a word, the achievement of the democratic constitutional state, at once normative and functional, consisted in the *exclusion of inequality*—the

[11] Niklas Luhmann, *Social Systems* (Stanford: Stanford University Press, 1995), 374.
[12] On law as a medium for the transformation of the world and the deep historical roots of this, see Berman, *Recht und Revolution.* On law as freedom, see Immanuel Kant, *Metaphysik der Sitten, Rechtslehre*, in *Werke VIII* (Frankfurt: 1977), 345. For the English translation see: part I (the doctrine of right) of Kant, *The Metaphysics of Morals*, in *Practical Philosophy*, ed. Mary J. Gregor (Cambridge: Cambridge University Press, 1996), 353–603. Niklas Luhmann is skeptical on this point. See Luhmann, "Subjektive Rechte: Zum Umbau des Rechtsbewußtseins für die moderne Gesellschaft," in *Gesellschaftsstruktur und Semantik*, vol. 2 (Frankfurt: Suhrkamp, 1981), 45–104, 62f. See also Thore Prien, "Fragmentierte Volkssouveränität—Recht, Gerechtigkeit und der demokratische Einspruch in der Weltgesellschaft" (Dissertation, University of Flensburg, 2008).
[13] Still useful for the typology of crisis is Jürgen Habermas, *Legitimation Crisis,* trans. Thomas McCarthy (Boston: Beacon Press, 1973), originally published in German as Habermas, *Legitimationsprobleme im Spätkapitalismus* (Frankfurt am Main: Suhrkamp, 1973).
[14] On both sources, see Brunkhorst, *Solidarität*, Kap. I; in English, see Brunkhorst, *Solidarity*, ch. 1.

clearing away of unequal rights and intolerable inequality in all three dimensions of basic rights: freedom of mobility, political participation and social security, and equality of opportunity.[15] Of course, the development of the social or welfare state was already, as we will see, closely bound up with the 20th-century revolution of world law and pointed from the very beginning beyond the boundaries and possibilities of the legally sovereign national state (which was itself dependent on international law).[16]

2 THE REVOLUTION OF WORLD LAW

From the early 19th up until the last third of the 20th century the modern state was limited to the *regional societies* of Europe, America, and Japan. These had in turn transformed broad swaths of the rest of the world into *imperial spheres of control (Großreichen)* dominated by *national states.* There emerged first a European, and then a North Atlantic, form of *world rule* (*Weltherrschaft*) without as yet any normatively integrated *world society* (*Weltgesellschaft*). Imperialism was by no means a stranger to the sovereign national state, but rather belonged to its very essence.[17]

The long history of the imperial state bent on world domination, accompanied by *its* own "international" law, runs from June 7, 1494, when the Spanish and Portuguese signed the Treaty of Tordesillas, to the unconditional surrender of the German Reich on May 2, 1945. The Treaty of Tordesillas already divided the world into two halves. On the one side, occupying the center and radiating out from the apex, there were the "civilized" Christian dynasties of Europe, out of which the system of European national states later grew and among which the *jus publicum Europaeum*, European public law, was valid. On the other side of the world was "triumphal perdition (*Unheil*)."[18] The immense, "uncivilized," and pagan regions outside of Europe lay in the "heart of darkness."[19] In the Congo, Europe's *public affairs* ended and the dusky realm of its *private obsessions* began. Even the late 19th-century Belgian genocide was justified by the humanist European jurists, who in 1873 had joined together at the *Institut de droit international* in Geneva in the name of freedom, equality, humanity, world peace,

---

[15] Rudolf Stichweh, *Die Weltgesellschaft* (Frankfurt am Main: Suhrkamp, 2000), 52.
[16] On this point in agreement, see Hans Kelsen, *Das Problem der Souveränität und die Theorie des Völkerrechts* [1928, 1st ed. 1920] (Aalen, DE: Scientia Verlag, 1960); Carl Schmitt, *Der Nomos der Erde im Völkerrecht des Jus Publicum Europaeum* [1950] (Berlin: Duncker & Humblot, 1988), 169f, 175, 181, translated into English as Schmitt, *The* Nomos *of the Earth in the International Law in the* Jus Publicum Europaeum, trans. G. L. Ulmen (New York: Telos Press, 2003).
[17] Craig Calhoun, *Nations Matter* (London: Routledge, 2007), 33f, 137.
[18] Max Horkheimer and Theodor Adorno, *Dialektik der Aufklärung. Philosophische Fragmente*, Ges. Schriften 3 (Frankfurt: 1997), 5.
[19] Joseph Conrad, *Heart of Darkness* (New York: Norton, 1988).

parliamentarianism, and progress with the argument that only European actions of the Belgian King fell under the *public* international law of Europe, whereas his actions in the Congo fell under the *private law* of property, with which the owner could do what he wished.[20] These jurists were sorry comforters. A global crime like genocide against blacks did not yet count as a threat to world peace. The fundamental distinction that constituted the *Jus Publicum Europaeum* was that between *equal rights for European states* and *unequal rights* for what Derrida called "the other heading."[21] The Berlin Conference on the future of Africa held between 1884–1845 offered (in Article 35 of the closing text) those who were colonized, and those who were made available for colonization, "authority" instead of "jurisdiction," an arbitrary, executive-made law instead of a stable statutory law: *the horror, the horror.*[22]

The horror remained, but in the second half of the 20th century at least the law was supposed to be transformed from the ground up. The 20th century has been described as the "age of extremes"[23] and any attempt to paper over the abyss that separates the extremes would be, in Adorno's phrase, "false reconciliation."[24] At the very least, this century was the catastrophe that irredeemably "damaged" life, in Adorno's terms.[25] But it was *also* the century of a great legal revolution and earth-shattering normative progress, through which *democracy was universalized, state-based law was transformed into global law*, national *human rights* into *the rights of world citizens*, and merely *constitutional rule of law* into a *democratic and social rule of law*.[26]

The world legal revolution began in 1917 with terrifying events: the Russian revolution and the entry into World War I by the United States, whose President Wilson immediately dictated revolutionary war aims to the resistant Western powers. Vladimir Lenin, leader of the October Revolution, devout Marxist and social revolutionary, and Woodrow Wilson, Calvinist Kantian, believer in the Social Gospel and a personal mission from God, both understood World War I—though from very different perspectives—as the beginning of a world revolution and as a revolutionary war to end all wars. Wilson wanted to renovate *international law* in accordance with the

---

[20] Martti Koskenniemi, *The Gentle Civilizer of Nations* (Cambridge, MA: MIT Press, 2001), 98ff. On the whole era, see Antony Anghie, *Imperialism, Sovereignty and the Making of International Law* (Cambridge: Cambridge University Press, 2005).
[21] Jacques Derrida, *The Other Heading: Reflections on Today's Europe* (Bloomington, IN: Indiana University Press, 1992).
[22] See the last part of Conrad, *Heart of Darkness*.
[23] Eric Hobsbawm, *The Age of Extremes: The Short Twentieth Century, 1914–1991* (New York: Vintage, 1989).
[24] Theodor Adorno, *Aesthetic Theory*, trans. Robert Hullot-Kentor (Minneapolis: University of Minnesota Press, 1997).
[25] Adorno, *Minima Moralia: Reflections From Damaged Life* (New York: Verso, 2006).
[26] Cf. Art. 20, Par. 1 of the German Basic Law.

plan of Kant's *Toward Perpetual Peace*, and unite the peoples of the world into a great *league of democratic states* under the sign of the *right to self-determination*: "to make the world safe for democracy."[27] Lenin wanted to revolutionize *social relations* and establish a *socialist and council-democratic world polity*. The Treaty of Versailles and the founding of the League of Nations were events every bit as revolutionary as the Russian Revolution itself. While the victory of the October Revolution for the first time brought about the fundamental reform of the right of property within an entire region of the world and subordinated the entire legal order to social policy and social-pedagogical aims, with the peace treaty of Versailles "the legislative action of a league of nations stepped into the place of the *jus publicum europaeum*."[28] Both sides had to react to each other, hostile brothers from the beginning. The West saw itself forced to deflect the attack on private property and the powerful, globally resonating social-revolutionary impulse into a "peaceful revolution" that was supposed to discover a legal, constitutional path to socialism.[29] The Soviet Union had to finally jump into the boat of international politics—founding the United Nations *together* with the United States—and sign the various declarations and conventions of human rights on which it choked in the end. Who exactly influenced whom is a secondary question, because the upheavals of the 20th century led in the east and in the west to, respectively, pre-rule of law, pseudo-democratic and democratic rule of law variations of *the same* legal reforms:[30]

- The bourgeois concentration of *equal rights* on a core of property rights is superseded and transformed into a *comprehensive system of norms of anti-discrimination*.[31]

---

[27] On Wilson and Kant, see Gerhard Beestermöller, *Die Völkerbundidee* (Stuttgart: Kohlhammer, 1995); Oliver Eberl, "Demokratie und Frieden. Kants Friedensschrift in den Kontroversen über die Gestaltung globaler Ordnung" (Dissertation, University of Bremen, 2007), 85ff.

[28] Eberl, "Demokratie und Frieden," 75.

[29] Stafford Cripps, "Can Socialism come by Constitutional Methods?," in *Problems of a Socialist Government* (London: Victor Gollancz Ltd., 1933), 35, 38f.

[30] Compare to Berman, *Law and Revolution II*, 16ff.

[31] See Cass Sunstein, *After the Rights Revolution* (Cambridge: Harvard University Press, 1993). Franklin D. Roosevelt's famous "Second Bill of Rights" speech from January 1944 stands at the beginning of a "rights revolution" that reaches deep into the 1970s and 1980s and in which comes wave after wave of anti-discrimination law. In this speech before Congress, he names, without any mention of the right of property, "free speech," "free press," "free worship," "trial by jury," and "freedom from unreasonable searches and seizures" as the existing "inalienable political rights" of the Constitution. These rights, he declares, are valid, but insufficient to cope with conditions in a highly complex society. In the latter part of the speech, he lists a whole series of social rights, which he says are necessary "to assure us equality in the pursuit of happiness" (Roosevelt, quoted in ibid., XI). On the Soviet development of social anti-discrimination rights, see Harold Berman, *Justice in the USSR* (Cambridge: Harvard University Press, 1963).

- Legislation switches from straightforward, if-then "conditional programming" to an orientation of law toward the achievement of substantive social objectives (*Finalprogrammierung*).[32]
- A comprehensive, administrative *planning* is tested in World War I and II, and embodied in specific *legal forms* (*Planungsrecht*).[33]
- A completely new system of laws regulating family, socialization, and behavior is produced. One can speak with Niklas Luhmann of a *law aimed at transforming persons*, with Harold Berman of "parental law," or a "nurturing" or "educational role of law," with Michel Foucault of a policing of discourse and bio-power.[34]

Just like the first one, the second World War was also understood by the sitting American president, in this case Franklin Delano Roosevelt, as a revolutionary war. It was not simply waged in the national interest, but was also intended to bring forth a new democratic order, the "One World" that Roosevelt invoked again and again. The new kind of law and the new institutions of this "One World" all emerged in the time between the end of the First and the end of the Second World War; the general outline of their current form was established by the end of the 1940s. They did not just *emerge evolutionarily*. They were also *intended* as *revolutionary* change, as a new foundation for the world social order, and therefore also represent compromises from the perspective of the various actors in the social struggles that led to them.

The never-ending debate about the extension of the concept of a constitution to the international legal community had already begun in 1917, and in the period between the wars for the first time the statutes of an international organization, the International Labor Organization (ILO), were officially described as a *constitution* ("Constitution of the International Labor

---

[32] Dieter Grimm, ed., *Wachsende Staatsaufgaben—sinkende Steuerungsfähigkeit des Rechts* (Baden-Baden, DE: Nomos, 1990). Also cf. Dieter Grimm, "Der Wandel der Staatsaufgaben und die Krise des Rechtsstaats," in *Die Zukunft der Verfassung* (Frankfurt: Suhrkamp, 1991). Compare also Niklas Luhmann, *Das Recht der Gesellschaft* (Frankfurt: Suhrkamp, 1993), translated into English as Luhmann, *Law as a Social System* (Oxford: Oxford University Press, 2004); also compare the classic statement of Luhmann, "Der Funktionswandel des Gesetzes im Recht der bürgerlichen Gesellschaft," *Zeitschrift für Sozialforschung* 6, no. 3 (1937): 542–96.

[33] For a historically instructive perspective from a New Deal activist, see William Seagle, *The Quest of Law* (New York: Alfred A. Knopf, 1941). Also relevant is Hartmut Maurer, *Allgemeines Verwaltungsrecht*, 16th ed. (München: Beck, 2006), §16.

[34] Niklas Luhmann, *Politische Theorie im Wohlfahrtsstaat* (München: Olzog, 1981); Berman, *Justice in the USSR*, esp. 277ff. On an astounding and curious parallel between Soviet paternalistic (*erzieherischen*) law and the Puritan code of the Massachusetts Bay Colony, the "Body of Liberties" of 1641, see Harold Berman, *Recht und Revolution*, 64f. With a view toward the beginning of the 1930s, see Christian Joerges and Navraj Singh Ghaleigh, eds., *Darker Legacies of Law in Europe: The Shadow of National Socialism and Fascism over Europe and its Legal Traditions* (Oxford: Hart Publishing, 2003).

Organization").[35] But it was only in the period between 1941 and 1951 that the overthrow of all the fundamental norms of international law that began with the Versailles Treaty and the creation of the League of Nations became irreversible. The first truly *global constitutional order*, a new *system of inter-, trans-, and supranational institutions*, was created in the 1940s. This is the time of the most important groundings and foundational documents of the new international community: the Atlantic Charter of 1941; the Bretton Woods Agreement of 1944; the International Monetary Fund (1944); the World Bank (1944); the United Nations and the UN Charter (1945); the Nuremburg and Tokyo Tribunals in 1945, which became the paradigm for all later inter- and supranational criminal justice; the General Agreement on Tariffs and Trade (GATT) (1948), from which the World Trade Organization (WTO) later emerged; the Universal Declaration of Human Rights of the same year, a document that at first lacked any legally binding force but was step by step converted into positive international law and regional human rights instruments starting in 1966; and finally the grounding of the first European Community in 1951, from which further enterprises of this kind have followed in almost all regions of the world.

The system of post-national institutions has not only been sustained since the end of the Second World War, it has grown ever stronger and more influential. With its help, the entire surface of the earth was converted into the territory of legally equal national states subject to international law. Whether they wanted it or not,[36] these states became *legally open*.[37] They became unexpectedly ever more dependent on a continuously thicker network of inter-, trans-, and supranational organizations that they themselves had created and whose main actors they still are. Things simply cannot function anymore without the World Health Organization (WHO), the WTO, the Organization for Economic Cooperation and Development (OECD) Council, the Basel Banking Committee, the European Council, and the UN Security Council. To an increasing degree, these bodies no longer simply *supplement* the functions of the state, but also are beginning to *substitute* for them more and more often (and not just on purely technical matters), even when they are formally still organized as intergovernmental entities. At the same time, a larger proportion of the purely technical norms created by international committees of experts going back

[35] Bardo Faßbender, "Grund und Grenzen der konstitutionellen Idee im Völkerrecht," in *Staat im Wort: Festschrift für Josef Isensee*, eds. Otto Depenheuer, Markus Heintzen, Matthias Jestaedt, and Peter Axer (Heidelberg: Müller, 2007), 73–91, 74.

[36] Just think of the apartheid regime in South Africa, Iranian atomic politics, or Guantanamo; even the death penalty in the United States or the intervention of the Russians in Georgia have long since become public affairs of the international community.

[37] On the concept of open states, see Rainer Wahl, *Verfassungsstaat, Europäisierung, Internationalisierung* (Frankfurt: Suhrkamp, 2003); Udo Di Fabio, *Das Recht offener Staaten: Grundlinien einer Staates-und Rechttheorie* (Tübingen: Mohr, 1998).

all the way to the 19th century have become loaded with aspects that touch upon fundamental rights—from general conditions of labor, gender equality, environmental sustainability, and so on.[38] In the web of international organizations, interstate relations are mutating step by step into a strongly decentralized, pluralized, and fragmented *global polity without a state* (*Weltstaatlichkeit ohne Staat*).[39] Of course, the social dimensions of legal membership are highly fragmented, and that poses a problem for democracy and the rule of law, to which I will return. But it is no longer certain that the global legal community is more fragmented than states like Cameroon or Tanzania. Even India and China probably also have, internally, legal orders that are similarly highly fragmented. The European Union, the United States, and even classical national states like the Federal Republic of Germany or France are also not spared from the trend toward fragmentation.[40] From the perspective of the legal revolution of the 20th century, the classical national state, which even the anti-metaphysician Max Weber had still described using the metaphysical predicate of "unbreakability,"[41] appears to be a strongly idealized and short-lived (1850–1915), limiting case of a great diversity of federal and imperial political forms of organization in Europe—forms without a unified and thoroughgoing monopoly of

---

[38] For a commentary on Gunther Teubner's systems theory approach towards transnational law, see Rainer Nickel, "The Missing Link in Global Law: Regime Collisions, Societal Constitutionalism, and Participation in Global Governance. A Comment on Gunther Teubner's Systems Theory Approach Towards Transnational law," in *Globalisation, Law and Economy/Globalización, Derecho y Economía: Proceedings of the 22nd World Congress of the International Association for Philosophy of Law and Social Philosophy, Granada 2005,* vol. 4, ed. Nicolás López Calera (Stuttgart: Franz Steiner Verlag, 2007), 237–50.

[39] See the contributions in Matthias Albert and Rudolf Stichweh, eds., *Weltstaat und Weltstaatlichkeit* (Wiesbaden, DE: Verlag für Sozial, 2007); for an earlier statement than this, see Matthias Albert, "Politik der Weltgesellschaft und Politik der Globalisierung: Überlegungen zur Emergenz von Weltstaatlichkeit," *Zeitschrift für Soziologie* 34, Sonderheft Weltgesellschaft (2005): 223–38; See also Mathias Albert and Rainer Schmalz-Bruns, "Antinomien der Global Governance: Mehr Welstaatlichkeit, weniger Demokratie?," in *Demokratie in der Weltgesellschaft*, ed. Hauke Brunkhorst (Baden-Baden, DE: Nomos, 2009), 57–74. Generally and critically on the thesis of a world polity formation (*Weltstaatlichkeitsthese*), see alongside the just cited collection, Friedrich Müller, *Demokratie zwischen Staatsrecht und Weltrecht* (Berlin: Duncker & Humblot, 2003), 119; Matthias Lutz-Bachmann and James Bohman, eds., *Weltstaat oder Staatenwelt?* (Frankfurt: Suhrkamp, 2002). For a perspective critical of imperialism, see Bhupinder S. Chimni, "International Institutions Today: An Imperial Global State in the Making," *European Journal of International Law* 15, no. 1 (2004): 1–37.

[40] Prien, "Fragmentierte Volkssouveränität." On fragmentation, see also the contributions of Tanja Hitzel-Cassagnes, Nadja Meisterhans, and Jürgen Bast in *Demokratie in der Weltgesellschaft*, ed. Hauke Brunkhorst (Baden-Baden, DE: Nomos, 2009).

[41] Max Weber, *Wirtschaft und Gesellschaft*, Bd. II. (Köln: Halbband, 1964), 1060, translated into English as Weber, *Economy and Society*, vol. 2, eds. Guenter Roth and Claus Wittich (Berkeley, CA: University of California Press, 1978).

violence, territory, and people centered on a state and lacking in centralized sovereignty (whatever that is).[42]

The rapid evolution of a complex international system of institutions, the globalization of the national state, and the emergence of a global polity without a state have been made possible by the revolutionary founding acts at the close of World War II, which had their "constitutional moment" in the signing of the Charter of the United Nations on June 26, 1945 in San Francisco.[43]

First, the Charter supplemented the horizontal *law of coordination* inherited from the Treaty of Westphalia with a vertical *law of subordination* (Art. 103) that derogates all contrary international treaties and also expressly binds all non-members to the aims and principles of the Charter (Arts. 1 and 2). Second, it replaces the *imperative of coexistence* of the old *jus publicum europaeum* with a *duty of cooperation* (Art. 1, par. 2, 3, and 4; Art. 2, par. 6).[44] Third, it does away with the fundamental legal principle of the old international law—the equal right of (European, "Christian," "civilized") states to wage war (*jus ad bellum*) and to impose their "authority" on the remaining part of the world without states—and replaces it with the exceptionless *equality of all states and peoples before the law of the international community* (Art. 2, par. 1).[45] For the first time in history, *wars of aggression* and *annexations* are proscribed, *war is made illegal*, and *all warlike actions are submitted to the decisions of the Security Council* (Art. 2, par. 4).[46] Finally, the principles of *the right of self-determination of peoples* (Art. 1, par. 2) and *human rights* (Art. 1, par. 3), which had already been pronounced in the constitutional revolutions of the 18th century, are

---

[42] One thinks for instance of the National Rifle Association in the United States, Guantanamo, the Schengen borders or the Catalans and Scots, non-EU foreigners, foreigners with EU voting rights in some EU member states, or the Swiss Constitution, which, like the EU Treaties, leaves open the "sovereignty" question between "the Swiss people and the Cantons" (preamble). Are the citizens of the United States who live in Georgia the constituent people (*Staatsvolk*) of the union or of Georgia? That was at least not so clear to the judges of the Supreme Court just several years ago: it gave a five to four decision in favor of the priority of the national union. The dissenters declared that "when the people of Georgia pick their representatives in Congress, they are acting as the people of Georgia, not as the corporate agents for the undifferentiated people of the Nation as a whole" (514 U.S. 858 (Thomas, J., dissenting)). See Christoph Schönberger, "Föderale Angehörigkeit" (Habilitation, University of Freiburg, 2005).

[43] Bardo Faßbender, "The United Nations Charter as Constitution of the International Community," *Columbia Journal of Transnational Law* 36 (1998): 529–619.

[44] Wolfgang Friedmann, *The Changing Structure of International Law* (London: Stevens & Sons, 1964).

[45] In contradistinction to *equal sovereignty*, the *sovereign equality* of Art. 2, par. 1, UN Charter, means equality before the law. Faßbender, "The United Nations Charter."

[46] Since the coming into force of the Charter, there have hardly been any formal annexations of foreign state territory. The most striking case was the illegal annexation of the Western Sahara by Morocco in 1975.

declared to be the highest principles of the Charter. Symbolically polishing off the text, we have also a pluralization of the *democratic rhetoric* of the US Constitution in the preamble: "We the Peoples of the United Nations."

In the meantime, from a constitutional perspective, the legal revolution in the world of states has *delegitimated almost all nominal alternatives to democracy*. Between 1789 and 1945 there were only a small number of democratic constitutional documents. At the beginning of the 21st century, only Saudi Arabia dispensed with any reference to democracy in a brief constitutional text that prescribes an Islamic hereditary monarchy, and China and Iran were almost the last formal constitutional regimes that combine democratic popular power with undemocratic theocracy or party dictatorship—very much in the way the English constitution of the 18th century or that of the German Reich in the 19th century combined citizen self-determination with an area of arcane, executive special powers or princely rights of initiative, veto, and prerogative. By now there is even talk of a fourth generation of human rights, the "emerging right to democratic governance,"[47] and an international legal principle of *democratic inclusion* that steps in beside the community of states as a second level of political legitimation in the eyes of citizens.[48]

Last but not least, the global legal revolution has transformed *human rights* into *rights of world citizenship* and thereby recognized the *international legal personality* of individual human beings.[49] For better or worse, the implementation of the Charter and Universal Declaration have made the Security Council, and more recently the International Criminal Court, guardians of individual human rights. In doing so, of course, rather arbitrary and often disproportional military interventions have been justified as police actions.[50] Not only that, the Security Council has effectively

[47] Thomas Franck, "The Emerging Right to Democratic Governance," *American Journal of International Law* 86, no. 1 (1992): 46–91; Christina M. Cerna, "Universal Democracy: An International Legal Right or the Pipe Dream of the West?," *New York University Journal of International Law and Politics* 27, no. 2 (1995): 289–329; Müller, *Demokratie zwischen Staatsrecht und Weltrecht*, 52.

[48] Susan Marks, *The Riddle of all Constitutions* (Oxford: Oxford University Press, 2000).

[49] Kay Hailbronner, "Der Staat und der Einzelne als Völkerrechtssubjekte," in *Völkerrecht*, 4th ed., ed. Wolfgang Graf Vitzthum (Berlin: de Gruyter, 2007), 157–264, 167ff, 228 ff. Kelsen had already derived the international legal personality of individual human beings from the Versailles Treaty (Arts. 227–230). See Hans Kelsen, "Der völkerrechtliche Strafanspruch wegen völkerrechtswidriger Kriegshandlungen," *Neue Freie Presse*, September 8, 1920 (Wein), 3–4. Hans Kelsen, "La Théorie générale du Droit International Public," *Recueil des cours (de l'Académie de droit international)* 42, no. 4 (1932): 117–351, 141ff, 155 ff; see also Cristina Hoss, "Kelsen in Den Haag. Die Haager Vorlesungen von Hans Kelsen," in *Rechts-Staat*, eds. Hauke Brunkhorst and Rüdiger Voigt (Baden-Baden, DE: Nomos, 2008), 157f; Jochen von Bernstorff, *Der Glaube an das universale Recht: zur Völkerrechtstheorie Hans Kelsens und seiner Schüler* (Baden-Baden, DE: Nomos, 2001), 128f.

[50] Hauke Brunkhorst, ed., *Einmischung Erwünscht? Menschenrechte und Bewaffnete Intervention* (Frankfurt: Fisher, 1998).

declared every single person to be a potential risk to world peace in the intense "listing of terrorists" in which it has engaged since the 1990s under chapter 7 of the Charter. So it is no longer the case that only states or recognized parties to civil wars can be threats to world order. Compared to this legal practice, Guantanamo's illegality is child's play. However, the listing of terrorists reveals the individual citizen to be, at the very moment when he or she stands eye to eye with states and the world of states as subjects of international law, suddenly without effective rights, a *legal subject* in the classical sense of *sujet* or *subjectum*; a dominated body.

But even this dark side of the law of world citizenship (*Weltbürgerrecht*) shows the growing juridification of world law (*Weltrecht*) and the continuation of the revolutionary rebirth of 1945—after all, even the French Revolution brought forth not only, as Marx said, an "Eden of the innate rights of man,"[51] but also a new secret police. And the first post-revolutionary constitution of France was anything but democratic and republican and nevertheless was a product of the revolution, the *Charte Constitutionelle* of the reestablished, but now *constitutionalized*, monarchy. The constitutional question could no longer be avoided in Europe.[52]

The constitutional question was also placed on the agenda by the global legal revolution of the 20th century, and the UN Charter was conceived from the very beginning as a *constitution* of the international community with the "typical features of a (state) constitution" and was also adopted as such by its signers.[53] It marks the first appearance in history of a genuinely

---

[51] Karl Marx, *Capital*, vol. 1, trans. Ben Fowkes (New York: Penguin Books).

[52] Volker Sellin, *Die geraubte Revolution* (Göttingen: Vandenhoeck & Ruprecht, 2001).

[53] Faßbender, "The United Nations Charter," 77. On the UN Charter as the constitution of the international community, see Pierre-Marie Dupuy, "The Constitutional Dimension of the Charter of the United Nations Revisited," *Max Planck Yearbook of United Nations Law* 1 (1997): 1–33; Faßbender, "The United Nations Charter." On [the UN Charter as] only the constitutionalization of international law, see Jochen A. Frowein, "Konstitutionalisierung des Völkerrechts," in *Völkerrecht und Internationales Privatrecht in einem sich globalisierenden internationalen System. Berichte der Deutschen Gesellschaft für Völkerrecht,* vol. 39, eds. Klaus Dicke et al. (Heidelberg: Müller, 2000), 427–47; Christian Tomuschat, "International Law as the Constitution of Mankind," in *International Law on the Eve of the Twenty-First Century: Views from the International Law Commission* (New York: United Nations, 1997), 37–50; Brun-Otto Bryde, "Konstituionalisierung des Völkerrechts und Internationalisierung des Verfassungsbegriffs," *Der Staat* 1 (2003): 61–75; Andreas Fischer-Lescano, *Globalverfassung: Die Geltungsbegründung der Menschenrechte* (Weilerswist, DE: Velbrück Wissenschaft, 2005), Kap. 5f; Gunther Teubner, "Globale Zivilverfassungen," *Zeitschrift fur auslanderisches öffentliches Recht und Völkerrecht* 63, no. 1 (2003): 1–28; Andreas Fischer-Lescano, "Die Emergenz der Globalverfassung," *Zeitschrift für ausländisches öffentliches Recht und Völkerrecht* 63, no. 3 (2003): 717–60. Andreas Fischer-Lescano and Gunther Teubner, *Regime-Kollisionen: Zur Fragmentierung des globalen Rechts* (Frankfurt: Suhrkamp Verlag, 2006); Robert Uerpmann, "Internationales Verfassungsrecht," *JuristenZeitung* (2001): 565–73; Armin von Bogdandy, "Constitutionalism in International Law: Comment on a Proposal from Germany," *Harvard International Law Journal* 47, no. 1 (2006): 223–42.

universal law of treaties between peoples (*Völkervertragsrecht*), and as such a *formal constitutional law of peoples* (*formelles Völkerverfassungsrecht*). The Charter of the United Nations is what the League of Nations, according to its "idea" and purpose, was meant to become: the formal constitution of the "comprehensive community of states,"[54] the "constitution" of the "community of states" "in a formal sense,"[55] which "derogates" any contrary, preexisting international customary or treaty law and "in whose light" the entire body of international law "must be interpreted."[56] The constitutional task of 1945 was also put into action by the international community. The Vienna Conference on the Law of Treaties of 1971 and the *Barcelona Traction* decision of the International Court of Justice of 1970 made the principle of *jus cogens* and obligations *erga omnes* into the foundation of all international law.[57] *States are thus immediately accountable to and subjected to*[58] the "international community as a whole,"[59] even if it has not only an address in Geneva or New York, but many changing addresses that may have constitutions that are in stark conflict, both with each other and with the UN Charter.[60] In Resolution 554, the Security Council even declared a state constitution, that of South Africa, to be "null and void" on this basis.[61]

---

[54] Alfred Verdross, *Die Verfassung der Völkerrechtsgemeinschaft*, 2nd ed. [1926] (Berlin/Vienna: Springer, 1950), 112.

[55] Ibid., 74, cited in Faßbender, "The United Nations Charter," 77.

[56] Alfred Verdross and Bruno Simma, *Universelles Völkerrecht* (Berlin: Springer, 1984), VIIf.

[57] Vienna Convention on the Law of Treaties, Art. 53. See Stefan Kadelbach, *Zwingendes Völkerrecht* (Frankfurt am Main: Duncker & Humblot, 1992), 41ff.

[58] On the way this (hesitantly) creates a positive legal transition from a law of coordination to a law of subordination, see Christian Tomuschat, "Die internationale Gemeinschaft," *Archiv des Völkerrechts* 1, no. 7 (1995): 1–20; comprehensively, see Andreas Paulus, "Die internationale Gemeinschaft im Völkerrecht," (Dissertation, University of Munich, 2000); cf. also Christian Walter, "Constitutionalizing (Inter) national Governance—Possibilities for and Limits to the Development of an International Constitutional Law," *German Yearbook of International Law* 44 (2001): 170–201; Christian Tomuschat, "Die völkerrechtlichen Grundlagen der Zivilgesellschaft: Internationale Abkommen als Garanten internationaler Solidarität," in *Transnationale Solidarität*, eds. Jens Beckert et al. (Frankfurt am Main: Campus, 2004), 135–47; Anne Peters, "Compensatory Constitutionalism: The Function and Potential of Fundamental International Norms and Structures," *Leiden Journal of International Law* 19, no. 3 (2006): 579–610; and more recently, Ulrich K. Preuß, "The Twilight of Constitutional Law: Demise or Transformation?," paper presented at the Workshop of the Wissenschaftskolleg zu Berlin, June 19–20, 2008. For a skeptical view about world federalist inferences, see Stefan Oeter, "Internationale Organisation oder Weltföderation? Die organisierte Staatengemeinschaft und das Verlangen nach einer 'erfassung der Freiheit,'" in *Globalisierung und Demokratie*, eds. Hauke Brunkhorst and Matthias Kettner (Frankfurt am Main: Suhrkamp, 2000), 208–39, 229; Fischer-Lescano, *Globalverfassung*.

[59] On the key passage from the *Barcelona Traction* decision of the International Court of Justice, see Paulus, "Die internationale Gemeinschaft im Völkerrecht."

[60] On the latter, see Fischer-Lescano and Teubner, *Regime-Kollisionen*.

[61] Tomuschat, "Die internationale Gemeinschaft," 18.

Just as in the then revolutionary theories of international law developed in the 1920s by Hans Kelsen, Alfred Verdross, and Georges Scelle, state constitutions have become *component constitutions* of a trans- and supranational network of constitutions. At the time, those theories were opposed, lampooned, and ridiculed by supposed "realists" and adherents of *realpolitik*.[62] The old order of international law of the Peace of Augsburg, the Treaty of Westphalia, and the Vienna Congress—which found its constitutional credo in the positivist focus on the "will of the state" in late 19th and early 20th-century jurisprudence a "logical imperialism" of atomistic sovereign states—has given way to the *civitas maxima* of a world legal community that *normatively* stands above states which are no longer even constitutionally autonomous. The formal organs for the "development, application and implementation of international law," whose limitation to states (Art. 39 of the International Court of Justice (ICJ) Statute) was still bemoaned by Kelsen in 1920 as the great flaw of a "primitive" legal condition,[63] have long since grown into a highly differentiated (and multiply fragmented) *global system of the division of powers*. In this order, states and their often very autonomous bureaucratic agencies, which even partly become decoupled from the state's constitutional order, must play their part *above*, *alongside*, and *beneath* the other (public and increasingly also private or hybrid) organs developing, applying, and implementing international law.[64]

Meanwhile, international lawyers are already speaking of an internationalization of the *pouvoir constituant*, the constitution-generating or constituent power. [65] In any case, it has been true at least since 1989 that there is no founding of a state or constitutional revolution that is not more or less intensively regulated by the international community. Even a regime like that of contemporary Iran cannot entirely defy the international legal duty of cooperation (*Kooperationsgebot*), and even China must live with the normative pressure of positively binding human rights that limit its constitutional autonomy.

World law no longer has any exterior. Today the United States itself can only operate *within* this system of universal law.[66] It can break the law without always having to reckon with sanctions (just like any intrastate agency

---

62 Kelsen, *Das Problem der Souveränität*; Verdross, *Die Verfassung der Völkerrechtsgemeinschaft*; Georges Scelle, "Essai de Systematique de Droit International," *Revue Générale International de Public* 30 (1923): 116–42.

63 Kelsen, *Das Problem der Souveränität*, 320.

64 Christoph Möllers, *Gewaltengliederung: Legitimization and Dogmatik im internationalen Rechtsvergleich* (Tübingen: Mohr, 2005).

65 Philipp Dann and Zaid Ali-Ali, "The Internationalized *Pouvoir Constituant*—Constitution-Making Under External Influence in Iraq, Sudan and East Timor," *Max Planck Yearbook of United Nations Law* 10 (2006): 423–63. See also the debate between Arato, Dann, and Kemmerer in Brunkhorst, *Demokratie in der Weltgesellschaft*.

66 Michael Byers, "Preemptive Self-Defense: Hegemony, Equality and Strategies of Legal Change," *The Journal of Political Philosophy* 11, no. 2 (2003): 171–190.

too, as the case of the Bavarian government in the "Kreuzurteil" case of the German Constitutional Court shows). But it cannot escape the legal code that classifies each of its actions as legal or illegal—even at Guantanamo. Like any intrastate actor that has the necessary power or sufficient influence, even the United States can only attempt to make the international legal order amenable to its interests.[67] The success of the United States in this endeavor is comparable to that of groups like the Republican Party, the aerospace industry, or the National Rifle Association within its own national legal system, where these actors have pursued their own interests with similarly robust strategies as George W. Bush used regarding international law. However, the decisive point regarding the legalization and constitutionalization of world society is that the formation of hegemonic status is now only possible through legal action and the development of new law and is no longer bound to territorial centers.[68]

Beyond this, between 1941 and 1951, the Atlantic Charter, the Philadelphia Declaration (1944) of the ILO and texts of the UN Charter, the Universal Declaration, and the global and regional human rights covenants with their heavy load of social rights have created all the essential presuppositions, if not of a global welfare state, then a global form of state-like policy implementation regarding social rights and socialization in general: "the ideal foundation of global social policy was already part of the founding international legal documents of the world society in the form of social human rights."[69] It was only after the Second World War that *democratic welfare capitalism* became unleashed all over the OECD world in the crucible of *national* welfare state formations (*Staatlichkeit*). But even *before* the actual development of national welfare state regimes the programmatic outlines of *welfare internationalism* had already been formulated. In this development towards a global welfare regime the "strong role of the law" is notable: "global social policy is, even more than at the national level, global social law."[70] Even the *educational policy* of the states of the world has become considerably unified since the 1940s. This development is due above all to the "soft law effects" set off by several UNESCO studies and the permanent, solidly institutionalized PISA comparisons of educational systems, or through (highly divided) arrangements like the Bologna process.[71]

---

[67] Ibid., 189.

[68] On the de-territorialization of hegemony in world law, see Fischer-Lescano and Teubner, *Regime-Kollisionen*.

[69] Lutz Leisering, "Gibt es einen Weltwohlfahrtsstaat?," in *Weltstaat und Weltstaatlichkeit*, eds. Matthias Albert and Rudolf Stichweh (Wiesbaden: VS Verlag, 2007), 185–205, 189.

[70] Leisering, "Gibt es einen Weltwohlfahrtsstaat?," 200.

[71] Instructive here is John W. Meyer, "World Society and the Nation-State," *American Journal of Sociology* 103, no. 1 (1997): 144–81; Meyer, *Weltkultur* (Frankfurt am Main: Suhrkamp, 2005).

As we saw above, until the middle of the 20th century the dark side of the *national state's exclusion of inequality* consisted in legally fixated inequality for all those individuals, organizations, and political regimes that did not belong to the world of states centered on the North Atlantic. A juridically compelling claim to the exclusion of inequality at the global level did not exist.

That changed dramatically after the Second World War. Of course, massive human rights violations, the social exclusion of entire regions of the world, and outrageously arbitrary and discriminatory treatment have not disappeared. But now, for the first time, human rights violations, lawlessness, and political and social inequality are understood as *our own problem*, as a problem that affects *every* actor in the world society, and finally there are serious and *legally binding* claims to the *global exclusion of inequality*.[72] For the first time the *inequality* produced by increasing *difference* (functional and cultural differentiation) can be *characterized* as *legally unacceptable* (*unzumutbar*) and *experienced* as a *violation of law* that is, in Kant's words, "felt everywhere."[73] To that extent one can no longer speak with Luhmann of a merely functionally or negatively integrated world society, but must speak with Rudolf Stichweh of a *normatively integrated world society*.[74]

3 WORLD SOCIETY AND WORLD CULTURE

The world legal revolution created all the presuppositions for the radical change in the *social structure* of the world society that has occurred since the end of World War II. Functional systems have globalized themselves in such a way as only to allow states to occupy their places as organizing subsystems that must share their labor with ever more influential international governmental and non-governmental organizations. The globalization of functional systems, in particular international markets and national educational institutions, has led to a situation in which the *life chances* of all people who live in the beginning of the 21st century are without exception determined by *functional differentiation, being primarily dependent on success in school and in the labor market*. All of the social, cultural, political, and regional differences that distribute these chances unequally do not at all

---

[72] Most recently, Regina Kreide, *Globale Politik und Menschenrechte. Macht und Ohnmacht eines politischen Instruments* (Frankfurt: Campus-Verlag, 2008).

[73] In English, see the section on "cosmopolitan right" (*Weltbürgerrecht*) in Immanuel Kant, "Perpetual Peace: A Philosophical Sketch," in *Kant: Political Writings*, ed. Hans Reiss (Cambridge: Cambridge University Press, 1991), 93–130, 108. In German, see the section on *Weltbürgerrecht* in Kant, *Zum ewigen Frieden*, in *Werke* XI (Frankfurt am Main: 1977), 191–251.

[74] Rudolf Stichweh, "Der Zusammenhalt der Weltgesellschaft: Nicht-normative Integrationstheorien in der Soziologie," in *Transnationale Solidarität. Chancen und Grenzen*, eds. Jens Becker et al. (Frankfurt am Main: Campus, 2004), 236–45.

change the fact that the fortunes of each and every person (since the annihilation of the last household-based economies in the wake of decolonialization and de-Sovietization)[75] are subject to the high selectivity of these two systems, which do not eliminate, but rather strengthen and enlarge, social and cultural differences (if there is no corrective intervention).[76] The basis, the *social structure of functional differentiation,* is everywhere the same. And along with the other discursive powers of modern society and its state, the *police*, the *clinic*, the *military*, and the *prison*, *involuntary membership in schools and firms* produces everywhere the same *disciplinary individual*.[77]

Along with the material base, the cultural semantics, collective consciousness, and knowledge of the world, society changes: "the entire, monstrous superstructure undergoes upheaval more or less rapidly."[78] Lone human individuals are not just exposed to an external, *compulsory individualization* by this uniform social structure. A thoroughly *secular world culture* shapes the secular *as well as* the (predominantly) non-secular *lifeworlds*, *intrinsic motives*, and "habits of the heart," in the sense of a modern *individualism* and *rationalism*, whether it be communitarian ("Asian values") or liberal ("Western values"). In this way the various diverse regionally and locally shaped, religiously minded or atheistic, liberal or paternalistic ancestral cultures have fallen into *a dependent relationship* with globally accessible cultural knowledge and secular value orientations. Within a very short period, individualistic and consumerist life styles have spread through all regions of the world, in poor, fundamentalist areas as well as rich, liberal ones. The global cultural revolution is particularly easy to observe in religious fundamentalism. Instead of preserving and renewing religious traditions, it annihilates and decontextualizes them, politically instrumentalizes them, individualizes and atomizes them even to the perversion of a (highly individualistic) suicide bomber.[79] And even when it reaches a higher state, it transforms them into the functional equivalent of the protestant work ethic.[80]

---

[75] Even in the Soviet Union the old form of *household common property* was preserved, a kind of *oikos* within the *Kolchosen* economy that had its own types of rights and property distinct from private property and state property. For an informative view of the legal history, see Berman, *Justice in the USSR*.
[76] Still paradigmatic here is Marx, *Capital*.
[77] Foucault, *Discipline and Punish*.
[78] Karl Marx, *A Contribution to the Critique of Political Economy* (New York: International Publishers, 1904), 12 (translation emended).
[79] Peter L. Berger, "The Desecularization of the World: A Global Overview," in *The Desecularization of the World: Resurgent Religion and World Politics*, ed. Peter L. Berger (Washington, DC: Ethics and Policy Center, 1999), 1–18; Olivier Roy, *Der islamistische Weg nach Westen. Globalisierung, Entwurzelung und Radikalisierung* (Bonn: Bundeszentrale für Politische Bildung, 2006); Manuel A. Vasques and Marie F. Marquardt, eds., *Globalizing the Sacred: Religion Across the Americas* (New Brunswick: Rutgers University Press, 2003).
[80] Berger, *The Desecularization of the World.*

The superstructure also shapes the base. The surprisingly high degree of *uniformity in action* on the part of world-societal actors (individuals, states, organizations) cannot be understood simply on the basis of the purely negative (necessary) conditions of global functional systems. As John W. Meyer and the empirical investigations of the Stanford School have shown, this requires the assumption (functioning as a sufficient condition) of a constitutive world culture that shapes all actors of the world society (in a macro-phenomenological sense): an almost isomorphic organizational structure, a high degree of similarity of goals, and an extensive agreement in value orientations and social techniques and socialization practices that has only existed in the last several decades.[81] During recent educational reforms one saw almost everywhere the same 6-3-3 schema of school stages applied and the same model of student-centered instruction introduced. The law of almost every state has been thoroughly positivized and academically professionalized; constitutional and ordinary laws have been separated. In the shortest time, an extensive and influential constitutional jurisprudence has emerged almost everywhere. Governments resemble each other in their organizational structures as one egg does another. Everywhere there are ministers and secretaries of state, educational and environmental agencies; almost everywhere, there are anti-discrimination quotas, women's rights, and officials overseeing the enforcement of equal civil rights. And the political leaders of every country, whether they are communists or capitalists, religious fundamentalists or secularist atheists, promise progress, growth, peace, environmental protection, and social justice—in this George W. Bush was no different than Vladimir Putin or Mahmoud Ahmadinejad. They refer to each other constantly and form each other into Ego and Alter just as George Herbert Mead described. Their political programs are almost exchangeable and everywhere one sees the same gap between progressive rhetoric and slow, limping achievement. For some this is the spur to further efforts (United States), and for others it is grounds for resignation (Brazil). For some, it is a motive for upholding international law (Gerhard Schröder), for others a reason to break it (George W. Bush).

This unified world culture does not make cultural differences disappear, but is precisely what makes them visible and turns them into the object of collective projections of identity. In fact it continually produces new cultures of every kind and fashion. Without it there would neither be the requisite patterns (usually invented in Paris, London, or New York, from "national liberation" to "cultural studies" to "postcolonialism") nor the possibilities of comparison necessary for sharply contoured boundaries and self-identifications. In Indian villages, one no longer compares oneself with the neighboring village or the English, but rather with *the* West or *the* global hegemon (*Weltmacht*).

---

[81] See, for example, John W. Meyer, *World Society: The Writings of John W. Meyer*, eds. Georg Krücken and Gili S. Drori (Oxford: Oxford University Press, 2009).

Finally, only the intertwinement of the "hard law" of international positive human rights with the soft medium of a world culture to which human rights belong as a cultural object of identification ("a culture of human rights")[82] explains the astonishing effectiveness of *global blaming and shaming* in the struggle against the torturing agents of dictators and totalitarian rulers.[83] The *society-wide* structure of functional differentiation, which is everywhere the same (despite quite different *social* structures), has created problems that affect all human beings *simultaneously*. But only the unified world *culture* turns global problems into the controversial affairs of a world public. The complementary development of society and culture has already led to the formation of political frontlines that cut right through states and on both sides of which the parties of a transnational world domestic policy driven from below are beginning to appear. The partisans of Venus and Mars, of human rights and *realpolitik*, of global redistribution and Fortress Europe-Japan-North America are as numerous in Europe as they are in the United States, and come from all over the world. They are linked to each other across borders and continents through the Internet and networks of non-governmental organizations (NGOs) and thereby diminish the significance of the old geopolitical blocks. With that I come to the controversial problems of the world public.

4 CONSTITUTION AND DEMOCRACY

Even if protagonists of the *civitas maxima*, the League of Nations, world law, and democracy, like Hans Kelsen or Georges Scelle, have in the end been proven right against Carl Schmitt and Hans Morgenthau, the *civitas maxima* in which and with which we must live today is far from having a good constitution. Legalization, constitutionalization, and the rule *of* law do not *per se* lead to democracy, but always strengthen the form of rule or domination (*Herrschaft*) that already exists or is coming to be. There is no stable and efficacious dictatorship without rule *through* law (and thus at least a minimum of the rule *of* law). The power of both democratic and undemocratic rule, as the Roman senators and emperors already knew, first becomes stable, effective, and, above all, augmentable through law.[84] The

---

[82] Richard Rorty, "Human Rights, Rationality and Sentimentality," in *On Human Rights*, eds. Stephen Shute and Susan Hurley (New York: Basic Books, 1993), 112–34.
[83] Thomas Risse, Stephen C. Ropp, and Kathryn Sikkink, eds., *The Power of Human Rights* (Cambridge: Cambridge University Press, 1999); Thomas Risse, Anja Jetschke, and Hans-Peter Schmitz, eds., *Die Macht der Menschenrechte. Internationale Normen, kommunikatives Handeln und politischer Wandel in den Ländern des Südens* (Baden-Baden, DE: Nomos, 2002); Nicole Deitelhoff, *Überzeugen in der Politik. Grundzüge einer Diskurstheorie des internationalen Regierens* (Frankfurt: Suhrkamp, 2006).
[84] "Roman law," writes Uwe Wesel, "was the law of the nobility. Classic means of course exemplary. And so Roman law is called since the end of the eighteenth century. But classical law was also class law, the law of the propertied among each other, in other words, civil law. With the others one made short shrift using means outside the law" (*Geschichte des Rechts* [München: Beck, 1997], 156).

constitutionalization of world law, world politics, and the world economy is therefore not by itself the solution to the problem of overcoming undemocratic rule (between and above states), but rather *part of the problem.* The contemporary constitution of the world society is a network of rights and organizational norms that reflects a pervasive contradiction between democratic solidarity and hegemonic world polity formation (*Weltstaatlichkeit*). Its basic law (*Verfassungsrecht*) is on the whole not democratic, but constitutionalist. The might of hegemonic powers that are halfway constitutionally limited is growing (quite rapidly too) at the expense of democratic solidarity—and the simultaneity of legalization and deformalization, and of unification and fragmentation transforms world law into a flexible and elastic order of great power spheres of influence, or *Grosraumordnung* (to use a favorite phrase of Carl Schmitt's from the 1930s), whose contours vary with the perspective of the given hegemon. In this way, the increased ability to hold together greater variety that our multicultural, highly individualized, and ever more specialized society obtains from constitutionalization[85] is accompanied by ever more intolerable differences between capital and labor, the included and the excluded, the mighty and the powerless, the believers and the unbelievers, the knowledgeable and the uneducated, the entitled and the rightless.[86] The division of the world into people with good passports and people with bad ones is reflected in the constitutional structure of the world society, which regularly allows egalitarian *ius cogens* rights and democratic lip service to be shattered and rendered mute by the hard law of undemocratic, organizational norms.

The systemic restabilization of the world society via the structural coupling of politics, law, and economics (functional constitution-making) enables the formation of *new forms of class rule*. With the establishment of world political and world legal structures *the ability of the national state to exclude inequality effectively disappears*, without any post-national compensation in sight.

This is particularly clear with regard to the three great structural problems (see above) with which modern society had to struggle when it was still a regional society ("the West") and which it once solved through the formation of states: the problems arising from the out of control, mutually blind, insensitive, and independent development of markets, executive powers, and religious value spheres.

The globalization of the former has turned the *state-embedded markets* of *national* late capitalism into the *market-embedded states* of *global* turbo-capitalism. The new capitalism, which has gratefully exchanged the

---

[85] Niklas Luhmann, "Arbeitsteilung und Moral. Durkheims Theorie," in *Über soziale Arbeitsteilung* (Frankfurt am Main: Suhrkamp, 1992), 19–38, 25.

[86] See Cristina Lafont, "Alternative Visions of a New Global Order. What should Cosmopolitans Hope For?," in *Demokratie in der Weltgesellschaft*, ed. Hauke Brunkhorst (Baden-Baden, DE: Nomos, 2009); Regina Kreide, "Why a Minimalist Notion of Justice is Not Enough," in the same volume.

narrow and rigid framework of democratic constitutional law for the light clothes of a flexible and elastic world law, has plunged the half-democratic, half-bureaucratic welfare state of the West into a deep crisis just as it was jubilantly celebrating its triumph over the dictatorial state of the East.[87] Once again the freedom *of* markets is being unleashed *at the expense* of freedom *from* their negative externalities, and the competitive struggle for fossil fuels is becoming ever more destructive: *There Will Be Blood.*[88]

What is good for capitalism is good for religion. Fundamentalist religious sects and networks and the Catholic Church have experimented with world polity-type organizational forms for almost a thousand years. They are the great winners of globalization, whereas the protestant state churches are the losers. The second great transformation has turned *state-embedded religions* into *religio-embedded states*. The anarchic freedom *of* religions that is gained thereby already threatens freedom *from* religion, while the instruments of the bureaucratic agencies of states and supra-state organizations do not seem sufficient to recivilize the unchained, destructive potential of the world religions: *There Will Be Blood.*

However it is not just *capitalism* and *religion* that have formed inter-, trans-, and supranational networks and torn loose from their state-based legal and organizational anchors. The same has occurred with *public executive powers*. The third great transformation turns *state-embedded public powers* into *power-embedded states*. Everywhere the winners of globalization are the fast and mobile executive branches, which have long since learned to act in globally networked and coordinated ways. As a consequence, here too the freedom *of* public power grows at the expense of freedom *from* public power.[89] For those of us in the North Atlantic, there is soft Bonapartism. For the others with the bad passports, there is the full severity of the state of exception: *There Will Be Blood.*[90]

---

87 Wolfgang Streek, "Sectoral Specialization: Politics and the Nation State in a Global Economy," paper presented on the 37th World Congress of the International Institute of Sociology, Stockholm. July 5–9, 2005.

88 *There Will Be Blood*, DVD, directed by Paul Thomas Anderson. 2007; United States: Miramax, 2008.

89 In other words, today the same problems of the misuse of power and law that the classical state constitution tried to solve are posed beyond the state. The discussion of the solution of these problems should no longer be intellectually disarmed by the caricature of the world state as a supposedly universal despotism: "The anti-world-state rhetoric overlooks the fact that today public power is already being exercised at the international level with an intensity that was unknown to the average modern state. So everything turns on just what exactly one means by 'world state' or a 'world government' and how one proposes to *organize* and *control* the exercise of international public power, which is long since a reality, *in a hierarchical ordering of legal norms* (*Stufenbau des Rechts*)" (Faßbender, "Grund und Grenzen," 79, see also 87f).

90 See China Miéville, *Between Equal Rights: A Marxist Theory of International Law* (Leiden: Brill, 2005); for a critique, see Susan Marks, "International Judicial Activism and the Commodity-Form Theory of International Law," *The European Journal of International Law* 18, no. 1 (2007): 199–211.

If the executive organs beyond the national state were *unified*, perhaps they could produce the power necessary to democratically reconstitutionalize the freedom of markets, religions, and executive organs and exclude the inequality of rights not only in a formal, legal sense, but effectively as well.[91] For that, however, they lack the *interest*. The interest in increasing one's power, which at least in countries like the Federal Republic of Germany is entirely democratically legitimated, binds together the united executive branches with the other global players, frequent travelers, and professionals, with the boards of firms, powerful NGOs, media tycoons, and television stars into a new *transnational class* with its *own class interests*, its own habitus and symbolic capital. The active *cosmopolitanism of the few* is separated from the passive *cosmopolitanism of the many*, who form a global precariat[92] that is only loosely networked and weakly organized by NGOs.[93]

The three great transformations of the world society have not only converted democratically legitimated power into the legitimation-free power of a *political-economic-professional ruling class* with its own "coterie of advocates, professors and spin doctors"[94] and the media stars of television and tabloid journalism. They have also led to a new transformation of the public sphere—this time of the world public sphere, of which the national and subnational public spheres have long become parts. Meanwhile, through an entire arsenal of techniques of bypassing public law and public opinion, almost every spontaneously emerging movement of the unorganized public, almost every untamed and anarchic formation of communicative power flows right past the center of the political decision-making process to be poured out into empty space. Picking up an idea of Jürgen Habermas's theory that traces back to Bernhard Peters,[95] it appears as though the filter that is supposed to cash out public opinion into political decisions has turned into a kind of reverse thrust that permanently provides for the silencing of the public. This is the European model! It is one of White Paper democracy, informative and transparent, deliberative and participatory. During the Bologna process there was a representative of civil society alongside those of states—namely, the delegate from the Bertelsmann firm. But there

[91] Whether that actually works is, as always, another question. But the point is of course to try.

[92] Pierre Bourdieu, "La Précarité est Aujourd'hui Partout [Precariousness is Everywhere Nowadays]," in *Contre-feux* (Paris: Raisons d'agir, 1988), 96–102.

[93] Craig Calhoun, "The Class Consciousness of Frequent Travelers," *The South Atlantic Quarterly* 101, no. 4 (2002).

[94] Karl Marx, *Der 18. Brumaire des Louis Bonaparte*, MEGA Bd. I/11 (Berlin: Deitz, 1985), 120.

[95] Bernhard Peters, *Der Sinn von Öffentlichkeit*, ed. Hartmut Weßler (Frankfurt am Main: Suhrkamp, 2007); Jürgen Habermas, *Between Facts and Norms: Contributions to a Discourse Theory of Law and Democracy*, trans. William Rehg (Cambridge, MA: MIT Press, 1996), originally published in German as Habermas, *Faktizität und Geltung* (Frankfurt am Main: Suhrkamp, 1992).

were no citizens, and no populism—no referendum, no genuine elections, no visible leaders or alternatives. In short, this was deliberation *instead* of democracy, public spirit *instead* of public opinion, good governance *instead* of democratic government.[96]

Under the pressure of the new hegemonic powers, legality degenerates ever further into a *concrete legal order*, and in the end to law as a mere instrument. For instance, the heads of the large central banks meet regularly behind closed doors in the rooms of a private bank in Basel and lay down the guidelines of global financial and monetary policies in a purely informal, but highly effective, soft law.[97] The news programs report about disagreements and spats at the G8 and European summits, but not about the fact that the most powerful heads of state are in agreement about most points of their ever longer agendas, and that for a long time now they have exercised something akin to a directorial competence to issue directives for the world society. The protests that regularly accompany these summit meetings may be hapless and often poorly justified, but they make the legitimation problem of the world society visible to everyone. What they allow us to see is the blockage in the democratic legitimation cycle symbolized by the fence that separates the included executive powers and TV journalists from the excluded power of citizens, who have created a new form of anarchic communication for themselves on the Internet. More than a democratic deficit, there is an institutional deficit that lies between those inside and those outside. No lawmaker has assigned competences to the loosely associated conferences and summit meetings of the executives, frequent travelers, and

---

[96] See the contributions of Gertrude Lübbe-Wolff, Alexander Somek, and Stefan Oeter in *Demokratie in der Weltgesellschaft*, ed. Hauke Brunkhorst (Baden-Baden, DE: Nomos, 2009).

[97] Christoph Möllers, "Transnationale Behördenkooperation. Verfassungs-und völkerrechtliche Probleme transnationaler administrativer Standardsetzung," *Zeitschrift für ausländisches öffentliches Recht und Völkerrecht* 65 (2003): 351–89. Transnational administrative law, which studies transnational networks of governance agencies, has become its own academic subdiscipline in the last few years. Compare Anne van Aaken, "Democracy in Times of Transnational Administrative Law: The Case of Financial Markets," in *Demokratie in der Weltgesellschaft*, ed. Hauke Brunkhorst (Baden-Baden, DE: Nomos, 2009). See further Christian Tietje, "Die Staatsrechtslehre und die Veränderung ihres Gegenstandes," *Deutsches Verwaltungsblatt* 17 (2003): 1081–164; Nico Krisch and Benedict Kingsbury, "Symposium: Global Governance and Global Administrative Law in the International Legal Order," *European Journal of International Law* 17, no. 1 (2006): 1–13; Benedict Kingsbury, Nico Krisch, and Richard B. Steward, "The Emergence of Global Administrative Law," *Law and Contemporary Problems* 68, no. 3/4 (2005): 15–61; Christoph Möllers, Andreas Voßkuhle, and Christian Walter, eds., *Internationalisierung des Verwaltungsrechts* (Tuebingen: Mohr Siebeck, 2007); Andreas Fischer-Lescano, "Transnationales Verwaltungsecht," *Juristen-Zeitung* 8 (2008): 373–83. On the globalization of (so to speak, de-state-ified, *entstaatlicht*) executive power beyond the state, see Klaus Dieter Wolf, *Die neue Staatsräson—Zwischenstaatliche Kooperation als Demokratieproblem der Weltgesellschaft* (Baden-Baden, DE: Nomos, 2000).

global players. No administrative court is responsible for their completely free association. Where the result of deliberation is not a legal norm but simply a drafted protocol, there can be no plaintiff or judge, and the comprehensive power of parliament grasps at straws.

The legal revolution of the 20th century was successful, but it is incomplete. Constitutionalism *instead of* democracy blocks the implementation of human rights and is ill at ease with festive democratic declarations. However, Kant is still correct that even human rights and democratic constitutional rhetoric—whose implementation is distorted by the legal form of existing organizations—are still *law* and not *philanthropy*.[98] Thus they cannot appear in legal and constitutional texts without consequences. They can recoil and strike back.[99] Once again the hegemonically legalized and constitutionalized world society shares with the constitutional law of the 18th century and the Western legal tradition as a whole a double structure: to be at once the immune system of society and the medium of its transformation, at once to accommodate the interests of those who rule and nevertheless to give space for the formation of emancipatory interests. As long as the constitution of world society (and all constitutions, not just state constitutions, are constitutions of society) is not democratically organized, the paradoxical simultaneity of juridification and deformalization, of equal rights and inegalitarian organizational norms will lead to the formation and stabilization of informal rule and domination.[100] But the same law that stabilizes and increases the power of the new, transnational class rule makes possible a counterhegemonic politics of global protest[101] and reform in accordance with principles;[102] principles that press toward the formalization of undemocratic organizational law in order to finally turn it into a law that enables democratic politics within legally protected spaces.[103]

Translated by Jonathan Trejo-Mathys

---

[98] Kant, *Zum ewigen Frieden*, 213f; see also Seyla Benhabib, *Another Cosmopolitanism* (Oxford: Oxford University Press, 2006).
[99] Friedrich Müller, *Wer ist das Volk? Eine Grundfrage der Demokratie, Elemente einer Verfassungstheorie VI* (Berlin: Duncker & Humblot, 1997), 56.
[100] Nickel, *The Missing Link in Global Law*.
[101] Brunkhorst, *Solidarität*, 184ff; Buckel, *Subjektivierung und Kohäsion*; Sonja Buckel and Andreas Fischer-Lescano, eds. *Hegemonie gepanzert mit Zwang: Zivilgesellschaft und Politik im Staatsverständnis von Antonio Gramscis* (Baden-Baden, DE: Nomos, 2007).
[102] In connection with Kant, see further Claudia Langer, *Reform nach Prinzipien. Untersuchung zur politischen Theorie Immanuel Kants* (Stuttgart: Klett-Cotta, 1986). On the linkage of protest and reform, see Prien, "Fragmentierte Volkssouveränität."
[103] Ingeborg Maus, "Volk und Nation im Denken der Aufklärung," *Blätter für deutsche und internationale Politik* 5 (1994): 606–12; Christoph Möllers, "Verfassungsgebende Gewalt—Verfassung—Konstitutionalisierung," in *Europäisches Verfassungsrecht*, ed. Armin von Bogdandy (Berlin: Springer, 2003), 1–57.

BIBLIOGRAPHY

Aaken, Anne van. "Democracy in Times of Transnational Administrative Law: The Case of Financial Markets." In *Demokratie in der Weltgesellschaft*, edited by Hauke Brunkhorst, 195–214. Baden-Baden, DE: Nomos, 2009.

Adorno, Theodor. *Aesthetic Theory*. Translated by Robert Hullot-Kentor. Minneapolis: University of Minnesota Press, 1997.

Adorno, Theodor. *Minima Moralia: Reflections From Damaged Life*. New York: Verso, 2006.

Albert, Mathias. "Politik der Weltgesellschaft und Politik der Globalisierung: Überlegungen zur Emergenz von Weltstaatlichkeit." *Zeitschrift für Soziologie* 34, Sonderheft Weltgesellschaft (2005): 223–38.

Albert, Mathias. *Zur Politik der Weltgesellschaft*. Weilerswist, DE: Velbrück, 2002.

Albert, Mathias, and Rainer Schmalz-Bruns. "Antinomien der Global Governance: Mehr Welstaatlichkeit, weniger Demokratie?" In *Demokratie in der Weltgesellschaft*, edited by Hauke Brunkhorst, 57–74. Baden-Baden, DE: Nomos, 2009.

Albert, Mathias, and Rudolf Stichweh, eds. *Weltstaat und Weltstaatlichkeit*. Wiesbaden, DE: Verlag für Sozial, 2007.

Anghie, Antony. *Imperialism, Sovereignty and the Making of International Law*. Cambridge: Cambridge University Press, 2005.

Aristotle. *Politics*. Translated by C.D.C. Reeve. Indianapolis: Hackett, 1998.

Bast, Jürgen. "Das Demokratiedefizit fragmentierter Internationalisierung." In *Demokratie in der Weltgesellschaft*, edited by Hauke Brunkhorst, 186-–194. Baden-Baden, DE: Nomos, 2009.

Beestermöller, Gerhard. *Die Völkerbundidee*. Stuttgart: Kohlhammer, 1995.

Benhabib, Seyla. *Another Cosmopolitanism*. Oxford: Oxford University Press, 2006.

Berger, Peter L. "The Desecularization of the World: A Global Overview." In *The Desecularization of the World: Resurgent Religion and World Politics*, edited by Peter L. Berger, 1–18. Washington, DC: Ethics and Policy Center, 1999.

Berman, Harold. *Justice in the USSR*. Cambridge: Cambridge University Press, 1963.

Berman, Harold. *Law and Revolution II: The Impact of the Protestant Reformation on the Western Legal Tradition*. Cambridge, MA: Harvard University Press, 2006.

Berman, Harold. *Recht und Revolution*. Frankfurt: Suhrkamp, 1991. Published in English as: Berman. *Law and Revolution: The Formation of the Western Legal Tradition*. Cambridge, MA: Harvard University Press, 1983. Bourdieu, Pierre. "La Précarité est Aujourd'hui Partout [Precariousness is Everywhere Nowadays]." In *Contre-feux*, 96–102. Paris: Raisons d'agir, 1988.

Brunkhorst, Hauke. "Demokratie in der globalen Rechtsgenossenschaft." *Zeitschrift für Soziologie* (2005): 330–48.

Brunkhorst, Hauke, ed., *Demokratie in der Weltgesellschaft*. Baden-Baden, DE: Nomos, 2009.

Brunkhorst, Hauke. "Die Globale Rechtsrevolution. Von der Evolution der Verfassungsrevolution zur Revolution der Verfassungsevolution?" In *Rechtstheorie in rechtspraktischer Absicht*, edited by Ralph Christensen and Bodo Pieroth, 9–34. Berlin: Dunker & Humblot/FS Müller, 2008.

Brunkhorst, Hauke, ed. *Einmischung Erwünscht? Menschenrechte und Bewaffnete Intervention*. Frankfurt: Fisher, 1998.

Brunkhorst, Hauke. "Globalising Democracy Without a State: Weak Public, Strong Public, Global Constitutionalism." *Millenium: Journal of International Studies* 31, no. 3 (2002): 675–90.

Brunkhorst, Hauke. *Solidarität. Von der Bürgerfreundschaft zur globalen Rechtsgenossenschaft*. Frankfurt: Suhrkamp, 2002. Translated into English as:

Brunkhorst. *Solidarity: From Civic Friendship to Global Legal Community*. Translated by Jeffrey Flynn. Boston, MA: MIT Press, 2014.

Bryde, Brun-Otto. “Konstituionalisierung des Völkerrechts und Internationalisierung des Verfassungsbegriffs.” *Der Staat* 1 (2003): 61–75.

Buckel, Sonja. *Subjektivierung und Kohäsion. Zur Rekonstruktion einer materialistischen Theorie des Rechts*. Weilerwist, DE: Velbrück Wissenschaft, 2007.

Buckel, Sonja, and Andreas Fischer-Lescano, eds. *Hegemonie gepanzert mit Zwang: Zivilgesellschaft und Politik im Staatsverständnis von Antonio Gramscis*. Baden-Baden, DE: Nomos, 2007.

Byers, Michael. “Preemptive Self-Defense: Hegemony, Equality and Strategies of Legal Change.” *The Journal of Political Philosophy* 11, no. 2 (2003): 171–90.

Calhoun, Craig. “The Class Consciousness of Frequent Travelers.” *The South Atlantic Quarterly* 101, no. 4 (2002): 869–97.

Calhoun, Craig. *Nations Matter*. London: Routledge, 2007.

Cerna, Christina M. “Universal Democracy: An International Legal Right or the Pipe Dream of the West?” *New York University Journal of International Law and Politics* 27, no. 2 (1995): 289–329.

Chimni, Bhupinder S. “International Institutions today: An Imperial Global State in the Making.” *European Journal of International Law* 15, no. 1 (2004): 1–37.

Conrad, Joseph. *Heart of Darkness*. New York: Norton, 1988.

Cripps, Stafford. “Can Socialism Come by Constitutional Methods?” In *Problems of a Socialist Government*. London: Victor Gollancz Ltd., 1933.

Dann, Philipp, and Zaid Ali-Ali. “The Internationalized *Pouvoir Constituant*—Constitution-Making Under External Influence in Iraq, Sudan and East Timor.” *Max Planck Yearbook of United Nations Law* 10 (2006): 423–63.

Deitelhoff, Nicole. *Überzeugen in der Politik. Grundzüge einer Diskurstheorie des internationalen Regierens*. Frankfurt: Suhrkamp, 2006.

Depenheuer, Otto, Markus Heintzen, Mathias Jestaedt, and Peter Axer, eds. *Staat im Wort: Festschrift für Josef Isensee*. Heidelberg: Müller, 2007.

Derrida, Jacques. *The Other Heading: Reflections on Today's Europe*. Bloomington, IN: Indiana University Press, 1992.

Di Fabio, Udo. *Das Recht offener Staaten: Grundlinien einer Staates-und Rechttheorie*. Tübingen: Mohr, 1998.

Dupuy, Pierre-Marie. “The Constitutional Dimension of the Charter of the United Nations Revisited.” *Max Planck Yearbook of United Nations Law* 1 (1997): 1–33.

Eberl, Oliver. “Demokratie und Frieden. Kants Friedensschrift in den Kontroversen über die Gestaltung globaler Ordnung.” Dissertation, University of Bremen, 2007.

Faßbender, Bardo. “Grund und Grenzen der konstitutionellen Idee im Völkerrecht.” In *Staat im Wort: Festschrift für Josef Isensee*, edited by Otto Depenheuer, Markus Heintzen, Matthias Jestaedt, and Peter Axer, 73–91. Heidelberg: Müller, 2007.

Faßbender, Bardo. “The United Nations Charter as Constitution of the International Community.” *Columbia Journal of Transnational Law* 36 (1998): 529–619.

Fischer-Lescano, Andreas. “Die Emergenz der Globalverfassung.” *Zeitschrift für ausländisches öffentliches Recht und Völkerrecht* 63, no. 3 (2003): 717–60.

Fischer-Lescano, Andreas. *Globalverfassung: Die Geltungsbegründung der Menschenrechte*. Weilerswist, DE: Velbrück Wissenschaft, 2005.

Fischer-Lescano, Andreas. “Globalverfassung: Verfassung der Weltgesellschaft.” *Archiv für Rechts-und Sozialphilosophie* 88 (2002): 349–78.

Fischer-Lescano, Andreas. “Transnationales Verwaltungsecht.” *Juristen-Zeitung* 8 (2008): 373–83.

Fischer-Lescano, Andreas, and Gunther Teubner. *Regime-Kollisionen: Zur Fragmentierung des globalen Rechts*. Frankfurt: Suhrkamp Verlag, 2006.

Foucault, Michel. *Discipline and Punish: the Birth of the Prison*. New York: Random House, 1975.

Foucault, Michel. *The History of Sexuality*, vol. 1: *An Introduction* [1976]. London: Allen Lane, 1979.

Franck, Thomas. "The Emerging Right to Democratic Governance." *American Journal of International Law* 86, no. 1 (1992): 46–91.

Friedmann, Wolfgang. *The Changing Structure of International Law*. London: Stevens & Sons, 1964.

Frowein, Jochen A. "Konstitutionalisierung des Völkerrechts." In *Völkerrecht und Internationales Privatrecht in einem sich globalisierenden internationalen System. Berichte der Deutschen Gesellschaft für Völkerrecht,* vol. 39, edited by Klaus Dicke, Waldemar Hummer, Daniel Girsberger, Katharina Boele-Woelki, Christoph Engel, Jochen Abr. Frowein, C. F. Mueller, 427–47. Heidelberg: Müller, 2000.

Grimm, Dieter. "Der Wandel der Staatsaufgaben und die Krise des Rechtsstaats." In *Die Zukunft der Verfassung*. Frankfurt: Suhrkamp, 1991.

Grimm, Dieter, ed. *Wachsende Staatsaufgaben—sinkende Steuerungsfähigkeit des Rechts*. Baden-Baden, DE: Nomos, 1990.

Habermas, Jürgen. *Between Facts and Norms: Contributions to a Discourse Theory of Law and Democracy*. Translated by William Rehg. Cambridge, MA: MIT Press, 1996. Originally published in German as: Habermas. *Faktizität und Geltung*. Frankfurt am Main: Suhrkamp, 1992.

Habermas, Jürgen. *Legitimation Crisis*. Translated by Thomas McCarthy. Boston: Beacon Press, 1973. Originally published in German as: Habermas. *Legitimationsprobleme im Spätkapitalismus*. Frankfurt am Main: Suhrkamp, 1973.

Hailbronner, Kay. "Der Staat und der Einzelne als Völkerrechtssubjekte." In *Völkerrecht*, 4th ed., edited by Wolfgang Graf Vitzthum, 157–264. Berlin: de Gruyter, 2007.

Hobsbawm, Eric. *The Age of Extremes: The Short Twentieth Century, 1914–1991*. New York: Vintage, 1989.

Horkheimer, Max, and Theodor Adorno. *Dialektik der Aufklärung. Philosophische Fragmente*, Ges. Schriften 3. Frankfurt: Fisher, 1997.

Hoss, Cristina. "Kelsen in Den Haag. Die Haager Vorlesungen von Hans Kelsen." In *Rechts-Staat*, edited by Hauke Brunkhorst and Rüdiger Voigt, 149–68. Baden-Baden, DE: Nomos, 2008.

Joerges, Christian, and Navraj Singh Ghaleigh, eds. *Darker Legacies of Law in Europe. The Shadow of National Socialism and Fascism over Europe and its Legal Traditions*. Oxford: Hart Publishing, 2003.

Kadelbach, Stefan. *Zwingendes Völkerrecht*. Frankfurt am Main: Duncker & Humblot, 1992.

Kant, Immanuel. *Metaphysik der Sitten, Rechtslehre*. In *Werke VIII*. Frankfurt: Suhrkamp, 1977. For the English translation, see: The doctrine of right, part I of Kant, *The Metaphysics of Morals*. In *Practical Philosophy*, edited by Mary J. Gregor, 353–603. Cambridge: Cambridge University Press, 1996.

Kant, Immanuel. "Perpetual Peace: A Philosophical Sketch." In *Kant: Political Writings*, edited by Hans Reiss, 93–130. Cambridge: Cambridge University Press, 1991.

Kant, Immanuel. "Zum ewigen Frieden." In *Werke* XI. Frankfurt: Suhrkamp, 1977. Translated into English as: Kant. "Perpetual Peace: A Philosophical Sketch." In *Kant: Political Writings*, edited by Hans Reiss, 93–130. Cambridge: Cambridge University Press, 1991.

Kelsen, Hans. *Das Problem der Souveränität und die Theorie des Völkerrechts* [1928, 1st ed. 1920]. Aalen, DE: Scientia Verlag, 1960.

Kelsen, Hans. "Der völkerrechtliche Strafanspruch wegen völkerrechtswidriger Kriegshandlungen." *Neue Freie Presse*, September 8, 1920.

Kelsen, Hans. "La Théorie générale du Droit International Public." *Recueil des cours (de l'Académie de droit international)* 42, no. 4 (1932): 117–351.

Kesselring, Thomas. *Die Produktivität der Antinomie. Hegels Dialektik im Lichte der genetischen Erkenntnistheorie und der formalen Logik*. Frankfurt: Suhrkamp, 1993.

Kingsbury, Benedict, Nico Krisch, and Richard B. Steward. "The Emergence of Global Administrative Law." *Law and Contemporary Problems* 68, no. 3/4 (2005): 15–61.

Kitzel-Cassagnes, Tanja, and Nadja Meisterhans. "Konstitutionalisierungsperspektiven eines fragmentierten Weltrechts." In *Demokratie in der Weltgesellschaft*, edited by Hauke Brunkhorst, 159-185. Baden-Baden, DE: Nomos, 2009.

Koskenniemi, Martti. *The Gentle Civiler of Nations*. Cambridge, MA: MIT Press, 2001.

Kreide, Regina. *Globale Politik und Menschenrechte. Macht und Ohnmacht eines politischen Instruments*. Frankfurt: Campus-Verlag, 2008.

Kreide, Regina. "Why a Minimalist Notion of Justice is Not Enough." In *Demokratie in der Weltgesellschaft*, edited by Hauke Brunkhorst. Baden-Baden, DE: Nomos, 2009.

Krisch, Nico, and Benedict Kingsbury. "Symposium: Global Governance and Global Administrative Law in the International Legal Order." *European Journal of International Law* 17, no. 1 (2006): 1–13.

Lafont, Cristina. "Alternative Visions of a New Global Order. What Should Cosmopolitans Hope For?" In *Demokratie in der Weltgesellschaft*, edited by Hauke Brunkhorst. Baden-Baden, DE: Nomos, 2009.

Langer, Claudia. *Reform nach Prinzipien. Untersuchung zur politischen Theorie Immanuel Kants*. Stuttgart: Klett-Cotta, 1986.

Leisering, Lutz. "Gibt es einen Weltwohlfahrtsstaat?" In *Weltstaat und Weltstaatlichkeit*, edited by Matthias Albert and Rudolf Stichweh, 185–205. Wiesbaden: VS Verlag, 2007.

Loughlin, Martin. *Public Law and Political Theory*. Oxford: Clarendon Press, 1992.

Lüdtke, Alf. "Genesis und Durchsetzung des 'modernen Staates.'" *Archiv für Sozialgeschichte* 20 (1980): 470–91.

Luhmann, Niklas. "Arbeitsteilung und Moral. Durkheims Theorie." In *Über soziale Arbeitsteilung*, 19–38. Frankfurt am Main: Suhrkamp, 1992.

Luhmann, Niklas. *Das Recht der Gesellschaft*. Frankfurt: Suhrkamp, 1993. Translated into English as: Luhmann. *Law as a Social System*. Oxford: Oxford University Press, 2004.

Luhmann, Niklas. "Der Funktionswandel des Gesetzes im Recht der bürgerlichen Gesellschaft." *Zeitschrift für Sozialforschung* 6, no. 3 (1937): 542–96.

Luhmann, Niklas. *Politische Theorie im Wohlfahrtsstaat*. München: Olzog, 1981.

Luhmann, Niklas. *Social Systems*. Stanford: Stanford University Press, 1995.

Luhmann, Niklas. "Subjektive Rechte: Zum Umbau des Rechtsbewußtseins für die moderne Gesellschaft." In *Gesellschaftsstruktur und Semantik*, vol. 2, 45–104. Frankfurt: Suhrkamp, 1981.

Lutz-Bachmann, Matthias, and James Bohman, eds. *Weltstaat oder Staatenwelt?* Frankfurt: Suhrkamp, 2002.

Marks, Susan. "International Judicial Activism and the Commodity-Form Theory of International Law." *The European Journal of International Law* 18, no. 1 (2007): 199–211.

Marks, Susan. *The Riddle of all Constitutions*. Oxford: Oxford University Press, 2000.Marx, Karl. *Capital*, vol. 1. Translated by Ben Fowkes. New York: Penguin Books, 1992.

Marx, Karl. *A Contribution to the Critique of Political Economy*. New York: International Publishers, 1904.

Marx, Karl. *Der 18. Brumaire des Louis Bonaparte*, MEGA Bd. I/11. Berlin: Deitz, 1985.

Maurer, Hartmut. *Allgemeines Verwaltungsrecht*, 16th ed. München: Beck, 2006.

Maus, Ingeborg. "Volk und Nation im Denken der Aufklärung." *Blätter für deutsche und internationale Politik* 5 (1994): 606–12.

Maus, Ingeborg. *Zur Aufklärung der Demokratietheorie*. Frankfurt: Suhrkamp, 1992.

Meyer, John W. *Weltkultur*. Edited by Georg Krücken and Gili S. Drori. Frankfurt am Main: Suhrkamp, 2005.

Meyer, John W. "World Society and the Nation-State." *American Journal of Sociology* 103, no. 1 (1997): 144–81.

Meyer, John W. *World Society: The Writings of John W. Meyer*. Edited by Georg Krücken and Gili S. Drori. Oxford: Oxford University Press, 2009.

Miéville, China. *Between Equal Rights: A Marxist Theory of International Law*. Leiden: Brill, 2005.

Möller, Kolja. "Subalterne Konstitutionalisierung. Zur Verfassung von Evolution und Revolution in der Weltgesellschaft." In *Kritische Systemtheorie? Zur Evolution einer normativen Theorie*, edited by Marc Amstutz and Andreas Fischer-Lescano. Frankfurt am Main: Suhrkamp, 2012.

Möllers, Christoph. *Gewaltengliederung: Legitimization and Dogmatik im internationalen Rechtsvergleich*. Tübingen: Mohr, 2005.

Möllers, Christoph. "Der parlamentarische Bundesstaat—Das vergessene Spannungsverhältnis von Parlament, Demokratie und Bundesstaat." In *Föderalismus—Auflösung oder Zukunft der Staatlichkeit?*, edited by Josef Aulehner, Andreas Dengler, and Karlheinz Konrad, 81–112. Stuttgart: Boorberg: 1997.

Möllers, Christoph. "Transnationale Behördenkooperation. Verfassungs-und völkerrechtliche Probleme transnationaler administrativer Standardsetzung." *Zeitschrift für ausländisches öffentliches Recht und Völkerrecht* 65 (2003): 351–89.

Möllers, Christoph. "Verfassungsgebende Gewalt—Verfassung—Konstitutionalisierung." In *Europäisches Verfassungsrecht*, edited by Armin von Bogdandy, 1–57. Berlin: Springer, 2003.

Möllers, Christoph, Andreas Voßkuhle, and Christian Walter, eds. *Internationalisierung des Verwaltungsrechts*. Tuebingen: Mohr Siebeck, 2007.

Mouffe, Chantal. *The Democratic Paradox*. London: Verso, 2000.

Müller, Friedrich. *Demokratie zwischen Staatsrecht und Weltrecht*. Berlin: Duncker & Humblot, 2003.

Müller, Friedrich. *Wer ist das Volk? Eine Grundfrage der Demokratie, Elemente einer Verfassungstheorie VI*. Berlin: Duncker & Humblot, 1997.

Neumann, Franz. "Der Funktionswandel des Gesetzes im Recht der bürgerlichen Gesellschaft." *Zeitschrift für Sozialforschung* 6 (1937): 542–96.

Nickel, Rainer. "The Missing Link in Global Law: Regime Collisions, Societal Constitutionalism, and Participation in Global Governance. A Comment on Gunther Teubner's Systems Theory Approach Towards Transnational Law." In *Globalisation, Law and Economy/Globalización, Derecho y Economía: Proceedings of the 22nd World Congress of the International Association for Philosophy of Law and Social Philosophy, Granada 2005*, vol. 4, edited by Nicolás López Calera, 237–50. Stuttgart: Franz Steiner Verlag, 2007.

Oeter, Stefan. "Internationale Organisation oder Weltföderation? Die organisierte Staatengemeinschaft und das Verlangen nach einer 'erfassung der Freiheit.'" In *Globalisierung und Demokratie*, edited by Hauke Brunkhorst and Matthias Kettner, 208–39. Frankfurt am Main: Suhrkamp, 2000.

Paulus, Andreas. "Die internationale Gemeinschaft im Völkerrecht." Dissertation, University of Munich, 2000.

Peters, Anne. "Compensatory Constitutionalism: The Function and Potential of Fundamental International Norms and Structures." *Leiden Journal of International Law* 19, no. 3 (2006): 579–610.

Peters, Bernhard. *Der Sinn von Öffentlichkeit.* Edited by Hartmut Weßler. Frankfurt am Main: Suhrkamp, 2007.

Polanyi, Karl. *The Great Transformation.* Boston: Beacon Press, 1957.

Preuß, Ulrich K. "The Twilight of Constitutional Law: Demise or Transformation?" Paper presented at the Workshop of the Wissenschaftskolleg zu Berlin. June 19–20, 2008.

Prien, Thore. "Fragmentierte Volkssouveränität—Recht, Gerechtigkeit und der demokratische Einspruch in der Weltgesellschaft." Dissertation, University of Flensburg, 2008.

Risse, Thomas, Anja Jetschke, and Hans-Peter Schmitz, eds. *Die Macht der Menschenrechte. Internationale Normen, kommunikatives Handeln und politischer Wandel in den Ländern des Südens.* Baden-Baden, DE: Nomos, 2002.

Risse, Thomas, Stephen C. Ropp, and Kathryn Sikkink, eds. *The Power of Human Rights.* Cambridge: Cambridge University Press, 1999.

Rorty, Richard. "Human Rights, Rationality and Sentimentality." In *On Human Rights*, edited by Stephen Shute and Susan Hurley, 112–34. New York: Basic Books, 1993.

Roy, Olivier. *Der islamistische Weg nach Westen. Globalisierung, Entwurzelung und Radikalisierung.* Bonn: Bundeszentrale für Politische Bildung, 2006.

Scelle, Georges. "Essai de Systematique de Droit International." *Revue Générale International de Public* 30 (1923): 116–42.

Schmitt, Carl. *Der Nomos der Erde im Völkerrecht des Jus Publicum Europaeum* [1950]. Berlin: Duncker & Humblot, 1988. Translated into English as: Schmitt. *The* Nomos *of the Earth in the International Law of the* Jus Publicum Europaeum. Translated by G. L. Ulmen. New York: Telos Press, 2003.

Schönberger, Christoph. "Föderale Angehörigkeit." Habilitation, University of Freiburg, 2005.

Seagle, William. *The Quest of Law.* New York: Alfred A. Knopf, 1941.

Sellin, Volker. *Die geraubte Revolution.* Göttingen: Vandenhoeck & Ruprecht, 2001.

Stichweh, Rudolf. "Der Zusammenhalt der Weltgesellschaft: Nicht-normative Integrationstheorien in der Soziologie." In *Transnationale Solidarität. Chancen und Grenzen*, edited by Jens Becker, Julia Eckert, Martin Kohli, and Wolfgang Streeck, 236–45. Frankfurt am Main: Campus, 2004.

Stichweh, Rudolf. *Die Weltgesellschaft.* Frankfurt am Main: Suhrkamp, 2000.

Streek, Wolfgang. "Sectoral Specialization: Politics and the Nation State in a Global Economy." Paper presented on the 37th World Congress of the International Institute of Sociology, Stockholm. July 5–9, 2005.

Sunstein, Cass. *After the Rights Revolution.* Cambridge: Cambridge University Press, 1993.

Teubner, Gunther. "Globale Zivilverfassungen." *Zeitschrift für ausländisches öffentliches Recht und Völkerrecht* 63, no. 1 (2003): 1–28.

There Will Be Blood. DVD. Directed by Paul Thomas Anderson. 2007; United States: Miramax, 2008.

Tietje, Christian. "Die Staatsrechtslehre und die Veränderung ihres Gegenstandes." *Deutsches Verwaltungsblatt* 17 (2003): 1081–164.

Tomuschat, Christian. "Die internationale Gemeinschaft." *Archiv des Völkerrechts* 1, no. 7 (1995): 1–20.

Tomuschat, Christian. "Die völkerrechtlichen Grundlagen der Zivilgesellschaft: Internationale Abkommen als Garanten internationaler Solidarität." In *Transnationale Solidarität*, edited by Jens Beckert, Julia Eckert, Martin Kohli, and Wolfgang Streek, 135–47. Frankfurt am Main: Campus, 2004.

Tomuschat, Christian. "International Law as the Constitution of Mankind." In *International Law on the Eve of the Twenty-First Century: Views from the International Law Commission*, 37–50. New York: United Nations, 1997.
Uerpmann, Robert. "Internationales Verfassungsrecht." *JuristenZeitung* (2001): 565–73.
Vasques, Manuel A., and Marie F. Marquardt, eds. *Globalizing the Sacred: Religion Across the Americas*. New Brunswick: Rutgers University Press, 2003.
Verdross, Alfred. *Die Verfassung der Völkerrechtsgemeinschaft*. Berlin/Vienna: Julius Springer, 1926.
Verdross, Alfred. *Die Verfassung der Völkerrechtsgemeinschaft*, 2nd ed. [1926]. Berlin/Vienna: Julius Springer, 1950.
Verdross, Alfred, and Bruno Simma. *Universelles Völkerrecht*. Berlin: Springer, 1984.
von Bernstorff, Jochen. *Der Glaube an das universale Recht: zur Völkerrechtstheorie Hans Kelsens und seiner Schüler.* Baden-Baden, DE: Nomos, 2001.
von Bogdandy, Armin. "Constitutionalism in International Law: Comment on a Proposal from Germany." *Harvard International Law Journal* 47, no. 1 (2006): 223–42.
Wahl, Rainer. *Verfassungsstaat, Europäisierung, Internationalisierung*. Frankfurt: Suhrkamp, 2003.
Walter, Christian. "Constitutionalizing (Inter)national Governance—Possibilities for and Limits to the Development of an International Constitutional Law." *German Yearbook of International Law* 44 (2001): 170–201.
Weber, Max. *The Protestant Ethic and the Spirit of Capitalism*. Translated by Talcott Parsons. New York: Routledge, 1992. Originally published in German as: Weber. *Die protestantische Ethik und der Geist des Kapitalismus*. In *Gesammelte Aufsätze zur Religionssoziologie*, vol. 1, 17–206. Tübingen: J.C.B. Mohr, 1978.
Weber, Max. *Wirtschaft und Gesellschaft*, Bd. II. Köln: Halbband, 1964. Translated into English as: Weber. *Economy and Society*, vol. 2. Edited by Guenter Roth and Claus Wittich. Berkeley, CA: University of California Press, 1978.
Wesel, Uwe. *Geschichte des Rechts*. München: Beck, 1997
Witte, John. *Law and Protestantism: The Legal Teachings of the Lutheran Reformation*. Cambridge: Cambridge University Press, 2002.
Wolf, Klaus Dieter. *Die neue Staatsräson—Zwischenstaatliche Kooperation als Demokratieproblem der Weltgesellschaft*. Baden-Baden, DE: Nomos, 2000.

Contributors

Amy Allen is Parents Distinguished Research Professor in the Humanities and Professor of Philosophy and Women's and Gender Studies at Dartmouth College. Her research and teaching interests are in continental philosophy, with a particular emphasis on the intersection of critical social theory, poststructuralism, and feminist theory. She has published widely on the topics of power, subjectivity, agency, and autonomy in the work of Foucault, Habermas, Butler, and Arendt. Her publications include two books: *The Power of Feminist Theory: Domination, Resistance, Solidarity* (Boulder, CO: Westview, 1999) and *The Politics of Our Selves: Power, Autonomy, and Gender in Contemporary Critical Theory* (New York: Columbia University Press, 2008). A third book, *The End of Progress: Rethinking the Normative Foundations of Critical Theory*, is forthcoming from Columbia University Press. She is Co-Editor of the journal *Constellations: An International Journal of Critical and Democratic Theory*, Series Editor of the Columbia University Press book series *New Directions in Critical Theory*, and Executive Co-Director of the Society for Phenomenology and Existential Philosophy (SPEP).

James Bohman holds the Danforth I Chair in the Humanities and is Professor of Philosophy and Professor of International Studies at Saint Louis University. His primary areas of research include political philosophy (deliberative and transnational democracy) and the philosophy of social science (rationality and normativity). He has also done work in German philosophy (critical theory and German idealism). He is the author of *Democracy across Borders* (Cambridge, MA: MIT Press, 2007), *Public Deliberation* (Cambridge, MA: MIT Press, 1996), and numerous articles on republican political theory.

Hauke Brunkhorst is Professor of Sociology and Head of the Institute of Sociology at the University of Flensburg, Germany. He is the author of *Solidarity: From Civic Friendship to a Global Legal Community* (Cambridge, MA: MIT Press, 2005), *Critical Theory of Legal Revolutions: Evolutionary Perspectives* (New York: Bloomsbury, 2014), and

Das doppelte Gesicht Europas—Zwischen Kapitalismus und Demokratie (Suhrkamp, 2014). He has also authored books on Theodor Adorno, Hannah Arendt, Karl Marx, Jürgen Habermas, and Herbert Marcuse.

Barbara Buckinx is Associate Research Scholar in the Woodrow Wilson School of Public and International Affairs at Princeton University. She has held research and postdoctoral fellowships at the UCSD Center on Global Justice, Frankfurt's Centre for Advanced Studies "Justitia Amplificata" and Institute for Advanced Studies in the Humanities, and the Political Theory Project at Brown University. Her work has appeared in *Critical Review of International Social and Political Philosophy, Ethics & International Affairs,* and *Global Justice: Theory Practice Rhetoric.*

Rainer Forst is Professor of Political Theory and Philosophy at Goethe University Frankfurt am Main, and Co-Director of the Cluster of Excellence on the "Formation of Normative Orders" and of the Centre for Advanced Studies "Justitia Amplificata: Rethinking Justice—Applied and Global." His publications include *Contexts of Justice* (Berkeley, CA: University of California Press, 2002), *Toleration in Conflict* (New York: Cambridge University Press, 2013), *The Right to Justification* (New York: Columbia University Press 2012), *Justification and Critique* (Cambridge: Polity Press, 2013), *The Power of Tolerance* (with Wendy Brown) (New York: Columbia University Press, 2014) and *Justice, Democracy and the Right to Justification* (a dialogue with critics) (London: Bloomsbury, 2014). In 2012, Rainer Forst was awarded the Gottfried-Wilhelm-Leibniz Prize, which is the most important research award the German Research Foundation (DFG) accords.

Stefan Gosepath is Professor of Moral and Political Philosophy in the Institute for Philosophy at the Free University Berlin. He is the Director of the Centre for Advanced Studies, "Justitia Amplificata: Rethinking Justice—Applied and Global." He has previously been a professor at the universities of Frankfurt, Bremen, Giessen, Potsdam, and Vienna. He is the author of *Einführung in die politische Philosophie* ("Introduction to Political Philosophy," with Robin Celikates) (Reclam, 2013), *Gleiche Gerechtigkeit. Grundlagen eines liberalen Egalitarismus* ("Equal Justice. Foundations of a Liberal Egalitarianism") (Suhrkamp, 2004), and *Aufgeklärtes Eigeninteresse. Eine Theorie theoretischer und praktischer Rationalität* ("Enlightened Self-Interest. A Theory of Theoretical and Practical Rationality") (Suhrkamp, 1992). He has also published widely on global justice, democracy, and human rights, as well as on social and legal philosophy.

Duncan Ivison is Professor of Political Philosophy at the University of Sydney. He is the author of *The Self at Liberty* (Ithaca, NY: Cornell University

Press, 1997), *Postcolonial Liberalism* (Cambridge: Cambridge University Press, 2002), and *Rights* (Stocksfield, UK: Acumen, 2008). He is Editor (with Paul Patton and Will Sanders) of *Political Theory and the Rights of Indigenous Peoples* (Cambridge: Cambridge University Press, 2000) and *The Ashgate Research Companion to Multiculturalism* (Burlington, VT: Ashgate, 2010). He is currently Dean of the Faculty of Arts and Social Sciences at the University of Sydney.

Terry Macdonald is Senior Lecturer in International Relations at the University of Melbourne. She has previously held positions at Merton College, Oxford University, the Centre for Applied Philosophy and Public Ethics at the Australian National University, and Monash University. She is the author of *Global Stakeholder Democracy: Power and Representation Beyond Liberal States* (New York: Oxford University Press, 2008) and co-editor of *Global Political Justice* (London: Routledge, 2013), and has published work in journals including *Ethics & International Affairs*, *Political Studies*, and *The European Journal of International Law*.

John W. Maynor is Professor of Political Philosophy at Middle Tennessee State University. He is the author of *Republicanism in the Modern World* (Cambridge: Polity, 2003) and co-editor (with Cécile Laborde) of *Republicanism and Political Theory* (Malden, MA: Blackwell, 2008). His work on republicanism, democratic theory, and liberalism has recently been published in the *Critical Review of International Social and Political Philosophy*, *The European Journal of Political Theory*, and *Politics*.

Thomas McCarthy is Professor Emeritus of Philosophy at Northwestern University. He is the author of *The Critical Theory of Jürgen Habermas* (Cambridge, MA: MIT Press, 1978), *Ideals and Illusions: On Reconstruction and Deconstruction in Contemporary Critical Theory* (Cambridge, MA: MIT Press, 1991), *Critical Theory* (with David Hoy) (Malden, MA: Blackwell, 1994), and *Race, Empire, And the Idea of Human Development* (Cambridge: Cambridge University Press, 2009), and the general editor of the series *Studies in Contemporary German Social Thought*.

John P. McCormick is Professor of Political Science at the University of Chicago. He is the author of *Machiavellian Democracy* (Cambridge: Cambridge University, Press, 2011), *Carl Schmitt's Critique of Liberalism: Against Politics as Technology* (Cambridge: Cambridge University Press, 1997), and *Weber, Habermas and Transformations of the European State: Constitutional, Social and Supranational Democracy* (Cambridge: Cambridge University Press, 2006).

Charles W. Mills is John Evans Professor of Moral and Intellectual Philosophy at Northwestern University. He works in the general area of oppositional political theory, and is the author of five books: *The Racial Contract* (Ithaca, NY: Cornell University Press, 1997), *Blackness Visible: Essays on Philosophy and Race* (Ithaca, NY: Cornell University Press, 1998), *From Class to Race: Essays in White Marxism and Black Radicalism* (Boulder, CO: Rowman and Littlefield, 2003), *Contract and Domination* (with Carole Pateman) (Cambridge: Polity Press, 2007), and *Radical Theory, Caribbean Reality: Race, Class and Social Domination* (Kingston: University of West Indies Press, 2010).

Philip Pettit is L. S. Rockefeller University Professor of Politics and Human Values at Princeton University and Distinguished Professor of Philosophy at the Australian National University. Among his books are *The Common Mind: An Essay on Psychology, Society, and Politics* (Oxford: Oxford University Press, 1996), *Republicanism* (Oxford: Oxford University Press, 1997), *The Economy of Esteem* (with Geoffrey Brennan) (Oxford: Oxford University Press, 2004), *Made with Words: Hobbes on Language, Mind, and Politics* (Princeton, NJ: Princeton University Press, 2008), *A Political Philosophy in Public Life: Civic Republicanism in Zapatero's Spain* (with José Luis Martí) (Princeton, NJ: Princeton University Press, 2010), *Group Agency* (with Christian List) (Oxford: Oxford University Press, 2011), *On the People's Terms: A Republican Theory and Model of Philosophy* (Cambridge: Cambridge University Press, 2012), and *Just Freedom: A Moral Compass for a Complex World* (New York: W. W. Norton, 2014). *Common Minds: Themes from the Philosophy of Philip Pettit*, ed. Geoffrey Brennan et al., appeared from Oxford University Press in 2007.

Jonathan Trejo-Mathys is Assistant Professor of Philosophy at Boston College. He has been a Fulbright Scholar at the J. W. Goethe Universität and a Postdoctoral Fellow at the Justitia Amplificata Centre for Advanced Studies, both in Frankfurt am Main, Germany. He has published articles and reviews in journals such as *Philosophy & Social Criticism*, *Constellations*, and *Contemporary Pragmatism*.

Timothy Waligore is Assistant Professor of Political Science and Global Professional Studies coordinator at Pace University in Pleasantville, New York. He has been a Democracy and Diversity postdoctoral fellow at Queen's University, a Justitia Amplificata postdoctoral fellow at the University of Frankfurt, and an Andrew W. Mellon Postdoctoral Research Fellow and Postdoctoral Fellow in the Research Group on Constitutional Studies/Groupe de Recherche Interuniversitaire en Philosophie Politique at McGill University. He has published and forthcoming pieces in *Politics, Philosophy & Economics*; *Public Reason: Journal of Moral and Political Philosophy*; and *Analyse & Kritik*.

Index

For Product Safety Concerns and Information please contact our EU representative GPSR@taylorandfrancis.com
Taylor & Francis Verlag GmbH, Kaufingerstraße 24, 80331 München, Germany

www.ingramcontent.com/pod-product-compliance
Ingram Content Group UK Ltd.
Pitfield, Milton Keynes, MK11 3LW, UK
UKHW022115190926
475702UK00013B/1454
* 9 7 8 0 3 6 7 1 4 4 1 3 5 *